MW01502677

About this book

Child Witch Kinshasa is the first part of a two-volume novel. The second part is *Child Witch London* (Nicoaro Books, 2014).

MIKE ORMSBY

ChiLD WiTch
KINSHASA

Stretch
Your
Mind

Nicoaro
Books

This novel is a work of fiction. Characters, names, places and incidents are products of the author's imagination or are used fictitiously. Any resemblance to actual persons living or dead, to events or locales, is entirely coincidental.

Nicoaro Books
Copyright © Mike Ormsby, 2013

🐦 *NicoaroBooks*
🐦 *OrmsbyMike*

ISBN-13: 978-1479285129
ISBN-10: 1479285129

www.childwitch.com

Cover design by Doug Proctor and Matthew Young

Interior design by Victor Jalbă-Șoimaru

Map by Sorin Sorasan

Author photo by Cosmin Bumbuț

For Angela wherever we go, and Kilanda
wherever you went.

If one does not accord the voyage the right to destroy us a little bit, one might as well stay home. A voyage is like a shipwreck, and those whose boat has never sunk will never know anything about the sea.

Nicolas Bouvier
(translated from The Paths of Halla-San*)*

Chapter 1

God, what a racket. Frank Kean rolled over in bed, half asleep, listening to drums and chanting from the streets beyond his *hotel.* Numb to the bone after a twenty-hour trip, he fumbled for his watch and squinted in darkness at glowing digits. *01:27.* A mosquito buzzed overhead like a helicopter low on fuel. Frank sat up, elbows tucked at his sides, listening. Some novice was cranking chords from an electric guitar down in the neighbourhood. Frank looked towards the sliding glass door. *Forgot to shut it?* Long net curtains shimmered in the balmy breeze like silver angels come to prophesy. *You'll get malaria.* The music reached a climax and stopped. He heard a boy wailing. Pleading for mercy, by the sound of it.

Frank rose naked from tangled sheets, wrapped a towel at his waist and stepped through swirling curtains onto the balcony, its terracotta tiles and steel handrail still warm eight hours after sunset. Balmy equatorial heat dropped like a python from a tree and curled around his ribs, squeezing the breath out of him. The boy's howls faded. About time, too.

He lit a cigarette and peered into an inky city dotted by pinpricks of yellow light. Hotel Maisha sat among a labyrinth of backstreets; a motorbike puttered by and some dog was barking up the wrong alley. Frank sucked smoke, scanning rooftops with a wry smile, savouring the slow promise of a vast, unknown land. *This makes ninety-nine countries; visit one more and I can join Travelers' Century Club. Something to write home about? Or maybe not; better just go home, bide my time?* He mulled his options, pausing mid-drag, ear cocked.

The music resumed, quietly at first then louder: drums, choir and tinny guitar, surging like surf up a midnight beach, rushing around his feet and spreading upwards on crashing waves of song. The chanting built to a climax that quickly faded to a simmering silence punctuated by the howls of a boy. The kid sounded delirious. Adrenaline prickled through Frank's veins triggering a reflex older than time, urging him to do something. Perhaps call the front desk. *And say what?*

A baritone voice boomed across the rooftops. Someone was addressing a crowd, like a practised politician or stand-up comic, pausing for yips and whoops from his audience. Frank shifted a few paces to hear better, but thunderous applause for the orator made it pointless trying. He spotted two uniformed guards under a solitary bulb in the car park, nattering the night away, rifles slung across their knees, the toecaps of their black boots shining like aubergines. One guard glanced up at the pale figure on the balcony. Frank gestured towards the noisy neighbourhood. The guard resumed chatting with his colleague. Frank stepped back into his room and slid the glass door shut. *Whatever.*

From the bed, he aimed the remote at the TV. The screen fizzed into life, revealing an earnest-looking priest yapping in French, bug-eyed and bombastic, catastrophe due any minute. Frank flipped channels. CNN offered more of the same, this time from Wall Street. On the next channel, three beefy dudes in oversize bling were smooching bikini babes to a hip-hop beat. Catchy tune, but not that catchy. Frank poked the red button and they vanished.

He nibbled a sesame biscuit and sipped water, considering the task ahead. His new contract would last several weeks. A tricky one too, potentially. Four cities, fifty people at least. It was becoming a routine but how else to pay the bills back home? The details blurred and swam in his head like tropical fish in a knobbly reef. *Get in, get out and move on.* Fatigue enveloped him like warm water until he was floating in time and space, fingers twitching. He sank back on his pillow and, finally, he was gone, slack-jawed and dribbling for England.

His soccer kit was red, white and blue. He ran across a sloping field of patchy grass in blinding sunshine, chasing a misshapen ball that bounced all wrong. Why even bother? Chanting fans packed the terraces and a young African player told him, *Mister, we are losing.* Frank shrugged. *Doing my best.*

The ball spun loose and Frank lashed an audacious volley that sent it dipping over the grasping goalie. The net rippled in slow motion and a bank of cheering fans rose, ecstatic, their chants spiralling to a blue sky, pealing like the bells of heaven. Muscle-bound men pummelled big drums and a burly woman stood twanging a guitar like some vintage blues starlet – Sister Rosetta Tharpe? Frank turned to salute the crowds but they had vanished. Instead, he saw a barefoot boy sitting alone on the grass, sobbing into puny fists. Frank moved towards him but was soon sinking in mud, his boots popping gloop. A mosquito buzzed his ear as the boy's sobs mutated into howls, louder and louder.

There it is again.

Frank opened an eye and looked towards his balcony, listening to the incessant scratching of a thousand crickets. *Welcome to the Democratic Republic of the Congo.*

Chapter 2

Night came quickly to the village. Dudu lay on his bamboo bed, listening to a monkey screeching in the bush, not far away. It was caught in a trap, perhaps. Uncle Moses nosed through the ragged curtains, picking at his teeth, face half in shadow. "Goats?"

"Done, Uncle."

"Firewood? Henhouse?"

"Yes, Uncle, done."

"Did you fetch water?"

"No, Uncle, but first thing tomorrow."

A shaft of moonlight fell across Moses' pinched face. He looked like a rat sniffing for scraps. Dudu noticed how his mouth curled a little from a shrapnel scar, as if he would be forever smiling about his lucky escape from the war. *Not like Tata, blown to bits by the same landmine. It seems unfair.* Dudu turned away, gazing at the ceiling. Moses clicked his teeth.

"First thing, good and early. Don't be late. We must clean up Heroes' Corner. My bar is dusty, probably why I'm losing clients. Tables and floor need a scrub. What d'you say?"

Dudu lay watching a moth wriggle in a spider's web. "Yes, Uncle."

Moses spat a shred of tobacco. "*Yes Uncle, no Uncle.* Go to sleep, and no peeping."

The curtain closed and Dudu slipped silently from his bed to watch through the crack. He saw Moses lie down and snuggle into Mama, complaining about something. He seemed skinny compared to her, pawing at her robe now and kissing her face. Mama did not seem to mind. *How can she let him do such things; has she forgotten Tata?* Uncle Moses turned his head towards the curtain. Dudu shrank away and crept back to bed. He covered his brother with a blanket. Little Emile's withered leg stuck out like a branch on a small dead tree.

The house smelled of vomit and diarrhoea; worse every day, because of Nana Kima. Dudu wrinkled his nose and watched silver moonlight paint the crusty wall, while questions wriggled like snakes in his head. *Will Uncle never take Nana to the clinic? Why does Mama not insist?* He stared at the tufts of dried grass that Moses had stuffed in a hole in the roof. They resembled the hair in his stinky armpits. Tata would have fixed that hole with wood.

Dudu watched the moth struggle on. But when you were caught, you were caught. The spider darted from darkness, orange and white, fat as a bean, and spun a fine cloak around the moth, pausing briefly to inspect it, perhaps whispering *hello,* or more likely *goodbye.*

He heard Mama gasp and give a little yelp, like the time she had stubbed her toe in the yard. Moses groaned as if someone were strangling him; Dudu wished it were true and closed his eyes. *How can Mama lie down with Moses, night after night?*

"Because she needs *security,*" Ginelle said, early next day, in her matter-of-fact way. They were walking to the spring and Dudu's pretty neighbour had all the answers, as usual.

"What's *security?*" asked Dudu.

"Something important, so my tata says."

Ginelle strode along the muddy path swinging her empty bidon of scuffed yellow plastic. Dudu swung his too, back and forth, trying to keep time. The forest rose in a bank of rippling green to their right. To their left, hills rolled gently to the plain where distant villages lay in a smoky haze. "And Uncle Moses is the best you can hope for," Ginelle concluded.

Emile was lagging behind again. Dudu turned and hissed at his brother to hurry and Ginelle said, "It's not Em's fault. Why are you bossy? You're not the boss around here."

She paused to regard him, as though daring him to disagree; her fine neck arched just so. Silhouetted against dazzling sunlight, Ginelle resembled a beautiful statue, like in Dudu's picture book. A goddess from Ancient Rome. But he did not tell her. Emile shuffled past them and muttered, "Slowcoaches."

Ginelle pointed towards the bend in the path. "You first, Dudu. Unless you're scared."

"Of what?" Dudu pretended to adjust his satchel and Ginelle walked on, smiling as though she knew a thing or two. Around the corner they joined the bigger track with deep ruts and walked in single file to avoid tripping into them.

"How's your Nana?" said Ginelle.

Dudu shrugged. "Worse. Uncle keeps saying we can't take her to the clinic because the white nurses will kill her and sell her insides. No one ever gets out alive. Is that true?"

"Moses is a donkey," Ginelle replied.

Emile giggled, swinging his bidon. "Moses is a donkey."

Dudu frowned at Ginelle. "You shouldn't say that."

"Why not? Listen, neighbour, if people die in the clinic, it's because they went too late. Here's something else you don't know: last night I dreamed I met a handsome warrior."

"Another one?"

"His father was *mwami*, a chief. They had a big house, water from a brass tap."

Dudu sighed. "I dreamed of Tata. We went fishing."

"Not again! Don't you ever dream of me?" Ginelle scooped up a rock and weighed it in her hand. Dudu wondered how to reply. If he said *no,* it might hurt her feelings, but if he said *yes,* she might tease him. So he said nothing. Besides, the dog was coming.

It hurtled up the path, blocking their way, barking and snapping, black fur all clumpy and its torn ear dangling like a dry leaf. As ever, the dog seemed mostly interested in Dudu and circled him with a nasty look, but Ginelle distracted it by pretending to offer food, and when it approached, curious, she threw the rock, bang on target. The dog squealed and ran.

Dudu clapped his hands. "Good shot."

"You owe me." Ginelle walked on, leading Emile by the hand.

They reached the spring and joined the long queue of children clutching plastic bidons. Most kids wore old clothes like his; some had smart uniforms, ready for the school bus. Dudu watched Ginelle chat to a friend in shoes, not to some scaredy-cat barefoot neighbour like him. The tall twin boys in Adidas caps were looking Ginelle up and down.

Dudu squatted at the back of the line and took his picture book from his satchel. It was soon snatched from his hands; the twins stood over him in white shirts and red ties. One of them was mocking Emile's wobbly walk and the other pretended to read aloud, turning Dudu's pages. "*Dear Diary: my uncle drinks, Nana stinks and fetching water is girl's work.*"

Dudu stood up and tried to make himself as tall as them. "Can I have it back, please?"

The twin turned pages. "*Famous Places. Rome. Paris.* Where d'you get this rubbish?"

"From my tata. He got it from school. When he was little."

"Why don't *you* come to school, are you too thick?"

"I help Uncle Moses. Can I have it back, please?" Dudu thrust out his hand.

"Or what?" said the other. The twins even sounded alike.

"Or you'll get a headache," said Ginelle, approaching with a rock in each hand.

The book was flung at Dudu and the twins wandered off, working their way down the queue, mocking Emile's wobbly walk and pushing the smaller kids.

Ginelle dropped the rocks, picked up her empty bidon and walked quickly away. Dudu trotted after her, dragging his little brother by the hand. "Ginelle, where are we going?"

"Somewhere else. And bring Emile."

They followed Ginelle towards the river and, along the way, she offered *free advice*.

"You're twelve, Dudu, and I'm thirteen. So listen carefully: you'll never amount to much if you can't stand up for yourself. Agree?"

"I'll get slapped by Moses if I don't fill his bidon. We should be at the spring."

"We'll go back when there's no queue or bossy boys."

"But Moses is waiting. I have to mop Heroes' Corner, so it's clean for clients."

"What *clients*? My tata says that Moses has none, these days! Let me tell you something else, Dudu. My mama says your Uncle Moses is too bossy to manage a bar. Anyway, donkeys can last a long time without water. So don't be boring. Come along."

She led them to the riverbank and climbed the big tree with the sloping trunk, her knickers showing. Dudu watched with interest and Ginelle was soon straddling the fat branch that extended out over the water. She smiled down and said, "Come up, if you dare."

"What about Emile? He can't climb."

"Emile is a brave warrior guarding my boxes of jewels. Isn't that right, Emile?"

Emile nodded and set the three bidons in a row. Dudu hauled himself up the tree and joined Ginelle, high over the river. He watched her elegant brown fingers trace names that sweethearts had gouged into the bark: COLETTE & DIDIER, JEAN-LUC & MARIE.

"Still carving your funny little animals in the yard, Du?" She spoke quietly now.

He watched the brown river curling away towards the next village. "Sometimes, yes."

"Do you think someone will carve my name in this tree, one day?"

Dudu wondered what to say. If he offered, she might make fun. "Perhaps, Ginelle."

She sighed and seemed troubled. "You know your problem, neighbour? You're not brave. Or romantic. If the beautiful daughter of a chief set you a task, you wouldn't do it."

"Do what?"

Ginelle picked her nose with a dainty finger. "Jump in the river. To find a box of jewels, the one she lost long ago."

Dudu looked down. "I'll get wet."

"Perhaps I should ask the twins, what do you think? They seem big and strong."

Dudu peeled off his T-shirt, walked along the branch and jumped. He tucked his knees up and hit the water with a satisfying splash, whooshing down to the reeds, where he held his breath, so Ginelle would think this brave warrior had drowned. Would she weep? *Maybe.*

He shimmied up to the sunlight, flicking his feet. He broke the surface, shook water from his eyes and heard Ginelle yelling above. She sounded upset and that pleased him, until he spotted the bossy twins on the riverbank, slapping their thighs, laughing and pointing. Emile was sobbing and the three yellow bidons were floating swiftly away downstream.

Chapter 3

Frank wandered the hotel lobby, double-checking his watch. *Ten a.m. sharp but no sign of my driver.* He sank onto an old leather sofa to watch the place empty and fill, a constant flow of come-and-go. Porters with worn heels pushed shiny brass trolleys laden with luggage. Some clients fretted over lost bags or frantically patted their pockets. Others chatted and smiled. A Congolese couple emerged from the elevator, the young woman looking regal in her purple robe, her hair sprung with wire and beads, her briefcase made of pink lizard or crocodile skin. The middle-aged beau at her side was Denzel Washington-handsome, suited and booted, tugging his cuffs. Teenagers in T-shirts moved aside for the two swells to pass.

A lanky guard in combat fatigues and mirror sunglasses stood clutching a machine gun, the wooden stock worn smooth. His head turned towards Frank, who averted his gaze to an abstract painting and adopted a studied air, chin on knuckles. Soon bored of modern art, he scrolled in his phone for DRIVER and sent a text: *I'm in lobby as agreed, where are you?*

The reply came soon enough. *I'm very fine, I shall arrive in 20 minutes, Claude.*

Frank took his laptop from his bag and set it on a coffee table. He booted up an Excel document showing his list of countries visited and typed DR *Congo, #99,* at the bottom. He felt better already. In the next column he typed: *3-month contract, first gig for Unicorn Trust, Spring 2002.* The sofa wheezed as someone else joined him, someone who said, "Awful weather."

The voice was deep, the tone ironic, the accent British. The tanned stranger sounded friendly but looked scary – head shaved to the bone and deep-set eyes with a piercing gaze. Strong shoulders bulged under a blue cotton V-neck and brown toes peeped from battered sandals. He was ogling Frank's screen and looked puzzled, or perhaps envious. Frank closed the document and extended a hand. "Certainly is warm. I'm Frank Kean, by the way."

"Jerome Braddock. No worries." The fellow had a no-nonsense grip. He lounged back like he owned the place and plopped a newspaper on the table. Frank looked at the smudged print and wonky headlines, and Braddock said, "So Frank, what's your game?"

"I train radio journalists. And you?" Frank had a feeling they had met before.

"Journalists, eh? Good luck with that." Braddock jabbed a tanned finger at his newspaper on the table. "You can have that local rag, if you like. Full of shite anyway."

Frank reached for the freebie. "Cheers."

"What you teaching 'em, how to spin even more propaganda?"

Frank scanned the front page. "We were due to cover the peace talks, but…"

"Dead as a dodo, mate."

"Exactly. I need a Plan B. That's probably what's on the agenda at HQ, if my driver ever turns up. Seemed reliable last night but now I'm starting to wonder. Thing is, I'm not even supposed to be in this hotel. I was supposed to have my own flat, move straight in."

"So, what happened?"

"God knows. Last night my driver mentioned a problem with the rent."

"Still, at least they put you in a decent place. Well, not bad, apart from this lot, every day and night." Braddock gestured towards the window. Two raggedy kids were gawping in from the car park, rubbing their bellies in melodramatic anguish.

Mister, we could kill a croissant. They waved and Braddock waved back. "Who's funding you, Frank, the Brits?"

"No, USAID." Frank loosened his tie and glanced down at Braddock's sandals; perhaps he was on vacation. "And you, Jerome, what brings you to Kinshasa?"

"Fine and dandy, thanks." Braddock pointed at the laptop. "Wife and kids, eh?"

Frank glanced at his screensaver. The random sequence of family photos had paused on a shot of Ruth in a summer top, flanked by little Dylan with sun-bleached blonde hair and Billie in her Goth phase – black eyeliner and a barnet like a dead crow. "Yup, that's my tribe. We were on holiday in South Wales; nice spot. My father-in-law's got a cottage."

"Teenager looks a bit peeved, what's her problem?"

"Long story. You married, Jerome?"

Braddock chuckled. "Tried and failed. So, are you going to the east as well? Teach the rebels to tell even bigger whoppers? Those boys are taking orders from Rwanda."

"That's the plan. But first, I do a five-day seminar in Kinshasa; probably take a couple of weeks to set up. Then I head east: Goma, Kisangani and Bukavu, if they'll have me." *Head east.* Frank pictured himself as a lonesome cowboy at a campfire. Except cowboys went west.

"The rebels will have you, all right," said Braddock, rooting in his pocket for a beeping mobile. He fished it out and cupped his hand over the screen.

"How do you mean?" asked Frank.

"Well, if the RCD see your little boxes, list of countries? They'll insist that east Congo is *a sovereign state, a new one.* But it isn't. It's a bloody mess. So watch your back."

"Thanks for the tip."

"*Avec plaisir.*" Braddock got up and wandered off, barking into his tiny phone. Frank watched and wondered. The fellow was helpful, bordering on nosey. Not to mention cagey.

Frank closed the laptop, a yawn splitting his face. He sat back, watching the raggedy kids outside thump each other.

Braddock drifted back with a knowing smile. "Jet-lagged?"

"Just tired. I had a six-hour wait in Nairobi."

"*Nairobbery*... great town. Any hassle here in Kin, at the airport? They're buggers."

"Luckily my boss sent a fixer. Godwin someone."

Braddock seemed amused. "Let me guess. Small guy? Built like Mike Tyson and wears a black fedora? Met you on the tarmac and walked you through immigration?"

"How did you know?"

"That's Godfrey, best *expéditeur* in town. You ever need any help, he's your man."

"I'll bear it in mind," said Frank, stifling another yawn. "Actually, could he find me a quieter hotel? I hardly slept. God knows what was kicking off around the back, last night. Sounded like the Third World War at times. Woke me up three times."

"Weapons?" said Braddock, one eyebrow rising like a furry caterpillar.

"Not exactly. Drums booming, kids howling, people chanting, guitars and speeches."

"Oh, that? That's not war. That's a pile of bollocks."

"I beg your pardon?"

"*C'est une délivrance*, mate. Twice a week in public, a right bloody din. They usually start around midnight when the Devil is abroad. But most of time, he's in Kinshasa."

A familiar voice echoed across the lobby. "Mr Frank! So sorry I am late...!"

Claude the driver approached, wearing an anguished smile and a UN baseball cap. Frank rose from the sofa and glanced back at the talkative stranger. "*Une délivrance?*"

"Exorcism," said Braddock, thumbing his phone.

Chapter 4

Dudu shuffled through the doorway of Heroes' Corner, his clothes all wet and muddy. Moses looked up from the bar, a cigarette dangling. "What the hell happened, boy?"

"I fell in the river."

"I can see that. Where's my bidon?"

"That fell in too. I lost it. Sorry, Uncle."

Moses closed his eyes and rubbed his head as if this were the worst news ever.

There was only one client. Nkusu seemed to be talking to the wall, wobbly already from too much beer. It was hard to believe that he, Old Koosie, one of the original *heroes,* would end up like this, drinking himself into pickle. Why did he do it? Depending who you listened to, it was because his wife had died from *Slim,* although others claimed Koosie had lost his wits in the war, after the explosion that killed Tata and the others. Koosie turned and squinted in the dark. "Dudu? Hah! Looks like someone put a spell on you too!"

Dudu thought about Ginelle: *there is something magical about her.*

Moses hissed across the gloomy room. "Hush, Koosie, no more of that."

Koosie offered his empty beer bottle. "Some more of this, please, *patron.*"

Moses popped the caps on two beers and Koosie said, "What about Du?"

"What about him?"

"Put it on my tab," Koosie said. Moses rolled his eyes and popped a bottle of *sucré.* He pushed it to Dudu, raised his beer and said in a mocking tone, "To my clever stepson."

"I'll fetch another bidon," Dudu said. "I'll fill it quick and mop up. Clean for clients."

"No need," Koosie said. "*I found out* why nobody comes here. Why that TV broke."

Dudu looked at the dusty screen behind the bar, grey and lifeless. "What?"

Koosie was smiling, his few stumpy teeth like white pebbles in a riverbed. But before he could explain Moses boomed at him. "Koosie, shut up or get out!" Koosie sipped his beer.

Moses turned to Dudu, with a fierce look. "You were supposed to bring water in my bidon, not your pockets. So, for the last time, what happened? I want the whole story."

Dudu explained, as best he could, but it was hard with Moses glaring at him. The tale had sounded convincing when Ginelle had invented it, but not now. Moses folded his arms and spat a shred of tobacco. "My bidons *floated away?* It's a pity *you* didn't float away! Get out, boy, I don't need your muddy feet in my bar. Just wait until I tell your mother!" Moses pointed to the doorway and Dudu slithered outside. He could hear Nkusu protesting, calling him back, but the drunkard's amazing discovery, whatever it was, would have to wait.

Dudu trotted off, keeping to the edge of the village, but even so, people pointed and laughed, nudging each other. The little black dog spotted him too, came snapping at his heels.

When Dudu reached home, Mama threw him a clean pair of shorts and sat on a chair inspecting the rip in his soggy ones. "So, all three bidons fell in, and you swam after them?"

Dudu nodded. "It was muddy. I got tangled in bushes trying to catch them."

"I see. Was this before, or after you got tangled in the tree with Ginelle?" Mama glanced up. She did not look angry, just disappointed. "Don't fib, Dudu. Emile told me everything."

She tossed the wet shorts aside. "I'll have to sew them up. More work!"

Dudu stared at the goats tethered in the sunny yard. They stared back as if to say, *not our fault.* He put his head in his hands, wondering whether to ask Mama to sew Emile's mouth up, but she seemed in no mood for jokes. She tucked her wooden bowl between her feet and pounded the big wooden pole up and down, until the cassava flour rose in a fine white cloud. She shook her head as if her eldest boy were the biggest fool in the village.

"Should I fetch wood?" he said.

"You've caused enough trouble for one day. Make a drink for Nana. She's lonely."

Dudu poked the embers of the fire and added a few twigs. He filled the dented steel pan with water from the white enamelled jug and, while it was heating, he crushed a handful of dried leaves – eucalyptus, fennel, butterbur, garlic and camomile – and dropped them in the pan. When the water bubbled and darkened, he poured some of it into a plastic mug and took a deep breath before opening the squeaky door to the tiny room at the back of the house.

Nana Kima was hunched in the shadows on her bamboo bed, thin and sick. It was hard to believe, seeing her like this. Not long ago, she had been walking about, full of jokes. She beckoned him with feeble fingers and a wheezing croak. "Come, Dudu. Is that for me?"

The place stank but Nana's wrinkled hand reached out, like an old leather glove shrunken by rain and sun, urging him to enter. She gazed at him with watery eyes that knew what he had done. "Don't look so sad, Du! I'm ready for my journey." She sounded strange. He helped her sip from the mug of the tea and said, "Nana, you're too ill to go anywhere."

"I'm going in the hills, Dudu, where the plums are sweet. Remember?"

He nodded, trying to remember. *I was smaller than Emile, that time.*

"And perhaps," Nana said, "I'll go to the creek where the big fish hide. I'll meet your tata. Do you remember how he liked to cook them on a fire and watch the sun melt away?"

Dudu soon understood, but wished that he had not. "Please don't go, Nana."

"We all go sometime, Dudu. Shall we light a candle for *ekeko*?"

"For the Power Figure?" He shook his head. "Moses will count them and find out."

Nana coughed until her ribs rattled like dried beans in a can. "One candle, please."

Dudu opened the old cupboard at the wall and took out the heavy wooden Power Figure with rusty nails sticking from its breast. It had a tortoise shell for a belly, deep slits for eyes and three goat horns on its head. Shards of mirror, buttons and brass had been added over many years, fine beadwork too. He placed the figure on the floor and its head was level with his knee. He got some matches, lit a fresh candle and set it in melted wax at the figure's wooden feet. He sat cross-legged and watched the golden glow cast spooky shapes across the floor and up the wall, like black hoods. He noticed Emile peeping through the doorway, too scared to enter. Perhaps he knew he would get a slap for snitching. Dudu avoided his gaze and looked back at the Power Figure. "Can *ekeko* really make you better, Nana?"

"I hope so. Your grandfather carved it. Perhaps he is watching over me."

"Uncle Moses told me this is old-fashioned. Pagan stuff, voodoo."

"Because he's envious of what your tata and grand-tata did. Not everyone can carve figures like this one, only a master carpenter – *nswendwe*. You should be proud of them."

Dudu edged closer to the *ekeko*. "Because they carved figures for the *nganga buka*?"

"So you remember. For *nganga buka,* yes, the great sorcerer. Because they were *nswendwe*. You could be too, some day, if you practise hard with your little knife."

Dudu sighed. "Me? Moses says it's not much of a job anymore, *nswendwe*."

"It's not just a job, it's a privilege, a gift. Your tata had it, and so do you."

"Moses says the old days are gone. Nobody needs wooden dolls anymore." Dudu looked into Nana's eyes, murky and brown as a river. She smiled, as if sensing his confusion.

"Moses is right, in some ways, the old ways are dying, Dudu, but talent does not die; it is passed down. I have seen you sitting quietly, like your tata, carving wood in the yard."

"*Making funny animals.* That's what Ginelle says. You know what my problem is?"

Nana cackled and pointed at the window. "One day, my boy, you must stop listening to who's out *there* and listen to who's in *here*." She prodded him in the chest. "Understand?"

"Think so." He wrinkled his nose as Nana caressed his face; her hands smelled bad.

"You're very young, Du, and have a long way to go. Go now. Thank you for my tea."

Nana Kima coughed and lay back. He watched the candle. It had burned too far and Moses would notice. He blew it out and hid the Power Figure back in the cupboard. He stood in the darkness, listening to Nana's wheezing breath. What did she mean – *a long way to go?*

Moses came stumbling home at noon, bellowing like a giant. "Solange!"

Dudu was cleaning the hencoop but slipped out to watch. Moses would be complaining about his *fish-brained stepson*, any minute now. Mama appeared in the yard and Moses jabbed a finger back at the village, as if someone had done something bad.

"Solange, guess how many clients? Zero. But at least, now, I know why!"

"Because you're turning into a bully and a bore, I heard."

"Watch your tongue, woman. It's because someone is out to get me. It's envy."

"I see. Envy? It's not because you argue with anyone who disagrees with your opinions? Not because your TV is still broken and your prices are higher than elsewhere?"

"It's *sorcery!* Koosie says someone wants to ruin me. And they're succeeding."

Mama's eyes went as big as clocks. She looked as scared as the day the militia had taken Tata. She gathered up her robe and glanced around the yard. "Sorcery?"

Dudu ducked into a bush, peeping through the leaves. Moses was pacing about.

"Yes! But Koosie knows what to do. Because everyone is talking."

"About us?" Mama covered her mouth.

"No, about a pastor, from the Church of Victory Over Satan; he's very clever and has found a witch in every village. *Every village.* Sometimes two, even three witches."

Mama surveyed the yard as if looking for a snake. "Is he coming to *our* village?"

"If I invite him, perhaps he will. He's downriver, in Fansha. Koosie says I should go and ask him to come to Mavuku, to save my business. It's a good idea, don't you think?"

Mama sat down, looking puzzled. "I see. You'll go downriver to save your bar, but not to save my mother? Every time I ask you to take her downriver, to the *mundele* clinic…"

"I refuse, yes, because the *mundele* nurses will steal her insides. She'll die."

"She won't live, unless she gets help!"

"The pastor will help! I just realised! Nana's illness is because of sorcery too. Someone wants her out of the way. They want to destroy our family! Yes, why not?"

"*They?*"

Mama was soon firing questions about how to stop the sorcerers who wanted to kill her mother. Moses burped and confessed he did not exactly know how to do that, but the pastor would. "I'll leave first thing tomorrow! Buy two seats in a pirogue. I'll take Koosie."

"That drunken halfwit? No, this is serious, Moses. You must go, but not with him."

"What if I fall in the river? I cannot swim. Who will save me?"

"Take Dudu; he swims like a fish and his fare will be cheaper."

"So, why did he not swim after the bidons, bring them back? Fish brain, you mean." Moses tugged at Mama's robe and slipped a hand inside. "You will compensate me. Come."

Moses led Mama into the house and Dudu crept back to the hencoop. He stood among the feathers and mess, his heart thumping, staring at the walls. *Sorcery in Mavuku?* He spotted one of Tata's rusty nails in a beam, from the days when this had been his workshop. How proud Tata would be to see his son going in a big pirogue to meet a famous pastor who had found witches in every village. Dudu practised what to say to Ginelle before the trip.

"Sorry, Ginelle, I cannot come to the spring, I have to help catch sorcerers."

"Dudu, how brave. But aren't you scared? Let me give you some advice."

"I don't need any. I even know who the witches are, but don't tell anyone. Not yet."

"Oh, Dudu, may I kiss you farewell?"

"If you like."

Chapter 5

Frank climbed into the front passenger seat of the Unicorn jeep. Claude told him to get in the back, instead. Frank obeyed and Claude pointed to the seat belt. "Buckle it up, please, and listen carefully. First, we'll visit HQ to meet Mr Hector and everyone else, then we'll go to the Ministry of Information. Later, we'll visit radio stations. Any questions?"

"Why can't I ride in the front?"

"In case of accidents. And beggars. You must beware. Safer in the back."

Claude smiled and drove with deft movements, his forearms smooth as charcoal, his ivory bracelets chinking. His dress code was NGO chic: safari vest with pockets, a clean white T-shirt and baseball cap, pale blue, UN logo. Frank gazed ahead from the back seat. A cigar stub protruded from a bullet hole in the windscreen and rosary beads dangled from the rear-view mirror; a penitent's pendulum from the mists of time. They reminded him of Ruth, or rather, of the rosary beads he had spotted in her room, on their first night together, long ago. Frank asked Claude about exorcisms and the driver shrugged. "This is Kinshasa."

The busy Boulevard du 30 Juin was lined with office blocks and white villas. Bulging minibuses careened around corners and a white UN jeep cruised past, its black aerials swaying like antennae. Lurid signs offered backstreet worship: JESUS OF THE HOLY FIRE, and CHRIST THE WARRIOR. Frank spotted a few more and asked, "You a Catholic, Claude?"

"Of course. What is your religion?"

Frank paused to think about that one. "Travel. I believe it

broadens the mind."

Claude frowned. "*Travel makes one a stranger*. Do you know this?"

"My wife does. What's that place?" Frank pointed. "It was lit up last night, I think."

Claude beamed. "That is our Palais de la Nation. And over there, this is our Banque Centrale du Congo, do you see? And those are the *cambistes*." He pointed at buxom women on stools brandishing bricks of banknotes.

"*Cambistes?*"

"Change mamas; they are selling currency. And the new US dollar is worth less than the older ones, because the president's head is printed smaller now. Remember, *small-head dollars* are worth less than *big-head dollars*. And how is your hotel, Frank?"

"Noisy but not bad. You serious about the dollars?"

Claude flashed a sparkly smile. "But of course. And I am sorry about your room, but you should know that if not for our Bernadette at Unicorn Trust, things could have been worse. She has good contacts. Remember that, too."

Frank watched men stroll the kerb in ostentatious shoes with toes curled up like the snouts of amphibians. Stiff-backed women laboured under bundles balanced precariously on their heads. A wizened granny in a headscarf squatted beside three battered pans, doing a brisk trade in doughnuts. Kinshasa seemed as lively as any city but he glimpsed real despair amid all the activity – teenage mothers in threadbare shawls begging for change that would not come; young men on crutches wandering amid roaring traffic as if death had no dominion. "War veterans," said Claude, beeping his horn.

Mucky kids clustered in gangs at every corner; dusty daredevils, from small boys to lanky teenagers perched on walls and dangling their heels or strutting around shouting the odds. Most wore ragged vests or singlets and shorts; one tiny tot wore nothing at all. They spat and sprawled, scuffled and laughed, watching a world that seemed to have forgotten they existed or was perhaps trying not to notice. "We call them *shegués*," Claude said.

"*Sheh-gay?*"

"Short for *Che Guevara*. It comes from the song 'Kao-kokokorobo', by our famous Papa Wemba. He sang about kids who fight to survive like Che. So now we call them *shegués*. But we use a different word if a child fights as a soldier on the front line, for the army or a militia. For them, we say *kadogo;* that's 'little one' in Swahili. So, you're learning, already."

"They're everywhere, these *shegués*."

"Thirty thousand in Kinshasa. Three generations. Be careful. Because, usually, a *shegué* has only two choices: live or die. So, most beg and steal to survive. Although some are very hard-working, they often find jobs fixing flip-flops, dancing for musicians, running errands, selling water and fuel, or whatever they can, like these fellows." Claude pointed up the road, and his ivory bangles slid down his forearm.

A wiry young man stood at an intersection selling snacks from a tray. The next fellow carried a cage of five grey parrots with scarlet tails, eyes as black as caviar, beaks curled like sabres. Claude slowed the jeep and a third teenage salesman came a-grinning, holding up a flat wooden frame containing some wizened black creature, splayed flat. It stunk to high heaven. The stench filled the car. "Fried bat," said Claude. "Welcome to Kin la Belle! Or, *la poubelle*."

"Kinshasa the dustbin. I've heard that one before."

"*Mais c'est beau aussi, regardez le minibus!*" Claude pronounced it *minibiss* and directed Frank's gaze to a rusty camper van with a rainbow paint job. Passengers sat packed inside, faces glistening. Frank unbuttoned his collar and removed his tie. "My God, it's hot. Will my apartment have AC?"

Claude's grin faded. "As I told you, the landlord will not release your keys until he gets rent plus deposit."

"But wasn't that sorted out weeks ago? Hector emailed me; DC had promised to wire the cash, any day."

"Mr Hector discovered yesterday afternoon that the money

has not been sent."

"Great. What happened, someone forgot?"

"A lady named Puffer. I met her recently."

Frank groaned. "Misti Puffer forgot to wire my rent?"

"Probably a misunderstanding. She is a nice person; she visited Kinshasa to teach us managerial effectiveness."

Claude braked sharply at an intersection and Frank recoiled in his seat. "So how long will I stay in the Maisha?"

"Who can say, Frank?"

They sat watching a white-shirted traffic cop standing in her wooden cubicle high above the din, blowing a silver whistle and whirling her arms as if conducting an avant-garde concerto. A barefoot *shegué* stood at the kerb, sniffing the contents of a dirty plastic bag; dazed, happy and harmless. The kid wobbled towards the jeep and Claude said, "Window." Frank closed his window. The kid gawped in, eyes like boiled tomatoes and teeth like pearls as he wailed, "*Papa, j'ai faim.*"

Fifteen minutes later, the jeep eased into a cul-de-sac of shaggy palm trees and red brick walls. Rue Farahilde was a quiet place and provided immediate respite from cross-town traffic; Frank spotted familiar logos in bright colours – WORLD RELIEF, OXFAM – all the big agencies had nice villas in this street. The faded UNICORN TRUST logo was pinned askew on warped steel gates that swung back to reveal a bungalow in a parched garden. An ageing guard saluted. Frank disembarked and followed Claude on a path through dried-up flower beds. A scrawny kitten crouched among grey stalks and a generator sputtered out back, *bad-bad-bad.*

In the lobby, they passed three armchairs of faded chintz and a low table with a beer mat tucked beneath one of it legs. A handsome Congolese woman rose from a wide reception desk; she was big-boned, headscarf twisted like origami. She had sausage fingers and a motherly grin. "You must be Frank. I'm Bernadette; how was the hotel?" They shook hands.

He decided not to be frank. "Very nice, Bernadette! Thank you for saving my bacon."

"Your *bay-kon?*" She gave an imperious giggle and reached for a jangling red telephone. The communications console on her desk was a defiant display of '70s corporate kitsch, studded with lights, one flashing green. "Probably your landlord," Bernadette added.

A squeaky door disgorged a tall, reed-thin young man in shirt and tie, with a winning smile. "I'm Marc, Deputy Head of Training, welcome!" He led Frank on a guided tour of flow charts and graphs pinned to the walls. "Our throughput is consistent, you see?" Frank gazed at a baffling matrix of lines and dots.

A stout lady introduced herself as Rose from Accounts, all scarlet nails and vague resentment. She seemed to expect more than a handshake so Frank quickly produced a box of duty-free chocolates, which went down very well, in three minutes flat. Rose led him to a colour photo in a frame. "Miss Puffer put this up, to remind us of her instructive visit."

"As if we'd forget," said Bernadette, munching.

The photo showed the local Unicorn staff huddled around a young white woman in a safari suit with short blonde hair and a cheesy grin. Lilac-coloured font below announced:

Thanx everyone! I am blessed by your FRIENDSHIP *and will never forget our week* CO-CREATING *a vibrant social and economic landscape in* THE CONGO. *Bestest,* MISTI x

"She forgot my rent," said Frank, but Rose was reading the chocolate box.

"For every problem, a solution," Bernadette said, firmly. "My contact at the Maisha says you may stay longer."

"Thank you," replied Frank, and looked closer at the photograph. "Is this Hector?" He pointed at the large pug-nosed white fellow in a bright African robe standing in the middle of the picture, next to Misti. Rose nodded. "Come and meet."

She beckoned Frank down a poorly lit corridor and opened the door of a broom cupboard en route, pointing inside. It contained a desk, a chair and a framed photo of David Hasselhoff. "This will be your office, is it quite OK?"

Frank tried to look thrilled. "I'll be travelling quite a bit."

"That's what I thought," said Rose, with an air of satisfaction. "Mr Hector's in the seminar room. Wait here."

She left Frank at a door with a narrow section of glass in it. In the room beyond stood the big man from the photo, rugby arms going like a windmill as he addressed a group of well-dressed Congolese sitting in rows, transfixed by his every utterance. The three words on the whiteboard behind him seemed to suggest a marketing mantra. SELL THE SIZZLE!

Hector Harris stood about six foot four in his shiny brogues and boomed like a foghorn. He wore swathes of bright fabric; gone native, or nuts. A bumbag of wrinkled leather dangled below his sizeable stomach, half sporran, half scrotum. He had bushy black eyebrows, tufted ears and a beard shaped like a shovel. Frank felt hot just looking. An amulet of ebony and silver hung from Hector's bullish neck. He didn't look like a business advisor, or ex-Special Forces, come to that. He looked more like an ageing hippy. Was this really the man who had recently boasted to Frank, on a dodgy phone line to Kingston upon Thames, of having spent *a week in a cave with no food*? Perhaps he had said *a week in a rave*.

The confusion seemed mutual because Hector was now staring at Frank in return, momentarily baffled by the pink face and curly blonde hair, perhaps. The penny dropped. He checked his watch, called a halt and emerged, speaking in a Glaswegian burr, corners rounded off. "Frank Kean! You're on my patch now!" Hector's brief handshake was lukewarm, as though reticence lurked by default, despite the booming bonhomie. Perhaps you had to bayonet someone to earn his trust.

"Caffeine?" He stood rolling his ham-shank hands like a cartoon miser.

A Congolese trainee stepped into the corridor. "But Mr Hector, we haven't—"

Hector raised a podgy palm. "Sorry, I'm done for now, Gustave. I have a guest. I'm taking a break. Non-negotiable."

"But *everything's* negotiable," suggested the trainee, prompting giggles all round.

Hector walked on. "They learn fast, tomorrow's movers and shakers. Take a pew."

Frank followed him into a large office that stunk of cigars. It had elegant French windows and stunning African masks, eyeholes ogling the newcomer. A murderous wooden statue, three feet high with rusty nails protruding from its torso and feathers sprouting from its head, guarded a corner. Hector sat in a squeaky swivel chair, feet up. His tasselled brogues seemed out of place; a last grasp at conformity. "So, Frank Kean! Settling into Kinshasa? How's the Maisha?"

Frank related his first impressions, while Hector's right brogue rocked back and forth. *Been there, done that.* "Congo's no picnic, Frank, but you'll survive. And, to be honest, I wouldn't complain too much about the Church of the Barking Mad. Strictly *entre nous*, some of those pastors have friends in high places and I don't mean heaven."

"I'll try. How's your marketing seminar going?"

Hector grinned like Blackbeard. "Ducks to water, those young managers! The new generation." He lit a fat cigar stub from a brimming ashtray and puffed smoke at the ceiling, watching the plumes grow. "Years to come, Africa will reap the democratic dividend, the population will double as the birth rate declines, more people of working age but less kids and old folks. Congo can be Africa's engine, Frankie; it just needs fuel, not to mention an axle and wheels. We're the garage, if you see what I mean." Hector paused to stare out of the French windows, ear cocked. The generator beyond puttered to a stop and the AC unit on the wall whirred itself out. "Hear that? Janitor forgot diesel. I've only told him three times."

Frank looked into the garden. "I hear Misti forgot to wire my rent."

"Fine young lady," replied Hector, rather too soon, with a stuck-on smile. He handed Frank a printed sheet. "Let's talk training: here's a list of local FM stations. You asked me for reporters, a mix of rookies and veterans? Visit the stations; their managers will decide who attends. You'll do one seminar in Kinshasa and three in the east. Twelve trainees per seminar, so you'll need forty-eight wotsits. Here's fifty." Hector offered a bulging A4 envelope.

"Fifty what?"

"Look inside."

Frank looked. The envelope contained fifty diplomas with the Unicorn logo, signed by *Konrad Mott II,* whoever he was. Frank looked closer. The signature was pre-printed. *Classy.*

"Be sure to touch base with Rossi at AID," Hector said. "Claude will hire you a seminar room uptown. Rose will issue your per diem. Insist on big-head bucks. Know why?"

"Sure, better exchange rate. But, why can't I host my Kinshasa seminar here?"

"Sorry, all booked. Now, about these peace talks, the Inter-Congolese Dialogue… what do you think?"

Frank gazed at the generator. "Dead as a dodo."

"Correct. Which is why we've decided on a few changes to your training. Did Misti update you?"

Frank shook his head and Hector smiled. "Poor little Misti, always tons of work. Same when she was here. She set up base in my office, spent hours drafting proposals and God knows what for HQ. Anyway, here's the skinny: your seminars will be the first we have offered for journalists in DRC, so they must go well. They must be substantial. That means, Frank, that you can no longer focus on the peace talks."

Frank watched the kitten rolling in a flower bed. He wanted to say, *I suggested that a while ago and Misti ignored my email.* But something about Hector's defence of her dissuaded him. "Fair enough, you're saying we need a Plan B?"

"Bang on, Frank, because if there is no peace process, journalists can't report it, can they? And if you train them to second-guess the talks, God knows what rumours they'll broadcast, or how the local authorities might react. Not just Kabila's government here in Kinshasa but the rebels in the east: the RCD-Goma, all those boys, yes? In short, USAID could end up accused by both sides of trying to influence media coverage, which is the last thing they need right now. Because America wants elections here, free and fair, one fine day. Not trouble. So we mustn't provoke any. Write it down."

Frank was already scribbling. "I had a feeling about this. Where does it leave me?"

"Focus on community, that's what local radio does best. *Here is the news: a big hole has appeared in the road and police are looking into it.* In other words, keep it simple, stupid. Drop the rebel factions, forget the war crimes."

"*Alleged* war crimes. But thanks for the advice and the list. I'll bone up on local."

"Anything to help. I'm no newsman but I know radio. Congo's ripe for a boom once the economy picks up. With radio comes information, education, and let me tell you something: Scotland, my country, was among the most backward in Europe at the start of the seventeenth century. By the start of the eighteenth century, it was one of the most advanced. Guess why."

"Because you ate porridge?"

"Education. We knuckled down, swotted up. That's how we *grew our potential,* as Misti might say. That's what Dr Livingstone was all about. He was a Scot, like me. So get to work. Start small, think big and be careful what you promise."

"Meaning?"

"Congo has been shafted by too many foreigners, white *and* black. Trust me."

"If you say so." Frank surveyed the walls of Hector's office. Rows of wooden faces stared back. "Nice masks you've got, Hector. My wife would love them. Wants me to bring her *something really ethnic.* How long have you been in Africa?"

"Too long. My doctor recommends less stress. As if! This is non-stop. Make sure you see Alphonse at MONUC for your flights. You're going east. Watch yourself out there, laddie."

"Dangerous?" asked Frank, as a curvaceous girl in jeans and a tight top brought them a tray of coffee.

Hector smiled. "Well, the rebel zone is certainly… interesting. But let's not twist our knickers on Day One, eh Frank? You're new but try to relax and enjoy the delights of Kin la Belle. How's Blighty by the way? You're in Kingston upon Thames, as I recall. Good rowing, decent stretch of river. Do you row? Doesn't look like it. You'll need to register."

"For rowing?"

"For work, at Min-Info; lovely place if you like exercise." Hector smiled at the girl serving coffee, *thanks love.* He watched her sashay out, and said, "Christ, the arse on that."

Chapter 6

Frank trudged up five floors, following Claude in the gloom. By the tenth he was gasping in the fetid heat. *Too many cigarettes.* The concrete steps of the Ministry of Information spiralled up and up, endlessly. Sweat dripped from his nose, blotched a step and dried in seconds. "Claude, are we sure I need press accreditation? I'm not a reporter."

Claude brushed dust from a forearm. "They can stop your seminars, Frank."

"Great, and what happened to the elevator?"

"War happened."

Eventually, they reached the seventeenth floor and entered a large office reeking of mildew and echoing with the clacks of gargantuan typewriters. Frank stood with a hammering heart, filling forms and counting out big-head dollars. He gave them to a po-faced military clerk and sank into a sofa dotted with cigarette burns. He plucked a faded newspaper from a dusty pile. *La Voix* had musty pages of skewed text and grainy photos of sportsmen, soldiers, diplomats. It was slim pickings, news-wise, until Frank reached page nine and spotted a small article under a karaoke ad. Even its title made him wonder.

FOUR PARENTS ARRESTED FOR CHILD MURDER

The parents of two children aged 3 years, and 4 months, respectively, were arrested for their murder last Tuesday, in south Kinshasa. Two relatives were also arrested and will be tried.

According to Police in Kalamu, the parents claimed the children had been possessed by the Devil. They performed exorcism on the children in the shantytown, where Police came after neighbours heard screams.

The parents said they drove out the spirit of a deceased aunt who had possessed the children and wanted to harm the family. The children suffered atrocities before death.

Sweat tickled his scalp and typewriter bells jangled. The journalist in him spotted a few howlers but the parent in him reeled at the basics. *How could anyone hurt children? Four months old? Jesus. Ruth is due late summer; our new baby will be that age by Christmas; as for "three years old," Dylan was eating Lego at that age. Diabolical behaviour but kids are kids.* Frank glanced around and coughed as he tore the page out. *Because if it bleeds it leads, except in Kinshasa?* The clerk called Frank's name as if it were an infectious disease. Frank folded the page into a pocket and walked to the desk. The clerk gave him a press card, a scrawled receipt for two hundred and fifty dollars, and a stern look. "Mr Kean, you are permitted to train but not report. Understood?" Mr Kean nodded.

Claude emerged from the men's room, holding car keys. "No water in there. Ready?"

"You bet." Frank strode to the stairs. "And it's downhill all the way, easy-peasy."

Claude promised *an interesting detour* in the jeep and turned off the main drag into a quiet neighbourhood of royal palms, grand houses and heavy gates. Indolent guards squatted beside nests of sandbags, belts of brass cartridges drooping down from their long-barrelled machine guns. Security cameras swivelled on a wall, carefully tracking the progress of the car.

"This place is like Beverly Hills with guns," said Frank. Claude chuckled and dipped the jeep down a back lane. A few metres below, silent and unannounced, swirled a sudden expanse of brown water, miles wide, throbbing in the sun. Frank gawked at it. "Is this the Congo?"

"Three thousand miles long," said Claude. "Fifteen miles wide, in places."

They parked on a bluff. Frank walked to the edge, staring out. "My God."

"I thought you didn't believe?" Claude leaned from the jeep. "She is beautiful, no? That water comes from highlands far away, even Lake Tanganyika. Our famous Congo flows both north and south, which foxed even your Dr Livingstone."

"No wonder he got lost." Frank stood watching the vast slow-rolling river. There was something about water. It made you wonder. He recalled a similar sensation at Niagara Falls, where spray and roar had numbed his wits until he could hardly think. But this was different. Here, some conspiracy of the wet unknowable whispered: *don't even try.* He pointed to a big patch of bright green vegetation, low trees, out in the middle. "Anyone live on that island?"

Claude laughed, pushing up the frayed peak of his UN cap. "That's weed, water hyacinth, brought to our country by Belgian ladies for their gardens many years ago. Now it grows everywhere and is often choking the river. It's too bad."

The opposite bank smouldered in a blur of docks and cranes, but something was missing. Frank glanced left and right. "No ships or boats?"

"When war starts, my friend, everything stops. Upstream, the government controls one side of the river and the rebels control the other so trade is difficult. If it were easier our economy would grow. In the 1970s, one Congolese franc was worth two US dollars. Imagine that." Claude drummed fingers and his bracelets *chink-chinked* like the distant gunfire. Frank wondered about the stalled peace talks. So far, nine countries had spent more than four years tearing this place apart. Imagine that.

"When I was a driver for the UN," Claude said, "someone there told me that one thousand, two hundred Congolese die every day, mostly from malnutrition and malaria. Four million so far, Frank. I do not think this is fair. We are a very rich country."

"That's why there's a war. But peace will come, Claude, and the UN is helping."

"MONUC?" Claude removed his cap and smirked wistfully at the UN badge. He did not seem bitter, just bored. "*Le Mission de l'ONU en Congo.* I worked for them. Big maps and fine vehicles. But it won't stop the war."

"At least there are peace talks. Well, there *were.*"

"In my country, only money talks. Let's go."

As they drove alongside the riverbank, Frank spotted wood-smoke and a clutch of mud huts where barefoot kids with yellowing hair crouched beside stick-boned adults swatting flies with slow sweeps of the hand. The scene offered a glimpse of primordial hunter-gatherers, as if Congo were moving backwards in time. These people were surely among the poorest of Africa and the only modern aspect of their lives seemed to be the threadbare T-shirts that clung to their skinny bodies: *2Pac; Tyson.* They stared at Frank in the gleaming vehicle and their elfin faces expressed little except the certainty that he would not be dropping in.

"We should pull up," he said. "Give them money."

"And tomorrow?" Claude asked, and kept going. They drove slowly up a slope, back towards the VIP zone.

Frank's phone beeped with a text message from his wife. *How's it going? xxx*

He gazed at soaring palms. Ignorance was bliss. He thumbed a reply. *Great! On my way to a radio station ☺ xxx*

Frank stood in the newsroom, soaking up the familiar atmosphere. Or lack of it. Choice FM had seen better days. The bulky grey computers looked ready for the scrapheap. A faded poster of a Harley curled up the wall. A pretty young woman with exposed shoulders and big earrings had the place all to herself. She was sprawled on a chair, watching TV: some soap opera. On-screen, three worried-looking men stood exchanging glances across the cheap-looking set.

The skinny woman in the singlet tugged a bra strap and glanced at Frank. "If you want the manager, he's out. You should have phoned first."

"I tried. He didn't answer." Frank told her about the seminar. He asked her about life at Choice FM. She told him her name was Nadine and listened with one eye on the TV. "I'm just a presenter but the boss knows about your seminar."

"Will you be attending?"

"Me?" said Nadine, gazing at the telly.

Frank circled a battered desk strewn with the usual detritus – headphones and editing blades, tape spools and cassettes. The single computer had a ghostly glow and the porthole on the studio door was cracked. Frank cupped his hands and saw a good-looking male DJ inside, pouting into a microphone. He turned back to Nadine. "When's your next bulletin?"

"Forty minutes."

"Do you have a news archive?"

"A what?"

"A folder, in the computer maybe, somewhere you keep old news stories?"

"I write mine by hand."

"I see. And what happens after you read them, on air?"

"Papa Johnny plays a tune."

"I meant, do you save the stories, archives for three months say, for reference? Or in case anyone takes legal action?"

"They wouldn't dare." Nadine rooted under a pile of newspapers and pulled out a block of wood. A six-inch nail protruded from the centre, with a wad of scrawled notepaper impaled on it. "Do you mean this?"

"The spike. Yes, excellent, thanks. May I?" Frank prised

off the sheets of notepaper, flicking quickly through the hand-written stories. Some were legible, some not, but he soon discerned a pattern to Choice FM's news agenda. The station seemed to prioritise stories about government VIPs, pop concerts, sport, and traffic accidents. Most showed a date and an hour but the news writing was weak and the story Frank hoped to find was conspicuous by its absence. He dipped into his back pocket and offered Nadine the page he had torn from *La Voix*.

"Did you run this one? Four adults arrested for murder? Of two kids, allegedly."

Nadine read the story and handed it back. "Can't remember. Probably not."

Frank folded the inky page into his pocket. "Any idea why not?"

"That *ndoki* stuff happens all the time. Sorcery, I mean. With *shegués* too." Nadine gazed at her soap opera.

On the steel staircase leading down to the car park, Frank stepped aside for a chunky young man in a red tie, bounding up two steps at a time, clutching a stubby microphone and a minidisc recorder. He wore an ID tag on a lanyard. Frank spotted the first name: *Thony*. The staircase rattled as Thony trotted past, no time to lose. Frank walked down to the jeep and texted the manager, asking if Thony could come to the Unicorn seminar. That kid was keen.

Frank climbed aboard and buckled himself in. "Where next, Claude?"

"Radio 21 then Radio Hope, depending on traffic."

Frank spent the rest of the day in a blur of discussions with managers, editors and journalists, in newsrooms that buzzed with activity or needed a shot in the arm. He checked names against Hector's list and discussed the local news agenda.

He outlined his seminar, shook hands and said goodbye.

Early evening on the boulevard, Claude slowed the jeep to a crawl and stopped. Frank looked around and noticed every other vehicle had stopped too and every pedestrian was standing erect, facing the same direction, motionless. It was bizarre, like a scene from some corny old sci-fi movie. The aliens had landed or soon would. "What's up, Claude?" he said.

Claude brandished his watch: 6 p.m. sharp. He seemed unfazed, tapping his fingers to military music that came blaring from the sky and filled the world with pompous promise. Eventually, he pointed to a Congolese flag fluttering down a pole behind a high wall of peeling stucco. The music stopped, the traffic roared and the pedestrians went on their way.

"Twice a day," said Claude, driving on, beckoned by the whistle-blowing cops in their white gloves, doubtless happy to be in charge once more. Two junctions on, he slowed again, stuck in a traffic jam. A scabby street kid waved at Frank with a stoned smile. Frank waved back and within seconds half a dozen *shegués* were clambering up the Unicorn jeep, knuckles rapping, hands burrowing at windows. "*Papa! Donnez-moi! Pesa ngai mbongo!*"

Claude clicked his teeth. "Never encourage them, Frank. They may steal your laptop. Wing mirrors are costly."

A whistle peeped, Claude floored the gas and the boys dropped like spiders. Frank watched from the back window. "What if they get hurt?"

Claude poked the radio and Congolese rumba boomed out. He did not answer the question until two blocks later, as he spun into the car park of Hotel Maisha. "Frank, please, do not worry about *shegués*. Relax and have a nice evening. I'll be here tomorrow morning. We must visit USAID and MONUC. That is why you came. Not for our *shegués*. Beware."

Frank watched the jeep circle away. Claude smiled at him, wagging a finger from the driver's window. *Beware.*

Chapter 7

Ruth Kean was praying in a pew near the back of the silent church, when she heard footsteps clicking towards her. She opened her eyes and smiled up at the grizzled priest in his black soutane. He leaned closer, with a friendly whisper. "Afternoon, Ruth! Thought it was you. How's your nomad, got there OK?"

"Yes, thank you, Father Lynch. And how are you?"

"Weather like today? I'd rather be back in Africa, but he can't quote me!" The priest tapped his bulbous nose and walked on. He opened one of two shiny black doors a few metres away and vanished into the tiny confessional beyond, like a ghost through a wall.

Ruth watched a hunched crone in beige stockings shuffle up and enter the adjoining compartment of the confessional to spill her beans. The crucifix shimmered in the stained-glass glow above the marble altar and Ruth felt a phoney. She had been to confession how often, since her conversion? *Maybe twice. It's too... medieval. What are you supposed to confess? Bless me, Father, I nagged Billie about her revision? As if God would care.* She made the sign of the cross and closed her eyes. She prayed for Frank to be safe, for their son not to miss him too much and for Billie to do well in her exams. She prayed for her dad not to be lonely in South Wales and for her mother-in-law Betty, likewise, up north. Last of all, she offered a quick prayer for the baby in her womb. She felt a kick inside and waddled from her pew.

She stood outside under fat raindrops from ancient oaks, waiting for the drizzle to ease off. Surely, to confess, you must first *feel* like a sinner? Did she? No. Just a bit lonely, as usual when Frank went abroad, but it would pass. She checked her watch. Dylan would be waiting at school. She pulled up her collar and walked to her red Mondeo parked by the lichen-covered wall. She drove away listening to The Supremes' "You Keep Me Hangin' On".

Ruth arrived outside St Edward's Primary at 4.25 p.m. and walked along the privet-lined path towards the neon-lit annex, stepping aside for more punctual parents with boisterous offspring coming the other way. Dylan waved from a window of Kids' Club and came out flapping into his coat like a baby bird trying to fly. Ruth assisted and ruffled his blonde curls. She tried to peck his face but he recoiled, too busy glancing back at a pretty young girl with curly blonde hair watching from the window. She could have been his twin sister. Something in the air. "Who's she?" asked Ruth.

"New girl, Aubrey Price. Her daddy works in China."

"She's pretty. Is she nice?"

"Yes, and posh. Baxter makes fun of her voice."

"But you don't, I hope. Where does she live?"

"The Lindens. She told me it's a little street that goes nowhere. By Richmond Park."

"She means a *cul-de-sac,* I know the one. Her folks must be rich. You're moving up, buster."

They stopped at Mr Singh's on the way home. The burly newsagent was sitting behind his counter reading *A Farewell to Arms,* scratching at his silver beard. Ruth cancelled delivery of *The Daily Telegraph.* "Because Frank's gone to Africa for a couple of months and I won't have time to read it." She reached for a carton of skimmed milk.

"Not even do the crossword?" said Mr Singh, opening his blue ledger to scribble in a column.

"I'd rather quilt. Ernest Hemingway, that's who you remind me of. His photo is on the back of your book."

"Frank told me the same, one time. When will he be back?"

"When he's shot a few elephants. I'll take this milk and a French baguette, *s'il vous plaît.*"

Walking up her garden path five minutes later Ruth pictured ivy crawling up her house, like in those houses in The Lindens. But no, it would look presumptuous. *Pretentious?* Something like that. You either had ivy or you didn't.

Dylan kicked off his shoes in the hall and Billie appeared on the landing in her grey school uniform, arm over the banister, pouting like she was in a fashion shoot. She certainly had the looks – caramel-coloured skin and increasingly slender curves. Bordering on skinny, she was. Once, she would have been labelled *half-caste* but now she was *mixed-race.* It sounded like an Olympic event. She looked pleased. Weird. Perhaps it was the fluoxetine. Ruth unlaced a shoe.

"Looking chirpy, Billie. Is it the new meds or do you have some good news?"

"It's a free country. Good day at the *orifice?*"

"Old jokes, folks. But yeah, not bad thanks, some bridgework and a couple of extractions."

"How's Purple Jane, still getting on your tits?"

"Language, please. She wore a red scarf today, can you believe it? And the boss has new a watch."

"Cost a bomb I bet, knowing Simon." Billie's brow kinked. Something else on her mind. "You any good at the subjunctive?"

"I'm better at the subnormal. Why do you ask?"

"Three of 'em in French homework, apparently."

"Sorry, my French stopped at seventeen. *Où est la gare?* Why don't you ask Frank?"

"Because he's not here, *comme d'habitude.*"

"I meant by email. You know he likes to help. If you give him a chance."

Billie scrutinised a cuticle and Dylan said, "Guess what, Billie?"

"No idea. Guess Jeans?" Billie spoke sideways, too busy chewing a fingernail.

"Baxter caught a frog with three legs. It's at school, in a glass jar."

"Baxter has three legs?"

"No, the frog. And guess how many times Aubrey has read *Harry Potter*?"

Billie came down to tickle him. "Who cares. Guess who got invited to Glastonbury?"

Dylan writhed in her grasp, whooping it up. "Stop! Invited where?"

"To a pop festival," said Billie. "Biggest in Europe, and I'm going."

"Says who?" said Ruth.

Billie released Dylan and turned, staring. "Mother, I'm eighteen, you can't stop me." She shrugged and held the pose, arms out and palms up, *got it?* The scars on her inner wrists were still visible – translucent bracelets that would take years to fade.

"You're seventeen, Billie, and actually I could stop you. But, hey, it's free country, right? Live and learn."

"Learn what?"

"This and that." Ruth tried to sound blasé. Thousands of people went to Glastonbury every year, camping out, listening to bands and chomping exotic food sold by happy hippies. Yes, it was perfectly possible to pass a fun weekend in deepest Somerset and emerge sweaty but relatively unscathed. Not everyone got blasted out of their skulls, shagged their wife's best mate and spent Sunday weeping in a muddy ditch. Only fools did that, such as her first husband. The memory died hard and so had Max, eventually. Ruth glanced in the hall mirror at her crow's feet. Time passes, we move on.

"So I can go?" Billie stood alongside, her face unlined, her gaze unwavering.

"Sure," Ruth replied, "if you can afford it. A pop festival is not cheap. I went to Glastonbury a few times with your dad and it cost us a bit even then. A lot more now, I reckon. Transport and ticket, food and fun. So, who's inviting?"

"Chloé, actually." Billie turned away and Ruth knew that her doe-eyed daughter was lying, actually.

"I see. Chloé who hates camping?"

"Uh-huh. She changed her mind."

Ruth tapped Billie's arm. "Stop chewing your nails, how many times do I have to tell you?"

"Can I go?" asked Dylan, standing between them.

"And jump in a lake? Yes." Billie trotted upstairs, bum on her like a Bunny girl.

Chapter 8

Early evening, Frank smoked a cigarette on his balcony, observing the neighbourhood below. Church of the Barking Mad was down there somewhere. Would they kick off tonight?

He spent time online in his room researching local issues – nutrition, women's rights and malaria. He took a short nap and a long shower; mid-evening, he went down to the dining terrace in T-shirt and jeans. The swimming pool glowed aquamarine and a big blue lizard was doing press-ups in short grass, its orange head bobbing to cocktail jazz. Stars dotted a purple sky to herald a rising moon mottled grey and white like a wheel of Brie.

Frank settled into a wicker chair and heard a familiar voice from the bar. He turned to watch Jerome Braddock, the tanned Brit from the lobby this morning, chatting with two Congolese guys. One wore a gold-buttoned blazer, the other was in army uniform. Frank eyed the menu, again with a feeling he had met this Braddock fellow before. How come? It seemed unlikely.

Grilled fish or steak? Mining consultant or arms dealer? He glimpsed movement and sensed the riddle would soon be solved because Braddock was making a beeline. "Evening, Scoop. How was your first day? Mind if I sit? Famished."

"Please do, Jerome. What do you recommend, grub and beer-wise?"

Braddock clicked fingers and a waiter in a green waistcoat glided up like an ice skater. Braddock gave him the once over. "New waistcoat, Patrick? Smart. You look like a leprechaun. We'll have two beers, Primus. And one Nile perch."

"*Oui*, Monsieur Jerome, *merci.*"

Frank watched the waiter scoot away. "Thanks, Jerome. What brings you to Kinshasa, by the way?"

Braddock stifled a yawn. "Didn't I tell you? I'm here for the baddies."

"What baddies?"

"Big ones. Oh, and I totted up all the countries I've seen. I reckon forty-nine. How did you get to *ninety-nine?*"

"On a plane from Heathrow. What *baddies?*"

"Proper journalist, you are, eh? I'm a war crimes investigator, if you must know. Ex-Met."

Frank sat back. *Braddock was a policeman?* That explained it. He had the manner, the eyes and the reticence. Frank had interviewed plenty, back in the day job. "You're a bobby?"

"Was," Braddock said, with a wistful air, "London police, started out digging up Dennis Nilsen's place in Cranley Gardens, Muswell Hill. Serial killer, remember? Chopped people up, boiled 'em on his stove, poured the sludge in buckets, buried it in his garden, solidified by the time we found it. Soon I was on the beat but I preferred the mobile stuff. Eventually, I got restless and did a law degree, practised for a bit. Saw Rwanda on the news one night and applied for a job with the Tribunal, to help catch the *génocidaires*. I'm with the ICTR. You know about that?"

"International Criminal Tribunal for Rwanda. So, you work for the UN?"

"Bingo. I chase Category A, the ringleaders." Braddock grinned as the waiter returned and poured cold Primus. They sipped beer and he changed the subject. "So, Frank, ninety-nine countries? You sound like a fugitive. I should know. Wife doesn't give you gyp?"

"Sometimes. But I was a nomad before we met. Ruth knew the score."

"No jobs closer to home?" said Braddock, and Frank detected a prosecutor's guile at work, as though a case were being built. The deep-set eyes drilled into him.

"I like training, Jerome. And travelling. So now you know how I got to ninety-nine countries."

"Let me know when you need a divorce lawyer. What's with the itchy feet?"

Frank shrugged. "I grew up in Gripturn on the Mersey Estuary, the sticks. Dad gave me a blow-up globe, smelled like grapefruit. He told me *every colour is a country* and read out the names of cities. *San Francisco,* I liked how that sounded, beautiful. As a kid, I never went further than a caravan in Wales. I went to San Fran, eventually. Got mugged."

"That'll teach you." Braddock was picking at the corner of the yellow label on his beer bottle. "Why journalism?"

"I wrote for the student rag at college then bummed around Europe, trying to be a travel writer. Ended up as a waiter. Came back to London and looked up my room-mate Saul; he was a part-time DJ on hospital radio. I used to help out, read jokey news on his show, skits for the patients. Those were the days. A hospital is a special place: all that fear, all that love."

"All that crappy food. Then what?"

"Got a job in FM radio, spent three years zapping around the Smoke like a blue-arsed fly. For what? One day, I spotted an ad for training jobs in Eastern Europe, the end of communism. I thought *every colour is a country* and that was that, bye-bye newsroom. I've still got my globe. Once a month, Ruth threatens she'll stick a pin in it. She gets fed up holding fort with two kids. But that was the deal, like I said. And Billie was trouble long before I showed up. My stepdaughter, the mixed-race girl on my laptop?"

"I did wonder."

"Billie's father topped himself when she was seven. She's Ruth's first kid."

Braddock peeled back the label. "Sounds tricky. How's life as a stepdad?"

"Up and down. One minute, Billie's as sweet as a nut, next minute she's just a nut. She's on meds for depression, self-harm and so on. To be honest, I reckon she's happier when I'm abroad. Ruth reckons I should *communicate* more."

"Good luck with that. I saw a few suicides on my beat. Never easy on the kids they leave behind."

"Well, she gets along fine with our Dylan, the youngest. Plays practical jokes and so on. Ruth keeps me up to date."

"Any separation anxiety, as the psychobabblers say?"

"Well, I must admit, I do miss home; but I'm usually fine once I get settled in."

"I meant your son."

"Oh, yes, he misses me. But he knows that Daddy is making the world a better place."

"Because you told him?"

"Proper copper, you are. Anyway, how do you catch a *génocidaire?*"

"Think I'd tell a journalist?"

"I'm just a trainer."

"Use your loaf, is how. First you gather evidence: oral, real, documentary – sufficient to warrant the issue of an indictment. Then you find the fucker, triangulate his phone calls, follow his money and watch the airports. There's no single route to a collar. Plenty of dead ends, though; literally, in many cases." Braddock's eye glazed over with commitment to a goal. Athletes had it. Politicians had it. Coppers had it, sometimes. They saw more than most of us and did not blink.

"So, Jerome, when you find one of your *baddies,* what happens – you grab them in a dawn raid?"

"I'm present at the arrest but a local cop does the cuffs. We lack jurisdiction."

"And how does the baddie react?"

"Some get stroppy, some blank you. One guy cried his eyes out. Wouldn't you, looking at thirty-five to life, probably in a shitty prison? Some actually seem relieved the game is finally up. What they *all* do, on the run, is think they're bloody clever, which suits us fine, because they slip up. We nabbed one guy…" Braddock paused, folding his arms.

"Scout's honour," said Frank, with a three-fingered salute.

"Somewhere in Europe. I'll never forget his face, sitting in a café in his silk cravat. We sat down at his table. *Good morning, you're nicked.* He couldn't believe it. A rabble-rouser from '94, organised massacres, chopped up dozens himself, pregnant women a speciality, one sick bastard. Took us years, but we got him. Magic, that."

"Will he go to jail?" asked Frank.

Braddock raised a thumb and finger. "Our file is this thick and so is he."

"And now you're working on a fresh case, a new lead?"

"Multiple files, concurrently," said Braddock. The waiter brought a steel platter and whisked off the shiny lid to reveal a grilled fish the size of cricket bat nestling among steamed vegetables. Braddock pointed at a mound of wallpaper paste. "That's our *fufu,* by the way, made from cassava flour. *Lazy man's crop,* grows anywhere, staple carbohydrate, low in nutrients. Hence their skinny arses. Tuck in."

Braddock ate with his fingers, plucking *fufu* into a ball and dipping it in sauce. Frank used cutlery. The fish was tasty but the *fufu* was bland. He tried the red condiment and winced, dangling his tongue like a parched dog. "Christ, that's hot."

"That's *pilipili,* Frank. Good cure for jet lag."

"Jet lag? I'm not jet-lagged. We're on UK time, plus one hour. I just need kip."

"So let's hope the Devil's abroad, and not in Kinshasa, like last night?"

"Seems to me the Devil's here a lot," said Frank, reaching in his back pocket. He passed Braddock the inky page he had torn from the local newspaper. "What d'you make of this, constable? Found it in *La Voix.*"

Braddock wiped his fingers and pulled on his specs, holding the cutting at arm's length as he read it. "Murder, sorcery, the usual. Least they caught the buggers. I mean *suspects.* Why do you ask?"

"I visited three FM newsrooms today but none had ever

run that story. How come?"

"Perhaps an exorcism isn't very interesting." Braddock refolded the page and passed it back.

"What about child murder, Jerome? Should be interesting to local radio journalists, should top at least one bulletin. They should be covering this stuff in detail. Why does it happen? Who's responsible? What, when and where? Then follow up with analysis and debate, later."

Braddock shrugged. "Sure. We can go if you like."

"Go where?"

"To an exorcism." Braddock dipped a glistening chunk of Nile perch into hot sauce. "Usually starts around midnight. If you can stay awake, Mr Nomad."

Chapter 9

Frank followed Braddock out of the hotel. A sleepy-eyed guard in the car park nodded as if to grant them permission to proceed into the dark warren of backstreets beyond. The moment they did, three grinning urchins trotted up, hands out. Frank slipped the first a tatty banknote, sidestepping the rest. "Beggars belief," he said.

Braddock shrugged. "What do you expect? These kids are just symptoms of something much bigger. Vast. You should bone up on the causes, the context."

"I intend to. I've been too busy. Filing my reports and expenses for Ukraine. I was there for a month. Love the travel but hate the paperwork, the admin. Worst part of it."

"Count yourself lucky. And do some reading. When the Belgians pulled out of this place in the 1960s, they left thirty Congolese graduates to fill four thousand senior administrative posts, in a country as big as Western Europe. Think about *that*. Mind your step." Braddock hopped a pothole. "Look at the state of the roads. No wonder people lose hope. There's a material and spiritual vacuum, once the shooting starts. Beer?" He pointed to a knot of men clinking bottles. Frank spotted white faces under the flickering red neon of Bar Blue.

"I thought we were going to an exorcism?"

"Soon, there's a connection." Braddock shepherded him towards the counter. "Your round, I believe. Where was I?"

"In a vacuum, Jerome."

"Right, so living in this vacuum are millions of poor families. They're Christians but still believe in witchcraft, in their culture from way back. So, if someone loses a job or has an accident, they often blame a kid: *it's not bad luck; it's sorcery.* They pick a scapegoat – the stepson with a stammer or the girl who answers back – *here's our witch.* They pay a pastor for an exorcism or do it themselves, like in your article. Cheaper, see. Either way, it often amounts to the same thing: *put the kid's feet in the fire, chase the demon.*"

Frank felt a tug at his shirt tails and looked down. A kid in a mucky singlet gazed up, squashed between the clients at the bar. Braddock offered a banknote and the kid grabbed it, slithered away. They watched him go. "Most of these *shegués* have been accused of sorcery, Frank. Parents call 'em *ndoki.* You'll hear it around, quite often."

"Already did." Frank turned back, signalling to the doe-eyed barmaid: *I'm next.*

"*Ndoki* means *sorcery, child witch,* all that stuff the pastors love to hate."

"By pastor, do you mean priest?" Frank wiggled fingers at the barmaid. *Please?*

"Nah, a pastor is more of a chancer; a salesman who spotted a gap in the market."

"What market?"

"Redemption, salvation. He flogs tickets for heaven, the best show in town."

The barmaid uncapped two bottles of Primus and Braddock reached to grab one. "Hallelujah."

"How does a chancer become a pastor?"

"Frank, stop being a journalist. We've got ten minutes. Drink up."

The church of Christ the Warrior was a brick-walled hut the size of a tennis court, with benches and a tin roof. The place was heaving when they arrived but Braddock found a spot near the door, with a decent view. Frank stood on tiptoe, gazing at rows of people young and old. The better dressed sat in front clutching bibles, the rabble at the back craning to see.

The choir and musicians wore grey military tunics, red berets and satin sashes. An obsequious youth fluttered about a concrete dais as if backstage at a fashion show, helping a large fellow into a white cassock. Braddock provided a running commentary, over Frank's shoulder.

"There's our chancer. Last time I came, he had a tent and five people. Now look."

Frank looked at the big guy checking his cuffs, the youth buffing his shoes. "So how did he start?"

"Probably wandered into a place just like this. Heard the singing, saw people donating cash, heard a pastor say *I had a vision*. Our chancer goes home, drinks banana beer and has a vision: *I'll be a pastor too*. Next day, he buys a Bible and starts preaching, preferably in a quiet neighbourhood with little competition. If folks don't like him, he tries elsewhere. There are fifty-three million people in Congo, Frank, mostly illiterate, superstitious and needy. Our man can't lose, because he provides a sense of community, helps people to cope with grief, illness and bad luck. In time, he sets up an *église en bâche* – a tarpaulin church. He gives folks what they want – fire and brimstone. They give cash for a new brick church. Win-win. Some pastors go abroad to raise money. But they usually drop the nasty stuff from their sermons."

Frank turned. "How do you know all this?"

"From the horse's mouth. A Congolese friend brought me here. I met the pastor. When the chips are down in DRC, you have two ways to move up: find God or join a militia. Why do peace talks stall? Plunder. The longer this war lasts, the longer the top dogs can loot the land and sell minerals. But *poor* folks turn to guys like this, spiritual leaders."

One of the poor folks made a face at Braddock. *Hush.* Frank replied in a whisper. "Talking of peace talks, Jerome, my boss says I should focus on community issues instead."

"Good idea. The Inter-Congolese Dialogue is dead as a dodo, I told you. Because half a ton of raw rock sells for fifty thousand dollars. They use child labour in the mines and ship

the ore to Asia. Out comes the coltan, cassiterite and baux-
ite for our gadgets. For example…" Braddock pulled his tiny
phone from his pocket, held it up. "We're all complicit, Frank,
through these little things, and more. Big business drives the
trucks, not politics or ideology. Rwanda's in on it too, partly
why they can't keep out of Congo. You think Kagame is just
chasing psycho Hutus? As for two kids murdered for sorcery,
it all connects, but it's not news, and that's why they were not
on page one, or on the radio. Showtime, here we go."

Braddock pointed his phone and Frank turned towards
the dais. The drummer tapped his sticks to count the band in.
The guitarist twanged a chord, the bass boomed and a woman in silk stood to sing *Hosanna*. She sounded like Aretha
Franklin and Braddock was grinning like he had been born
again. "Watch the choir, Frank. Mexican wave, coming."

The choir rose as one, *Lord, Lord*. The walls seemed to
shake. The pastor's young assistant swung a silver pot on a
chain and incense billowed from its pointy lid. He walked
around, eyeballing the faithful. Most bowed their heads as
he approached, to prove their piety. He spotted Frank and
sauntered up. Frank closed his eyes but opened one a moment later, to peep. The youth with the incense smirked and
moved on. "Very friendly," Frank said. "Where does the Vatican stand on all of this? How about the Anglicans?"

Braddock shrugged. "They stand and watch, like us."

"I mean about kids getting killed during exorcisms. Surely they could intervene."

"If they tried, would these folks listen? Think about it,
Frank, from their perspective: if the older churches had any
clout with the Almighty, would Congo be in such a mess?
No. Most of these people want to be *born again*, to speak in
tongues, all the stuff Catholics and Anglicans don't sell. The
big churches are already shrinking. If they opposed something *more* popular, it would be theological suicide."

The congregation bellowed as if in agreement, *Hosanna*.
Frank spoke over the din. "So what's this church? Evangelical?

Pentecostal?"

Braddock chuckled. "*Church?* This is a cult, Frank. This is brainwashing. You'll see."

The music stopped and the big pastor spoke in a familiar baritone voice. "*Bienvenue!*"

Frank whispered back at Braddock. "This is the guy who woke me up. Same voice."

"God works in mysterious ways. Listen and learn."

The pastor gave a rambling speech, sometimes in French, sometimes in a local language. Braddock elbowed Frank. "Kiswahili and Lingala, covering all his bases; pity President Kabila can't do the same."

Next came a bombastic reading from a battered Bible the size of a headstone. A scuffed wooden bowl was passed around and soon stuffed with banknotes crisp and new, filthy and torn. The pastor spoke in French, sounding peeved, blaming the West for AIDS, *the gay plague*. A row of baleful eyes gazed accusingly at Frank and Jerome. The pastor changed tack, ranting about drugs and prostitutes as he paced up and down the concrete dais. A woman yelled *Amen*. Braddock put a banknote in the wooden bowl, clapped his hands and shouted. "Hallelujah." Frank gave him a puzzled look. Braddock winked.

A young girl in a print dress and jelly sandals walked onto the dais and knelt down. The pastor was poking her hard in the arm, accusing her of sorcery, yelling at Satan to flee or else. The girl slid to the floor, eyes shut. The congregation roared approval. *Good riddance!* The girl staggered up and stumbled away, rubbing her elbow. "She's hurt," Frank said.

"*Hurt?* This is the mild stuff," said Braddock. "It gets worse in private. That's when the gloves come off."

"What about UNICEF, Save the Children, can't they do anything?"

"Seems they try but their efforts are a drop in the proverbial."

"What about local council leaders, don't they have some

charter to protect kids?"

"A charter?" Braddock laughed. "The pastor is the one with a charter. It's called a licence. He buys it and the money travels up, protects him unless he bungles big time. Did your article mention a pastor? No. Because some politicians call themselves pastors. And a lot of well-educated Congolese attend these churches. They believe this stuff and we would too, in their shoes. Visit any middle-class home; once a week, they'll watch some chat show or Nigerian soap. Sorcery is a common theme. So be careful when you focus on community issues, because you're playing with fire."

The band started up and Frank turned. "What about rule of law, national government? Everyone is implicated, as you said, so nobody intervenes?"

Braddock shrugged. "Congo had local government and justice, once. Tribal chiefs were accountable, through debate and decree. Until we arrived, put a spanner in the works."

"So it's our fault? White man's burden?"

"Yes and no. We didn't invent slavery, we industrialised it. What I meant was, Stanley and the Belgians smashed the old system, chopped hands off when the rubber quota was low. Accountability went out the window and when Congo tried democracy in the early '60s, the CIA eventually bumped off the first elected prime minister – because he was cosy with the Soviets – and installed Mobutu, a cocky soldier. Cue decades of financial rape and pillage. Eventually, Laurent Kabila took over but squabbled with Rwanda. The Hutu maniacs found a safe haven in Congo, which is why I'm here. Anyway, enjoy. Do your bit and go home. But remember, kids are bottom of the pile and sorcerers are fair game. Yours sincerely, the Devil."

Frank looked towards the dais, where the burly pastor was haranguing a young boy in a faded Nike top. The kid seemed to relish the attention. Frank slipped his camera from his bag. Jerome nudged him.

"Hey, tourist, be discreet. Do not use a flash."

Frank checked the settings on his trusty Nikon, tricky in the shadows. He lodged the camera under his chin and clicked. The flash lit the hut silver-white. Heads turned and Braddock hissed, "Are you *crazy?* Let's go. Now." Braddock spun on his heel, pushing through the crowd. Frank tried to follow but was jostled by the faithful. Strong arms barred his way and eager hands prised the camera from him. His protests were drowned in a wave of fury and curses. He felt a sharp slap on his head as he made for the door.

Braddock was waiting halfway down the narrow street. "You idiot!"

Frank trotted up. "They stole my fucking Nikon! Where's the Christianity in that?"

"Are you deaf? I warned you, *no flash.* They hate cameras!"

"It was an accident, thought I'd checked. Thieving bastards. Can't you arrest them, Mr Copper?"

"Oh, sure. Where do you think you are? Law and order takes time. Congo needs fifty years of peace to get back to the prosperity of 1960, so they say. Try to remember that, next time you start snapping."

Frank stopped to look back. "That camera's been all over the world. Fuck."

"Let's go into town," Braddock said, summoning a taxi. "Nightcaps on me. I know a piano bar…"

"No, I'm done with the guided tour, thanks."

Frank walked alone back to the hotel, cursing his luck and the potholes.

In his room, he kicked his empty rucksack. The Church of the Barking Mad was still going strong down in the valley of darkness, so he turned the TV on, loud, and sat watching the ads. One showed a sweaty guy sipping Skol after work, the plump wife cooking him a plump chicken, watched by their happy kids. Above the kids hung a crucifix. Frank hissed diabolic oaths, until he realised how to make the world a better place. *Maybe. I'll discuss it at USAID tomorrow, with what's-his-name. Or should I ask Misti, first?*

Chapter 10

Frank ordered breakfast from room service and ate it on his balcony as the sun came up, listening to the birds and typing an email to his boss in DC.

> *Dear Misti, hello from Kin, hope you are well. Update: I'll meet USAID today (Rossi). I've had an idea. Suggest we add street kids / abuse of 'child witches' to my training agenda? Journalists could / should do more on this. I can teach them. I will pitch it to Rossi, test water. Claude chasing seminar room. PS. Please wire rent for my flat?*

He read it again and clicked *Send*. Why wait? Kinshasa was five hours ahead of Washington; by the time Misti replied, the meeting at USAID would be over, his chance gone. Anyway, Rossi would say no. It was just an idea. Frank munched a croissant, watching the neighbourhood. All quiet on the exorcism front.

He showered and dressed in chinos, shirt and tie, grabbed his bag and took the elevator to the lobby, watching the glowing digits.

In the car park he found the Unicorn driver reading a book in silvery sunshine. Claude folded the corner of a page and tapped the book against Frank's arm, all matey. "And how is Mr Frank today?"

"Older and wiser. How is Mr Claude?"

USAID lived behind steel barriers, razor wire and sentry boxes stuffed full of marines with biceps like ballast tanks. One of them walked around the Unicorn jeep, combing the underside with a mirror attached to a long pole. Claude tapped his fingers to music on the CD.

"You like this singer, Frank? He's Luambo, very famous, from TPOK Jazz. Good for dancing. My girlfriend likes to dance. I told her about you."

The soldier waved them through, Claude parked between two sleek saloons with little US flags on the front and Frank climbed out. "Back soon, don't get shot."

Three heavy doors and two security checks later, he was in an air-conditioned corridor, sitting among potted plants and browsing a glossy magazine full of USAID success stories. It seemed most people in sub-Saharan Africa, from grinning Kenyan farmers to white-coated Angolan pharmacists, were on the receiving end of Uncle Sam's financial largesse. A door squeaked and Frank glanced up. A slender Congolese woman invited him in. Her accent was American and her perfume smelled of frangipani.

The office had big maps and white walls. Alberto Rossi wore an office shirt with the sleeves rolled up. He had an expensive-looking watch and the smile of a diligent undergraduate, eager to please but rather young for Chief Bean-Giver. They shook hands and chatted, or rather, Alberto chatted and Frank sipped coffee, soon convinced he was in the presence of a superior intellect. Rossi exuded a bright-eyed passion for projects and a wealth of regional experience. He summarised Congo's complex politics with the laconic tone of a seasoned observer then paused for questions. Frank tried to think of a good one.

"Off the record, Alberto, what do you make of Joseph Kabila, compared to his dad?"

"I'd say the current president is defying all expectations. Kabila *fils* has made his mark by lifting a ban on political parties and agreeing to peace talks – AKA the Inter-Congolese Dialogue – which have stalled."

Frank nodded and Rossi breezed on, sounding a bit glum, apparently convinced Congo was heading for a half-baked peace deal that would unite Kabila's Kinshasa government with warring factions upcountry. "As for elections, Frank, Kabila will probably team up with the Congolese Liberation Movement, the Ugandan-backed rebels. Their leader Jean-Pierre Bemba is due to become Congo's prime minister. But here's the thing: the other rebel faction – RCD-Goma – will no doubt refuse to sign on the dotted line, because they're backed by Rwanda in the catbird seat. So, it's not looking too rosy, right now."

Catbird seat? That was a new one. "Leaving us where, exactly?" Frank asked.

"That question is above my pay grade. But peace would be nice. Because if Congo stabilises most of sub-Saharan Africa stabilises. It's politics 101. We'll see." Rossi was smiling. Frank spotted a small maroon pennant on his wall: *Harvard*. "Anyway, Frank, you know the big picture, I'm sure. So tell me about Unicorn's input; I hear from Hector you'll focus on community issues. Sounds good. First steps?"

"I'll visit participating radio stations, talk to managers, draft the journalists, junior and senior."

"Excellent, send Hector my regards. And how's young what's-her-name, your backstop in DC?"

"Misti Puffer. Always busy."

"I can imagine. Rising fast, I hear. So, any further questions before we wrap up?"

"Just one. Can I include kids on my training agenda?"

Rossi seem puzzled. He sat back, hairless forearms folded. "You want to train *kids?*"

"Not quite. I want to train radio journalists to provide more coverage of the *abuse* of kids, specifically those accused of sorcery, *les enfants sorciers*. Objective coverage. Quiz the cops, pastors, talk to *shegués*—"

"Actually, it's *enfants* dits *sorciers*, *so-called* child witches, to be politically correct." Rossi steepled pale fingers under a smooth chin. "But I interrupted. Go on?"

"Well, it seems the subject doesn't get much coverage, apart from pastors on talk shows, who have a vested interest, from what I've heard. They buy licences. Money talks, as you probably know. So, it's right up our street: local news, community-based, a conflict of ideas. Media could mediate, offer debate."

"Media could mediate. I like that. But how?" Rossi glanced at his watch.

"We train journalists to cover both sides; to broadcast phone-ins where listeners talk anonymously; to interview street kids, ask how they feel about it all; interview local residents, pastors, police, parents; make vox pops, call local leaders to account, talk to NGOs about their efforts, challenge the Bible-bashers. In short, we get local people talking and thinking about both sides, not just about Satan-in-our-midst."

"I see." Rossi fingered his foppish fringe. "And you've been in-country how long?"

"Landed two nights ago. Am I missing something?"

"Not home, by the sound of it." Rossi moved from his chair to the window and stood with his hands in pockets, broad-backed and legs apart, watching the street. Probably a college athlete, back in the day. He turned to the big maps on his wall, one issued by the UN, the other by USAID, and both dotted with coloured pins.

"And if it works here," said Frank, sensing he was home, "it might work in the east."

"East as in Goma?"

"Exactly. I'm also going to Kisangani and Bukavu. I could cover it there too, if you like the idea."

"Like it? Frank, it's a no-brainer. Send me a concept note for our files. And you should apply for your flights, if you didn't already. It takes time. I'll have someone call Alphonse, he's in logistics at MONUC. Oh, and the best place to swim in Kin is Cercle Sportif. You should join. Are we done?"

Frank wondered, for a moment, whether he should tell

Rossi that he had been to Harvard on a day trip, but instead he pointed to the paperweight with the baseball logo and said, "Red Sock Nation."

Alberto smiled with the well-tested tenacity of a Fenway fanatic. "We like to think so, eh?"

The administrative headquarters of the UN in Congo occupied a compound in Avenue des Aviateurs, a side street in the downtown Gombe quarter of Kinshasa. A big blue MONUC flag fluttered above a white gatehouse and razor wire festooned the top of the walls. Congolese men and women were queuing below, clutching documents. Hawkers worked the line selling bananas and snacks. Street kids trailed after the passers-by, pleading. Frank watched for a few moments from the Unicorn jeep then climbed out and quickly crossed the busy street. A keen-eyed soldier in a pale blue beret beckoned him to a different door where he filled in a security form under the eye of an unshaven Arab whose open khaki shirt revealed a white singlet and hairy chest. Frank was frisked with a beeper and entered the compound.

The world within was very different – compact office blocks, clean white Portakabins and neat gravel paths lined with well-clipped bushes. Frank stood for a few moments, unsure of where to go but content just to take it all in. Congolese pop music bounced from a staff restaurant where soldiers lounged on a sunny terrace in their UN caps and Ray-Bans, cradling their cans of Coke and espresso cups, watching female civilian staff totter past in heels and tight skirts, clutching paperwork and mobile phones. The place had a relaxed yet businesslike air. An agreeable combination. It just needed a helpful sign. *Welcome to the peace-industrial complex.* Frank could not help notice how every woman who walked by seemed to be young, good-looking and slim – as if this somehow qualified her for a job. It was Club Med with machine guns.

"Need help?" said a podgy guard, pistol sagging at his thigh and a gold bracelet hanging from his wrist. Frank mentioned *Alphonse* and the guard pointed to a gravel path.

Frank walked up the path and entered an office, its shelves stacked with box files. Alphonse was small and stocky, wearing red braces like a Wall Street banker and yapping into a phone about a *manifest,* rummaging through faxes. He looked Congolese but had a British accent. His bald head reminded Frank of a mooring post worn smooth from barge rope, like the ones he used to sit on as a kid, on the canal towpath back home in Gripturn. Alphonse glanced up and nudged a stack of documents across the desk. Frank took a seat and was scrutinising flight request forms when the phone dropped with a clatter onto its cradle. He looked up. Alphonse swigged Evian, wiped his mouth and said, "*Bonjour.* And you are?"

"Frank Kean from Unicorn. About these forms—"

"Talk of the devil. So you're the new guy with Hector Haggis, who's training out east? Good luck; you'll need it. Whereas right now, what I need," Alphonse said, pointing at the forms, "is for you to complete that lot. Copy them on the machine and leave me the originals. Have you been to Min-Info?"

Frank pulled his new ID card from a pocket. "You mean this? I walked up every floor."

Alphonse beamed. "Good start, but it won't mean much on the other side, so email Dr Hitimana." Alphonse scribbled a note with a fountain pen and handed it over. The handwriting resembled hieroglyphics: *rebels2002@yahoo.fr.* He capped his pen. "And don't forget to CC me. For now, just pop your forms in my box, up the corridor, when you're done. Add your phone number. Corridor, see?"

Frank craned his neck. A slim woman was walking along the corridor towards him, one arm laden with files, the other sweeping the air, her gaze unseeing, as if she were walking through the pages of *Vogue.*

"And bide your time," Alphonse added. "Requests take a

while; depending on who you are, of course. Keep your bag packed just in case you get lucky. On the other hand, a VIP might bump you down the list, so, as I said, be patient." Alphonse raised a sheet of paper. "Oh, and you'll need this. It's my list of friendly fixers in the east. Some numbers may be out of date, but, best I can do. Anything else?"

"Who's Dr Hitimana?"

"VIP on the other side, works for the rebels, decent guy. Handles visitors like you, journalists and stuff. So, write and pitch him your gig. Ask him nicely to authorise your entry into RCD territory."

Frank checked the note. Alphonse stepped closer.

"All OK? You've heard of the RCD?"

"Of course." Frank nodded. "Rally for Congolese Democracy, biggest of the rebel factions."

"And don't they know it. Anyway, back to work. Would you mind? There's a chair up the corridor."

Frank went out and sat down to complete his forms. It took twenty minutes and he was almost done when Alphonse emerged to use the photocopier. A tall Latina woman strolled by. She grinned at Alphonse, who turned to watch her. "The UN's not perfect but we try. Ever thought of applying, Frank?"

"Not until recently." Frank looked at his forms, checking one last time.

"You should. By the way, there's a trip to Namibia, if you're game."

Frank glanced up. Namibia would make one hundred countries. "A *trip*, Alphonse?"

"So I'm hearing. A bunch of us usually hire a jet for some R & R, split the cost. Makes for one heck of a weekend. You weren't around for the São Tomé junket but Namibia will be fun. Sand dunes and shrimps *this* big." Alphonse spread his hands. "From all that plankton that comes up the coast. Or so they say."

"You rent a jet?"

"Sure. Boeing 727 and a couple of pilots. Why not?"

"You rent a jet from an airline?"

Alphonse gave him a pitiful look – *no, from a video shop.*

"When?" Frank said.

"Around the time you get back from the Wild East." Alphonse winked and strode away, heels clicking, a man on a mission. Frank photocopied his forms, thinking the offer through. Namibia would be perfect, a well-earned break at the end of his stint in-country. And if he went, Ruth would break his neck. He carefully placed his forms in a pigeonhole, folded the copies into his bag and walked out, across the yard, past the swarthy guards in the gatehouse and back into the real world.

The wind was up, rain clouds looming. The queue of weary-looking Congolese had lengthened in his absence. He glanced up at the ragged MONUC flag, fluttering away and trying its best. There was no solemn music and no stiff-backed locals gazing at it in awe, but why would they?

He spotted the Unicorn jeep at the opposite kerb. Claude was slouched inside, dozing under his pale blue baseball cap. The crowd of street hawkers parted to let Frank through, as if his emergence from the UN compound had conferred upon him some hallowed status. He could only hope they were right.

Mid-afternoon, he found a seat in a busy cybercafé on the boulevard, between two young men in suits typing CVs. Misti Puffer had sent him an email marked *URGENT* that steamed with displeasure.

> *Frank, Re-street urchins. Bad idea! Advise me soonest*
> *of Rossi's response. As Project Manager I am best placed*
> *to handle fallout. Kindly desist from future unilateral*
> *proposals on strategy. Please read Scope of Work, Terms*
> *of Employment & Partner Briefs. Bestest, Misti.*

Frank tapped his thumbnail at his teeth. He typed a reply, trying his bestest.

Rossi liked my idea, asked me for a concept note.
I have read my contract but did not
receive partner's briefs. Please send.

If Puffer detected insolence, he would blame it on a typo, due to chronic fatigue, due to lack of sleep, due to noisy neighbours, due to her not wiring his bloody rent. He emailed Ruth, emphasising the positive.

Claude is brill, dead reliable.
Radio managers keen. Great meeting with USAID.
You?

He did not mention the legions of unlucky little beggars sleeping in doorways, the infants dying in exorcisms in Kalamu; Ruth would only get upset. He was ready to log out when he heard a *ping*. Misti had replied. Frank read it twice, marvelling at her U-turn.

Hey there Frank, please send me your rough basics
ASAP. I will formulate a Concept Note for Alberto
to consider. If USAID wishes to adopt a tactical
amendment, he may have a point. Misti

Talk about rising fast. Frank typed slowly, outlining his idea about including street kids and sorcery on the training agenda, with a feeling it might not be his for much longer.

Chapter 11

On the morning of the trip downriver, Dudu stood straight while Mama tucked his best shirt into his best shorts. She wrapped chunks of *kwanga* in banana leaves and put them in his satchel. She fussed around Moses, smart in his dark suit, although he had cut his chin shaving. Mama thrust Tata's ebony walking cane into his right hand, dusted off her Bible and tucked it under his arm. "So you look decent, Moses." She stood back, taking a good look.

Moses patted his hair, admiring himself in the cracked mirror. "Am I not decent?"

Mama sighed. "You'll do. Try not to fall in the river."

"That's Dudu's job. Mine is to fetch a pastor, to end my misfortune. Time to go."

"First I must say goodbye to Ginelle," Dudu said, but Moses shepherded him out with the ebony cane as if he were a naughty goat. "No time for that. We have a canoe to catch."

Emile tugged Moses sleeve. "Take me! I want to—"

Moses shook his head. "Impossible. Very sorry, Em, but you're too small."

"You're a donkey," Emile said. Moses glared down, gripping the ebony cane.

Mama pushed Moses into the yard. "The pirogue will be full. Hurry, both of you!"

Dudu and Moses trotted through the village, all dressed up; they drew smirks from bleary-eyed men and giggles from girls with bundles on their heads. Moses bowed graciously and said, "Ignore them, Dudu, they won't be laughing when we find the witch. Hurry now!" Dudu strode past the scabby black dog and it was soon sniffing the air and barking, circling and glaring at him if to say, *I know you*. It fled when Moses raised Tata's cane. Dudu paused to watch. *It seems a good idea to carry a stick; maybe Mama would let me use Tata's too?*

When they reached the river, the big pirogue was packed with people and chickens and goats and bulging UN sacks and a chattering monkey with a red bottom that would soon be in someone's cooking pot. The pilot wore a cap and an oily singlet over strong muscles. His seemed a good job, perhaps even better than a carpenter's. Moses argued about the fee and handed over some money from his little leather pouch. The pilot yanked a cord, the engine sputtered blue fumes and the pirogue swung from its mooring leaving a creamy whirlpool in its wake. It spun into the middle of the river, caught the current and surged downstream.

Dudu settled on a narrow wooden bench to watch the last traces of dawn mist licking the mossy banks. The forest drifted past on either side. Parrots swooped from high branches and naked kids splashed in the shallows. Moses seemed misty-eyed. "Time passes so fast."

After a few miles, the smell of fermented cassava bread tickled Dudu's nose and he peeped into his satchel at the neat parcels of *kwanga*. "Hungry, Uncle Moses?" But Moses was not listening. He was gripping the edge of the pirogue and gazing into the swirling water. "Crocodiles and mud-suckers! What if we fall in? Our lives are in God's hands." Moses uncorked a small silver flask that glinted as he sipped. Dudu looked at the river. It was a nice day for swimming. "Don't worry, Uncle, we won't."

About twenty minutes later, the clever pilot cut the engine and let the pirogue drift sideways towards a wooden jetty and dock with a gentle bump. Dudu helped Moses walk up smooth stone steps, past women frying bushmeat, a man selling scratch cards and barefoot kids sitting in trees.

Moses approached a group of respectable-looking ladies who seemed pleased to answer his questions. Some carried black Bibles with red pages, like Mama's. A lady with a wooden Jesus Cross around her neck pointed up the busy road and Moses bowed. He took Dudu's hand. "Come, dear child." Dudu trotted along, grinning. *Moses is nice, sometimes.*

They walked towards the sound of singing and the smell of sweet smoke, and soon came upon the Church of Victory Over Satan. Dudu stared. It was just a clearing packed with dreamy-faced people who stood in rows, singing and swaying like reeds caught in a powerful current. *Hallelujah!* Moses looked puzzled. "Oh, well, at least we arrived safely, eh, Du?"

Dudu stood on tiptoe and saw a small man at the front wearing fine robes of white and purple, standing behind a wooden table. Flames flickered like golden tongues from two torches, wisping into black smoke. From the man's neck hung a Jesus Cross as big as a hammer. His arms were spread and his shiny gold spectacles had pink lenses; he looked very wise, a man of God. Dudu tugged Moses' coat and asked, "Is that the famous pastor?"

"That's him, found a witch in every village." Moses was already worming his way forward. Dudu was dragged by the hand until they stood a few yards from the table. Moses had a strange look now, mouth open as he watched and listened. The pastor was pointing a bony finger out at the crowd and looking a bit annoyed with them. "Upon the wicked, He shall rain snares, fire and brimstone, horrible tempest: this shall be the portion of their cup!"

"Psalms 11:16!" cried a man wearing a black suit, standing just behind the pastor.

The pastor summoned a boy who stood rolling his head and gabbling in a strange language that rumbled from his belly like burps. "This is Paul," the pastor said, "I met him yesterday for the first time. He has admitted sorcery and unspeakable acts! Told me how he bartered with Satan, took the

Devil's bread in exchange for Christian souls. He is damned."

The crowd said *ooh* and made the sign of Jesus Cross on their chests. Moses tried to copy them, except the wrong way round. Dudu giggled and people stared at him.

The pastor walked in a circle. "Paul brings misfortune upon his family, because he is a lost sheep, rejected and despised. Because he is *possessed*. So, brethren, what should I do?"

"Bring him to Jesus," said a man in an old straw hat. "You should purify him!"

"*Délivrance totale!*" yelled a voice from the back. "He is damned, wicked!"

The pastor twisted one of Paul's wicked ears. "*Bima molimo mabe, molimo ya Satana, bima mopepe ya ndoki!*" He slapped Paul's face. "Come out, Jezebel! Stop this sorcery!"

Paul squirmed, fell, and lay still as a rock. The crowd gasped. After a few moments, Paul sat up and seemed a bit confused. The man in black helped him to rise and the pastor said, "Jezebel is banished! God's work is done. I must rest. If you need my help, queue up."

Everyone clapped and sang *Hallelujah,* arms waving. Dudu noticed a pretty girl walked about holding a stick with a small green velvet bag tied at the end by a gold ribbon. She thrust it at the people and most put money in the bag. Moses watched with big eyes.

"Hallelujah! Dudu, did you see that? Pastor Precious is the man we need. But we haven't got time to queue. We have urgent business. Come, stay close, don't get lost."

The pastor was resting in a comfy-looking chair on a sort of platform. The man in the black suit was fanning him with a big leaf. Moses explained that they had come all the way from Mavuku. The man smiled. "If you want to confess, line up with this lot." He pointed at the queue of anxious-looking people nearby. Moses frowned, scratching his head.

"*Confess?* Confess what?"

"Your sins, Mr Moses. Pastor Precious must purify you before he can help you."

Moses sighed and joined the queue. Dudu stood along-side near an old lady with a squint who said, "Satan hides closer than we think, but Pastor Precious will find him."

The pastor invited those queuing, one by one, to kneel close by and confess. He tilted his head to listen. One by one, the people confessed and shuffled away. Moses and Dudu edged up the line. Moses turned to whisper. "Dudu, what am I supposed to tell him?"

Dudu shrugged. "Some good sins, I expect."

As each person finished, Pastor Precious made the sign of Jesus Cross and his shiny gold ring glinted in the sun. When Moses knelt to confess, Dudu settled behind to listen. *Will Uncle tell Pastor he shot ten men in combat? Was that a sin or just being a hero?*

Moses sounded confused. "It's like this, Pastor. I came back from the militia with some… resources. I opened a bar, Heroes' Corner. It used to be popular, but not any more. People get envious, you see! Someone made sorcery. Perhaps you could come and find…"

The pastor nodded, loosening his round white collar. "Yes, but have you sinned?"

"Not recently."

The pastor sat back. He looked bored. Moses looked worried. "Although during the war I did it with a girl who said *no*. I shot a bullet up her. Is that good enough? I mean…"

Pastor Precious leaned forward. "Tell me more."

"She lived in a village. We came for supplies, beer. Her father told us to leave but we stayed. We did it with the girl, made him watch. I shot a bullet up her for a bet, to see how long she would last. So, will you come to Mavuku? You could stay at my home."

The pastor took off his glasses and rubbed the corner of his robe across the pink lenses. He appeared tired without them, tired from catching witches. "And the girl, Moses?"

"Oh, I won. I spent most of my winnings on my bar. Now I have only two left."

Pastor Precious made a puzzled face. "Two what?"

"Oh, diamonds. Will you come? Someone's doing sorcery. You must find the witch. Mavuku has no pastor. He ran off, long ago, with money for a church. We need your help."

The pastor glanced towards his keen-eyed friend in the black jacket. "No pastor in Mavuku? We must help. Moses, perhaps you have a vocation; perhaps Jesus sent you."

"Solange sent me. She's my wife, sort of."

People in the queue were tutting and yawning. "Hey mister, are you finished?"

Moses turned and Dudu looked him straight in the eye.

It was late afternoon, the sky darkening as they walked along the path back to the river. Moses talked a lot, mostly about the pastor. He did not talk about sins, about shooting a village girl, about making nasty bets and winning diamonds. Instead he spoke of having a vocation, being sent by Jesus. He paused for breath only when some people appeared ahead, thumping drums and carrying flaming torches. They were dragging a boy and yelling orders.

"Make way, he's *ndoki!*"

"Stand aside, keep away! He's a witch!"

The boy slobbered and howled like a dog with the madness in it. His face bore cuts and bruises, his limbs crusty wounds. The noisy mob passed, the women at the rear dancing and singing *Hallelujah*. Moses pointed. "Another one! He needs to be purified. Hallelujah!"

They walked back to the river, Moses humming a tune, Bible tucked under his arm.

Back in the pirogue, rolling home on black water, his good spirits seemed to fade. He pointed towards the tree-lined bank with Tata's ebony cane. "Dudu, if you tell Mama how I won my diamonds, I'll take you into the bush and tie you to a tree. You will lose your ears."

Dudu looked at the forest. Leopards would do the rest.

He would lose everything.

When they reached home, they found no fire in the yard, no hot food waiting in the cooking pot. Moses marched indoors. "Success! Bring banana wine! A sip for Dudu!"

They found Mama kneeling in the back room, wailing at the walls. A ragged sheet was draped over Nana Kima's stiff body. Emile was teasing a beetle on the floor.

Chapter 12

Ruth lay in bed listening to raindrops drum gently on her leaded windows and the early morning traffic hiss along Tudor Lane. London could be a miserable place, at times. She thought of Frank off again somewhere new, usually warm. *Or is Congo a wet country too, all that rainforest?* She caressed her bulging tummy. "Don't worry baby, he'll be back." There was movement in there and she got a kick out of it. She slid from crumpled sheets and waddled onto the landing to peep into the next room. "Rise and whine, Billie."

Billie was still in bed, sucking her thumb and browsing a magazine. She unhooked her thumb from her mouth. "Mum, have you seen *My Beautiful Laundrette*?"

"No, just your dirty washing." Ruth pointed at clothes strewn on the floor.

Billie smiled. In fact, she almost laughed, which made a change. Probably those new meds, fluoxetine. *Prozac by another name?* Ruth bent down and scooped the clothes up. "And stop sucking your thumb. I'm not blind. You're eighteen."

"I'm seventeen. It tastes good. You can go now."

Ruth backed out to check on Dylan. Her son's bunk was empty, his school clothes neatly folded on his little chair. A zombie screamed from downstairs and Ruth leaned over the banister. "Dylan, get off that computer and get dressed. Do you hear me?"

After a few moments, a small voice echoed from the sitting room. "No."

She made coffee and toast for breakfast. Dylan munched cereal, reading the packet. Billie slurped milk from a carton. *Not hungry.* They left home in good time, Dylan sitting in the back of the Mondeo and Billie up front, checking her hair in the drop-down mirror, pushing it up for that crucial slept-in-a-hedge effect. Her cheekbones were too sharp and her wrists thin as broom handles. "You look anorexic," Ruth muttered, watching traffic.

"At least I'm not fat like Cakehole Chloé. Actually, we're meeting at the bus stop, so you can drop me there. I need to ask her about the subjunctive. We've got French today."

"Are you copying her homework? She's a nice girl, you shouldn't take advantage."

"It doesn't matter where I get it *from*, it's where I *take* it. Godard said that."

"Well, Godard help us. Started your revision yet?" Ruth accelerated past a Renault.

"Yup. Been looking at some universities too, for October. Can't wait."

"*If* you get the grades, Billie. Anyway, which college have you got your eye on?"

Billie pointed. "My stop coming up, after the traffic lights. Slow down, Senna."

Ruth crossed the intersection and pulled in at the bus bay. Billie slithered out. "Ta."

There was no sign of Chloé but a good-looking, dark-haired lad on a skateboard zoomed in front and alongside the car as Ruth pulled away. She touched the brakes and cursed him in her rear-view mirror. He toe-flipped the skateboard into his hands and pecked Billie's face. Dylan was staring out the back. "She's got a boyfriend, with a skateboard."

"And no brains. But hey, spring is in the air."

"I bet they do snogging. Probably in Richmond Park, people do it there."

"Trust you to notice. Maybe we should go for another hike one of these days, up to the park, see the deer?"

"Yes, please. Will they be rutting?"

"Good question."

When Ruth parked outside St Edward's Primary, Dylan pointed to the small blonde girl in a Barbour standing apart from the other kids in the playground, reading a book.

"There's Aubrey!" He hopped from the car. *Ants in his pants.* Ruth watched him scamper across the yard. Aubrey closed her book and clutched it tight. She smiled at him like a comely milkmaid. Spring was in the air.

Traffic into Richmond was slow and Ruth was a bit late getting to work. The boss's Porsche was already slotted under the sycamores and a purple bicycle sat chained to a black drainpipe alongside the Edwardian mansion. Ruth swung into her usual spot and parked.

Walking across the gravel, she pictured herself as a country lady soon to be welcomed by a deferential butler at the shiny black door. Instead, as Ruth entered the lobby, Jane the receptionist emerged from her cubbyhole wearing a scarf of lilac satin, a purple jacket and red earrings. *Very air hostess.* Jane walked towards the TV on the wall, pointing the remote control at it. "How cute is this, Ru?"

Onscreen, a brown duck was waddling around the trunk of a big tree, watching fluffy ducklings jump from a nest halfway up it. They flapped their stubby wings and dropped in slow motion – *plop* – into a bed of bouncing leaves. "I could watch this all day," Jane said, and probably would. "Love the earrings," Ruth said, reaching for the appointments book.

She scanned the list of clients due and passed it back. She strode up the black-and-white tiled corridor and into the changing room, put on fresh green scrubs and emerged to find Simon already in the surgery, admiring his new watch. He looked worried and the place was gloomy. Ruth opened the blinds. "Morning, Fearless Leader."

Simon sat caressing his stubble. "Do you think my watch says *grasping yuppie?*"

Ruth took a closer look. "It says *Rolex Daytona,* which is why you bought it."

"Cade called me a *grasping yuppie.* We had an argument for breakfast."

"Like cat and dog, you two."

"We used to be *cute as kittens.* According to you."

"Didn't we all?"

"Cade says we must *clarify our priorities.* Give to charity."

"Sounds good. But you told him, let me guess…"

"I suggested he should work for one. After his master's, I mean. Work for a charity like your Frank does. Then again, what if Cade had to go abroad, somewhere dodgy? I'd get lonely. I'd worry. I don't know how you cope. Is your wanderer doing OK, in Africa?"

Ruth opened the autoclave. "Fine, first seminar soon. But he's with an American NGO, not a charity. Actually, I can just see Cade back in Africa, helping the motherland."

"I think he has a guilty conscience. Probably misses home, deep down."

"So, you wrote a cheque? Tell me you wrote a cheque for Ethiopian refugees?"

"*Cade, love,* I said, *you're my African charity.* Well, African-Canadian, as he calls himself these days."

"Was this before or after the argument?" Ruth removed the tray from the autoclave.

"I don't trust charities. Working for them is one thing, but *giving*? Not me. Saw this documentary one time. It's quite a scam. Most donations go on overheads and salaries."

"But not on shiny watches that cost three grand."

"Four actually." Simon turned the shiny bezel of his Rolex with careful fingers.

"You know what you are?" Ruth said, and he nodded, eventually.

They had a busy morning of it – two fillings, one extraction and three crowns by lunchtime. The clients ranged from timid to tiresome and included a pimply thirteen-year-old who clutched his Game Boy console throughout, poking buttons whenever he could.

Some clients seemed to think they were doing you a favour, such as Tom Maddox who strutted in wearing a worn-out tracksuit, shoved his peroxide ponytail into an elastic band and said, "How long will you need me?"

Ruth got a whiff of his musty armpits and turned aside. Simon, too, wrinkled his nose and said, "Don't worry, Mr Maddox, you'll be on your way as soon as possible."

The next client, a waxy pensioner, surveyed the surgery with gimlet eyes and asked, "Painted your walls?" Simon glanced from his clipboard. "No, Wilfred, but good idea."

Wilfred Jennings's gaze fell on the small photo in a silver frame of Simon and a grinning African man, snuggling too close for comfort. Wilfred glared at Ruth, who was tempted to blurt out: *It was destiny, Mr Jennings, love at first sight. Cade was a smart Ethiopian refugee who won asylum in Canada and got a casual job as a waiter, catering for events and conferences. Simon attended one in Calgary, OK?* Instead, she just smiled.

Jennings frowned. "I've got another idea. Turn off that telly in the lobby, all them bloody *fish*." He lowered himself into the reclining chair and winced as if sucking a lemon. Simon promised to have a word with Jane. "But for now, open wide, Wilfred."

At lunchtime, sitting alone under the sycamores in dappled sunlight, Ruth ate prawn sandwiches. She texted Frank but got no reply. Jane was walking alongside the flower bed with her watering can, cooing encouragement at her purple pansies in their ochre pots. Simon emerged to smoke his daily Marlboro, gave Ruth a weary look and checked his watch.

The afternoon session was quieter – routine fillings – and

by quarter to four Ruth was in the yard dropping a rubbish bag into the incinerator. She pushed the green button, gazing at the lichen-covered brick walls, ticking off chores in her head. *Surgery and chair – cleaned, sanitised and surface barriers placed. Instruments washed, chemical soaked, dried, bagged and autoclave on. Sharps – all boxed safe. Bin – emptied.* The incinerator roared its usual response – *rubbish burning* – and she went back inside to change. Another day done.

At 4 p.m. grey clouds rumbled over the car park and when Ruth walked towards her Mondeo, Simon was looking peeved in his Porsche, phone at his ear. He dumped it aside. Ruth slowed her pace as she passed. "No golf then?"

Simon sat scowling. "Can you believe it? Cade just invited me to drive uptown and meet him outside some foreign embassy for a bloody protest. Do I look like an *activist?*"

"Just a pissed-off yuppie."

"Watch it, I wear the dress around here." Simon revved his engine. The gravel crunched and he was gone, her poor rich boss; up and down like a fiddler's elbow. Maybe he needed Prozac. Ruth drove away listening to Dire Straits, feeling glad she was not in them.

She took a detour, stopped at Sainsbury's for groceries and a nice bottle of Bogle red, before the rush. Heading past St Edward's High School minutes later, she spotted Billie and the new boyfriend walking hand in hand, Chloé playing gooseberry a few paces behind, face on her like a bag of spanners. Whatever Billie and lover boy were discussing, it wasn't homework; Billie looked far too happy. Ruth sighed. It would surely end in tears, as usual. She considered stopping to offer a lift. But no, Billie would freak and Dylan was waiting.

The heavens opened and rain fell in crashing volleys as she parked outside St Edward's Primary at 4.25 p.m. She pulled on her smelly rainproof and strode towards the neon-lit annex, stepping aside for parents and kids coming the other way under umbrellas and canopies of coats. She cupped a wet hand at the steamy window of *Kids' Club* and watched a boy wobble past like a puppet. A knackered-looking, petite, ginger teacher stood unblinking in her canvas smock. Ruth spotted Dylan sitting near a lurid painted frieze of anemones and starfish, ogling a big book with little blonde Andrea. *Audrey?* The New Girl, anyway. They could have been twins. Ruth flipped back her dripping hood and went inside.

The blonde girl wore a pleated kilt and was reading aloud in a plummy voice. Her hair was well cut. Dylan tried to turn a page but she blocked him. Ruth tickled her son's scalp and he looked up, blue eyes crinkled into commas, just like his dad. "Hi, Mummy. We're reading *Harry Potter*. Guess what. Aubrey's read them all, twice."

The girl rose and extended a hand. "I'm Aubrey Price, how do you do?"

Ruth shook the dainty fingers and noticed the confident smile. *Breeding, that was.* Ruth recalled Billie, at the same age, stuffing books down the loo. "Hello, Aubrey, and you?"

"Ah, waiting as usual, but we're having *such* fun, aren't we, Dilly?"

Ruth glanced at her son: *Dilly?* He nodded enthusiastically, *that's me.* She dangled his rainproof top but *Dilly* had other ideas. "Mum, come and see Baxter's frog. It's got three legs, not four. It's a freak."

Ruth was led towards the Nature Table – a motley collection of ferns, feathers and a glass box containing two stick insects named *Posh & Becks*. Dylan searched in vain for the frog. "It was in a jar by the bird's nest. Where's it gone?" Two other boys joined the hunt, checking under tables. Their tired-looking teacher suggested that maybe someone had released the frog or perhaps Baxter had taken it home. Aubrey licked a finger, turned a page.

"Who cares, Dilly? It was just a freaky frog."

The tallest boy giggled, peeping behind a display board. "Come out, freaky frog!"

Dylan had moved on. He was quizzing a pretty black girl whose mittens dangled on string. *Have you seen Baxter's frog?* The girl shook her head and departed with her mother. The exodus continued until only two kids remained – Aubrey and Dylan. She was chatting and he was listening. Ruth stood watching and waiting, with a patient smile. Her son seemed to be under a spell. The teacher unbuttoned her smock. "So nice to see Aubrey settling in. She's bright as a button but could use a friend. Lives near you, I believe, in The Lindens?"

Ruth smiled. "No, I'm on Tudor. I'll move to The Lindens after I win the lottery."

"Bye then," Dylan said, knotting his tartan scarf, but Aubrey was once again lost in her book. He seemed worried by her sudden and studied indifference, or the fact that neither of her parents had turned up to take her home. Ruth crossed the room and crouched alongside, speaking in a gentle voice. "Is Mummy or Daddy coming to fetch you, Aubrey?"

Aubrey traced text with a firm finger. "Daddy's in China. Mummy's en route."

"To China?" Ruth chuckled.

Aubrey looked up. "Are you making fun of me?"

Ruth shook her head. Dylan glided up to confide in a low voice. "Aubrey's mummy works in the city but she won't tell me which." He gazed at a wall map of the world.

Ruth heard the growl of a large car as blinding silver beams swept like searchlights across the rain-spattered windows of the classroom. She shaded her eyes, briefly dazzled until the beams faded, dimming to a faint glow in seconds. Aubrey rose quickly, dropped her book into a satchel and plucked a Barbour from a hook. Dylan peeped under a cupboard.

The long-legged woman who entered the annex moments later wore a business suit and a distant smile. She had bookshelf cheekbones, boudoir eyes and the rock of Gibraltar glittering on a finger. Her perfume did not smell like the stuff that shop girls sometimes sprayed at Ruth. Her scuffed

Barbour coat hinted at years of horseplay.

"Sorry, Aubs, foul weather, beastly traffic!"

That accent did not come cheap, either. She greeted Dylan – *hello young man*. He gawped as if he had lost the power of speech. Ruth gave her son a gentle nudge. "Say hello, Dylan."

The woman grinned down at him. "Ah! So *you're* Dylan, the-little-boy-down-the-lane? Best friends, I hear."

Dylan seemed puzzled about being *little* but squeaked a reply. "I'm six and a quarter. We lost our frog."

Ruth zipped his rainproof top and its cheap logo seemed too prominent. Aubrey went for a word with the teacher and Dylan followed. Aubrey's mother offered a hand to Ruth.

"Persephone Price."

Ruth shook it. Persephone had pipe-cleaner fingers, a no-nonsense grip and spoke quickly of working in town and having a *heck of a time, being on time.* She regretted being *habitually late* for Aubrey but was practically a single parent. She loved the proximity to Richmond Park but finding reputable dry-cleaners was, frankly, a wild goose chase. Her job in risk management was simply *endless* and rush hour traffic *beastly.* She had seriously been considering a Brompton foldaway bicycle until a school friend fell off one in Ken High Street. "So bugger that and pardon my French. Come, Aubs, let's away!" Persephone beckoned her daughter.

They all left together in light rain, Aubrey and Dylan hopping puddles, Persephone rooting in her expensive-looking handbag. "Lost my keys for the old banger." She gave Ruth a toffee with a Fortnum & Mason's logo. "It's my last one, but do try, frightfully chewy!"

Ruth chewed, despite a lingering aversion to sugar. *Wrecks your teeth.* Persephone's old banger turned out to be a sleek Range Rover grinning like a shark on steroids, all smooth lines and chrome gills. Dylan stood in the drizzle, ogling in respectful silence. Ruth's Mondeo resembled a terrified kipper in comparison. Persephone shook her keys, jubilant.

"Found them!" She beeped the car's doors. "Well, jolly nice to meet you both!"

She slid gracefully into her seat, twisting to buckle up. Her loose silk blouse revealed tiny freckles on a tanned cleavage. The car smelled of lavender. A mobile phone rang next to a slim leather briefcase. Persephone opened the glove box, tossed the ringing phone inside and shut the flap. She looked in the mirror and brushed raindrops from her perfect hair. Ruth watched and wondered. Persephone Price had almost everything she needed – heels, wheels and deals. What she didn't have, perhaps, was time? Local contacts and a man at home to share the burden? She seemed posh but not stuck up, successful but kind-hearted. Small wonder Dylan was smitten with little Aubrey – same good bones and easy charisma. Ruth stepped closer, trying to recall the word for what she was about to do, the word her best friend Carol used sometimes. It began with *A*. Perhaps it was *altruism*. And why not.

"If it would help, when you're stuck for time, I mean, I could always collect Aubrey and take her to ours for an hour. We're quite close." *Or we could be, m'lady.*

Persephone's chin dipped into that ballerina neck. "Gosh, really? How kind of you to offer. They *do* rather seem to be hitting it off, don't they? But Ruth, are you sure?"

"I finish at four twice a week. I'm on Tudor Lane. You could pick her up from there, it would save you a few miles. You'd have more time and less... beastly traffic?"

Persephone's pale brown eyes widened. "How utterly amazing, but, let me check." She spun round to speak to her daughter. "Aubs, darling, what say you?"

"Rath-er!" Aubrey sat forward. Persephone pulled a gold pencil from inside her suit jacket. The lining shimmered vivid lemon. "Then it's a deal! Ruth, your details, please!"

Ruth fished out a business card. "My mobile number is scribbled on the back, see?"

"Gosh, you're a dentist?" Persephone was reading the front.

"No, dental nurse. This is where I work."

"Amazing." Persephone tapped the card against her aquiline nose, keeping perfect time with the classical music that swirled from her stereo. "Do you care for opera?"

A man was bellowing on the CD, as if he had just whacked his thumb with a hammer. "Never been."

Persephone blinked, owl-eyed, then grinned because the new *Aida* at Covent Garden was *simply superb,* with a Welsh bass chappie raising the roof as the King of Egypt. Ruth grinned too and mentioned that she had actually grown up near Swansea; The Mumbles, Rum Cove, down by the beach. Persephone seemed puzzled so Ruth added, "It's in South Wales."

"Ah, and I'm sure it's *charming!* And what about the other days?"

"The other days?"

"When you don't finish at four, one assumes you finish either earlier or later?"

Ruth returned Persephone's gaze and wondered what risk management was. "On the other days," she replied, "I finish at six-thirty and my daughter Billie fetches Dylan on her way home from school. Billie's seventeen, quite reliable. Very reliable." She wondered why she had added the last bit. Perhaps because the conversation seemed to have turned into a job interview, that one ought to pass. She omitted Billie's colourful history of teenage depression, truancy and Selective Serotonin Re-uptake Inhibitors. "But why do you ask, Persephone?"

"Just curious." Persephone reached to squeeze Ruth's wrist. "And please, it's *Pippa*. Thank you, we'll talk. I'll find a way to compensate, time being money. Say *ciao*, Aubs!"

When Aubrey smiled Ruth noticed a black smudge on tooth number twenty-three, caries, labial aspect; too little oral hygiene, too many toffees? The Range Rover purred away and Ruth wondered what Pippa had in mind – a soirée at Covent Garden? *Very nice, if so.* One could do with a posh friend and Aubrey would be a good influence on *the-little-boy-down-the-lane*. Ruth walked to her car, which now seemed to resemble all those funny little ones Frank had photographed on a trip to Berlin, years ago. There was a word for that too. *Autosuggestion?*

Dylan crouched to peep under a hedge and Ruth crouched too. "Any sign, son?"

He stamped a shallow puddle. "Who cares? It was just some freaky frog."

"Oh well, never mind. The good news is – we're moving up in the world, *Dilly*."

"Up where?" Dylan clambered into the Mondeo.

"To nice places, maybe the opera." Ruth started the car, inched towards the exit gate.

"The opera?"

"Yes. It's when you get dressed nice and go to a theatre, listen to people singing their heads off, kings and queens and stuff. Not real ones, they pretend. It's like a school play."

"Sing about what?"

"One has no idea. It's in Italian. But one is going to find out. Do I sound posh?"

Dylan shook his head. "You sound a bit nuts."

Ruth flipped her indicator for home and frowned at the slippery road ahead.

Chapter 13

The general manager at XFM swivelled in his chair, nose snuggling into the zippered roll-neck of his tracksuit, brown eyes peeping warily over the top. "*Shegués?* Child witches?"

Frank smiled. "They're a community issue. You'll win listeners."

"Not if other stations report on child witches too. Are you asking them to do it?"

"Yes, but the trick is to be the best, to offer the most reliable local news."

"We are. We do. Ask Mr Hector. We sell the sizzle. Will you teach marketing?"

"No; news writing, interviews and presentation. A range of formats and subjects."

"Including child witches."

"*So-called*. They'll give you a strong local angle. It could help generate advertising."

Bertrand snuggled his chin deeper into his tracksuit, Claude peeped around the open door, brandishing a mobile phone. "Frank, I've found a room downtown. For your seminar."

Half an hour later, Frank and Claude were standing at a dusty window opposite a grimy block of flats, gazing down at a busy intersection. Claude shrugged. "Too noisy?"

"No, very convenient! Perfect for vox pops. Location, location. You're a genius."

Frank surveyed the room and rearranged the tight rows

of desks and chairs, pulling them into a wide, loose semicircle. "Less formal, more eye contact. You agree, Claude?"

"Yes, and please tell my girlfriend I'm *a genius*. She says I'm not a serious person."

"I will, beers on Friday, I'm buying. Meanwhile, I need a whiteboard. Any ideas?"

Claude pulled car keys from his safari vest. "Come. We can borrow one from HQ."

They drove to Unicorn where Claude asked the aged, indignant-looking janitor to unscrew a whiteboard from a wall. The janitor insisted on written authorisation but Mr Hector was absent so Claude strode off to ask Rose in Accounts. "Wish me luck, Frank."

Frank settled into his tiny office to check emails. Dylan had written to ask whether he had *seen any lyons*. Ruth had written to say the baby was kicking and that Billie had a new boyfriend. But from Misti Puffer in the concrete jungle of DC there was only silence.

Claude returned. "The whiteboard will be in your seminar room, Monday morning."

"Thanks, genius. Do I need authorisation to buy pens and jotters for my trainees?"

"Not if you use your own money." Claude adjusted the framed photo of David Hasselhoff. He stood back to check it was level and Frank raised a thumb. All was in order.

Friday night, they went out to see a Congolese band playing shrill guitars under a massive baobab tree. Frank stood at the bar sipping Primus, wearing the Hawaiian shirt Ruth had chosen for him in Gap; *take something ethnic, love*. He felt like a bit of a pineapple, love.

Coloured lights hung from the big tree, casting spooky shadows on the dance floor where buxom women gyrated. Their grinning partners shuffled and pranced in lightweight suits, snake hips pumping the air. *Go mama, go*. Two barrel-chested white guys sashayed onto the floor, clutching beer bottles, doing the gorilla. Frank lit a cigarette.

Claude emerged sweating from the crowd, followed by his gazelle of a girlfriend. He went to the bar to buy her a Fanta. She sent him back to fetch a straw. Ellen had beaded hair, a serious look and questions for the visitor. "Mr Frank, I don't think Claude is a *genius*. But do you think your Queen murdered Lady Diana?"

"Doubt it, but she might murder the Duchess of York one of these days."

Ellen wandered off, took her straw and went to friends to chat. Claude sidled up to Frank. "So, what do you think of my Ellen; she's not too skinny? She says she wants a bigger bottom. Like in the tune by Werrason. *Mwana natikaki moke sima e koli! A girl I left small, the buttocks grew big.* You know it?"

Frank shook his head. They chatted about music until Ellen strode past, heading back to the dance floor. Claude followed as if he were on a retainer. From the crowd, they beckoned Frank and he obeyed, doing his best – a shuffle to the left, a shimmy to the right. "Last time I had a dance was at Kew Gardens in England!"

Ellen looked puzzled, as well she might. "This is dancing, in England?"

Frank shrugged. Come summer, he would be bopping with Ruth. Those outdoor concerts at Kew were fun. Maybe he would take her a Congolese robe, *something ethnic.*

An owl fluttered from darkness and the balmy air smelled of roast meat. Hungry-eyed street kids loitered at the club's entrance. Frank watched and wondered. *How do they survive?* On their wits, probably, ever alert. How would his trainees react when he raised the subject – would they help to dispel some of the superstitious paranoia that hung like a storm cloud over *shegués,* or dismiss him as a do-gooder? He swayed to the beat, one eye on the kids. Braddock had advised him to look deeper. He was trying. It was not about doing *good*, just about doing *something*.

One kid was begging aggressively from a man entering the club who swiped out with a fist, silver bracelet flashing like a flying fish. The song ended and Frank returned to the bar. He glimpsed himself in the cracked mirror behind the rows of bottles. He looked tired – his blonde curls straggly with sweat, Harpo Marx on a bad hair day. But so what, it was hot tonight. Because he was in Congo. A new place. Vast. He'd seen it on that map at USAID. They had liked his idea: *no-brainer, Frank*. It was a good feeling. Something had altered his perception of both his task and of Unicorn, his employers. Frank Kean was in control now, had the horse by the horn. In country number ninety-nine. The barmen were all busy serving so he stood in line and turned to watch the dancers bubble and pop. *Go mama, go.*

Back at the hotel lobby, he scribbled a note. *Jerome, beer sometime?* That fellow Braddock could be a nosy bugger but a useful source of local information. Frank folded the note and gave it to the concierge, who shook his head and passed it back. Mr Jerome was gone, checked out. Frank crumpled the note. Somewhere, soon, a baddie had it coming.

He went up to his room and checked email, just in case. Sure enough, Misti had written a short but luminous message to Alberto Rossi at USAID, thanking him for his *invaluable flexibility on the strategic tweak to Unicorn's media training module that I am now proposing.* She had CC'd three other people whose names Frank did not recognise. His own name came last. He clicked to read the attachment, *by Misti B. Puffer.*

It was three pages long and began with a diagram of intersecting spheres to show how, by encouraging Congolese journalists to *engage with child welfare at grass roots, Unicorn would satisfy USAID's latest development objectives at Project, Program and Strategic Levels.* Frank popped a packet of peanuts and stared at the screen, reading quickly, crunching one nut for every bullet point. He read about the *Anticipated Outcomes and Impacts of Participatory Method, Monitoring and Evaluation, Domains of Change (definitions/usage), Story Collection Protocols, Secondary Analysis and Feedback Loops.* Finally, came the *Community Beneficiaries, reflective linkages and a gradual paradigm shift to enhance the Dialogic Process.* At the bottom of the last page, he noticed his name among the small print. *Additional input by F. Kean.* The font had shrunk in the whitewash.

He took a long shower, washing the stink of roast meat from his hair. He dried off and lay on the bed, caught the last few minutes of *The Sting* on Classic Movies. It looked easy to con people, if you knew how.

He woke up around 1 a.m. to the sound of drums, a chanting choir and a discordant electric guitar, but there was no wailing kid tonight. *Too many tourists, recently?* Frank hauled himself from bed and stood on the balcony wearing a damp towel around his waist. He lit a cigarette and blew three grey rings at a silver moon, trying to snare it.

Chapter 14

When you die, they wrap you in a raffia madiba and bury you, like Nana Kima, sitting in a pit, on this slope of scrubland between the village and the forest. It was a strange place to end up, neither here nor there. Unless, of course, you had got blown to bits like Tata because you had stepped on a land-mine. Dudu stood by Nana's grave, looking at her stiff toes protruding like stones from the end of the woven mat. One day it would be his turn, in a pit like this. Unless he trod on a landmine.

He watched Nana's wrinkle-faced friends come to wail and fling soil into the pit, their hands leathery like hers, their backs bent from lives of lifting and carrying, pounding and plant-ing. Most of the old folks were so small they looked as if they had shrunk in the rainy season. They wept because their friend was gone and probably because they knew their turn was com-ing soon. Dudu counted twenty sad faces. Younger men used shovels to add more soil until Nana disappeared, gone forever.

Uncle Moses stood solemnly in his black clothes, check-ing his watch and bossing people about – *stand back, move.* The men rammed a wooden Jesus Cross into the moist earth and set a semicircle of rocks, like stumpy teeth smiling at heaven. Mama dabbed her eyes and Emile sniffled. Ginelle stood nearby with her parents among the rest of the villagers, who looked as if they had seen a ghost or soon would.

The crowd drifted down the hill. Mama had invited them to her yard. Each guest brought an offering – a bottle of maize juice or a bidon of palm wine, a big bag of salty nuts or a plate of *kwanga*. Some of them sang, some of them danced, and a youth with wild hair played his drum. A man with few teeth told funny stories, mostly about Nana Kima: the time she fell in the ditch, saved the drowning goat, argued with a militia-man who wanted banana wine. Dudu watched Moses smacking his lips over a glass of fiery *lutuku* and bragging, to anyone who would listen, about how Pastor Precious from the Church of Victory Over Satan had encouraged him to read his Bible.

"To help my spiritual development," Moses added, puffing up his chest, and tapping it with a thumb. "In here, I mean." Moses moved away and Dudu glanced at Ginelle, who tapped the side of her head with a fingertip.

In the middle of the afternoon Dudu went with Moses to the riverbank to wait for the pirogue bringing the pastor, but it did not come. He sat on a rock and looked in his picture book, at the page about a clever bridge with arms that went up for ships to go under. Its name was printed alongside, next to a soldier in a red tunic and big furry hat: *London Bridge*. It was quite something. But there was no bridge like that on this river. He looked along the shimmering water. Still no pirogue. Moses walked up and down nearby with Mama's Bible, swinging Tata's ebony cane and practising how to look decent.

Eventually, a pirogue drifted into view, small at first then bigger, like a sly crocodile. Dudu glimpsed a purple shirt and a flash of gold. He waved and the pastor waved back. The pirogue swung towards the bank and the pilot with big muscles puffed a pipe while everyone got off. Pastor Precious and his friends came first. The man in a black suit, who introduced himself as Cyril, assisted him up slippery steps. Next came Paul the Purified Boy and the little girl who had collected the money downriver. The pastor shook hands with Moses and patted Dudu on the head as if he were a goat that would soon have its neck cut open.

Pastor Precious paused to wipe the pink lenses of his gold spectacles on a clean white handkerchief and, when he was ready, they all walked slowly up to the village. Moses led the way, proudly swinging Tata's ebony cane as though he had carved it himself.

The pastor was *sincerely sorry* to hear about Nana Kima. Moses looked around, grave-faced. "The sorcery was too strong, Pastor. I feel Satan in the air."

"My condolences. But Satan is not in the air. Mostly he is in *people*."

"Yes, of course Pastor, but the fear is spreading. You'll see."

"I shall visit her grave, pray for her soul then begin my inquiries. We have no time to lose. If there is a sorcerer in the village, I shall find him. Or her."

"Hallelujah! Your intervention will save my livelihood. In fact, I invite you to stop for refreshments at Heroes' Corner, so you can rest a few moments and see what I mean."

Dudu walked with Paul the Purified Boy and Cyril. They did not say much. Paul whistled and Cyril's trousers had ragged pockets. The little girl who had collected money in the velvet bag was the friendliest, and rather pretty too, with a big smile, which made you smile back. Her name was Awa and she came to walk with Dudu, chatting about where she had been, what she had seen. He found he enjoyed Awa's company but expected that Ginelle would give him some advice about that, if she found out.

When they reached Heroes' Corner, Moses unlocked the big rusty padlock and ushered his guests inside, but Pastor Precious did not want cold beer. "I need my wits." He asked for an orange *sucré* instead and Dudu smiled hopefully. "That's my favourite too." But Moses did not offer Dudu a free drink. He was busy watching the pastor pray over the bottle to chase any demons out. "I can see why this place was popular," Pastor Precious said, looking around. He took off his spectacles to wipe the lenses. Perhaps he needed new ones.

"Best bar in Mavuku," Moses said. "But not any more.

Sorcery is to blame."

"Why is it called Heroes' Corner?"

"In honour of my fallen comrades. Jean Luc, Marc, Pierre…"

"And Tata," said Dudu and they all turned to look at him.

"Yes," said Moses, "but let's not dwell on the past."

Pastor Precious looked sad. "Your father died in the war, young man?"

Dudu nodded. "Landmine, and Uncle shot ten men, risked his…" The words faded as Dudu pictured a girl with a bullet up her, bleeding to death, for diamonds.

"Salted nuts?" Moses said from the bar, and the others came to get some.

"Do you miss your Tata, Dudu?" said the pastor. Dudu looked towards Moses.

Moses' mouth was going round and round, chewing nuts, his eyes unblinking. Pastor Precious leaned closer. He had a smooth chin and a nice soapy smell. His voice sounded gentle and wise. "Dudu, I lost my Tata when I was your age. So I know about loneliness, bitterness. But I see the hand of Jesus. Do you see the hand of Jesus?"

Dudu shook his head. The pastor smiled. "Listen, I'll explain. Jesus has given you *two* heroes to emulate: Tata in heaven, Moses in Mavuku; such is your comfort."

Moses was smiling too now. "Very well put, Pastor. Hallelujah."

"Thank you. Perhaps you'll donate some of your *winnings* to my church, one day. Every little helps, every sinner can be saved, just like Cyril, Paul and Awa." The pastor gestured to his friends at the bar and they all smiled, because they were all saved. Or perhaps because they had free drinks and thought Moses was a donkey.

When it was time to lock up and leave Moses sighed and seemed rather glum. He led his guests through the village, past wide-eyed ladies who made the sign of Jesus Cross when they saw the pastor's purple shirt. Moses strutted alongside, swishing the ebony cane. He was soon smiling again, at friends and neighbours. Some of them smiled back.

"So, Dudu," said Awa, coming close, "you couldn't see the hand of Jesus?"

He shrugged and wondered how to reply. It seemed a strange question.

"Pastor can see it quite easily," said Paul the Purified Boy, strolling along with his hands in his pockets. "And the work of Satan. Although, sometimes, it can take a while."

Awa frowned. "But sometimes Pastor is very quick, Dudu! Like the time we went to see a man whose wife died having a baby. Her baby had survived, of course, because Satan had *possessed* it. Pastor found out quite soon." She clicked her fingers. "He's *that* clever."

"And what did Pastor do?" Dudu said, sidestepping a grazing goat.

"Pastor told the man to bury that bad baby too. And the man did."

Dudu slowed down, thinking about that. "Was the baby *alive?*"

"Not for long," Awa said, skipping ahead.

Chapter 15

As they got closer to home, the scabby black dog came trotting towards Dudu with its tail up, barking as usual. Moses swung his cane and the dog dodged, circling, fangs bared. Pastor Precious looked a bit worried until Moses said, "Don't worry, it wants to bite Dudu, not you." The pastor watched the bad-tempered dog retreat, then walked on, glancing back.

By the time Moses and Dudu arrived with four special guests, a few not-so-special guests from the village were tagging along – bored-looking youths in hats, and a girl in wobbly sunglasses. They were muttering about sorcery and witches and helping themselves to leftover food and drink while the pastor chatted with Mama. He put a hand on her arm and asked about Nana Kima. She wiped her eyes and pointed to the scrubland.

Soon the pastor was walking up there followed by his three friends, by Moses and a long line of inquisitive villagers, most of whom had not attended Nana's burial but seemed suddenly keen to pay their respects, jostling each other to get closer to the important visitors. Dudu was pushed aside. Something was different now, excitement rippling the balmy air.

The crowd reached the scrubland and the pastor's shiny shoes sank into soft soil as he stood alongside Nana Kima's grave. Everyone listened – even those chewing gum – when he spoke. His voice was loud but calm, his hand raised and his eyes closed tight.

"Again he said unto me, Prophesy upon these bones, and say unto them, O ye dry bones, hear the word of the Lord."

Cyril in the black suit stood alongside. "Ezekiel 37:4,

Book of Job."

"Hallelujah," cried a toothless villager, sucking a piece of sugar cane.

"Find some sorcerers," said another.

"Yes, before they steal the body at night," said the girl in sunglasses. Latecomers shuffled on tiptoe, gawping and whispering, perhaps curious to hear more about that book of jobs. A worried-looking youth retied the bandana on his head and said to Pastor Precious, "Never mind big speeches. I thought you came to find Jezebel and banish Satan? We've got a sorcerer, in case you forgot."

Some of the others began chanting, louder and louder. "Banish, banish!"

"Very well," said the pastor, beckoning pretty Awa to his side. "Yesterday, I met this girl. She admits to sorcery and taking the Devil's bread in exchange for Christian souls."

Awa shut her eyes and rolled her head, gabbling in a strange language, more like little growls. Dudu stared at her, puzzled. The crowd gasped as one and some of them made the sign of Jesus Cross. "This girl brings tragedy to her family," said the pastor. "She is a lost sheep. Despised, because she is possessed by Jezebel. What should I do?"

Some of the villagers exchanged glances. Cyril sighed. "Bring her to Jesus."

"Purify her!" said Moses. "*Délivrance totale*. It will cleanse her soul."

Most of the crowd nodded; *yes!* But some looked less certain; *well, maybe.*

"Not yet," the pastor said. "I need to conserve my energy if I am to save your village. First, I will find your sorcerer, perhaps several, then I will purify them all."

"Will you purify Moses?" Old Koosie lurched through the crowd with shirt open and his ribs showing like the rungs of a ladder. His voice was wobbly from beer.

Moses glared. "Shut up, Koosie, you're making a fool of yourself."

Koosie flopped at Nana's grave and wept, his bony shoulders heaving. Moses turned to Pastor Precious and said, "My apologies. Nkusu sometimes loses his wits."

"And his decorum," said the pastor, and strode downhill. Dudu followed quickly, because he did not want to get pushed aside in the rush. The pastor was urging the people to fetch family and friends. "We'll assemble at Moses' house. Inquiries will begin forthwith. I will accept your help and donations, no matter how small, to build the Church of Victory Over Satan, one day. Perhaps here, in Mavuku. What do you say?"

"Yes!" yelled the youth in the bandana. "I can help with jobs!"

Dudu walked downhill listening to the villagers' fearful gossip. *Satan is in the old woman's cat; Satan is in Koosie's empty head; Satan was in my food last night – it tasted bad.* The youth in the bandana was soon taking bets about where the pastor would find Satan. Ginelle came scurrying from behind and slipped her arm through Dudu's. *For the first time ever.* He liked how it felt, until she pinched his wrist and spoke in a worried voice.

"Hey, neighbour, keep away from Miss Chatterbox. I know she's pretty but she's possessed. Didn't you notice, Dudu?"

Dudu glanced back at Awa walking with Cyril. "She seemed normal earlier."

"So did *you*. But now you're ignoring me. Behaving rather strangely, in fact."

"I'm not ignoring you. I'm helping the pastor. I know who made sorcery."

"*What?* You know who sent Nana Kima to *hell*? You'd best tell me, quickly."

Dudu was wondering whether he should, when Koosie stumbled up and hissed in his ear, "Ask your pastor if Moses will go to hell!" Koosie had stinky breath and was staring with bloodshot eyes. "Your tata deserved better."

Dudu stopped to listen but the crowd swept Koosie

downhill. Emile stumbled past on his weak leg and Dudu steadied him. "Easy, Emile, plenty of time."

The villagers turned left at the bottom of the hill and marched quickly along the main street, pouring into Mama's yard where inquiries would begin forthwith. Dudu slipped through a gap in the fence and watched them wriggle for places like nursing piglets; he felt very proud that such important events could happen here. He strolled into the house, taking his time, with many envious eyes upon him, because the clever pastor had chosen this house to start his search for Satan. He just needed a little help.

Chapter 16

It was gloomy indoors but the pastor's purple shirt shimmered in a beam of sunlight. He knelt and put his palm on the wall near Mama's chair, then made the sign of Jesus Cross.

"Submit yourselves therefore to God. Resist the Devil, and he will flee from you."

"James 4:7," said Cyril. Moses flicked the crinkly pages of Mama's Holy Bible, straining his eyes in the gloom as he tried to read the tiny words. The pastor rose slowly and Mama patted the best chair for him to sit in. "Come, please tell me: did a sorcerer kill my mother?"

"He certainly killed my business," said Moses.

"Why do you suspect a male?" asked Pastor Precious. "Men practise *butsi*. But women make *kiswenene;* more powerful. Maybe the sorcerer is female, perhaps a girl?"

"Actually, Pastor, it's the twins," said Dudu. "They've got it in for us."

Everyone turned. The pastor smiled. "Thank you for your opinion, young man."

"Whoever did it, I want them punished," said Mama. "Today, Pastor."

"I do not punish, I redeem. For ye are not under the law, but under grace."

"Romans 6:14," said Cyril, and Moses flicked through his Holy Bible.

"Very well, Pastor," said Mama. "You redeem, I'll punish. Just tell me who."

The pastor raised an eyebrow. "Madame Solange, I appreciate your concern, but please be patient. It may take time for me to find and exorcise The Evil One."

"The Evil Two," said Dudu, and got a sharp poke in the head from Moses.

Mama edged closer to the pastor. "Whoever it is, how long will this take?"

"There are six stages. The exorcism of Nicole Obry lasted two months."

"Two *months*? First I've heard of it. What village does she live in?" said Mama.

"She lived in Laon, in France, in 1566. She levitated, among other things," said Pastor Precious. Moses gawped like a goat and made the sign of Jesus Cross.

"Is my nana in hell, Pastor?" Dudu asked.

"Let's hope not, young man. You've been giving it some thought, I see?"

"Yes, Pastor. And also, when we were in Heroes' Corner, you said, *Awa is a sinner saved.* But, later you said, *Jezebel is inside her.* When we were up the hill."

The pastor seemed surprised. Perhaps he had forgotten. "Go on, Dudu."

"I also remember that Awa was with you two days ago, downriver."

"Correct," said Cyril in the black suit. "What are you suggesting?"

"Well, Pastor said they *first met yesterday*. He must have forgotten. That's all."

The room was silent, except for the sound of a dog barking in the distance. The pastor looked first at Cyril and then towards the window. He did not seem interested in Dudu's opinions. "Madame Solange, please tell me more about your family."

While Mama was talking, Dudu got another poke from Moses, who whispered, "Be quiet, or I'll cut off your little tongue and your big ears. Do you understand?"

Dudu nodded and sat watching Mama wipe her tears as she spoke in a sad voice about Tata. "Then the war came,

99

Pastor. The militia took my husband Félicien to help build their camps. Lots of our men were marched off; Moses and old Nkusu too. I watched from the forest, hiding with my two boys."

The pastor seemed puzzled, turning the gold ring on his finger. "Your *two* sons?"

Mama summoned Emile from a corner. The pastor patted Emile's head and briefly inspected his withered leg. "Félicien was the father of this boy and of Dudu too?"

"Yes. They have his eyes. And his boldness."

The pastor turned to Emile. "What do you think of Uncle Moses?"

"Moses is a donkey."

Someone giggled among the neighbours and the pastor said, "Emile, you seem tired today, perhaps after a restless night? What do you dream, when you go to bed?"

"About a big house with a brass tap for water. I'm guarding the jewels."

"I see, and tell me about Dudu. Is he a good boy for Mama and Uncle?"

Emile shook his head. "Dudu lost the bidons. And he lights the candle."

"The candle?"

Moses leaned in. "A candle for his tata's Power Figure. I consider it wasteful."

The pastor rubbed his chin, looking at Emile's leg. Mama said, "Poliomyelitis."

Cyril whispered to the pastor who said, "Indeed. Do you dream of Tata, Dudu?"

Dudu grinned. This was an easy one. "Yes, Pastor; we cook fish on a fire."

"What sort of fish?" The pastor glanced back at Cyril, as if they already knew.

Dudu shrugged. "I can't remember. We just eat it."

"Do you ever dream of faraway places?"

"Sometimes. Last week I dreamed about my picture book.

The Eiffel Tower. That's in France. Or London Bridge; the arms go up and down. Do you want to see?"

"No, thank you. Do you meet Emile in the dreams? Does he *accompany* you?"

"Sometimes, but not always. He's probably in his own dreams."

"Indeed. And why do you light candles to pagan idols, worship false gods?"

"I don't understand."

"The Power Figure. Emile says you *light the candle*. Moses has confirmed it."

"Nana Kima wanted me to light it. Because she was very sick."

"And what does Tata ask? Does he ask you to defy Jesus?"

Dudu stared. "I don't understand."

"To spurn our Redeemer's immortal sacrifice?"

"What?"

"Listen closely, young man, even the black dog understands." Pastor Precious stood up and walked in a little circle with his hands behind his back, watched closely by everyone in the room. It was quiet, except for the creaking of his shiny shoes and the barking of a distant dog. Pastor Precious crouched before Dudu and said, "The Evil One may have fooled your family, but he does not fool me. Not even for a moment."

"Pardon?"

"You are possessed, Dudu. You are a witch. And so is your brother."

Chapter 17

Dudu watched Pastor Precious march about the room saying big words to Mama, Moses and everyone else. Pastor wiped the pink lenses of his spectacles and said, "I established my conclusions through observation, inquiry and fundamental deduction."

"But I'm not a witch," Dudu said.

"I am," said Emile, smiling at pretty little Awa, who smiled back.

Mama sobbed on Moses' scarred shoulder. "My own sons? Are you sure, Pastor?"

"Consider the evidence: Emile's withered leg. *Poliomyelitis,* yes?"

"Polio-my-ass," said Paul the Purified Boy and someone giggled.

"By day it seems a tragic disability," said Pastor Precious. "But by night? Emile can run faster than a cheetah. He can run to London in minutes, even with Dudu on his back. Madame Solange, even as a baby in your womb your youngest son had bartered with Satan and exchanged disability in *this* world for superpowers in the *underworld*. His pact with the Prince of Darkness brought misfortune into your home. That is how it started. Now, ruin."

Everyone gasped – even the mean-faced boy in the bandana stopped chewing bubblegum. Mama looked terrified. "I carried the Devil? I nursed The Evil One?"

Moses hugged Mama, kissed her head and asked, "What about Dudu, Pastor?"

The pastor raised a finger. "His case is more complicated.

Dudu accepted Devil's Bread, disguised as a fish, in exchange for Nana Kima's soul. He also bartered your livelihood, Moses, because he resents you as his stepfather. Witness the lost bidons, the insolence in your presence. Surely you know that when we raise another man's child, we raise an enemy?"

Moses stared. "It's true. Now I see. *Even the black dog understands.*"

"Exactly. That's why it barks at him, because it sees Satan disguised as Dudu."

"I'm not a witch," Dudu said.

Moses raised a finger. "Be quiet please. Pastor knows best; he is here to help you."

Dudu looked towards Mama. She gazed back, as if deaf. A worried-looking man in a straw hat slipped into the packed room and his whispers soon reached the pastor, who spoke to Mama and went out. His audience made the sign of Jesus Cross as he passed. The room emptied in seconds. "I should go too," Moses said to Mama. "Banza's wife believes her daughter may be a witch; she answers back too often. Banza has business problems, too."

"You're going to Banza's house? What about me? I've got two—"

"Put them in the back room, until I return. Pastor will search the rest of the village. We'll find as many sorcerers as we can and then decide what to do. We must act soon."

"We?" said Mama. Moses kissed her head, picked up the Bible and hurried out.

Mama wiped her eyes and frowned at Dudu and Emile. She pointed towards the stinky room where Nana had died and said, "Both of you. In there. Not another word."

Dudu led Emile into the back room and the door squeaked shut behind them. The place still smelled bad, even though Mama had scrubbed it. Emile wobbled about sniffing here and there like a dog scavenging for food. The wooden shutter was secured from the inside in case of burglars. Dudu slipped the rusty bolt and pushed it open. He stood looking towards the distant trees. He could easily jump out and run away, deep into the jungle; but then what – hunt bushmeat until a snake squashed you? And what about Emile?

"Tell them it's not true." He turned to his little brother. "Do you hear me, Emile? Tell the pastor you're not a witch. Or they'll bury you alive, Awa told me so. You'll see."

"No they won't," Emile said, squatting to watch a shiny centipede. "You'll see."

Dudu slumped down and stared at the crusty wall. After a bit, he heard weeds rustle and Ginelle peeped in from outside. "Hello, sorcerers! People say I should stay away."

"So why are you here?" Dudu replied.

"To visit the prisoners," she said, resting her elbows on the ledge.

"I'm not in prison. I could escape easily," said Dudu.

"So why don't you?"

"Why should I? It's not even true. I'm not a witch."

"That's what *you* think. Satan tricked you. Are you smarter? I don't think so."

"Thanks for coming. Perhaps you should stay away, like people say."

"Don't you want to hear my news? They've found more sorcerers. There's going to be an exorcism and you're all invited. They'll use Banza's yard because it's big. Oh, and now Mrs Banza has *two* mobile phones. You can rent one to call friends. Well, not *you*, because you haven't got any, except for Koosie and he's a drunk. By the way, Koosie told people that *Moses* is The Evil One. So Moses punched him on the nose. Everyone is gossiping and Mrs Banza is getting rich. I'll bet she buys another dress. I want a phone. What's wrong? Where are you going?"

Dudu moved to the door, listening, just in case. He returned to Ginelle and spoke in a low voice. "I'm thinking about something Koosie said; something strange. He told me *Tata deserved better*. Can you ask what Koosie meant, if you see him?"

"He meant a better *son,* probably. Not a sorcerer, for example."

"But he said it up the hill, *before* Pastor told Mama I was a witch. Can you ask?"

"I might, if I feel like it. Any more final requests?"

"Tell those bossy twins to go and jump in the river. This is all their fault."

"Doubt it," said Ginelle, and disappeared. The weeds rustled farewell.

Emile was pointing a finger at the centipede, to count its legs. Dudu poked him with his toe. "*Carry me fast on your back to London?* Em, you can't even walk, never mind run."

"At night I can," said Emile. Dudu groaned and put his head in his hands.

The room was getting hot and stinky when the weeds rustled again and a different face peeped in from outside, this time with an unshaven chin and a bloodstained nose. "I hear you have a question. Me too. How's jail?" Old Koosie propped his elbows on the ledge and coughed, his chest rattling like rain on a roof. Dudu stood up and leaned out. Music crackled from a distant radio and a white heron floated slowly by, towards the bush. It looked easy.

"Thanks for coming, Koosie. Why did my Tata *deserve better*? What do you mean?"

Koosie looked puzzled, watching the heron. "Forget it. War's a dirty business."

"You asked Pastor if Moses will go to hell. You mean because he shot a girl?"

Koosie suddenly seemed worried. "Who told you about that? Not me. Was it me?"

"No. Uncle confessed to Pastor Precious, when we went downriver. I listened."

"Well, listen to this: forget whatever you heard. Because when we were in the militia, Moses was a bad man. A very bad man. He used to collect the enemy's ears. He'll collect your nose if you stick it in his business! Be careful. I've said enough. Time to go."

Dudu gasped, thinking fast. "Did Tata tell you he deserved a better *son* than me?"

Koosie shook his head. "I meant your tata deserved a better *comrade*. Moses claims he risked his life? To rescue the injured that day and bury the unlucky ones? The only thing Corporal Moses ever buried was the *truth*. Word travels fast in the bush, Dudu. I was in a different unit but I heard all about it. I saw the skeletons later, picked clean by beasts and vultures. That's all I'll say. Best you know that much before I die. God's truth."

Dudu swallowed hard, his ears burning. "Before *you* die? I don't understand."

"I've got *Slim,* same as my wife." Koosie was nodding. His head seemed ready to fall off. He grasped Dudu's wrist. "Don't tell Moses what I said about him! He'll open you up. He's trouble, always gets what he wants, including your sweet Mama. Don't you see?"

Dudu gulped, his skin tingling all over as if a ghost had passed by. The door swung open, Koosie ducked away and Mama entered carrying a tray with two bowls of food.

Chapter 18

Dudu was half asleep when he was hauled to his feet, bundled from the back room and into the sunny yard. Moses gripped his arm. "Sorcery, eh? Time we purified you. Come."

Cyril in the black suit carried a grinning Emile on his shoulders. They went quickly through the village to Banza's house, accompanied by a crowd of squawking busybodies.

Banza's yard was the biggest Dudu had ever seen, with two Toyota jeeps – one old, one new – parked under a huge baobab tree. The place was packed with people too: men sitting in the tree, youths squatting on the high walls, kids huddling on the well-swept flagstones, women gawping from windows, up and down. Mrs Banza strolled about in a nice pink dress, offering her phone for people to call friends, if they could pay. Banza's handsome son wore Adidas from head to toe, selling snacks and cold drinks while a kettle puffed steam on a brazier, for hot tea if you wanted to buy some. The yard gates hung wide open so passers-by could enter to see the wicked sorcerers. "And buy refreshments," said Banza, waddling about with his fat belly hanging over his trousers and rings on his fingers. No wonder some people called him *Mercedes Banza*. He would probably buy one, any day.

Moses shunted Dudu and Emile towards a bench. "Sit, don't budge." They took their places alongside a line of girls and boys – some smiling, some not. Ginelle strolled up and stood nearby, arms folded, offering advice. "They're all witches, just like you, neighbour."

She had sprung her hair with wire and tied yellow beads in it. Her head seemed to be shooting stars. She pointed at the row of well-dressed adults at the front of the crowd.

"There's your Mama, sitting in a chair, see? Guess what she told Pastor? *Satan must be banished, please purify my sons, pray all night if need be.* Guess how long they prayed for Nicole? Two months! She levitated to heaven, in a different village. Oh, and Pastor said today won't be easy, especially for Emile, because lots of demons got inside him a long time ago, when he was first in your Mama's belly, like this." She raised finger and thumb: *tiny.*

Dudu gestured to Mama who seemed to be in a daze, leaning with her elbows on her knees and her chin in her palm. The women sitting alongside her were chatting away.

"And what did the pastor say about me?" Dudu said, looking back at Ginelle.

"Not much. Just that your case is easy, as the demon got in you after your tata went away, which was, what, only two years ago? I remember my blue dress still fitted and your tata said it was nice. Oh, Moses said you're not smart and Satan sent a stupid demon to trick you and it will be easy for the clever pastor to chase it out. But the thing is, Paul told me there is no such thing as a stupid demon, only *stupid people.* He's quite handsome, I think."

"So what are they going to do?"

Ginelle shrugged. "Well, your best friend Miss Chatterbox said sometimes it's better if you just admit it and get it over with, because Pastor is clever and Satan can never win. But Paul told me it gets more interesting if you refuse to admit to sorcery. It all depends."

"On what?"

"Pastor, of course. Don't you think Paul is nice? I do. He let me swing his smoke box, but it wasn't lit, so he promised I could swing it again later, when it is. They're all staying in Banza's house, by the way, not yours. Moses complained about that until Banza's son threatened to burn down Heroes' Corner. Anyway, I'm not even supposed to talk to you, so, see you later, sorcerer. And don't forget to wave during the thing.

The exercise."

Dudu watched her skip away into the crowd on legs too long for her body, like a spider in a dress. He spoke to the boy sitting alongside. "I'm not even a sorcerer; are you?"

The boy nodded and seemed pleased, even though he had only green underpants for clothes. The next boy was too busy picking a scab on his elbow. Emile got up to take a look.

"Here they come!" cried a man in the tree, pointing towards Banza's garage.

Uncle Moses came first, carrying Tata's ebony cane and a plastic bag that bulged, like the time he had taken too many noisy kittens to the river, except this bag did not wriggle and meow. Next came Cyril carrying two unlit torches, then Paul the Purified Boy swinging his pot of smoke, then the pastor in robes of white and purple, carrying his Holy Bible. Last of all came pretty Awa, holding her green velvet bag on a long stick. Dudu shaded his eyes, watching carefully. It was hard to tell whether she was still possessed, or a sinner saved.

Cyril walked to the big wooden table and placed his two torches, lighting them. Black smoke rose and the pastor bowed his head. Moses upended his plastic bag on the ground and out tumbled the Power Figure and some smaller carvings that Tata had made, including a wooden fetish to cure the polio in Emile's leg, which had never worked. Perhaps Nana was wrong and Moses was right – the old days were gone.

Pastor Precious pointed to the pile of carvings and then at the crowd, talking in a big voice. "You have spent enough time doing what pagans do – living in debauchery, lust, drunkenness, orgies, carousing and detestable idolatry!"

Cyril uncoiled a length of rope from his pocket and said, "Peter 1, 4:3."

"They have made themselves a golden calf and have worshipped it."

"Exodus 32:8."

Pastor Precious gestured to Moses. "Bring the youngest. I'll need all my strength."

Moses led Emile from the bench and the pastor walked about, talking to the crowd.

"This boy admits sorcery! As a baby he offered his limb – a gift from God – in exchange for superpowers in the underworld. He welcomed Satan and brought misfortune upon his family. Having established the Presence, I will now force the demon to reveal itself in the Pretence." The pastor turned to Emile and said: "Speak your name; who are you?"

"Emile. But I'm not a witch."

"Liar! You're possessed! You confessed this morning! Tell me, are you Abaddon the Destroyer? Naberius, Marquis of Hell? Sabnock? Valac with his thirty legions?"

"I'm Emile."

The pastor reached out, twisting Emile's ear. "Or perhaps Xaphan the Fallen Angel?"

Dudu stood up and said, "Pastor, stop hurting him."

Moses pointed a finger. "Silence, Dudu!"

Emile kicked Pastor Precious in the shin. The pastor yelped and people laughed.

"The demon awakes!" the pastor whimpered. "The child loses control of his limbs!"

Cyril yanked Emile to the ground and looped his rope tight around his legs as if trussing a goat for the knife. Emile wriggled and clawed Cyril's face. Moses put his cane on the table and came to help, pinning Emile down. "Got him! Pastor, do what you must!"

Cyril strode across the yard to Banza's son and jabbed a finger at the steaming kettle on the hot brazier: *give me that!* Dudu looked at Mama. She was still watching in a daze. Pastor Precious rubbed his shin and circled Emile, looking angry and wagging a finger.

"God exacteth of thee less than thine iniquity deserveth!"

"Job 11:6." said Cyril, trotting up with the steaming kettle. He poured the boiling water over Emile's bad leg. Emile screamed and howled. Moses held him firm. Dudu raced forward, seized Tata's ebony cane from the table and swung it down hard on Cyril's hands. The ivory knob gave a smart crack and Cyril cried out, dropping the kettle. The lid popped and the water gushed towards Moses, who scrabbled away on his knees. Mama lurched from her seat, grabbed Emile and waddled towards the open gates. The crowd parted before her.

Dudu followed, backing slowly across the yard, his stick poised and ready, but nobody dared approach – *because he was Satan?* Pastor Precious pointed a finger at him. "Who warned you to flee from the wrath to come?"

Cyril rubbed his sore hand and said, "Luke 3:7."

Moses approached. A knife appeared in his hand as if by magic as he strode forward, growling curses. Dudu raised his stick. "Leave us alone, Uncle, or I'll tell her everything."

Moses stood blinking in the sunlight, watched by the listening crowd. Mama was gone, through the gate, with howling Emile. Dudu turned and ran after them.

Chapter 19

It was late when Moses came home to argue with Mama, cursing and yelling. Dudu watched them through the gap between the ragged curtains. Mama shouted and wailed, wiping tears. "Keep that crazy pastor away from my boys! I swear, if he lays one finger—"

"Solange, you agreed that Satan must not elude us."

"I agreed the pastor could say *prayers,* not torture Emile!"

"We have to purify the village."

"*We?*"

"Pastor Precious says I have a higher calling, a vocation. Pastor says *all hard work brings a profit, but mere talk leads only to poverty.* Proverbs 14:23. He says that's probably why my bar is failing, because people just drink and talk nonsense, like old Koosie."

"Koosie told us to fetch the pastor. What do you have to say about that?"

"Divine providence. Where is Emile?"

"Somewhere you can't find him."

"Where's Dudu? Whatever he says do not believe it. Satan speaks through him."

"Oh really? Well Satan says I shouldn't trust *you.* Moses, and I believe that much. Have you lost your mind, letting that pastor scald my child? He's a brute. How could you?"

"I need a job, a future. Pastor can help me."

Mama paced the room, running her fingers through her hair. "You call that *helping?* We don't need that kind of help. I certainly don't. Keep him away from my boys!"

"He wants to exorcise Dudu, *lest Satan flourish unchecked.*

And if I don't do as Pastor asks, I will look like a fool. I invited him to Mavuku in the first place! Think of that!"

Mama sat down, rubbing her chin, staring at the ground. "I've got an idea, Moses. We'll send him to Kananga, first thing tomorrow morning. That's the only solution."

"Send the pastor to Kananga? Why? His work is here, he has a sacred mission."

"I mean send *Dudu*. Tell Pastor, *Satan got scared and escaped*. You can blame me."

Moses walked about. He seemed to be thinking it over. "Why Kananga?"

"Because you've got family there. So, here's what to do. Go back to Banza's tonight and borrow his phone. Call your aunt in Kananga. Ask her if Dudu can stay for a while."

"My aunt will never accept a sorcerer in their home. Who would?"

"Don't tell her any of *that*. Just tell her Dudu is sad about Nana and needs a change. Tell her… you want him to work in their restaurant for free, to train as a waiter and barman; you're preparing him to work in Heroes' Corner, because business is booming. Well?"

Moses rubbed his chin. Mama glanced towards the ragged curtains as if she knew they were being watched. Dudu retreated to the shadows, thinking hard. *Go to Kananga?*

"Actually, it might work," Moses said. Dudu edged back to the curtain and heard Mama whispering the rest of her plan.

"Moses, of course it'll work. But don't let anyone overhear you phoning. Be careful. Tomorrow, tell Pastor that Satan fled. Pastor saves face. Dudu disappears, for a bit."

"Yes, exactly. Good idea."

Their voices faded and Dudu went to lie down on his bamboo bed, watching pale moonlight cast strange shadows. The house still smelled of Nana. He imagined worms sucking her cold toes and pictured Tata's bones picked clean by vultures, who knows what. He thought of Pastor Precious making plans that would not work; *Mama is smarter.*

Another stupid moth fluttered into a spider's web high in the corner. It twisted and dangled, struggling to free itself. Somehow it succeeded but flew into a bigger web and a fat spider came to spin its silver *madiba* and say goodbye. Dudu turned to watch the moon; tomorrow, he would say goodbye to Mama. *Why must I leave and not those twins, the real sorcerers? Why not Moses who shot a bullet up a girl?* The front door creaked and Moses said, "Remember, Solange, it was your idea." Moses' footsteps faded into the night. Dudu heard Emile weeping in Ginelle's house and Mama pattering up their path in her flip-flops.

Dudu woke early next day to find Mama crouched at his bed, stroking his forehead and quietly explaining. He pretended to be surprised at her plan. She opened his satchel to reveal spare clothes, water and snacks. "I packed some cigarettes too, for militia, see? Moses made a call, last night; someone will meet you in Lukamba village, near Kananga. Auntie has kids and ping-pong so you'll have fun. I'll call her when it's safe to come home." Mama handed him an old wallet. "This was Tata's. I've put a little money and Auntie's number inside. Keep it safe in your back pocket. You're a man now. Get up, Du, hurry, but quietly!" She pressed a finger to her lips, even though Moses was snoring loudly from behind the curtain.

Dudu dressed, watching Emile fast asleep with his leg bandaged and his eyes puffy from tears. Dudu kissed his forehead and said, "Bye Emile. If I ever see that pastor…"

From under his bed he took a small Power Figure that Moses had missed in the big clear-out. It seemed only yesterday that Tata had carved it in his workshop. He put the carving and his picture book in his satchel, glanced around one last time and went outside.

The goats gazed at him as if thinking, *there goes the* ndoki. He walked to Tata's old workshop, where the hens fluttered and fussed. He pictured Tata whistling while he stood on an upturned chair, balanced and grinning: *best way to test 'em, son.* A hen flew from its roost as Dudu took one of Tata's old penknives from a tin can and slipped it in his pocket.

Mama hissed from the rutted path: *come, for the bus!* He trotted across the yard to join her. She put Tata's old cap on him, tugging the peak low. "Walk a bit behind me, son."

Dawn cast long shadows through the village and woodsmoke curled like grey snakes. Mama walked quickly and Dudu followed, past yawning children carrying yellow bidons. He expected them to point at him but they were busy with their chores. On a quiet stretch of the path he trotted alongside Mama. "Do you think I'm a witch? Do you think I'm *ndoki?*"

"I think we live in strange times, Dudu, and the sooner you leave the better."

"I'm not a witch."

Mama paused and turned. She places her big strong hands on his shoulders, as if she would snap him like a dry twig. But she didn't try. Instead, she just looked him in the eye.

"Son, *I* know who you are, so I don't care what *others* say. This trouble will pass. Meanwhile, Tata and Nana will watch over you. Remember that. Do not shame us. Be good in Kananga. No stealing, fibbing or fighting. And watch your manners. *Please, thank you.*"

He nodded, she kissed his forehead and they continued together along the top road to the bus stop. A white UN jeep bounced by, with four Blue Hat soldiers chatting and grinning inside. He remembered how Tata would often point and say, *See those guys, Dudu? Peace will come!* But it hadn't. Instead, nasty militia had come and they had pointed at Tata: *You.*

At the bus stop, an old woman with wobbly hands blabbed proudly to Mama about her sweet daughter doing very well in Kananga with a clever and helpful husband. Dudu watched a wrinkly man with stick legs push a bicycle laden with bottles of palm oil. A familiar figure appeared with a bundle of wood under her arm. Dudu turned away, but too late.

"Going somewhere, neighbour?" Ginelle said. "Good idea. They say you bust Cyril's skull. Such fibs. Anyway, I say you stood up for yourself, which makes a change."

Dudu squinted down the dusty road, watching for the bus to come around the corner. But it didn't. Ginelle stepped closer. "Nice hat, neighbour. Should we kiss goodbye?"

"No thanks. You said I was a sorcerer. Perhaps you should kiss Paul instead."

"I already did. He's fourteen. Why, are you jealous?" She reached out and squeezed his arm and it felt quite nice but he pulled away, pretending to be more interested in Mama's chat with the old woman. He could feel Ginelle's gaze on him, until she turned and walked back down the road to Mavuku and her hand rose to her eye, perhaps to rub dust away.

The minibus came rolling up with a sign on the front. *Jesus saves*. The door hissed like an angry cat. Mama paid the fare and wept as she whimpered, "Bye, Dudu. Your stop is Lukamba village. Someone will meet you there on a motorbike. Don't fall off it."

The door hissed again and he found an empty seat. He waved from the rear window and Mama waved too, dabbing her eyes as the engine growled and dust whirled from the wheels in red clouds that swallowed her up. He sat down. Two boys turned slowly from the seats in front. They took off their sunglasses. Their faces were identical. The bossy twins.

"Look who's here!" said the one in the red shirt; the one in blue just smiled.

Chapter 20

The bossy twins seemed confused. The twin in red made a face. "Why are you on our bus? Shouldn't you be back in Mavuku, fetching water with the other girls?" They both stared as if Dudu were an unusual fish they had never caught before. The twin in blue moved to an empty seat behind Dudu and flicked his neck with a fingernail. "We asked you a question."

Dudu was careful with his answers and soon realised the twins had not heard about Pastor Precious and the exorcism in Banza's yard. "So, where are *you* going?" he said.

"Mind your own business."

"We're going to stay in Peka for a few days," said the twin in red, breezily. "Mama and Tata got divorced. We have two homes. We prefer Peka. We go on this bus a *lot*."

He smirked as if bumping up and down on squeaky seats was something to boast about. Dudu wondered how it might be to have *two homes*. He would find out in Lukamba.

"When are you getting off, Dudu? Soon I hope."

"Lukamba. It's seven hours' drive, about. That's what Mama said."

"And you believe her," said the twin sitting behind him.

Dudu looked out of the window, watching monkeys dangle from the trees. The forest was thick and dark, good for hiding. He wished he were in it. Little ramshackle houses sat alongside the road. He watched hens scuttling among nervous goats. Men were lounging on benches and dogs chased the bus or scratched themselves with jerky back legs. A tiny boy stood splashing in a puddle. A fellow in shorts was chopping wood; a woman was filling a bidon. Dudu thought about Mama and Tata and how it used to be, not so long ago.

"Pity about your bidons," chuckled the twin behind. "How's your stinky Nana?"

"She died," said Dudu. "Because of sorcery."

The twins' mocking smiles faded. They looked troubled and had nothing clever to say about that. They put their shiny sunglasses on and gazed out of the window.

"Think I'd prefer to sit near the front," Dudu said and moved away, up the aisle.

"Good idea. Getting a bit smelly back here," said one of the twins.

Dudu sat to watch the driver, who wore a shiny cap and shared jokes with a man in the first seat. Sometimes the other fellow said *slow down* but the driver only did so when he approached a village. He would announce each one by name. *Buanga! Kumbala! Sashidi!*

Sometimes he shouted a name but there would be no village, just a big circle of ash, charred trees and often a rusty jeep or truck, upside down in a ditch, torn with bullet holes. The bus passengers would make the sign of Jesus Cross and look sad. After a few more miles, the driver's companion pointed ahead and said, "Better slow down. Checkpoint."

Dudu watched a child soldier stroll into the road and raise a hand. *Stop.* His other hand rested on the rifle at his hip. One of the twins sauntered up the aisle behind Dudu and whispered in his ear. "That *kadogo* will board and want money. *To fight invaders.* Got any cash?"

Dudu turned. "Yes, a little. Why?"

"*Kadogo* might search your satchel. Put your cash in your back pocket, and sit on it."

"That's where it is, already. I have a wallet, you see."

The twin grinned. "You're no fool."

Dudu shook his head, staring ahead and wondering how smart that *kadogo* might be.

The bus slowed down and stopped at a piece of string,

stretched across the road like a washing line, with a human skull hanging from the middle. Dudu thought of Tata's bones and watched the soldiers lounging at the side of the road – three men and several *kadogos*.

The *kadogo* who entered the bus was aged about ten, chewing gum and making it pop. It sounded like a distant gun. Perhaps he did it to remind the passengers how the war had sounded and how quickly it could come back. He took off his black beret and held it upside down. The driver put money in and the *kadogo* strolled up the aisle collecting more contributions, his rifle swinging and bumping into the passengers as he walked. Some gave him money. Dudu gave the packet of cigarettes from Mama. When the *kadogo* reached the twins, the one in red said, "Sorry, no money or cigarettes. Tata forgot. Mama's been sick."

The *kadogo* pointed to their sunglasses and beckoned with a hand. *I'll take those.* After a moment, the sour-faced twins removed their sunglasses. He took them and walked down the aisle and got off the bus, without a word. Another soldier unhooked the string across the road and Dudu watched through the dusty window. The *kadogo* was wearing sunglasses now and put the other pair on the skull and held it up, to make the soldiers laugh. The skull stared at the bus as the driver continued along the bumpy road. *Bon voyage.*

Dudu turned around to look at the twins and said, "Pity about your sunglasses."

They glared as if he were to blame. He turned away and rested his head to doze with the sun in his face. *Serves them right for throwing my bidons in the river.* He thought about Ginelle climbing a tree and had a dream about swimming with her in a river that carried them to Heroes' Corner and flooded the place with frothy brown water; Moses got angry.

When Dudu awoke the twins had gone and he was glad. Through sleepy eyes he saw a bent road-sign – *N40* – with rusty bullet holes through the zero and he remembered Moses bragging in his bar about target practice, *when I was at the front.* Koosie had laughed at that and said, *even though you mostly were at the back?* Dudu wondered about the girl Moses had shot and about how war was a dirty business. *Where had Moses hidden his diamonds?*

Late in the afternoon, the bus hit a bump and everyone got off to listen as air hissed from the tyre and the driver walked about scratching his head. His companion rolled up his sleeves, inspecting the damage. "Jagged rock. I warned you to slow down. Didn't I say?"

Dudu sat on a log and watched them change the wheel with iron bars, a firm push with their foreheads and no jokes, while the sun kissed the grey horizon and made it blush.

The bus reached Lukamba later than expected. The place was not really a village, more of a busy town bubbling like a pot of soup, with lots of people, cars and trucks, even though darkness had fallen hours ago. The kerbstones were painted red and white. Blue flags hung from shops. A man wearing a cowboy hat hauled a steel trolley laden with heavy sacks. Two girls squatted on a street corner selling bananas. Surly *shegués* lurked in the shadows, street kids trading punches. Three policemen in yellow shirts and numbered yellow helmets stood in the road, watching traffic. Their belts had pistols and yellow whistles dangling down. Motorbikes whizzed about and glamorous ladies strolled with handsome men, chatting and smiling because they loved each other. Mama and Moses did not do that. Not any more.

The bus pulled into a busy car park and the driver got out to fetch luggage from the roof rack while his passengers stood kissing their families and friends under neon lights.

Dudu put his satchel over his shoulder and sat on a wooden bench, flip-flops dangling. Three *shegués* ambled from the shadows. They looked wild and smelled bad.

"What's in your bag?" said the tallest. Dudu walked away to a man in a white suit who seemed to be waiting, and asked, "Are you looking for Dudu from Mavuku?"

The man shook his head. "Am I who?"

A bright placard outside a kiosk offered *Calls In & Out, Best Rates!* Dudu knocked at the little round window and a lady opened it from inside. She had big eyelashes, big red fingernails, and a little television about the size of a pineapple. Her three mobile telephones were attached to chains so you could not steal them. She held her hand out, still watching TV. Dudu reached in his back pocket. He tried his other pocket. He looked in his bag. *No wallet?* The lady at the window frowned at him and swung it shut with a sharp click.

He ran back towards the bus, checking the ground. He climbed aboard and looked under all the seats. *No wallet.* He asked the driver who shrugged and wrote on a clipboard.

Different noises seemed to squash Dudu's head from all sides: shouting and laughing, gossiping and arguing, engines rumbling and buzzing, drivers calling destinations, dogs barking and scampering by. He closed his eyes and wondered what to do. Mama would curse his bad luck and Moses would say *fish-brain.* Auntie in Lukamba would be displeased and his cousins would make jokes. It was a good start. He walked back to the wooden bench and sat down, staring at the oily concrete. He sat there for a long time, watching feet pass by, some with shoes, some not. After a while, a voice came inside his head, like in a dream.

"Dudu? Dudu from Mavuku?"

He blinked at shiny, black boots and looked up. The man who had spoken wore a dark uniform, a crash hat and a walkie-talkie on his belt. He looked rather worried.

"Yes, that's me!" Dudu nodded, wiping tears. "I'm Dudu. Did Auntie send you?"

"Moses. Let's go."

He walked away and Dudu trotted alongside, telling him about losing Tata's wallet, but the man did not seem concerned about that, just serious about his job. They climbed onto a red motorbike and zoomed out of the car park, the man yelling *hold on kid* and Dudu squinting in the wind that whistled in his ears. His eyes filled with tears but he was not sad.

Bright signs flashed past: *Unique Motors, Star Motors,* and *Auto-Change.* A cardboard Jesus in white robes was pointing at the sky: *Paradise This Way, Follow Me.* The motorbike swung into a corner, Dudu tucked his heels and smiled, he had arrived safely in Lukamba and Mama had foxed that nasty pastor. He shouted as loud as he could, "Mister, what's ping-pong?" But the wind snatched his words and flung them at the starlit sky.

The man drove fast, probably because they were late and Auntie was waiting. Dudu watched restaurants and hotels fly by. *Perhaps this street, or the next?* He practised what to say, listing jobs he could do. *Graze goats; fetch water; lift crates of beer; clean the hen house; make hot drinks; chop wood; pluck weeds, any chores you wish.* A slow bend straightened into a wide road with big trucks that beeped and swerved. After a few miles, the motorbike slowed down, the driver turned off the road and puttered towards a big café with a brightly lit forecourt packed with all manner of vehicles and drivers filling their fuel tanks.

"We'll stop here, Dudu. Stretch your legs. I need a pee."

The driver disappeared behind some bushes and Dudu walked alongside a big truck, watching three grimy *shegués* begging for a ride. The truck driver told them to get lost. The kids moved on, pulling a dented cardboard carton from a bin and arguing about who saw it first, which of them should sleep on it. They were foul-mouthed and probably best avoided.

The rubbish they spilled twirled in the breeze and spun under a white jeep with UN on the side, parked outside a busy café with music playing inside. Dudu cupped a hand at the window to watch the clients eating nice-looking food at shiny tables and a waitress in a white shirt. Dudu's driver emerged from the bushes, talking on his walkie-talkie.

Dudu waited until he turned it off, then asked, "Is this Auntie's restaurant?"

The man climbed onto his bike. "This is where we say goodbye."

"But where does she live?" Dudu said, looking around. The man started his engine.

"Not here, and if you ever turn up, we'll set the dogs on you."

"What?"

"Moses told us all about you, Dudu from Mavuku. We don't want *ndoki*."

"I'm not *ndoki!*"

"And if you go home Moses will take you into the bush, show you how to cut meat."

Dudu watched the man slip his pedal. "But where are you going? What about me?"

"You?" The man twisted his handle to make the engine growl like an angry dog. "You never arrived. You got lost. We have no idea. Now go to hell. *Longwa kuna!*"

He zoomed away and his rear light was soon just a bright red dot, like Moses' cigarette at midnight.

Chapter 21

Frank spent most of Saturday editing his worksheets in the hotel's tiny, antiquated Business Centre, flitting between two ancient computers and a photocopier that hissed and lurched like a steam train.

Early evening he dined alone on Nile perch, carefully avoiding the red-hot *pilipili* sauce. The waiters took their time, perhaps because Mr Jerome had taken off.

Frank phoned Ruth from his room later, with one eye on MTV. She told him Dylan was glued to *The Sound of Music* and Billie had gone out to see a friend, *just a friend.*

Sunday morning, he had a long swim in the hotel pool and emerged gasping for a cigarette. He lay on a sun bed, listening to a cassette Billie had given him. The label said BRING IT BACK. Perhaps that was the album title. Dub reggae swirled in his headphones, heavy on the echo, *lovers' rock* and *baby mothers.* Still, it made a relaxing change from Billie's previous offering – an album by a sinister-sounding Australian who sounded like he wanted to chop you up. *But reggae, since when?* Frank felt stoned just listening. He bobbed his foot, sucking a ciggie; he would quit one day. Two tanned French women were chatting with a muscled dude in a UN hat, puffing their Gitanes. Or Gauloises. The distinctive aroma floating this way. Would they quit? *Mais non. Pourquoi?*

The reggae singer was warbling about *bump and grind* and Frank pictured Billie aged about ten, the time she had emptied a box of Ruth's precious vinyl in the back garden and set it ablaze with lighter fuel. Actually, it had been her dad's precious vinyl; poor Max must have turned in his grave. Maybe that was the idea. And how much reggae had melted on the lawn, that sooty day? Nor could you *bring it back*. Now this, seven years on. *Once more, Mistah DJ.* Frank closed his eyes, lulled by throbbing bass and plunking piano. Billie might be a handful but she was right; this stuff was *dead wicked*. And he would enjoy his time off.

Claude collected him from the hotel lobby on Monday morning and they drove across town to the seminar room. A few minutes before nine, they were hauling twelve desks and chairs into a semicircle, because some busybody had arranged them back into rows since their last visit. Frank placed a blue pen, a red pen, a jotter and a *Unicorn* folder on each desk. He opened a window for air and spotted a tubby woman hanging laundry on a balcony in the opposite block, her two kids at the railings. Frank waved. They gawped at the *mundele*.

He wrote on the whiteboard: UNICORN JOURNALISM SEMINAR. Just in case anyone might wonder, like that shy Bosnian woman who, in 1996, had waited until the first coffee break to ask him, *Excuse me, I thought this was about hotel management?* Wrong floor, wrong door.

Claude was poking the buttons of a dusty boom box, borrowed from HQ, scanning local radio for news. Frank checked his watch. A young man marched into the room, wearing a white shirt, red tie. Frank knew the face, but from where? *Ah, yes. Choice FM.*

"I'm Thony," the fellow said, shaking hands. He had a friendly grin and pearly choppers. "You texted my boss, Frank. Thanks for that." Thony chose a desk and sat down to inspect the freebies. "These for us? Nice." He pointed at the clock. "It's nine. You should start." Frank chose to bide his time, because two was company but twelve was a seminar.

Four women turned up, at five past the hour. The two

younger ones wore T-shirts and jeans; the older ones had on silky blouses and trouser suits, their diamanté brooches glittering. At quarter past, several men sauntered in. The tallest of them had the heavy eyes and goatee beard of a late-night sax player; the smallest wore a beige cap, slanted like a vol-au-vent. Frank smiled, shook hands, and waited for them to settle. They certainly took their time.

The trainees ranged from rookies to veterans, a blend of youth and experience, as he had requested. They cooed at their freebies. He asked them to tear a page from their jotters, write their names on it and fold it for him to see. Thony finished first, using huge capitals, underlined: _THONY_. The rest of the folded tags appeared one by one, in bold letters or emaciated scrawl. Henri in the pastry hat ran out of space and started over. A woman with a brooch wrote _Anais_ and turned it to herself, as if she might forget.

Frank offered a quick summary of his career and Henri said, "Do we get per diem?"

"Yes, at the end of the day. But for now, I'd like each of you just to say a few words about your own job, and about what you want from the seminar. One at a time, OK?"

Henri protested. _About my per diem._ Anais across the semicircle told him _be quiet._ Thony raised a hand. Frank gave him the nod. Thony sat erect, lining up his coloured pens.

"Me, well, let's just say I cover everything: news, sport, music. And, one day, I'll have my own radio station. And I support Chelsea, although I used to support Arsenal." He elbowed Maurice, the camp youngster in candy-striped cuffs, at his right. "Now you go."

Frank scribbled notes. Maurice from Hope FM spoke slowly, fingers trailing the air, as if spinning a fairy tale for children. He was new to radio and had been selected to attend this seminar, to help improve his chat show. "I hope to move into television, one day."

"If you're _new to radio,_ how come you got a chat show?" said Thony, chewing a pen.

"Because Maurice's brother is Deputy Ed," said Claire in the granny specs. "And now, Mr Frank, about me. I've been a reporter these last three years. No training. I think I'm quite good, considering. But you'll decide." She pushed her specs up. "That's it. Who's next?"

Remy with the grizzled grey curls rolled up his sleeves and confessed he *didn't know where to begin.* Nor did he know when to stop. Some of the others were less forthcoming, the shy ones drying up in seconds. Overall, they seemed a promising bunch. Frank spotted feet rocking with nervous energy, restless hands a-twiddle, as he distributed the first of his photocopied sheets. Thony hunched over the bullet points. "What's all this?"

"We'll mix theory and practice." Frank was pacing the room. "Discussion and exercises in class, outside for practical stuff. Five days is not long so be punctual, always."

"*Devil's Question.* What's that?"

"Basically it means a difficult question. You'll find out more, on the day."

"Coffee breaks?" said Louise in the shiny wig.

"Two, every day," said Thony, pointing at his sheet. "It's written at the bottom, see?"

The door creaked and several stragglers entered the room, slumping into empty seats. They wrote their name tags, made their pitch. Nadine, the presenter from Choice FM, looked tired already, tugging her bra strap, speaking with a languorous lilt. "Do we get a diploma?"

"Yes," said Frank and they all smiled, except the middle-aged fellow in the wrinkled suit who smelled of stale booze; his speech was short but could have been sweeter.

"As you know, I'm Jean Marie, twenty years on the job. So, not expecting much."

"Except, maybe, another diploma?" chuckled Bellidée in the Daffy Duck T-shirt.

"Thank you all." Frank pointed to the clock. "Time to move on; shall we?"

He got them started on the basics, asked them each to write a short bulletin of headlines, lasting thirty seconds, just an exercise. "Invent the news, OK? For example, President Kabila is flying to Washington. Or there was a fire in Kinshasa, a bomb in Paris, a row in Bukavu about child soldiers. Whatever you like."

"Invent the news?" said Nadine. "If I did that at Choice FM, I'd get sacked."

"It's an exercise. Are you deaf?" said Thony, scribbling. Jean Marie sighed. The rest sat muttering.

"Please work alone," said Frank, "you've got fifteen minutes. Coffee break is coming." He stood at the window. The laundry on the opposite balcony hung stiff in the sun. He spotted movement on the balcony below and watched a small monkey on a leash leaping around, teasing a grey parrot with a scarlet tail, cooped up in a cage. "Nice parrot, across the way," Frank said, and someone told him *quiet please*.

Jean Marie the veteran hack finished first and slapped his pen down with a triumphant smirk. *This is easy.* Frank asked him to read his work aloud and watched the clock's second hand sweep around as Jean Marie boomed the bulletin. It was badly written, revealed a poor grasp of news values and lasted almost two minutes. Thony was watching the clock too and, at the end, cried out, "That was way over!"

Jean Marie seemed puzzled. His gaze travelled around the semicircle of faces to Frank, who was pointing a finger at the clock. "Thony's right, Jean Marie."

"Me next," Thony said. His bulletin lasted a more respectable thirty-two seconds but was biased against the government, at least according to Jean Marie. Frank nodded, listened to the rest and walked them through News Values. "As journalists, we prioritise information. The important bits come first," he said, and was pleased to watch the pens scratching. Even Jean Marie was taking notes. Nadine just watched.

He went back over their headlines, showing how to cut the fluff and put the real story first. Their initial shock subsided to friendly rivalry, and before long they were shredding each other's work like hard-nosed subeditors. "Should we do it like this, every time?" Claire asked, pushing up her specs.

"Every time." Frank handed out photocopied sheets. *News Writing & News Values.*

"If you gave us these first, we wouldn't have to take notes," Nadine said, reading.

"Exactly!" Frank winked. She gave him a long hard look.

Bellidée raised a hand. "Why is the finance minister in the *second* line, not the first?"

"Because that's where he belongs," suggested Thony, with a wry smile.

"Ask yourself," said Frank, "who's the most important person in any radio story?"

Nadine tugged at her bra straps. Maurice was watching, apparently intrigued.

"It's the *listener*," said Frank, and, in the sweet silence that followed, he fancied he heard pennies dropping, one by one. "Got it?"

He watched them nod, one by one. They were either learning or ready for a kip.

"Mr Frank," said Lucy in the shiny wig, "we haven't got coffee."

Chapter 22

After coffee, Frank covered cues and despatches; how to nail the best angle, develop a news story, but reduce the padding. He set another timed exercise and watched with a familiar glow in his belly – the satisfaction of getting a new team of trainees up and running, of twiddling with the engine in a journalist's head, fine-tuning it. A dream job, this, with travel perks.

Around 1 p.m. a local caterer turned up wearing a white tunic and tall white hat like a five-star chef. He was carrying two trays of filled rolls and his assistant lugged a crate of soft drinks. The trainees, however, seemed unimpressed with their free lunch and Henri said, between mouthfuls, "Why not just give us the cash? Then we could buy *fufu*. It's cheaper."

After lunch, Frank slipped a cassette in the boom box and cued it, ready to roll. "You're going to hear a vox pop from Senegal about malaria. Listen up. It's your turn soon."

"To get malaria? We've already had it."

"I meant *your turn to make a vox pop*, on community issues. Listen up."

The audio ran twenty seconds, a sequence of opinions recorded on a busy street and tightly edited in a studio. Thony raised a thumb – *not bad* – but the other journalists mostly slouched, ready for a postprandial nap, until Frank said, "Time for you to choose a community issue. You can work in pairs. Once you're ready, we'll go. We need fresh air."

"Go where?" said Nadine.

The heat on the street hit Frank like a sandbag, dust coating his mucous membranes, the diesel fumes making his head spin. So much for fresh air. Trucks came honking past, blasting Congolese pop. The journalists clutched their recording gear; *testing one-two-three*. Frank beckoned them. "Remember," he said, blinking in sun, trying to remember. "Be polite. Ask open questions that invite opinions. Not closed questions, *yes* or *no*. And focus!"

"On community issues," said Anais. "Mine will be about maternity leave."

"I'm doing gay and lesbian rights," said Claire. "I changed my mind, OK, Frank?"

"Up to you. Everyone else happy?"

The others announced their topics and Frank surveyed the circle of faces, some eager, some worried. "So, off you go. Good luck. Be upstairs by half past three. That's a deadline, OK?"

The journalists scattered in pairs. The confident ones had no problem approaching strangers, the shy ones hung back: *you first*. Thony selected a plump woman leaning against a doorway with a beady-eyed chicken hanging upside down from her fist. Frank followed, to watch. Thony asked the woman if she had kids. She nodded, warily. He asked her, what if someone accused them of sorcery? The woman spat in the gutter. "I'd bash their brains in."

"Whose brains?" said Thony. She looked at him as he were soft in the head.

A small crowd gathered to gawp. Some giggled in fright when Thony turned to work his way around the group, holding the microphone out to record their various reactions. They seemed friendly enough but most had no time for little witches. A fellow in oily overalls said, "If my lot ever did that sorcery, I'd kick 'em on the street."

One pushy fellow demanded cash *for the inconvenience of listening*. A long-legged soldier wandered over, rifle dangling. Frank flashed his Min-Info ID but the soldier had a glazed look, as if only bullets might rouse him. Frank walked on, following Thony towards a man reading a newspaper. This fellow had a neat beard, specs like Malcolm X and answered Thony while flipping crinkly pages. "In my opinion, any talk of sorcery is paranoia. The government should help street kids. Or maybe the UN should?" He gave Frank a wry smile.

"*Mundele, donnez-moi de l'argent!*"

A gang of street kids trotted from an alley, jostling each other to be first to get to Frank. Their swaggering leader wore a long and filthy brown shirt, unbuttoned, and carried a mucky plastic bag. Thony intervened, brandishing his mic, all smiles. "Hi guys, I'm from Choice FM. Got a question. If someone called you a child witch, what would you say, huh?"

The gang leader glared in silence, swaying on his feet, stoned. His puffy-eyed lieutenant stepped up, chewing a stump of sugar cane. "*Witches,* us? Never. Who says so?"

Frank sensed unease rippling through the ranks. A goofy lad in cracked wraparound shades raised his fingers like horns, taking the piss. A fist smacked into his mouth and he tottered back. The gang fell upon one another, snarling and kicking, punching and gouging.

The lazy-eyed soldier laid into them with the stock of his rifle, cracking skulls like coconuts. One of the youths made a grab for Thony's recorder. Thony snatched it back and slipped away through the oncoming crowd. Frank quickly followed, mayhem in his wake.

By half past three he was back in the seminar room. The others returned in dribs and drabs and sat in tight groups playing their recordings, swapping tales. Frank circulated, offering advice on how they might edit the opinions. Henri the veteran failed to return; he had apparently gone home with a headache. Maurice was pestering Claire about her vox pop on gays and lesbians. He wanted to borrow it. Claire seemed reluctant. Maurice pouted. Eventually, she handed it over.

Frank rounded off with a quick recap of the day. "And

thanks for all your hard work! As I see it, a seminar is a two-way street. You'll learn from me, I'll learn from you." He pointed a finger firmly at his watch. "But, one thing I'll be stressing is that in a radio newsroom, the clock is God, OK? Doesn't matter whether we're Christian, Muslim, Jewish or whatever – we arrive on time, we respect deadlines. Not like today, ladies and gentlemen. Some of you came back an hour late. Anyway, enough, let's go home. Please collect your per diems from Claude on your way out; he'll need your signatures. Any questions?"

"Yes. What religion are you?" said Bellidée.

Frank mulled it over. "Me? I believe in travel. And stories. Yeah, that's about it."

"What about Jesus?"

Frank shrugged. "*Jesus was OK but the Apostles screwed it up*. John Lennon said that."

"No wonder he got shot," said Nadine, and the journalists rose as one, laughing.

Frank watched them go. He walked to the window, exhausted, and gazed at the roaring city. The first day of any seminar was the hardest; fun but it sapped you. As for lessons learned, he pictured a gang of surly street kids surrounding Thony. *A hornet's nest,* someone had said, about this child sorcery stuff. Braddock, probably. But it could have been worse. What if the rising star of Choice FM had suffered a broken nose, lost his tape recorder? What would Misti have said in DC; could she have *handled the fallout*? He heard a familiar voice.

Henri had returned and was counting out his per diem, banknote by banknote, in a serious tone, presumably because he thought Claude might have tricked him.

"Hi, Henri. How's the headache?" Frank asked.

"Better." Henri said. He signed Claude's ledger with a flourish. His signature resembled a miniature mushroom cloud. He pocketed his cash and strode off, whistling.

Claude jangled the car keys with an enigmatic grin.

"Frank, the problem is solved."

"What problem?"

"Rent problem. Unicorn paid. Do you want to move into your flat tonight?"

"That's a closed question, but I'll let you off."

Chapter 23

You cannot trust grown-ups; not really. Dudu felt the morning sun on his face but did not open his eyes. He stayed on his bed of squashed cardboard, listening to the rumble of trucks and buzz of motorbikes, smelling food from the café and wondering what to do.

You could not trust Uncle Moses or Pastor Precious, nor Cyril in the black suit and certainly not that drunken half-wit Koosie. Even Tata had broken his promise to come back safely from the militia. As for Mama, she had said, *just get on the bus Dudu; it will be fine.* But it wasn't fine. It was a mess. Had she known this would happen? Perhaps she had plotted with Moses, because they both believed the pastor. *Dudu is ndoki.*

And what about Nana Kima? *You have a long way to go, Dudu.* She had been right about that; Mavuku was far away. So, you could probably trust her. *But how do I get home? What if I try? Besides, what's the point of trusting someone who is dead?*

He heard meowing and opened a sleepy eye. The usual cat gazed down from the brick wall, as if wondering, *why are you still in my alley?* It was a good question. Dudu sat up and peeped carefully through a gap between two oil drums. There were no mucky *shegués* to be seen this morning. Perhaps they had all got rides in trucks or were scrounging breakfast outside the café? He stood up and watched a man opening a big steel door with keys. The man turned and seemed scared out of his wits. "Jesus, where did you come from?"

"Mavuku," Dudu replied.

"Well, go back, wherever it is. I don't need your sort outside my shop." The man shooed his hand as if to chase a scabby dog and went inside, locking the door behind him.

Dudu stood up and dusted himself down. *Your sort?* He looked at the trucks and motorbike drivers waiting for fuel. Some were sipping drinks, leaning against the vehicles, chatting and laughing. Perhaps the driver who had abandoned him would return and say, *just teasing, hop on the back, Du!* He walked across the forecourt to wash his hands at the little sink for the men. He peeped in the broken mirror. His T-shirt was getting grubbier, his hair thick with dust. A big man in oily jeans walked towards the sink. "Move, *shegué.*"

Dudu stood aside. "I'm not a *shegué.*"

The driver wiped his wet hands, chuckling. Dudu walked away, alongside the garage. He drank water from a dripping hosepipe, peeped in a bin and found an overripe banana that tasted OK. The smell of fresh doughnuts soon attracted him to the other end of the forecourt. He went to watch a jolly lady frying them in her big pan heated by a sharp blue flame from a gas bottle. Each dollop of batter made the oil fizz and each customer made the lady smile, but when she saw him she frowned. "You again? Pay up or else, young man."

The shiny white jeep parked nearby had long black aerials and UN in black letters on the side. Dudu sauntered towards it, with Tata's voice in his head. *Peace is coming and those Blue Hats will bring it.* He circled the empty jeep, standing on tiptoe, looking at the comfy seats, walkie-talkies, cigarettes, biscuits, a shiny magazine of naked ladies and the blue helmet dangling from a hook, just waiting for someone to wear it.

"Stop or I'll shoot," said a loud voice. Dudu froze and put his hands in the air.

"Turn, slowly," said the voice and Dudu turned to see a fat soldier with a bristly chin and a blue beret, pointing his finger like a gun "Hah, fooled you. Spying on us, eh, *shegué?*"

Dudu shook his head. Another soldier emerged from the café and said, "Hey, son, you can put your arms down." Dudu lowered his arms and watched the soldiers gobble chocolate. They had dark eyes and hairy arms, thick black moustaches and small coloured flags on their army shirts. They had a strange, spicy smell. One of them smiled at him. "Hungry?"

Dudu nodded. The soldier offered chocolate and Dudu gobbled some. It tasted better than the stuff Moses sold in Mavuku. He wiped his mouth. "Thank you, sir."

The soldier seemed surprised to hear it. "Hear that? Makes a change, for a *shegué*."

A third Blue Hat approached, sipping from a white plastic cup. Behind him trotted three dusty *shegués* and Dudu recognised them all. Bad boys, and best avoided. The smallest one was tugging hard at the soldier's shirt. "Papa MONUC, *donnez-moi!*"

The biggest *shegué* spotted Dudu, strode up and shoved him. "Still here, stranger?"

One of the soldiers pulled the *shegué* aside and said, "Hey, pick on someone your own size."

The *shegué* backed off, but made a finger-pistol against his head for Dudu to see: *you're dead.* The soldier chuckled, patting Dudu's arm. "Popular, eh? What's the problem?"

"It's their garage. They keep telling me to leave, or else."

"How long have you been here?"

"Two days."

The soldier sighed. "They're right. You'd better leave. Or stay and get beaten up!"

"Where am I supposed to go?"

"Don't you have a home somewhere?"

It was a difficult question and Dudu could not think of a suitable reply.

"Oh well, sorry about that," said the Blue Hat and moved away to stand with his friends, leaning against their car, puffing and chatting. Dudu watched the *shegués* making nasty gestures across the forecourt. The soldier came back and said, "What's your name?"

"Dudu. What's yours?"

"You can call me Major Monuc. You want a ride, Dudu?"

"Where to?"

"A safer place."

Dudu looked at the shiny white vehicle with black letters and aerials. "In your car?"

Major Monuc nodded, caressing his big moustache. "You could try my helmet."

"The blue one?"

"The blue one."

Dudu wondered if these soldiers would take him to Mavuku so that pretty Ginelle might see him wearing it, but no, Pastor Precious would still be there. *Better go to a safer place. If you could trust grown-ups to take you there.* "Where, exactly?" he asked.

Major Monuc glanced at the *shegués,* winked at Dudu and put a finger to his lips.

It's a secret.

Chapter 24

Dudu sat in the back of the UN jeep chewing his third biscuit and watching the road ahead. The helmet he was wearing wobbled because it was too big, but Major Monuc leaned forward from the seat opposite and squeezed his knee. "Keep it on, Dudu, so that if we meet militia, they won't try to recruit you as a *kadogo*. OK?"

Dudu nodded and the blue helmet wobbled again. He told the soldiers about the militia who had taken Tata. They had been mostly *kadogos* with big guns and eyes that stared. "Tata stood on a mine and vultures picked his bones," Dudu added.

"We know. You told us half an hour ago," said the smallest soldier, sounding bored. His eyelids drooped and he stared across at Dudu, as if waiting to see who would blink first. Dudu looked out the window down a steep slope at a silver track below. "There's a railway."

"It goes all the way to Ilebo," said the small soldier, "where our base is!"

Major Monuc poked the soldier with his toe, as if that were secret.

"Is Ilebo a safe place? Is that where we're going?" Dudu asked, but the soldiers were chatting among themselves in their strange language. He looked closer at the neatly sewn badges on their shirts: two swords, a moon and a star. Their chins were shaved smooth and they looked neat and smart; grown-ups you could trust. The driver slowed down, chuckling and muttering as they approached a ragged boy standing alone by the side of the road.

The boy was wearing big headphones and dangling a snake at arm's length. It squirmed and wriggled; the soldiers seemed amused by that but Dudu knew better. Teasing a snake was dangerous and stupid. He stayed in the jeep when the soldiers got out, but he opened a window to listen. The boy with the snake was chatting and pointing up the road. Major Monuc pointed to the jeep. The boy seemed unsure until he spotted Dudu. They stared at each other through the dusty window. The boy had eyes like a snake too; one was milky white and his face was sort of lopsided, not quite right, as if it were melting down one side. He held up the snake against the glass and said, "Hey kid, you hungry, in there?"

The soldiers laughed. Dudu shook his head. The boy swung the snake around, tossing it high through the air, into the bush. He spat on his hands, wiped them on his mucky trousers and hopped into the back of the jeep, grinning at Dudu, as if they were best friends.

"Move up, kid. I'm Kilanda. Why are you wearing that stupid blue hat?"

Kilanda smelled very dirty but the soldiers did not seem to mind. They gave him a packet of biscuits and he ate every one. He wore tatty flip-flops and a ragged T-shirt but a shiny CD player was clipped to his belt. He talked non-stop, mostly about his time as a child soldier, a *kadogo* in the *Mai-Mai*, although his stories were a bit confusing and seemed to tie themselves in knots, like vines up a tree. "Anyway, now he's rich," said Kilanda, proudly.

"Who is?" said Dudu, staring out of the window.

"My brother Luc. Aren't you listening?"

"And that scar?" said Major Monuc, pointing to Kilanda's eye.

"Sentry duty. Loose wire on the perimeter fence. But I'm more handsome now."

How the Blue Hats laughed. Dudu watched the forest, hoping Kilanda would soon be gone. "Where are you going?" he asked. Kilanda shrugged and said, "Who cares?"

Perhaps he was hoping to go to a safer place. But he smelled of trouble.

The smallest soldier unfolded a map on the seat, moving his finger across it. "Blue lines are rivers, red and green are roads, black is railway. Here's Mavuku, Dudu's village."

Dudu stared. It was hard to believe so many people could live in a black dot.

"Never heard of it," said Kilanda.

"I've probably never heard of your village either," said Dudu. "Where is it?"

"Here and there," said Kilanda, yawning.

"You should wear a helmet," said Dudu, and Kilanda laughed. The middle soldier was showing them small coloured photos of little girls in nice frocks – *my angels, see?* Dudu smiled but Kilanda just grunted, cocking his head for a better look at the soldier's rifle.

They drove for an hour or so, mostly listening to music on the radio. Sometimes the driver would chatter into his walkie-talkie then pass it back to Major Monuc who spoke into it and passed it forward again. Dudu wished he could wear a smart uniform with badges like them and be a UN soldier bringing peace to Congo, because it seemed quite an easy job. But he would need a smaller hat. This one was too big. No wonder Kilanda refused to wear one.

Approaching a bend, Major Monuc tapped the driver's shoulder. The jeep slowed and they parked on a rise above a wide valley. "Nice spot! Let's eat," said Major Monuc.

The soldiers climbed out, yawning and stretching their arms. Dudu copied them but Kilanda just stood looking at the valley, rather quiet and thoughtful now. Perhaps he was like Moses, whose moods went up and down like a monkey in a tree. He turned and stared at Dudu then at the soldiers. He seemed to be checking something.

Dudu shielded his eyes from the sun and looked along the road. On one side lay dense bush and on the other, the valley swept down to a plain. Something glinted in the distance, probably the railway track. Kilanda stood beside him. "Ever jumped a train, kid?"

"Yes, of course," Dudu replied, even though it was a lie.

The soldiers squatted behind the jeep, fiddling with fat silver envelopes. "Hot food," said Major Monuc, beckoning Dudu. "In magic packets. They heat up! Come, boys, enjoy!"

He put one of the packets in Dudu's hands. It was quite hot. They peeled off the tops and the food inside tasted spicy. Major Monuc sat licking his lips. "Reminds me of home!"

Kilanda ate only half his share and wandered off with his headphones on, slapping his thigh to the music. He turned and said, "Hey kid, come and listen."

Dudu followed and Kilanda let him try the headphones. "I've only got one CD but it's a good one. *Papa Wemba*. You like dancing?"

"Sometimes," said Dudu, taking off the headphones. "But this keeps jumping."

"Shut up and listen. You see that gun, leaning against the jeep?" Kilanda glanced over Dudu's shoulder with his snake eyes. "It's an AK-101. They've got nice pistols too."

"They're nice soldiers. They're bringing peace. Tata said so."

"That's what you think."

"What do you mean?"

"*MONUC eteki mboka na biso*. MONUC sells our country! They help the Rwandese conquer the east of Congo. I bet your tata never told you that, eh, kid?"

Dudu shook his head and Kilanda leaned closer. "I don't trust these guys. So, if it starts, do as I say."

"If *what* starts?"

"Just be ready, kid."

"I'm not a *kid*. I'm thirteen. Almost."

"You're a kid to them," Kilanda raised a thumb at Major Monuc. "So stay close."

They returned to the jeep and watched one of the soldiers make a cigarette by licking papers and adding green tobacco from a pouch. The sweet-smelling smoke soon reminded

Dudu of Paul the Purified Boy who had swung his silver pot of incense for the pastor.

Major Monuc took a puff from the cigarette and passed it along. The solders took turns, and eventually the cigarette came to Dudu. Kilanda nudged him as if to say *don't*, probably because he thought he was in charge.

But had Kilanda chased away the gang of *shegués*? No. Had Kilanda offered a ride in a nice jeep to a safe place? No. Kilanda had only teased a snake and said *stupid hat, kid*. Boasted almost non-stop. Dudu sucked the cigarette and the smallest soldier gave him a thumbs up.

"Hold the smoke in," said the major but Dudu coughed and they all laughed, except for Kilanda who squatted chewing a stalk and gazing at the track glinting silver in the valley.

Dudu sat back against the jeep. The trees seemed to be spinning and the parrots screeching louder than usual. Major Monuc patted his arm. "Come and see something."

"I'll come too," said Kilanda, getting up and Dudu felt a poke in his back. *Stay close.*

"And me," said the smallest soldier, rising. The driver stayed behind with the jeep.

Major Monuc picked up a rifle and strolled across the road, down a path into the forest. Dudu followed, glancing up at branches in case a hungry python planned to drop on their heads. The small soldier led Kilanda up a different path, scaring a red parrot into flight. The soldier waved his rifle, telling Kilanda to kneel, to pray to Jesus Cross perhaps.

"What are they doing?" Dudu asked.

"Don't worry about them," said Major Monuc, pointing up. "See that butterfly? What a beauty. I collected them, when I was young like you. Come, Dudu." He put his gun against the trunk of a huge tree where creepers hung down and ants ran up. "Kneel, Dudu."

"To pray?" said Dudu, kneeling down among the ferns.

"To say thank you. Closer." Major Monuc unzipped his trousers and let them fall. Black hair curled on his thighs and red underpants bulged in front. He pulled Dudu's head with strong hands and said quietly, "Do it, for me. Do it to say *thank you*, be a good boy."

"Do what?" Dudu tried to twist away but Major Monuc was stronger, forcing him closer. Dudu heard someone gurgle, as if they were choking, nearby.

"Do it!" said Major Monuc, breathing faster now, fiddling inside his underpants.

Leaves rustled behind them and Kilanda came crashing through the ferns, holding a rifle at his hip, ready to shoot. Dudu clambered to his feet. Major Monuc gasped in fright and Kilanda said, "Take off your boots. Step out of your trousers. Or you'll be bushmeat."

Major Monuc raised his arms. "Don't shoot. I have a family… I have money…"

"Take off your boots and step out of your trousers. Now."

Major Monuc obeyed, fumbling and stumbling. He placed his boots together and folded his trousers and Kilanda said, "Enough. Now salute me and stand at ease."

Major Monuc gave a stiff salute and stood with his legs apart and tears dribbling down his moon face. Kilanda stepped forward and kicked him in the groin. The major sank wheezing to his knees, staring with eyes like a lizard. Kilanda flipped the rifle around and cracked him smartly in the head. Major Monuc rolled sideways into the ferns and lay still.

Dudu watched dark blood trickle from his head. "Is he dead?"

"Who cares?" Kilanda grabbed the major's walkie-talkie and hurled it deep into the forest. He reached for the rifle by the tree, pulled out the banana-shaped cartridge and tossed it to Dudu. "You'll carry the clip." He strapped the major's belt around his waist, with the pistol dangling. Next, he rooted in the major's folded trousers, took out a wallet and threw the trousers high into a tree where they dangled like green snakes. He sat down to pull on the major's boots. "Hey, these fit good, better than I expected! Now it's your turn; follow me."

"My turn?" Dudu followed Kilanda back to the other soldier. They found him lying face down in the ferns with his trousers at his ankles and black ants crawling over a bloody gash in his right buttock. Kilanda pointed a finger. "Try his boots. But hurry."

Dudu noticed blood glistening on the soldier's neck. "Did you kill him?"

Kilanda shrugged, adding this soldier's pistol and dagger to his belt. He soon looked like a cowboy on TV in Moses' bar. "Stop gawping, Dudu. Try the boots. Get a move on!"

Dudu put on the soldier's boots. They felt better than flip-flops. He quickly tied the laces and trotted after Kilanda, out of the bush and back to the road where they found the driver snoring, arms folded and curled like a baby in the rough grass. Kilanda unsheathed the dagger and glanced down the hill. A truck rumbled around the corner, blowing black smoke.

Kilanda pointed his dagger at the MONUC jeep. "I'll do these tyres when that truck passes. You grab some of their maps, water and sweets. Think you can manage, kid?"

"I'm not a kid," Dudu said, watching the road. Up the hill came the truck, slowly, laden with plastic barrels and sacks lashed to the back. As it passed, Kilanda rammed the dagger into one of the jeep's tyres, then hopped like a frog towards the next.

Dudu opened the jeep's rear door and leapt inside to gather maps, a plastic bottle of water and a packet of biscuits. He stuffed them in his satchel and backed out, huddling low. Kilanda was waiting, crouched in the grass, clutching his dagger. "Time to go. Stay close."

They scampered down a sloping path towards the plain where silver tracks glinted in the sun, Kilanda jabbing the rifle at the sky and singing at the top of his voice, *Brothers we will surely die for our beloved Congo.* And he was probably right about that.

Chapter 25

Frank explored his new home while munching a meat pie from the *boulangerie* seven floors below. The pie was not bad but his apartment was too big and poorly furnished: one bed, a chair, and a card table. The kitchen needed work and the phone was iffy. He lit a cigarette on the balcony. The railings needed paint but he had a view of the river. He watched the busy street; it needed a bike lane. He rang Ruth on his satphone and she told him, *guess what,* their baby was kicking in her womb at the sound of his voice. Frank played along. *As if.*

"Guess what, Ruth. I can see the River Congo from my new balcony," he added, watching it shimmer in the distance, festooned with piles of floating green stuff. *Hydrangea?* Ruth told him this was unlikely. Frank heard his doorbell chime twice and they rang off.

Through the spyhole in his front door he saw a swarthy fellow outside in a silky black shirt with, due to the lens, a longish head shaped like a rubber dinghy. He opened the door and the fellow stepped in, reeking of Brut. "Frank! I am Yossef, your landlord, yes?" They shook hands and Yossef wandered about, as if considering whether to move in. Frank tagged along and, after five minutes of small talk, decided to broach the delicate subject of terms and conditions. "My friend Claude told me you promised to bring new furniture?"

Yossef turned on his heel. "Who is this Claude?"

"Works for Unicorn. You just missed him. He gave me the keys to the flat."

"That's how they are, the Congolese. Trust me." Yossef walked to the door and left, closing it behind him.

Frank peered at the spyhole. Yossef was outside, shaking his rubber-dinghy head, poking his phone until he vanished into the elevator. Frank went for a shower. The water pipe rattled, brown stuff dribbled and two cockroaches twirled their antennae as if to say, *you the new guy?* Frank went to bed and slept like a baby. No drums, no exorcisms and no shower.

For breakfast, he bought buns from the *boulangerie* and shared them with some *shegués*, while waiting for Claude. The kids tore into them, chewing away, sitting in a tight row on a wall, rocking their scabby knees. One wore tatty trainers, the others were barefoot. Frank sat alongside. The lads had a distinctive smell – diesel fuel mixed with woodsmoke and ground pepper. The biggest grinned at him, perfect teeth; Ruth would be proud.

"*Merci, Papa Boulanger.*"

"You bet," Frank said, chewing a bun. He was part of a neighbourhood now, more than a hotel guest. It was a nice feeling. The kids seemed to agree, rubbing their bellies. *Yum.*

Claude drove up eventually, wearing his baseball cap backwards. "Sleep ok, Frank?"

Frank climbed aboard. "Better, thanks. But Yossef did *not* promise new furniture."

Claude chuckled and flipped his indicator. "That's how they are, the Lebanese."

Day two of the Unicorn seminar started with revision, Frank pacing the room and firing questions off the cuff. "Louise, why is the word *allegedly* so important to us?"

"Because it means *perhaps they didn't do it.*"

"Good, and why should we mark our script before going on-air? Thony?"

"To minimise mistakes. To figure out where to breathe, how to emphasise."

"Good." Frank spotted an empty desk. "Does anybody know why Maurice is absent?"

"No idea," said Claire. "Perhaps he got in trouble."

"What sort of trouble?" Frank asked, checking his watch. *Almost 09:20.*

"He borrowed my cassette," Claire said. "And I certainly hope he brings it back."

"I see. Well, I'm sure he will, when he turns up." Frank popped a tape in the boom box. "But for now, let's listen to this round-table debate from Côte d'Ivoire, about safe sex."

"Why?" said Thony.

"Because it's your turn next." Frank pressed PLAY and noticed a familiar face peering into the room through the glass partition in the door. Maurice appeared to have aged twenty years overnight, unless this was someone else who looked like him. Frank beckoned.

The man came in and said, "I'm Bizima. Maurice's brother." His handshake was businesslike, his cufflinks gold. He pointed to the empty seat. "So, may I sit here?"

Frank let the tape play and took Bizima aside for a quiet word. "Is Maurice unwell?"

Bizima perched on the front edge of Frank's desk, nodding at the journalists, most of whom he seemed to know. He placed his black attaché on the desk. The scuffed lid bore plastic gold initials. "My brother is as well as can be expected, in the circumstances."

"The circumstances?" Frank said.

"Maurice is a junior, our least experienced presenter. Whereas, I'm deputy editor, with years of experience. So I shall be attending for the rest of the week. Unless you object?" Bizima's nostrils flared and Frank glimpsed grey hairs inside. Bizima was no junior; in fact, his age would mean one too many old-timers in the group. It would upset the balance.

"But where's Maurice?" Frank said.

"Well, let me put it this way: *a goat eats where it is tethered.* And, unfortunately, my younger brother is too easily influenced. Given to big ideas, as it were. He needs to learn."

"That's why he came. But now he's absent because…?"

"He's absent because I'm present, to judge whether your methods are appropriate."

"Appropriate?"

"For our radio station, Mr Kean; appropriate for Hope FM, for our broadcasts."

Frank folded his arms. "You're here to *judge my methods?*"

"Perhaps Maurice has exaggerated. Or perhaps your standards will improve."

Frank scratched his head, mainly for effect. "My *standards?*"

Bizima offered an encouraging smile. "You neglect your class, Mr Kean. I'll explain later. It's rather complicated. I'll just sit and observe, for the moment, if that's OK with you?"

Frank watched Bizima glide to the empty seat.

Thony was scribbling notes, one hand aloft. "I got some ideas, Frank."

The taped debate from Côte d'Ivoire ended, Frank moderated a quick discussion on its strengths and weaknesses then split his class into groups of three. "You've got ten minutes to choose a community issue for a live debate. I need two guests and a moderator in each group. You'll chat first, then take questions from your audience. That's the rest of us."

"But how will we broadcast it?" asked Nadine, looking exhausted already.

"We won't," Frank replied. "It's an exercise; role play. Any ideas for a subject?"

Nadine chewed her pen and turned to her partners, huddled in chat. Frank suggested to Bizima that he join one of the groups but Bizima declined, preferring to monitor each one from a distance. He rose and prowled the room with his hands behind his back, playing the gracious elder statesman, watching and listening. Frank went back to his own desk to sort through his worksheets, clicking his ballpoint. *Methods, standards.* What was that about?

He soon had other problems. Nadine was arguing with

Bellidée. She looked fired up, which made a change, since she had spent most of yesterday in the land of Nod. *Because I'm tired, Frank, four kids!* Whatever. His gaze drifted back to Bizima, whose rookie younger brother was absent and given to big ideas. *Meaning what?* Young Maurice had been given the chance of five days' training; continuity was crucial. Why had Bizima pulled rank on a rookie? And who was he to judge methods? And that stuff about a goat? Frank checked his watch.

"Time's up, folks." He walked to the whiteboard, uncapping a marker pen. The groups called out their ideas and he scribbled them in block capitals. Some topics sounded promising – STUDENT GRANTS, FUEL PRICES, DEMOBILISATION OF CHILD SOLDIERS. But Nadine and Bellidée could not agree; she wanted to role-play an actress. He wanted to discuss soccer.

"So find a compromise," Frank suggested.

Nadine rolled her big eyes. "Like what?"

"A community issue," said Claire.

"Like *shegués,* street kids, orphans, all that," said Thony.

"Good." Bellidée scribbled it down. "*Shegués* like playing soccer. That's an angle."

Nadine slammed her pen on the desk. "*Shegués?* Who wants to hear about them?"

"And yet I suppose, if you were a famous actress…" Frank suggested, with a smile.

"What?" She angled her head, doe-eyed. "I wouldn't be sitting here, that's for sure."

"Exactly. You'd be travelling the world because you're successful, talented, versatile."

"And rich. Move to Paris," Nadine said, sucking her pen. "What are you getting at?"

"I'm thinking if a director asked you to play a former *shegué,* you could do it. Yes?"

She gazed at Frank, long and hard. He circled the desks, rubbing his hands. "Bellidée, what if you play a pastor who thinks too many *shegués* are witches? Lester can moderate?"

Lester rubbed his beard. "Sure."

Bellidée nodded. "Sounds like radio. I'm in."

Frank wrote on the whiteboard: SHEGUÉS – FOR & AGAINST. He turned back to the class. "But we'll need someone to role-play a former street kid. If Nadine can't do it. Volunteers?"

Nadine raised her hand. "I can do it. But you'd better remember, I helped you out."

"Thanks, I will." Frank turned back to the board and wrote NADINE V. BELLIDÉE.

Claire called out, "Hey, now write, *Safe Sex for Prostitutes.* That's our topic."

"Anais against Remy," added Anais, pushing up her hair. "I'll be a local hooker who want condoms for free. Remy will play a politician who disagrees. Claire will moderate."

"Sounds like radio, well done," said Frank, scanning the eager faces. Bizima was glaring at him. Frank wiped inky hands on a damp cloth. "OK, moderators, listen. First, I want you to ask each guest to make a brief opening statement; then you'll host a three-way chat for five minutes. Then open the phone lines and the rest of us will call with questions."

"On our phones?" asked Nadine, unwrapping a stick of pink bubblegum.

"No," Frank said. "It's an exercise. We raise a hand and make a noise: *brrr-brrr.*"

Nadine chewed gum, round and round. "What sort of questions?"

Thony grinned at her. "Hard ones."

Lester stroked his beard like it was a furry pet. "If I'm moderating, for how long?"

"Each round-table should last about fifteen minutes. If so, we'll be done by lunch."

"But we've only got square tables," said Louise in the wig.

"Square is fine," Frank said.

"And the clock is God," added Jean Marie.

Frank raised a thumb. "Good man."

"*Brrr-brrr,*" said Nadine, hand aloft. "I want to be present-er, sit in the middle."

"No, you agreed to be a *shegué,*" said Bellidée. "You'll be good as a child witch."

"Get lost! They're not *all* witches, are they?" She looked at Frank.

"You tell us," he said. "That's the point of local radio. But hurry, the clock is God."

Bizima sat forward. "As a Christian, I object to such language."

Frank shrugged. "Sorry, Bizima, just a figure of speech."

"It's blasphemy, Mr Kean."

They locked eyes like cowboy gunslingers in a silent bar. Nadine blew a big pink bubble. It popped and she said, "Maybe you should have a debate. Frank versus Bizima."

By high noon, each team had presented a mock broadcast and, for the last period before lunch, Frank played back the recordings of each debate. The journalists howled at their gaffes, like when Lester lost his rag and Louise lost the plot; they grumbled about who had hogged the microphone or talked nonsense. To round up, Frank asked them each to suggest something they had learned from the session and he wrote their replies on the whiteboard.

"How to play Devil's advocate," said Claire.

"Know your facts," said Louise.

"If you're moderator, don't let guests annoy you," added Lester, stroking his goatee.

"Nothing of practical value," said Bizima, snapping shut the lid of his attaché case.

Frank paused, mid-scrawl. "Sorry, Bizima, perhaps my methods will improve?"

Bizima said nothing but his vacant gaze suggested Hope FM's deputy editor had made his judgement, and, when Claude brought sandwiches and drinks, he declined to partake, instead drifting off to stand alone at the window, observing the city and talking on his mobile. The others ate their lunch and went out. Bizima lingered still, with a question.

"Mr Kean, why did you insist on choosing such sordid and immoral subjects for your seminar? In my opinion, it will never do. These things… are an abomination."

Frank reached for a damp cloth and stood at the whiteboard. "How do you mean?"

"Prostitution! This is not a suitable subject for the broadcast spectrum."

"If you mean safe sex, I didn't choose that subject, Bizima. The journalists did."

Bizima rose from his seat. "But you encouraged them. You wrote it on the board."

"Because that's my job. We look at social issues, how to debate them."

"Such *issues* may be considered appropriate in the so-called civilised West, but here they are not. First, you bring disease and drug addiction, now you bring licentiousness."

"You've lost me."

"You must change your methodology or there will be consequences."

Frank wiped the whiteboard. The inky cloth stained his hands and it would be a bugger to wash off. "Bizima, my methodology usually gets results; that's why I'm here."

"To encourage prostitution? Such debates will not be aired on Hope FM."

"That's up to you, but some stations welcome *such debates,* because they attract listeners; a discussion raises awareness, even helps people to keep healthy and stay alive."

"To live in sin? A radio station should set standards, be a beacon of hope."

"I agree."

Bizima opened his attaché case and tossed a tape on the desk. "Did you agree that last night, Maurice should have broadcast, from this very cassette, your vox pop about sodomy?"

Frank picked up the tape. "Actually, I think he may have got this from Claire."

"It was abhorrent," said Bizima, with fire in his eyes. "And it was your idea."

"If you mean the vox pop about gay rights, Claire chose it. Maurice borrowed it."

"The source is irrelevant. Our listeners were scandalised! And today, you encouraged your trainees to defend sorcery. I have witnesses. Please, think twice about your duties!"

"Perhaps you should tell Maurice the same thing. That vox pop was just an exercise."

"You took advantage. He is young and impressionable. He knows nothing."

"That's why your boss sent him to my seminar, as far as I recall."

Bizima's eyes bulged in their sockets. He rapped his knuckles hard on the table. "Mr Kean, in my opinion your seminar and your methods are inappropriate! Do you understand?"

"Thank you for your opinion. And I do tell my trainees: *always seek your editor's.*"

Bizima's cheek muscle fluttered as if a subcutaneous butterfly were trying to flee his raging temple. "Maurice did *not* seek authorisation. And I would like my travel expenses."

"We usually distribute the per diems at the end of the day."

"I'd like mine now." Bizima gripped his attaché case, his spindly fingers flexing.

"Certainly, Bizima, although my colleague takes care of the cash." Frank gestured towards Claude, munching in a corner, wide-eyed. "So, will we see you this afternoon?"

Bizima ignored Frank's question. Claude approached, counting out the cash. Bizima signed the ledger, folded his money into a slim wallet and departed without another word.

Frank moved to the window and watched the grey parrot in its cage on the opposite balcony. He waved at the two kids on their bench but they did not wave back today. Bizima appeared soon enough, striding along the street below. Frank noticed other pedestrians step aside as if wary of the fellow's bad aura. Claude came to the window and said, "He's angry."

"He's a windbag. Empty vessels make the most noise. Know that proverb, Claude?"

"Frank, you should not insult the crocodile while your feet are still in the water."

Chapter 26

Dudu dodged a thorny branch and glanced backwards, up the scrubby slope. The soldiers' jeep was a little white dot on the ridge. "Do you think they're both dead?" he said.

"They can go to hell, the Dirty Blue Hat Bastards," Kilanda replied.

Dudu looked ahead, peering along the track into the bush. "Where are we going?"

"To a safer place, like they promised."

"How do you mean?"

"On a train," said Kilanda, pointing down to the valley. "Where are the sweets?"

Dudu reached into his satchel. "I could only find biscuits."

Kilanda stopped and frowned. "I told you to get their *sweets*. Are you stupid?"

"I'm not stupid. Anyway, you can talk. Playing with dangerous snakes."

"That harmless worm? I was just fooling around to attract their attention. I needed a ride, supplies, even a weapon. I knew those suckers would see me and stop. Wake up, kid."

"I'm not a kid. Are you saying that you *planned* to steal from the soldiers?"

"What do you think? Anyway, enough questions. In fact, no more talk unless it's essential, you hear me? We waste energy and give away our position. Silence on the march."

They trekked for hours in the morning sun, the slope gradually flattening towards the plain where the grass grew thick as fingers and high as a man's head. Kilanda eventually revealed that, actually, he had suspected those Dirty Blue Hats all along and it was *better to be a hammer not a nail.* Dudu told him Tata used to have lots of hammers in his workshop.

Kilanda stopped dead, raised a finger to his lips and dropped to one knee, yanking Dudu down into the bushes. He raised his AK rifle and squinted down the barrel. Dudu glimpsed something big and yellow with black spots, up ahead. *A leopard.* His skin prickled as Kilanda shifted position, cracking a twig underfoot. The leopard stopped.

"Don't shoot us," said a voice. *A leopard that talks?*

"Come," Kilanda said, head cocked and finger flexing on the trigger, ready.

Two barefoot men in baggy trousers and no shirts came up the path, shiny with sweat, carrying a wooden pole on their shoulders. Hanging upside down from it, tied by its front and back paws, was a leopard with its terrible white fangs in a wide smile, as if it did not mind being dead. "Sir, we are not poachers, truly," said the first man, his forehead ridged with tribal scars. Kilanda slung his rifle and stroked the leopard's spotty fur. Dudu did it too. The fur was soft and smooth. "So why did you kill it?" Kilanda said.

"Sir, it took many goats and a sleeping child. So, we set a box trap."

"Then what?" said Kilanda, in a bossy voice, but he had a rifle after all, and two pistols on his belt and a lopsided smile that invited you to try your luck, if you dared.

"Sir, we baited a box trap. When this leopard got stuck, we killed him with poison darts."

"And we are now taking it for our chief to see," said the other fellow, through cracked brown teeth. Kilanda stood aside to let them pass, watching carefully with his snake eyes. The men plodded off, leopard swinging, and Kilanda said, "Poachers. A clean kill for a high price."

Grey monkeys chattered their own opinions from the tight green forest. Kilanda walked ahead, pushing foliage aside with the barrel of his rifle. Dudu noticed the path growing wider as they left the slope. He heard bubbling water and soon saw it flashing in the sun, through the trees. The stream was three metres wide. They crossed a narrow bridge of lashed logs and lay on their bellies to drink and wash their faces, splashing each other like kids. Big-eyed frogs watched from the shallows as Dudu filled the water bottle. Kilanda sat back, taking a pistol from its holster to caress. "M1911, this is. Good condition too."

"Do you know how to shoot it?" said Dudu. Kilanda stretched his arm and pulled the trigger. The sudden bang made Dudu jump. Leaves rustled behind him and he turned to watch a grey monkey tumble and flip through branches. It landed with a soft thud among the ferns.

"You mean like that?" said Kilanda, and put his gun away. "Go fetch our dinner."

They walked until the sun was high and their shadows short, Kilanda always in front and Dudu behind watching the dead monkey bounce up and down on his new companion's belt. Mid-afternoon they rested again and Kilanda tossed Dudu a box of matches. "Fire."

Dudu made a fire from dry twigs while Kilanda spread the monkey then skinned and gutted it with the dagger; he poked a sharp stick up its bottom and set it to cook over the embers. The smell of roast monkey soon tickled their nostrils under an orange sun and they sat there not saying much, chewing the meat. Kilanda seemed worried. *About the soldiers?*

Dudu poked the embers and said, "Tata sometimes cooked monkey in a pit."

"If we keep east," said Kilanda, tugging at a bone with his teeth, "we'll reach the track before dark. Unless you want to live in the bush, that is. But it's no fun, I can tell you."

Dudu spotted a green parrot staring from a branch, as if it disagreed. They finished eating and Kilanda wrapped the left-over bushmeat in leaves and put it in Dudu's satchel without asking. He kicked out the fire and covered the ashes in earth, cleaning the monkey grease from his fingers. He dragged branches and leaves over the spot and walked on.

"So, did you live in the bush?" Dudu asked.

"I already told you. I was in the *Mai-Mai*, what do you think?" said Kilanda, with a chuckle. He boasted about his time as a *kadogo* who had protected Congo. He had big plans for the future. "One day I'll be rich like my brother Luc. He's a businessman in Kinshasa."

"Selling *premium vegetables*."

Kilanda laced tight fingers around Dudu's arm "How the hell do you know that?"

"You told the Blue Hats," said Dudu, pulling free. "Anyway, what's *premium?*"

"Means you get a car," said Kilanda, cocking an ear. "Quiet! Down!"

They ducked behind a rock and Dudu listened hard but could hear only bugs and birds. But soon some big ladies passed with bundles on their heads. When they had gone Kilanda said, "The fewer people see us, the better. MONUC will be asking around."

They kept away from villages but even so, they heard laughter, dogs barking and someone chopping wood: *tak, tak, tak*. It echoed through the humid air and reminded Dudu of Tata in his workshop, ankle-deep in wood shavings. It seemed a dream from long ago.

It was easier to walk on the flat land, but Kilanda kept stopping and crouching to look ahead because, in his opinion, *it was better to be a hammer than a nail*. At dusk, he pointed to the right, off the path. *There, you see it, Du?* Dudu looked and, eventually, he saw it too.

The skeleton glimmered white with its arms stretched high, both hands lashed to a tree. The skull had been cracked across the top and the ribs had been pulled apart, like two little white gates made of bone. The feet were missing and scraps of uniform with brown stains lay scattered here and there.

How come? The buzzing insects seemed to know why. A bird shrieked through branches: *mind your own business.* Kilanda pointed at the ribcage and said, "I reckon they took out his heart. Cut off his feet and probably everything else, too."

"Why?"

Kilanda shrugged. "Why not?"

Dudu doubled over and vomited monkey meat and when he straightened up to wipe his mouth the bashed-in skull was staring eyeless through the shadows: *bon voyage.*

They walked on and coming around a turn under red rock, they met a man as thin as a stick who was pushing a bicycle, laden with bidons of sloshing liquid. He wore flip-flops, shorts and a hat of banana leaves. He stopped to stare at Kilanda's weapons as if he had a good mind to turn around and go back the way he had come. Kilanda smiled and pointed.

"Relax, mister. What's in your bidons?"

"Not beer, sir. Just red palm oil, sir. And a little fuel, sir, for my village."

Kilanda poked at a rolled-up grass mat on the bike. "Where are you from?"

"Yitenge, sir." The man turned, pointing. "Fifty kilometres. Four days' walk."

"Where you going?"

"Kananga." He glanced at their boots, looking puzzled.

"Hungry?" Kilanda offered a slice of roast bushmeat from the satchel.

The old man gobbled it down like a starved dog. "God bless you, sir."

Kilanda offered the water bottle and the fellow drank until his chin was dripping.

"Last question," said Kilanda, "did you meet two boys with guns and nice boots?"

The man wiped his mouth. "Not me, sir."

"Good. That means I won't have to come to Yitenge and shoot you in the head."

"God bless you, sir." The old man walked on, pushing his

bike.

They reached the railway line at sunset and sat down to rest. Dudu watched the silver rails turn yellow and curl off to the plain like two little rivers of gold. Kilanda knelt and pressed his ear to the steel. *Nothing.* He unfolded a map. "If that's west, this is north, see?"

Dudu's head was banging in the heat, but even so, he spotted Kilanda's simple mistake. "Can't you read, Kilanda? That's south. This is north. Where does the train stop?"

"It doesn't."

"So how do we get on?"

Kilanda folded the map into a pocket and smirked, "Not so clever now, are you, kid?"

Chapter 27

Frank looked back over the daily schedule on Thursday morning; the week was almost over, vanished and gone like that busybody Bizima and his younger brother Maurice.

He split the team of journalists into two groups and spent the day helping them make a thirty-minute news broadcast combining all the elements they had worked on so far: headlines, three-paragraph stories, vox pops, despatches, live reports down the line, round-table phone-ins and even a cool jingle that Thony had put together after hours. Nadine spent a lot of time staring at Frank but when he asked why, she said vaguely, "We'll talk Friday."

But Friday was their final day, exam time. Frank handed out printed sheets with twenty-five questions, some multiple-choice. Nadine chewed her pen, sighing at the task ahead.

Jean Marie said, "When do we get our diplomas?"

"When our special guest arrives," Frank replied, to puzzled looks. The journalists sat their test and he marked their papers during his lunch hour. Mid-afternoon, he talked them through their results. Nadine came bottom of the group. After the 3 p.m. coffee break, he asked them to compile a five-minute bulletin. "For our special guest to hear." More puzzled looks.

Special guest Alberto Rossi from USAID arrived punctually wearing a blazer, chinos and loafers. His barrel-chested young minder had a ginger buzz cut and a military air, despite the grey suit. Rossi perched on the edge of Frank's desk to chat with the journalists, asking if they had enjoyed the seminar, but some seemed more interested in USAID's agenda.

"When will we have general elections?" said Thony.

"Good question," said Rossi, and Frank noticed the burly bodyguard glancing down at a black digital watch the size of an ice hockey puck. After half an hour of informal Q & A, some of it recorded with Rossi's consent for broadcast on the journalists' FM stations, Rossi listened to their five-minute mock bulletin and applauded at the end. He handed out the Unicorn diplomas and shook hands with the journalists, queuing one by one in their smart shirts and colourful robes. Claire curtsied, Henri doffed his vol-au-vent cap and Thony asked for a business card. Rossi was genial as ever, but sharp with it. On his way out, he drew Frank aside and said, "I gave diplomas to eleven journalists. I thought we'd agreed twelve?"

"Quite right, but unfortunately Hope FM pulled their rookie, lest I corrupt him."

Rossi sighed and moved on. "Oh well, we can't win 'em all. Take care, out east."

Frank tidied up, and took the trainees to a café on a sunny terrace for a round of drinks. They peppered him with a round of questions. *Mr Frank, are we good journalists? Mr Frank, how much do you earn?* Mr Frank sipped his beer and changed the subject.

"But I bet you've got a big house," said Nadine, popping peanuts.

"Not really. Just a big mortgage," Frank replied.

"And two kids, plus one coming."

"How did you know?" he asked.

"I'm a journalist."

Frank lit a cigarette and poked a folded banknote through the wrought iron railings at a street kid with one eye; the other was a smudge of scar tissue. Nadine tutted and looked away. Frank waited and wondered. Eventually, she glanced back at him, her chest heaving.

At dusk on the busy boulevard, he said goodbye to the journalists and got a peck on the cheek from some of the women. The men departed in giggling groups, nicely tipsy, leaving him all alone with Nadine. She gave him The Look and said, "We have to talk."

"About?"

"I have a problem, Frank."

"Narcolepsy?"

"What's that?"

"Sleepiness."

"You're teasing. That's not my problem. This my problem. I have no man."

They stopped at the kerb and pedestrians waiting to cross engulfed them. They gazed at each other like wartime lovers on the brink of a bombshell. "I beg your pardon?" he said.

"And too many kids."

"Four boys, I believe?"

"You remembered, that's sweet. Come." She took his hand and led him across the road amid the bubbling crowd, trucks growling left and right. On the far side, she unzipped her purse and pulled out a photo of four gap-toothed young lads grinning at the camera.

"Handsome boys," Frank said. "So, where's their father?"

"Their fathers, you mean. How should I know?"

"You must be very proud."

"I'm twenty-two, Frank."

He made a face and hoped it looked sympathetic. But she had made her bed and someone had lain in it. "He'll come back, Nadine. I mean, *they* will."

"No they won't, Frank. I've been praying. God sent you instead."

Frank raised his left hand, wriggling his ring finger. "See that?"

"Yes, you're married. But that's perfect. You can offer him a better life."

"Who?"

Nadine held up the photo. "Take your pick."

Frank stared at the four winning smiles. "Nadine, is this a joke?"

"Not to me. Adopt one of my boys. Take him to London. You have a nice house, enough money. They're not your precious *shegués* but they have rights. Good boys, see?"

"Are you crazy? Even if I agreed, which I won't, you hardly *know* me."

"I know men. You might be a nice one."

"Not that nice, Nadine. I'm very sorry but I cannot adopt one of your sons."

Her smile cracked like dropped crockery. She glared at him, turned and boarded the nearest minibus, swallowed by the throng of passengers. It lurched off, coughing a rebuke and Frank watched it trundle down the boulevard. He walked the rest of the way home, besieged by bands of *shegués*, most of them appearing to share Nadine's giddy delusions.

The knot in his stomach had transformed to a gnawing hunger by the time he reached his block. He spotted a restaurant – Pizza Pazza – and peeped in the gleaming window. The place was deserted, except for the balding waiter in a black tie at the window, beaming out.

Frank entered, chose a seat and a Neapolitan. He sat humming along to piped music – "Ain't That a Kick in the Head". Poor Nadine – what was in hers? He looked at framed black-and-white photos on the restaurant wall – Muhammad Ali fighting George Foreman. The waiter poured blood-red Chianti and Frank said, "I watched that fight live on TV with my dad. Rumble in the Jungle, Kinshasa '74. I should visit the stadium." The waiter smiled. *Yes sir.*

When his pizza arrived, Frank asked why the place was so empty on a Friday.

"Because of the robbery," said the waiter. "Two weeks ago four men came in wearing army uniforms, holding guns and plastic bags. They went table to table taking cash, jewellery and credit cards. Since then no clients, except you. So, enjoy!"

Frank wolfed his pizza listening to "'O Sole Mio" and left for home *rapidamente*.

Back at his block, he found landlord Yossef checking new furniture in the lobby: sofas, chairs, tables, bed and cabinets wrapped in transparent polythene. The place smelled of freshly sawn wood and luxurious leather. Frank could hardly believe his nostrils. Yossef was flipping pages on a clipboard, watched by five Congolese men in singlets, sweat glistening. Yossef hailed Frank like a long lost brother – perhaps because Unicorn had recently coughed up two months' rent plus deposit. The landlord lumbered across the lobby in a sequinned black T-shirt. "New furniture, Frank! Will you be upstairs, tonight? Let's say, in one hour?"

Frank smiled. "Certainly, thanks a lot."

He was upstairs on the phone to his wife – who was not into adoption but keen to know how long he had been into Nadine – when his doorbell rang. "Bye, Ruth," he said.

Yossef entered the flat followed by the Congolese delivery men. They worked fast, hauling in the stuff: dining table, chairs, stools, coffee table, desk, sofa, lamps, bookcase, sideboard, mirrors and more. Yossef paced about barking like a prison guard. *You, over here.* Twenty minutes later, the men were done and dusty and Frank's empty flat looked more like a well-stocked furniture warehouse, although, oddly enough, it did not smell like one.

"Is better, now?" Yossef stood rubbing his bear-like hands.

Frank forced a smile but something was amiss. There was no polythene, no aroma of sawn wood or new leather. Instead, the flat now smelled of stale sweat, perfume and… sex? He sat on the sofa. It sagged in the middle and a steel spring was burrowing up his back end.

He surveyed the room, puzzled. "Excuse me, Yossef, but…

166

is this furniture *new*?"

"New for this flat. Was quite empty beforehands, yes?"

"Sure. But this stuff seems… old. Where is the new furniture I saw in the lobby?"

"In my flat, upstairs. I have kindly donated my own, in here, for you. Is good, I can confirm." Yossef stepped closer, to whisper. "And perhaps you can tip your delivery men?"

Frank had more questions but Yossef was already yapping into his phone, heading for the door. Frank handed out cash to the sweaty guys with wiry muscles and sat on his brand-new, ancient stinky sofa as their flip-flops slapped away, down his hall.

He spent an hour wiping down the dusty furniture and hauling it around the room to his heart's discontent. His phone buzzed. *Ruth?* No, it was Hector Harris, the man himself.

Frank took the call on the balcony, lighting a cigarette. "Good evening, boss."

"Glad you think so," said Hector, gruff as a goat.

"What's new," said Frank. "Apart from my manky furniture?"

"Deputy editor at Hope FM wants your head on a plate."

"Oh, him. With *fufu* on the side, no doubt."

"You think this is funny? Tell me what happened with Bizima, Frank."

Frank obliged, watching headlights weave up the boulevard like glow-worms. When he was done, Hector took his time replying. "I see, Frank. So that's your version, is it? Oddly enough, Bizima's is quite different. He says that you were very rude, *confrontational*, even."

"And he was not, I suppose?"

"There you go again, Frank. We're not here to cause bloody trouble, matey."

"Hector, I was doing fine, until Busybody turned up."

"Bizima has connections. You'll have to apologise."

"For what?"

"A quiet life."

"Apologise to that sanctimonious creep?" Frank sucked his ciggie. "No way."

"Let's try this again. I will draft a letter of apology, Frank, and you will sign it."

"So, Bizima tries to hijack my seminar and you expect *me* to say sorry?"

"I'm not asking, I'm telling. Work with me, Frank. I know this town. You're new. Listen, what if we call it a *misunderstanding*, express our *sincere regret*. Would you sign?"

Frank considered his options. "Sure. If that's all it takes."

"We'll see. Now the good news: I've also had an email from Alberto Rossi. He enjoyed his visit to your seminar today and he *loved* Misti's concept note about reporting on street kids. Sounds to me like you were able to implement it, these last few days, correct?"

Frank laughed aloud. "*Implement* it? It was my idea."

"Frank, let me tell you something about Unicorn. We don't score points. We're a family, a team. Misti is a key member. She has brains and two master's, one in Peace Studies."

"In that case, maybe you should ask her to write to Bizima."

"Frank, really."

"How about field experience? Perhaps she just has rich folks and time on her hands."

"Keep it up, you'll go far."

"Misti too, according to Alberto Rossi. Good luck to her."

"Luck is when hard work meets opportunity. She works hard and grabs her chances. Did you see her concept note? Could you write that? I couldn't. She used all the right language, checked all the boxes. Had your name on it too, did you notice?"

"Sure. When I used a magnifying glass."

"Frank, your attitude is not helpful. In your shoes, I would think about damage limitation, as follows. I've already sent Bizima's email to Misti, so she's in the loop. But she's not very happy. She cares a lot about this project. In fact, she pretty much wrote the original proposal that got your job funded. So if I were you, I'd drop her a line."

"And say what?"

"First, you could thank her for such a well-written concept note, then apologise for the *misunderstanding* with Bizima. What do you say to that? Frank, are you listening?"

"Every word." Frank had spotted a gang of street kids in the car park below, huddling down for the night among cardboard cartons. One kid looked up, saw him watching and waved, yelling at him, *Bonsoir, Papa Boulanger.* It drifted up on a breeze, loud and clear.

"I can hear shouting," said Hector. "What's going on?"

"Just some satanic sorcerers, whose methods are probably inappropriate."

"This is no joke, Frank. Email Misti, keep your head down, stay out of trouble."

"Goodnight, Hector."

The kids below waved and Frank waved back. His phone rang again. He checked the screen and saw Claude's name. *What now, more advice about crocodiles in the classroom?*

"Hey, Frank!"

"Hey, Claude. My furniture arrived. It smells like defeat."

"I'm very glad to hear it. Anyway, my friend, so sorry to bother you, but I was thinking, from now on you have free time in your hands, before you go to the rebel zone…"

"Correct. Seems clearance might take a week or so. Why?"

"Do you want to meet some pastors, tomorrow? My neighbour knows Father Benoit. And also, I can take you to Reverend Ray. You could meet some kids accused of sorcery, like the ones Bellidée and Nadine discussed, only real ones, witches. You could see an exorcism."

"I've already seen one, in some nutty church behind Hotel Maisha."

"Those are for the public; tomorrow will be private. So?"

Chapter 28

"She wants Frank to adopt a kid?" said Purple Jane, clutching her watering can.

"She's a single parent," said Ruth. "Twenty-two. Four boys. Nadine No-Knickers."

"Bloody Nora, I'm thirty and still trying." Jane moved across the lobby to the scarlet poinsettias by the bay window, dribbling water into their parched pots. *Hello, my babies.* Ruth flicked through the appointment book, with one eye on the TV; a panting cheetah was nursing cute cubs. "Here comes money," Jane said, pointing her plastic spout towards the car park. Ruth heard gravel crunch and watched a navy blue Range Rover easing under the leafy elms.

Long-legged Pippa Price emerged from the car in jodhpurs, tweed cap and tight-fitting jacket. "Must be Simon's next client," said Jane. "Bit tall for a jockey though, eh?"

Ruth watched Aubrey slide out from the back seat, clutching a book. Pippa strode into the lobby, reeking of perfume, and something money could not buy. "Ru, *dearest*, how are you?"

Pippa had a firm handshake and Jane had a face like a stopped clock. Ruth winked at her colleague and led Aubrey up the corridor. "I hear you missed school. Not sick, I hope?"

"No," said Aubrey, "just visiting Uncle P in St John's Wood, except guess what, there *isn't* one!" Aubrey's smile faded as she entered the surgery and stared at the reclining chair like a medieval plotter seeing the torture rack. "Oh no. Not *fillings?*"

"That depends," said Simon, beaming. "What's that big book called?"

"*The Wolves in the Walls.*" Aubrey held it up, straight out, as if for protection.

"Sounds scary. Is it scary?" said Simon, patting the chair.

"Only when they come out," said Aubrey, climbing up. Ruth taped the bib in place and Simon selected a steel probe. "Ready for take-off, here we go. One three, distal."

"That hurt," garbled Aubrey. Ruth scribbled the details of where and why.

Simon shifted position, adjusted his spotlight. "One five, buccal."

"What?" Aubrey raised her head, eyeing the probe. "You've got scary tools."

"At least I don't have wolves in my walls."

"How do you know?" said Aubrey, and Simon raised a finger, *hush now.*

After the initial assessment, Ruth led Aubrey to a smaller suite. Aubrey lingered at the door, hanging back. "And what's in here? Knockout gas?"

"No."

"So what, then?"

"I need to clean you up. Your teeth need attention."

"They've just had some. What *sort* of attention? Can't you just tell me?"

"Plaque on the lingual part of your front incisors and interdental debris."

Aubrey looked up, her eyebrows in knots. "What?"

"Like to hear a joke?" Ruth said, and Aubrey nodded, glancing left and right at the various charts and vicious equipment. Ruth draped an arm across her shoulder. "Here goes. Do you know why the seashore is never hungry? It's because of all the sand, which is there."

Aubrey shrieked with hollow laughter. Ruth said, "Do you get it?"

"Not really," Aubrey said, frowning at her patent leather shoes.

"*Sandwiches there.* Never mind. Hop in this chair for me,

and let's get started, eh?"

Twenty minutes later they strolled back to the lobby, Ruth offering advice en route. "Remember to keep your teeth healthy. We call it *three times two*: brush twice a day with two centimetres of paste and leave at least two hours between any food. Can you try that?"

Pippa rose from the sofa to meet them and raised an eyebrow as if to say, *try two minutes.* "Excellent advice, Aubs! And now Mummy needs a private word with Mrs Kean."

Aubrey nodded, tucking her book under her arm. She ambled out to the car park and Ruth called after her, "Bye, Aubs. I'll watch for the wolves." The little girl turned, smiling.

"Wolves?" Pippa said. "Drive up to the City, you'll meet plenty."

"No thanks," Ruth said. "Besides, I don't like all that *beastly* traffic."

Pippa flashed a dazzling grin, the sort that presumably helped to open doors and close deals. "Actually Ru, that's exactly what I'd like to discuss."

Ruth listened, wary of the familiar tone but curious as Pippa explained that *one needed a workable child-minding strategy.* They strolled around the car park and Ruth ran a fingertip along Pippa's gleaming Range Rover as they passed it, intrigued by the implications of what she was hearing. Pippa confided that *live-in nannies were a pain*, she needed *flexibility*.

She handed Ruth a slip of paper and said quietly, "Sums. Negotiable, I might add."

Ruth cast an eye down the three columns of elegant but unfussy handwriting; they listed days, an hourly rate and running total. *Yikes,* the terms were certainly generous. Pippa pointed a polished nail. "And you'll see, here, that I took the liberty of adding a weekend rate; lest I get whisked off to Brussels or Paris. On business, that is. One never knows."

"And here's me thinking you'd forgotten my offer, our chat at St Eddie's, I mean."

"Sorry for the silence. We've been away, staying in town. But I hope you'll think it over. I do realise, of course, that once your baby comes bouncing, I'll probably have to dump Aubs with my parents in Berkshire at weekends and over summer; pity, since she so *adores* Dylan. Talks about him no end; best pals, I gather. Plus, you know how it is, Mummy and Daddy mean well but… going home can be *such* a chore. So many *questions*."

"There is that," Ruth said, staring at the high numbers scribbled on the note. "But, then again, Frank will be back before the birth, and Billie will be around over summer, so we could probably still help you out, as a family. Thing is though, you hardly *know* us."

"True, but I'm a good judge of character. Have to be, in my job. Ciao for now."

Ruth watched the Range Rover purr out of the car park. Aubrey waved from the back seat, gnashing her teeth like a demented rodent. Jane emerged from the lobby, sour-faced.

"So, you lot know each other? What was all that about, she invite you to Ascot?"

"One never knows," said Ruth, tucking Pippa's offer into her fist, out of sight.

She went to the loo and sat rereading the note. She washed her hands and stared at her reflection. Funny thing, a mirror – sometimes you don't really see who you are, until you see who you are not. She stood on tiptoe, her nose in the air, trying to affect the breezy allure of a *gel* about Knightsbridge. Fat chance. She looked more like a fishwife from Fulham. So much for her invitation to a night at the opera at Covent Garden to see the King of Egypt. No, Ruth Kean would never be Pippa's friend. She was Help Desk, period. She looked again at the note: money for old rope. Her phone beeped with a text from Jane. *Have you resigned?*

Ruth ignored it and quickly texted Billie. *Got an idea, call me when u r free.*

Billie replied moments later. *Battery crap. Units low. I'm skint.*

Ruth walked up the corridor, thumbing back. *Not any more.*

Several hours later, she was standing in her daughter's messy bedroom. Billie was dressing to go out and said, "I'll be revising at Chloé's. Hey, Mum, do my jeans look OK?"

Ruth nodded, wondering why it mattered. "Now answer my question."

"Pass me that T-shirt. What question?"

"Will you help with childminding, for top dollar?"

Billie tugged the black-and-yellow skull T-shirt over her head and mumbled from inside it. "Mum, can we talk later? In a bit of a rush." Ruth sighed and left her to it.

Carol Watt turned up early evening with her capacious quilting bag in one hand and her cake tin in the other. The tin appeared encouragingly heavy. Dylan trailed her down the hall to the kitchen, like a dog after a bone. "Auntie Carol, what did you bake this week?"

"Victoria Sponge." She exaggerated her flat northern vowels. Dylan tried to mimic the Liverpool accent and Carol played along, beaming. "Not bad for a southern softie!"

"Auntie Carol, are you going to do sewing?"

"Don't we always?"

They settled around the kitchen table and she opened her quilting bag. Ruth peeped into it with a familiar pang of envy; for all Carol's wild coils of silver-grey Einstein hair and scuffed corduroy pants, the bag was meticulously arranged: Japanese titanium needles, bodkins and reels peeped from their pockets and blocks of fabric were neatly tucked in compartments.

Ruth opened her own quilting bag and Carol covered her eyes in mock shock, peeping through her fingers. "God help us, Ruth, when are you going to tidy that mess?"

"One of these years." Ruth turned on her reading lamp.

They settled into armchairs overlooking the darkening garden. Carol's short needle was soon threading grey stitches through a scrap of navy cloth, in and out, up and down like tiny dolphins in a dark sea. "So, Ruth, how's your nomad, enjoying life in brightest Africa?"

"Yes, but he's been asking about tickets for Summer Swing. Can you get some?"

"Sure. Will Simon want some too, or is he still sulking after last year? Frank called his BMW *a hairdresser's car*, as I recall. I'll never forget the look on Simon's face."

"Frank was tipsy. Don't remind me. Probably why Simon upgraded to a Porsche."

"Simon's got a Porsche?" Carol eyed her careful stitches, taking her time.

"He's a *grasping yuppie,* according to his boyfriend. They're like cat and dog."

Carol traded staff gossip in return but, as soon she started talking in detail about her IT department at Kew Gardens, the conversation drifted into software problems and Ruth's ears turned to stone. It was like Medusa had dropped in; the wild hair didn't help.

"You look fed up. Am I too boring?" Carol paused to peer over her reading glasses.

"No. It's just that my stitches are a mess. Look!" Ruth thrust her block of fabric under Carol's expert eye and asked, "How come mine never look as nice as yours?"

"You rush them. It's not how many or how fast, it's how straight and even."

"I'm tired, we were mad busy today; it does my eyesight in, all those choppers."

"Remember, with quilting you should practise first. Ten minutes, get your rhythm. And if I had a pound for every time I've told you that, *I'd* be driving a Porsche."

"You could afford one, easy. You earn a packet. Plus, no kids and no partner?"

"Actually, I did treat myself to a garden spade at Arden Nurseries. You must come."

"To deepest Sussex? Maybe when Mr Arden brings his prices down. How much?"

"My spade? It's vintage. Edwardian. From a stately home in Yorkshire. Cost me ten times the price of a new one from Tesco of course, but she's a beauty, Ruth, dead retro."

"You've got more money than sense, like Pippa Price. And I need a cup of tea."

Ruth moved to the sink to fill the kettle. She told Carol about the childcare offer. "I'm thinking of asking Billie to help out. Thing is, she could do with the cash for college. She wouldn't have to do much to earn it. And it's about time she had more responsibility."

Carol raised an eyebrow "Is Billie up to it? How are the new meds, flux-something?"

"Fluoxetine. It's Prozac, basically. She certainly seems more stable. I'll talk to Frank. Either it's the meds or she's in love. Perhaps both."

"Pippa's offer is decent. Sounds like you're developing a head for business, Ruth."

"Not at all. I was just being *altruistic,* as you might say. Now I'm a childminder."

"Only if you accept," Carol said, poking Egyptian thread at Japanese titanium.

Chapter 29

"It's wrong to steal." Dudu was sitting beside the rifle and pistols, watching Kilanda walk about humming a tune and dragging dead branches and saplings along the wide rock ledge. He laid them flat and crouched to lash them together with grass, hopping on his heels, his hands fast and clever. By the time the dying sun flooded the horizon, he had made a shelter that sloped snug against the rock wall, with heavy stones to keep it in place. "Who taught you?" said Dudu, and Kilanda tapped his chest.

"Good camp, this," Kilanda said. "The high ground gives us an advantage and we get down to the track quickly when we hear the train. If we hear the train. That fire ready yet?"

Dudu lit the pile of dry twigs and they sat watching them crack and burn. He thought about the brazier in Banza's yard. He told Kilanda about Moses, but not everything. Kilanda chewed a grass stalk, glassy-eyed, grunting now and then. "So what about you?" Dudu said.

"Like I said, I was a *kadogo* in the *Mai-Mai*."

"But what about before?"

"What about it? My father kicked me out."

"Why?"

"Mind your own business. Why did Moses kick you out?"

"Mind your own business."

Kilanda chuckled. "You want me to shoot Moses in the head?" His face glowed in the firelight. "Just kidding." He offered a pistol. "You might as well learn how this works. Look, safety catch, see? You're on first watch. If a leopard or hyena comes, you know what to do."

"Shoot it in the head?"

"No, tickle its ears." Kilanda lay on his back, closed his eyes and was soon snoring.

Dudu sat cradling the heavy pistol at the entrance of the shelter. He glimpsed two eyes glinting in the bush, something small nearby or big far away. He raised his knees and pointed the gun at the darkness. *What if I shoot and miss?* The eyes vanished. He put the pistol down and yawned, exhausted from the day's walk and not much sleep the last few nights, back at that noisy garage with the nasty *shegués*. It seemed a long time ago, somehow. So did Mavuku. He thought of Mama and Emile. Had Ginelle really kissed Paul the Purified Boy? He closed his eyes and wished Ginelle were here kissing him instead.

He woke slumped inside the shelter with the sun on his face. The fire was out and Kilanda had gone; so had Dudu's leather satchel, although his picture book lay open on the ground and Tata's tiny Power Figure dangled from the shelter by a length of grass, as if Kilanda had tied it there as a sign: *goodbye, sorcerer.* He had left a pistol, too. How come? Dudu untied the Power Figure and put it in his pocket, gazing across the plain and wondering what to do next. The sun baked the savannah from grey to brownish-green and puffs of grey smoke rose from morning fires in distant villages.

He picked up the pistol, slithered down the rocky ledge to the railway track and pressed an ear against a cold steel rail, looking along it at the curling mist, arching ferns and the bush beyond. He saw red blossoms on tree trunks – *poisonous* – and blue flowers on the vines that only came out in the morning; but no Kilanda. He stood up, leaned against a tree and considered his choices. Find a village and say *I'm good with goats?* People would ask about the pistol or tell a MONUC patrol. *Wait for a train? What if it doesn't come? What if militiamen find me and tie me to a tree to cut out my heart, chop my feet?*

He heard a loud bang and turned to see a monkey tumbling through a tree. It landed with a soft thud and Kilanda appeared on the railway track a few moments later, swinging the bushmeat by its tail. Kilanda had the satchel over his shoulder. He walked up and raised the flap to reveal a dead cane rat and five big caterpillars. He pointed at Dudu's pistol. "Safety catch is off. If you shoot yourself and bleed out, can I have this satchel? It's useful."

After breakfast Dudu carved a long-armed monkey from a bit of branch. He gave it to Kilanda. "Thanks for the food."

Kilanda looked at the carving. "Did you make the Power Figure I found in your bag?"

"No. Tata did. He was *nswendwe*. Like his tata before him."

"*Nswendwe?*"

"It means he carved figures for the Great Sorcerer who put the Power in them."

Kilanda's eyes widened. He passed the wooden monkey back. "No thanks."

"It was just part of his job, he was an artisan, a carpenter. He wasn't a sorcerer."

"Neither am I," said Kilanda and they looked at each other in a strange way, both wanting to say more, or perhaps nothing at all. The tough and clever *kadogo* who had bashed the Dirty Blue Hats looked more like a little frightened kid, just another *shegué* whose past was nobody's business. It seemed they had shared a secret that would never be spoken.

"Why did you hang the Power Figure, Kilanda? To protect me while you were gone?"

Kilanda shrugged. "No. It was just a joke."

"*Matondi mingi.*"

Kilanda gave him another strange look; perhaps the tough *kadogo* was not used to people who said *thank you*. Dudu pointed to the silver tracks. "When will the train come?"

"Life is about patience. And water. Let's go, I think I know where to find some."

Dudu put the pistol in his bag and they clambered down from their ledge. They walked through the bush to a grove of trees and found a pond with tiny insects skating across it. They lay flat on their bellies to drink, fill their bottle and wash their dusty faces. Two old banknotes floated past them, curled in the water like dead fish. Kilanda reached to grab one.

"You shouldn't touch the money," said Dudu. "Someone left it, a gift for the gods."

"A gift for us, you mean." Kilanda plucked both banknotes from the pond.

Dudu seized his companion's arm. "No! You already stole money from the Blue Hats; we have enough. This is the start of a river, a sacred place. As *Mai-Mai,* you should know."

They stared at each other for a few moments. Kilanda tossed the wet banknotes into the buzzing pond and walked away. Dudu went after him and grabbed his elbow. The *kadogo* reached for his dagger and said, "Dudu, if you touch me again, I'll put my blade in your eye."

Dudu pointed into a tree ahead of them and said, "Snake. Walk around, not under."

A huge blue-green snake was coiled along a branch and watching their approach, perhaps waiting to drop and feast. Kilanda pointed his pistol at the snake but seemed unsure. He glanced at Dudu, who shook his head. They walked past the tree and Dudu watched the snake tracking him with tiny eyes. It lay there tonguing the air, as if to say, *I'll get you next time.* Or perhaps it wanted to say, *matondi mingi.* He glanced back. It seemed to vanish.

When they returned to their camp, Dudu pressed an ear to the hot steel rail but heard no sound. He sat in the shade carving a snake from a small branch. Kilanda squatted nearby watching the distant plain where woodsmoke curled and axes went *tak-tak-tak*.

Late in the afternoon, they made a fire to roast the big green caterpillars on sharp sticks until they were stiff and white. "I should've shot that big tasty snake, Dudu. You saw it was *nguma?*"

"Boa constrictor, yes. But she was guarding the pond, and too big for us to eat."

"Some people keep Mystic Boa in their houses, to vomit dollars. You know that?"

"I know *nguma* are clever; they drop on your head. You must always look up."

"Sometimes they sit in the grass, come up your leg and strangle you."

"Well, she didn't, Kilanda, so that's a sign. It probably means something good."

Kilanda sat looking at the plain, perhaps thinking about that snake. He took out his dagger and nicked his thumb, wincing as it bled, and Dudu said, "What are you doing?"

"Your turn." Kilanda reached for Dudu's hand and carefully cut his thumb. Shiny blood came out like a little red balloon; Kilanda pressed their hands together and it dribbled down their wrists like a river. "We're brothers. I saw this on TV in Mbuji-Mayi."

"My thumb hurts, Kilanda."

"Not as much as Major Monuc up your ass. Or some big snake round my neck."

When Kilanda released his grip, Dudu curled into the rock wall to suck his cut thumb and doze in the fading light, listening to the bugs and birds and monkeys chattering through the trees. He dreamed of a snake vomiting wet money at his feet, so much money he could not pick it up. The snake curled around his foot and squeezed, harder and harder.

"Dudu, wake up!"

He opened his eyes. It was darker now, already evening. Kilanda's hand was wrapped around his ankle, trying to pull him off the rock ledge. Dudu sat up and heard a distant rumble like thunder that would not stop; he watched the weeds twitching and wondered if spirits were passing through the land. He rose on stiff legs and followed Kilanda down to the track. He pressed an ear to the steel rail and heard a noise: *clacketty-clack, clacketty-clack…*

"Train's coming!" Kilanda yelled, clambering back to their camp on the ledge. A horn bellowed through the night like some desperate beast being dragged to the knife. Dudu stayed where he was, standing in the middle of the track, knee deep in ferns that tickled, watching a tiny light glimmer far down the track but getting bigger and bigger. He heard a thud as his satchel landed beside the track; Kilanda slithered down from the ledge with the rifle and stood tightening his belt with the pistols and dagger on, looking left and right.

"Oh, no! Just my luck!"

"What?"

"The train is going the wrong way. Ilebo will be crawling with Blue Hats!"

"Will they put us in jail?"

Kilanda snapped the bullet clip from the AK and tossed the rifle into the bushes. He shoved the clip into Dudu's satchel and said, "I'll sell this later. Ready to run, tough guy?"

Dudu nodded but the clip of bullets in his bag made it heavier than before. *Will I be able to run fast in these boots?* He watched the white light growing bigger and brighter, the engine thundering as Kilanda yelled, "Steady, Dudu, here it comes… run, now!"

They raced alongside the track, faster and faster as the train approached from behind, roaring down on them, a clanking monster that rattled and rolled. Dudu watched the huge carriages fly past in a blur of faded yellow and blue paint on rusty brown iron. Kilanda reached up and was yanked clean off his feet, as if the hungry monster had grabbed him from above. He spun and twisted, dangling by his arm, howling back on the wind, "Jump!"

Dudu ran with his fists bunched and elbows pumping. Orange sparks spat at his legs and he imagined tripping under the terrible wheels, cut to pieces. He snatched at a rusty rail but missed and the train hammered on. He tried again but his legs seemed heavy as logs, like in a dream. The train was passing too fast and without Kilanda he would soon be alone in the bush. He felt a sharp thump in the back that made him yelp and sent him flying through the air, swinging him up, until his boots were kicking at nothing and scrambling for a foothold on the train. He spun through the open door of a boxcar, landed inside with a bone-jarring crack and looked up at a grinning stranger who cackled down at him, "Hah! I got one! I got one!"

Chapter 30

Cold wind howled around the boxcar and brought a chill to Dudu's bones. He rubbed his back. It still hurt. The doors were open on each side of the rattling wagon, it had no roof and the iron wheels churned below, *clacketty-clack* down the track. The forest flashed by, its leaves all shiny and black under the rising moon. The fellow who had hauled him aboard was sitting opposite, cross-legged on a pile of old sacks, rocking from side to side wearing a wrinkled coat, wrinkled trousers with frayed string through the belt loops and squashed shoes that needed polish. His hair shone silver as the moonlight and he said, "I got you! I got you! Didn't I get you?!"

"Yes, sir," said Dudu. "*Matondi mingi.*"

"You have good manners, young man, but please, there is no need to call me *sir*, for we are now allies, travel companions. My name is Baptiste Bomoy but friends call me Bap. I still have one or two!" His toothless grin reminded Dudu of the mad woman who used to shout at militia trucks passing Mavuku; until the day one of them stopped and some soldiers jumped out, tied her to the back by her ankles and drove off. And that was the end of her.

"And what is your name, young man?" Bap said.

"Dudu."

"And where is your friend? Didn't you say he was travelling with us?"

The train slowed down, clanking up a slope. Dudu peeped out along the line of wagons but the wind made him blink. He crossed to the other side of the wagon to look out. He sat down, dangled his feet over the edge and the train's horn roared like a lonely lion.

"So much for friends," said Bap. "Let that be a lesson to us all."

Dudu slung his bag off and set it down. A pistol slid out and Bap stared at it

"Are you a *kadogo?* Militia?"

Dudu put the pistol back in the bag, wondering what Kilanda would say. Probably something clever. But he could not think of anything. "No, what about you?"

"I was a schoolmaster with a class of thirty. But no longer. Are you in school?"

Dudu shook his head. "I have to do jobs. Well, I *did.*"

"And yet, here we are. No jobs! Free as birds."

"What happened to your school?"

Bap brushed dust from his knees. "Long story. A pupil named Destin became disruptive. I asked him to show more respect. He accused me of favouritism towards my son and daughter, who were also in the class; they sat near the front and were smart, so perhaps he was envious. Things got worse and Destin left school and joined a militia. The next time we met, he was a *kadogo*, with his chest puffed up and his empty head filled with big ideas. He told my pupils to stand up, out of respect for him. I disagreed and, afterwards, well…"

Dudu waited but Bap seemed to have forgotten the rest, so he asked, "Then what?"

"I found it difficult to teach and my class of twenty-eight pupils found it hard to learn. So they stopped coming. As for my wife, well, now I'm an IDP and here we are."

"You're a what?" said Dudu, looking out at the curving line of wagons.

"IDP. *Internally Displaced Person.* It's like a refugee, except you don't go to Belgium." Bap chewed a fingernail. "So, what plans for Ilebo? Four days' ride, you know."

Dudu watched trees flash past. "Not sure. Will there be lots of Blue Hats?"

"Hats of every colour, I expect." Bap reached behind his

back and Dudu reached for his pistol. Bap produced a dusty old sack with holes for his head and arms, and put it on over his coat. "You may borrow one if you wish. These nights get quite cold. You'll see."

Dudu huddled into a corner with one hand on his pistol and one eye on his *ally*, just in case. He listened to the juddering wheels that seemed to ask, *where is Kilanda, where is Kilanda?* Soon more questions came. Should he get off before Ilebo? Go to Mavuku and point his pistol at Pastor Precious and Moses? Shoot the black dog, just to scare them? *Where is Kilanda?* It was difficult to be a hammer; far easier to be a nail.

The strange man sitting opposite seemed to be nodding in agreement but after a while Dudu realised that Bap had fallen asleep, so he closed his eyes too and thought about Emile and Mama and tried to forget that he was in a windy freight train thundering across the land. Instead he pictured himself sitting in a tree and carving *Ginelle* into a fat branch with a MONUC dagger. Ginelle was happy when she saw the results. Next, she was flicking water at him, at the spring; soon they were lying on their backs in long grass watching two hawks circle slowly, high in the sky; he asked Ginelle if he might kiss her; then she was gone and all that remained was her voice; she was singing in her garden up the slope, a tune he knew from somewhere else: *Brothers we will surely die for our beloved Congo.*

He heard scuffling and grunting above; opened his eyes to watch fingers grappling along the top of the boxcar. Next he saw wiry arms and a familiar face; the figure dropped into the boxcar, silent as a midnight cat. Kilanda crouched beside him. "So here you are! First train, brother? I knew it!" Kilanda's embrace tightened into a nasty headlock and Dudu gasped, struggling in vain.

"Stop that! What are you doing?" Bap's cry echoed around the rattling wagon.

Kilanda's laughter faded quickly and his steely arms fell away. Dudu heard the click of a safety catch. Kilanda rose, turned and said, "Me? I'm pointing a gun at you, mister."

Bap put his skinny arms in the air, because it was true. Kilanda jiggled his gun and made Bap turn and spread his arms against the wall of the boxcar. Kilanda quickly searched Bap's pockets and found a piece of chalk and two pebbles. "What's all this junk?"

"Pebbles for sucking. Chalk for writing. I'm not an invader, I'm a schoolmaster."

"Shut up. Or you won't be anything."

Kilanda took Dudu aside and spoke quietly. *Did this nut touch you? Want me to shoot him in the head?* Dudu whispered back, *No, he helped me, he's sort of a refugee; there's not much in his head.* Kilanda turned and growled across the boxcar, "Sit, tramp."

Bap settled cross-legged on a sack. "I used to wear a tie, I had a class of thirty. Thirty!"

Kilanda dangled the pistol, tapping the barrel against his thigh.

"Sometimes it's twenty-eight," said Dudu, and Kilanda's snake-eyes narrowed.

Chapter 31

Saturday morning, Frank and Claude strolled into the ward of a single-storey hospital, somewhere in Kinshasa. Under the tang of disinfectant, Frank smelled faeces and the coppery whiff of stale blood. He passed a woman dousing broken tiles with a ragged mop. Stucco curled from the walls like sheaves of grated Parmesan. Patients were playing cards near cracked windows, emaciated souls with glimmering eyes. Frank followed his driver past flies buzzing around a dark stain on the floor. "Nice place, Claude. Remind me, how do we know this guy?"

"Some of my neighbours go to his church. Well they did, until he got sick." Claude turned up the next aisle and stopped at a cot containing a spindly man in a faded robe, reading a Bible. A beautiful young woman with a catatonic gaze sat upright in a canvas chair nearby.

Father Benoit looked sixty although was perhaps younger; the eyes were lively, even youthful, but he had the gaunt cheekbones of a malnourished man and an air of quiet desperation. A bloodied dressing clung to his shin. He offered a feeble handshake. "I'm diabetic. This ulcer on my leg comes from too much contact with Satan. But I receive money for medicine from my congregation, such as..." He gestured to the woman nearby.

"Father Benoit, Frank wants to interview you," Claude said. The pastor smiled, his Bambi eyes lighting up as he replied, "My pleasure. But for whom, on what subject?"

"Private research into demonic possession," Frank said. "Given your reputation."

"My *reputation?*" The pastor's sensuous lips rolled it around.

"Claude tells me you are highly regarded, as an exorcist."

"Ah, God's work, not mine. I am his servant. Satan will flourish, unless checked."

Frank opened his jotter and took out a pen. "How does one identify a child witch?"

"Easy if you know how. There are happenings, even physical signs."

Frank clicked his ballpoint. "For example?"

"When a sorcerer seeks supernatural power, they make a pact with the Devil to obtain it by sacrificing a relative, because the soul of a relative confers the most power. So, when someone dies, we must wonder why. But some sorcerers choose instead to sacrifice one of their own limbs or an eye. They settle for less power."

Frank stopped writing and looked up. "How do you mean, *sacrifice a limb?*"

"I mean precisely that. For example, an arm will appear withered and useless, as if the child is quite disabled. But at night, the same arm becomes a torch, when they fly. Or, the eye that does not see during daytime can be used to see what is going on in private houses, by night. Or a damaged leg, which causes a limp by day, can become an aeroplane at night and transport the child from Africa to America in a split second. These are the signs."

Claude stood wringing his hat in his hands. He looked worried, or perhaps he needed a pee.

"But apart from physical appearance, we consider behaviour," the pastor went on. "It varies, but a pattern will soon emerge. For example, sorcerers wet the bed. They resent authority. They steal. They become sleepy during the day, with dreamy eyes."

"What if, as a kid, I used to steal sweets, argue with my parents?" Frank said.

Father Benoit stroked his chin. "You pose a clever question

but Satan is cleverer still. It takes a religious man to see the *perfidité* within the child. Sometimes their belly button glows in the dark. A religious man can see it. I can see it. Have you seen it?"

Frank shook his head. "No, Father. But tell me, what do you do, after you see it?"

"I am guided by a higher authority." The pastor raised a bony finger and looked at the ceiling, all scrawny neck and large head. *E.T. phone home.* He leaned towards Frank. "And, usually, I must open their belly button, to release the demon."

"How do you do that?"

"With my fingers, or scissors."

"Doesn't it hurt the child?" Frank saw doubt flicker in the leathery face and pressed the point. "Did you study as a surgeon before you were ordained, or perhaps afterwards?"

"God provides the knowledge I need. I had a powerful vision. I founded my Church. I have many followers. Perhaps I save souls; but I fail more often than I succeed, alas."

"I have something to show you." Frank opened his wallet and took out the neatly folded newspaper item from *La Voix.* He passed it to Father Benoit. "What do you think?"

Father Benoit read the clipping and handed it back. "Amateurs should not dabble."

Frank folded the clipping into his wallet. He spotted a pink gecko scuttling up a wall, eyes shining like black pearls as it gazed down on the discussion, eager for the next question.

"Father Benoit, is it true you've performed over five hundred successful exorcisms?"

"Yes, but some required several sessions. For example…" The pastor pointed at the woman in the chair. She sat perfectly still, eyelids drooping, apparently oblivious to the chat. "This poor soul is still possessed," he said, "so today I must try again. Observe, if you wish."

The pastor reached into a plastic bag and took out a dalmatic; the white robe was frayed and wrinkled. He tugged it awkwardly over his head and draped about his pipe-cleaner neck a stole of scarlet cotton with a yellow cross. Frank noticed the pitiful stitching, *Poor pastor, could nobody sew him a decent hem?* He thought of Ruth's stunning patchwork quilts, those multicoloured miracles that evolved over months of careful planning and nimble fingers. Father Benoit winced and slid slowly from his bed. He stood before the woman.

"Perhaps I should tell you, Mr Kean, this young lady wanted to travel abroad for work, to join her sister in Belgium. But their dead mother conspired with Satan to block her visa. Furthermore, a demon now resides in her very soul. This will be my third attempt." He caressed the woman's neck with bony fingers. She arched her back and gave a husky moan.

The pastor closed his eyes and chanted quietly, *Hallelujah, Hallelujah.* The woman swayed to the rhythm and he moved closer, caressing her arm. "Satan, are you present?"

The woman sat bolt upright as if electrocuted, and squeaked a timid reply. "Yes."

"Tell me, Satan, why do you so block this woman's ambition?"

"She must stay in Kinshasa. Her sister makes false promises. Antwerp is costly." Her tongue slithered, licking air; her glassy eyes rolled in their sockets. Father Benoit turned to Frank. "Do you wish to commune with Satan, for your research?"

"My research?" Frank glanced at Claude, who stood bug-eyed with his baseball cap twisted like a corkscrew in his hands. The lizard circled above with a beady gaze as if to say, *you chicken.* Frank cleared his throat and turned to the writhing woman. "*Bonjour,* Satan."

"*Bonjour, monsieur,*" she squeaked.

Frank paused. *What to ask the Prince of Darkness?* Father Benoit gave him a reassuring nod. *Just chat.* Frank edged closer. "So, Satan, how long will you be staying?"

The woman arched her back and rasped, "Depends."

"On what?"

"On me. I'll stay as long as I like."

Father Benoit smirked and wagged a bony finger. *We'll see about that.*

"Satan," said Frank, "why do you block the intentions of this woman?"

"Belgium is a bad place. I saw it on television."

Beelzebub has cable?

"But Father Benoit plans to cast you out. What do you think of that?" Frank asked.

"The pastor is powerful and does God's work. But I will do mine. That is all."

The pastor gave a modest shrug. *They've heard of me in Hades.*

"Goodbye, Satan," said Frank, "nice talking to you."

The woman nodded and squeaked, "*Enchanté, monsieur.*"

Frank moved aside. Father Benoit moved in and grabbed the woman's braided hair. He gave it a sharp tug and hissed in her ear. "By the power of Jesus, leave!"

The woman howled and squirmed in her tight dress until a button popped to reveal a glistening cleavage. Father Benoit slapped her head. "You will acknowledge the Christ!"

"Never!"

Father Benoit seized the woman's throat. "Do you acknowledge the Christ? Say it!"

The woman gasped for air, gargling her submission. "Yes!"

"Satan! Relinquish her! By the power of Jesus, I cast you out!" Father Benoit pushed the woman backwards. The flimsy canvas chair buckled beneath her and she crashed to the floor, weeping and wailing. Father Benoit grasped his cot and panted, "It is over."

The woman sat in a heap. She clambered to her feet as though waking from sleep. She fastened her buttons, smoothed her dress and gave Frank and Claude a haughty glance. *Yes?*

"She remembers nothing," added Father Benoit, climbing

back onto his bed. He wriggled into his shrivelled pillows. "And now, I will rest. Before my medication."

Frank opened his wallet and handed over some cash. "For your tablets?" Father Benoit bowed his head and accepted the donation. "Every little helps. May God be with you." Frank turned and walked through ranks of kneeling patients, their skeletal hands clasped together as if containing rare butterflies. He ambled back to the car park in a daze.

Driving away, Claude gripped the wheel, grim-faced, like a novice on his test. Frank poked the radio. Rumba guitar jangled shrill and sweet. "What are you thinking, Claude?"

"That woman is not cured, Frank. The Devil came out too fast."

"If at all," said Frank. "Next stop, twelve little witches. You still want to go?"

Chapter 32

The Unicorn jeep crunched up dusty tracks of hard red earth split by flood gullies. Claude grappled the steering wheel in silence – still brooding on Satan, perhaps. He shook his head at the power of evil, or at these unspeakable roads. After twenty minutes' drive, the busy city of Kinshasa seemed a world away; this neighbourhood looked more like Mars. They lurched into another pothole and Claude wrenched the wheel, the jeep bucking like a bronco, Frank's guts churning to mush. Claude cursed. "These roads wreck my suspension."

"This was your idea, Claude, not mine."

"Because you wanted the other side of the story."

"That was in my seminar, and I was talking about ethical balance. Not a day trip."

They stopped at a sunken crossroads to pick up some buddy of Claude's named Vern who wore a similar canvas bush vest but with a snazzier logo: *Helping Hand.* Vern seemed a genial fellow and his arrival certainly improved the atmosphere in the jeep. A walkie-talkie crackled on his belt next to a fat leather pouch embossed with the Swiss Army logo. His skin shone black as tar but his eyes were blue-green from a genetic mutation or a *mundele* ancestor. He sat up front, calling the turns in his sing-song voice and chatting affably in broken English. "I will take you to meet Reverend Ray, who does much good work, here in our community," he said. Frank's head slammed into the roof.

They drove through a row of tumbledown shacks perched along a ridge and shuddered to a halt beside a dead tree, its roots exposed and coiled like cooked spaghetti. Barefoot kids swarmed around the jeep, draping their puny arms on its wing mirrors and pulling at the door handles, only backing off when Claude emerged in his brittle mood.

Frank clambered out, pulled on his sunhat and stretched, doing the starfish. Some giggling kids mimicked him. Wary-looking adults watched from a mud-walled café, their solemn expressions in stark contrast to the grinning faces in the faded advert for mobile phones tacked to the café door. On corrugated tin roofs, rusty satellite dishes curled towards the sun. Garbage festooned the drainage ditches alongside the dirt road – plastic bottles, crumpled scratch cards, and used condoms. A yellow dog with washboard ribs turned tight circles, snapping at its tail. Claude gave bubblegum to a small boy with a runny nose. Frank produced three boiled sweets and the others wrestled for the goodies. *Cadeaux!*

Claude's buddy Vern vanished into one of the shacks, its tarpaulin door flapping like the ear of an elephant, but re-emerged moments later followed by a big man dressed in a black soutane, six foot five in his flip-flops. He was munching a bright red apple and it looked more like a cherry in his huge fist. He shared a joke with Claude then perused Frank with an inquisitive grin. "I'm Reverend Ray. How can I help?"

Frank told him about his work with local journalists, about USAID's interest in community issues, about ethical balance, minority voices and media's obligation to seek out those people marginalised by society. It was quite a speech, probably too long. Reverend Ray placed one foot on the jeep's bumper, chewing his apple. He ate the whole lot, core and pips, nodding at the dusty earth. "*Marginalised.* Do you mean like lepers?"

"I guess. Although that's not a story we've covered yet."

"Maybe one day. And how do you like our Congo?"

"Good weather, friendly people," said Frank, besieged by grinning kids.

"You know what some of them do, in the remote areas?"

"What?"

"They dig up the bodies of Ebola victims, to see if the white nurses took out their insides. They find no organs, of course, but they do catch Ebola. That's a story, one day."

Frank stared, stuck for a response. Reverend Ray led him to the shack. "Docile is conducting a group exorcism." He raised a finger to his lips, tugging at the tarpaulin door.

Frank peered into a dark and musty room where an adolescent girl in a bright headscarf was perched on a stool surrounded by squatting children, perhaps twenty in all, some as young as two years old. They turned towards the door, the whites of their eyes catching the glow of a single candle. The girl fastened her hands around the head of a tiny, kneeling boy. She pressed her thumbs to his eyelids and chanted, "*Délivrance totale!*"

After a minute or so, she beckoned the next in line, a girl of seven or eight, and repeated the ritual. Reverend Ray whispered in Frank's ear. "Sorcerers, all of them."

Frank watched candlelight dance. "How do you know?"

"Come and meet Lionel, their father."

"Can I talk to the kids?" Frank asked, but Reverend Ray shook his head. *Bad idea.*

They moved outside, and a grazing goat looked up at Frank, its eyes like bar codes. The long-limbed pastor strode ahead down the slope, soutane flapping. He led Frank, Claude and Vern to a sad-faced man sitting on a beer crate outside a ramshackle kiosk that sold snacks, but not many.

Lionel was a pockmarked fellow with an anxious look who bowed his head when Reverend Ray shook his hand. They gently bumped temples, Congolese-style, and the pastor murmured in his ear, presumably explaining who was who. Lionel greeted Vern and Claude and, finally, he glanced at Frank. "It's true, sir, twelve of those witches are mine." He looked away, distracted by rasping barks from the yellow dog. Two barefoot kids were teasing it.

Frank held Lionel's earnest gaze and said, "Twelve witches, are you sure?"

Lionel nodded. "Because I lost my job and could not find another. My wife thought evil spirits might be to blame. We asked our children. The first to confess was our eldest, Sophie. So, we brought her to Reverend Ray. Two days later, we went back to see her. We were worried but she seemed happy to be here, playing with her new friends, all of them witches. That confirmed our worst fears. That day my eldest sons Dan and Didier also confessed and said they wanted to stay here with Sophie, because they were witches too."

Frank noticed an elderly woman shuffling up to eavesdrop, her waxy hands clutching a walking stick. She wore a tight dress with puffy shoulders. She hunched closer, all ears.

Lionel drew a handkerchief to dab his eyes. "A few days later, we came again to visit Sophie, Dan and Didier. They seemed happy. But five more of my children confessed. *Papa, I'm a witch too.* We left them here. Then, on the way home, the others confessed: *Papa, we are sorcerers; we want to stay there.*" Lionel sobbed into his clenched fist, his chest wheezing like an accordion. "Twelve! Little wonder that I cannot find employment. What can I do?"

Reverend Ray placed a brawny hand on Lionel's shoulder. "We can pray."

"You offer reasonable terms, Reverend, but if Satan cannot be banished?"

A tiny boy pushed into the group, tugging at Lionel's shins. "Papa."

Lionel snuffled his tears and looked down with a tearful smile. "Didier."

This little witch seemed to crave affection. Lionel caressed his son's face but seemed wary. Didier hugged his father's legs, weeping aloud. Perhaps he was having second thoughts about being possessed. They drifted off to talk and Frank sat on the empty beer crate; he lit a cigarette, blowing smoke rings at the gawping goat. Reverend Ray had moved away to chat with Vern. Claude was kicking the jeep's tyres and squatting to check the suspension. The old woman in the dress with the puffy shoulders gave Frank a long look, shook her head and hobbled away; Lionel was leading his son back up the slope towards the mud shack with the tarpaulin door. It swung aside and Frank heard the chanting from within, *Délivrance totale!*

On the drive back, Vern turned in his seat. "So, Frank, what did you think?"

"Seemed like a game, at least to the kids. No wonder they all confessed."

Claude stared at him in the rear-view mirror. "A game, you say?"

"Sure. Those kids probably just wanted new friends, a new place to play."

"This is no game," Vern said. "They are dangerous, that's why Pastor is helping."

Frank sat back, watching trees. "Vern, let me tell you something. My son Dylan is about the same age as little Didier. He told his teacher he went scuba diving in South Wales."

"And?'

"Dylan can't even swim. He wears inflatable rubber wings in the local pool."

"If you mean children exaggerate, I agree. But sorcery is the work of the Devil."

Frank leaned forward, his chin resting on the top of the seat, above Vern's shoulder. Vern had a Maglite torch in his left breast pocket, a collection of pens in his right breast pocket and a head full of superstition. "There's something else," Frank added. "Regardless of how reasonable Reverend Ray's terms might be, I wonder if Lionel is getting ripped off."

In the awkward silence that followed, Vern's neck visibly stiffened. Frank wondered about discretion being the better part of valour, about politics being the art of the possible and Frank Kean being a bloody big mouth. Vern's reply, when it came, was diplomacy itself.

"When you've spent a little longer in our country, you will

understand our culture."

"No doubt," Frank said. He sat back again and tipped his sunhat low over his eyes.

Bouncing back down to the city, he thought about Reverend Ray, Lionel, young Docile with her magic thumbs and *délivrance totale*. They were not digging up bodies, just medieval prejudice, as cranky in their own way. But what puzzled him most of all was the image of the old woman who had eavesdropped, the one with the walking stick, narrow waist and puffed-up shoulders. She had looked almost Victorian. Or was it Edwardian? There was a name for that style. Leg-of-mutton? *La Belle Époque?* Early 1900s? Ruth would know.

"I have a question about clothes," he said, hoping to defuse the lingering tension. He pointed at two women in bright dresses with shoulders that ballooned, necklines cut low, the waists cinched tight, headscarves to match. "Why do Congolese ladies wear those dresses?"

"Colonial styles," said Vern, back to his affable self. "And part of our culture. Or, as my daughter will sometimes insist: *too old-fashioned!* It is a subject of hot debate in my home. My wife favours this traditional style and argues with my daughter, who will marry soon and has other ideas. Such squabbles! Maize cannot get justice in a chicken's court, as we say."

"That's a good proverb," said Frank, jotting it down with a pencil. "But I quite like those traditional styles. Old-fashioned, yes, but dignified too. There's room for both, no?"

"Yes!" Vern turned and beamed at him. "So, at least we agree on something. Personally, I like how my wife looks when we step out. And yours, Frank, is she very fine?"

Frank laughed and told him about Ruth, how she liked to sew. They sat swapping domestic gossip, chewing the fat and the bubblegum that Claude distributed with a grin.

When they dropped Vern off, Claude hopped out for a quiet word with him by the side of the road, perhaps apologising about the uppity foreigner in the back of the jeep. Frank stayed put, deep in thought, blowing pink gum until it popped like a bubble of ignorance. *We brought guns and pith helmets. We hacked ivory and tapped rubber. We laid down the law, grafted our will onto the roots of their culture. We said Jesus-is-Love, and whipped them until they believed us. We put Mobutu in charge and pulled his strings with our magic thumbs. And twelve little witches think evil is a game.* He noticed Vern approaching the vehicle, smiling.

"You look upset, Frank," Vern said at the open window. "What are you thinking?"

"Just that my wife might like a summer dress from Congo. Any suggestions?"

"Try a dressmaker, Kinshasa has many. I'm sure she'll like the result. Goodbye!"

They shook hands through the gap. Claude climbed aboard, the engine roared and Frank sat watching the suburban villages morph into a city. He thought about religion and the disciples who screwed it up. His phone beeped and he read a text from Ruth: *Guess who offered me a well-paid part-time job? Let's speak tonight if you are free, Ru xxx*

London seemed far away but reassuringly sane, and Ruth would look *very fine* wearing a Congolese robe at that annual concert in Kew Gardens, Summer Swing. He was thumbing a reply when Claude said, "Frank, there's someone else you must meet."

"Let me guess."

"A real priest, I mean."

Frank watched the rosary beads swing below the rear-view mirror, almost taunting him. "No thanks, Claude, some real priests abuse altar boys and participate in genocide."

"Not this one. He will change your mind."

Chapter 33

Billie arrived at Callum's house at 8 p.m. sharp, Chloé tagging along. The yellow door had a red handle and the bell played the *Batman* tune. Billie smiled and said, "Cheer up, they invited us for dinner, not a funeral." Chloé frowned at weeds sprouting along the path. "I could be revising. You only brought me for backup; I hope his dad can cook."

A tanned man with dreadlocks and baggy trousers opened the door, placed his palms together and bowed his head. "Billie Estephane, we meet at last! And Chloé? *Namaste.*"

Billie stared. "Mr Xavier?"

"Yes, but call me *Jay.*" He beckoned them down the hall and Billie followed, watching his thick dreadlocks bounce above his cute little bottom. He was super skinny, gliding over reed mats in his embroidered slippers, tiny bells pinging at his ankles. Billie walked past candles and carvings, and looking around said, "Wow, your house is so…"

"Eclectic?" Jay suggested, over his shoulder. "Come through, I hope you're hungry. I cooked *momo* in your honour. Callum is in the chill-out zone. Mind my bonsai."

Billie stepped around a glazed plant pot containing a tiny tree; *poor thing needs a proper garden or it will never grow.* She paused at a framed black-and-white photograph of a leathery-faced man in a turban among hills as grey as the moon. It was signed: *Jay, '83.* "Stunning, isn't it?" said Jay, scratching his chin. "I took it in India, got the light just right."

"You've got cobwebs," Chloé said, looking at the ceiling.

Jay led them into a long, open kitchen smelling of garlic and cat litter, then through French windows at the far end into a small back yard with rocks, pebbles and a glass roof. Callum was slouched on a beanbag, strumming a guitar. God, he was handsome: eyes like the night and a smile that cut Billie in half, all the way down. She kissed him, but not enough.

"You guys haven't got any chairs," Chloé said.

They drank fragrant tea from lacquered beakers, sitting cross-legged at a low table made from some ancient door. "This old thing? I picked it up in Bali," Jay said, as if talking about a paperback from the Oxfam shop. He served salad and small parcels of transparent white pasta with cheese inside. "*Momo*, from Asia," he said. They ate from old wooden bowls.

Chloé scrutinised her food. "Tastes like tortellini from Tesco."

"But more delicious," Billie said, and Jay smiled. "*Merci beaucoup*, Billie. I learned the recipe in Ladakh, between the Kunlun and Himalayas. Fascinating art they have, too."

Billie asked about his job and Jay sighed. "Graphic design, freelance. Next question?" Billie nodded, *coool*. Chloé asked about his wife. Jay explained he was divorced, *but not from reality*. Chloe asked for salt; Jay said it was bad for her and explained his *take on life*.

Jay had realised, after months of meditation on Mrs Xavier and the mortgage – which was also a bitch – that change to the system *comes from within, ladies*. He tapped his tanned chest; his baggy shirt sagged open – *très* sexy – and his love beads glinted. "Do you know where I'm coming from? In India, I learned that we're all one. The servants in the ashram called me *gandu*, which means *wise visitor*. I felt so blessed! Do you like my *kehwa* tea? I find it very energising. Once, we trekked for nine hours without eating. Just sipping a flask of *kehwa*."

Chloé inspected her beaker. "What's in this stuff?"

"Cardamom, saffron, almonds," said Jay. "We drank gallons of it in Kashmir. But then we had Gavin, my firstborn, then Callum and that was the end of my globetrotting."

Billie sipped tea. "My stepdad is into tourism, too. He's been to ninety-nine countries."

"I was more of a traveller, and consider the idea of keeping count rather competitive, which is why I never bothered. For me, it was more about the people and the journey."

Billie smiled and wanted to go somewhere with him. Jay offered her the last *momo.*

"Do you ever wash your hair?" Chloé asked.

"Not since I was twenty-two," said Jay, caressing his dreadlocks. "Gavin's age. But I think he's more mainstream than I ever was; that's Oxford for you, I suppose. I visit when I can; plant seeds of subversion in the groves of academe. They've never met anyone like me!"

Billie gazed back. *Neither have I.* Jay gathered their bowls and told them he did not feel emasculated doing it. Billie made a mental note to look that one up, later. When Jay went to the kitchen, she leaned towards Callum and whispered, "Jay's cool, just like his name."

"Short for Jasper but don't mention it," said Callum. "And don't be impressed with graphics; he designs leaflets for hotels, crap like that. Just play along and he'll probably let me borrow the van for Glasto. I reckon that's why he invited you around, to check you out." Callum craned his neck. "Probably went for his stash. If he skins up, go with the flow, babe."

Billie winked. "Got it, babe." Chloé yawned and said, "Why don't you call him *Dad?*"

"Because that would reinforce the hegemony of the oppressive state apparatus!" Jay said, trotting back into the room. Chloé stared. Billie made a mental note to look that up too, if she could remember. Jay sat down with red eyes and a runny nose. "Spot of hay fever, ladies." He plucked crumbly tobacco from a silver box and rolled a fat spliff with his nice, almost girlish hands. He lit it and offered it to Chloé. "Chill! Try a little skunk."

"No thanks, that smells like a big one."

Jay passed the spliff to Billie and she went with the flow, but this stuff was stronger than Callum's usual ganja and soon the room was whirling around her ears. Yikes. Jay grinned.

"Head-spinner, Billie? Be one with the spirit, if you know where I'm coming from."

Billie went to sit on a beanbag of faded yellow velvet. Jay reached for the guitar and plucked it like a handsome cowboy. His dark eyes shone like the studs of jet in his earlobes. He sang a nice song with words he had written himself:

Born of my loins, this universe joins us,
forever and a day, no matter how far… away.

He kept looking at Callum. The oneness of their spirit made Billie want to cry and she almost did. The music echoed around the rock garden and off to the stars. A Siamese cat curled into her lap and gazed into her soul. Jay stopped singing and Chloé said, "I didn't expect country and western."

Jay winced as if someone had trodden on his foot. Billie said, "Frank likes Johnny Cash but I gave him one of Cal's reggae tapes as a wind-up. He didn't even say thanks."

"You're in pain, Billie," said Jay, raising his palm. "I can feel it in your aura."

"She's on fluoxetine," said Chloé. "For depression."

Billie glared and Jay said, "Cal tells me you've been in therapy, Billie?" She noticed that he was staring at the lurid scars that criss-crossed her inner wrist like a dark pink bangle.

She pulled her sleeve down. "Not for a while. They treat you like a guinea pig. Half the time my shrink couldn't remember what he'd prescribed, and his coat had elbow patches like dried prunes. Mum asked him, *is Billie with a bad crowd? You know what he told her, right in front of me? Mrs Kean, Billie is the bad crowd.* I just take the meds now."

Chloé sighed and said, "Can we put a CD on, listen to something happy?"

Jay slipped a CD in the slot. "Perhaps we could all use a healing mantra."

Sitars and gentle drums – *dup-dup-dup* – came floating around Billie's head. It was very relaxing at first, until a familiar and chilling emptiness crept up, from her toes to her head. "This music reminds me of when Dad came home from India," she said.

Jay sat alongside on a beanbag. "He died when you were seven, Cal told me?"

"Topped himself," said Chloé, like she knew all about it. Billie closed her eyes and listened to the purring cat in her lap. She stroked its ear and it meowed, at one with her spirit.

"Do we know why, Billie?" Jay's gentle voice seemed to float from deep inside her. Billie shrugged, lost in the music now, picturing herself as a child swimming at Rum Cove with Mum and Dad, all happy. But the image soon faded and, next, she imagined herself walking along the beach looking for Dad, as if she had gone to India in her head. "All I know is he went to Goa and came back depressed," she said. "That's it. So my mum told me."

"Your mum probably knows more than she lets on. Parents usually do," Jay said.

Someone cracked a pistachio shell and Billie opened an eye. She glanced at her phone, to check the time. Its screen was blank. Crap battery. "Anyone got a watch?"

"Not me," said Jay, rolling a spliff. "But linger awhile, I'll balance your chakras."

Billie watched his delicate fingers teasing the skunk and tobacco into shape. She glimpsed his aura glowing in the gloom. Or maybe it was the candle behind his head. She closed her eyes, breathing deeply, going with the flow. "Balance my what?"

"Your chakras, if you ladies know where I'm coming from?"

"No thanks," Chloé said. "I'll get a cab; coming, Billie?"

Billie shook her head, eyes still closed; she heard feet clomp off, a door slam far away. Good riddance to Chloé and her big gob. Someone nudged Billie's arm. "Smoke this."

They dropped her home around midnight. She climbed slowly

from the vw van, pecked Callum and waved at Jay. He signed *peace* and called out, "Big love, Billie!"

She wobbled woozily up the path and slipped her key in the door. It was yanked open and she stumbled into a storm of questions from her bug-eyed mother: *what the bloody, who the hell… it's midnight, we agreed ten-thirty, are you even listening?* Billie sat on the bottom stair, untying her baseball boots. The laces took longer than usual, tangled like strands of wet tagliatelle. Her mother was pacing about in pink socks, ranting like a madwoman. If anyone needed medication, she did. "Billie, you told me you'd be at Chloé's again, *revising.* So I rang her house. Chloé's dad told me you'd gone to Surbiton. *To revise?* I said, like a bloody fool!"

When Billie stood up, blood came roaring into her head. She felt queasy but when she looked in the mirror, her face seemed serene. The contrast was reassuring. "We *started* at Chloé's," she said, "but it was harder than we expected, because although Jean Anouilh never openly criticised the Nazi occupation of Paris, if you read his work allegorically, he doesn't approve. So, we went to a friend's, to look for… algorithms and stuff."

"In Surbiton? Which friend? I called your mobile. Not a dicky bird. How come?"

"Crap battery, I told you." Billie sat, toeing off a shoe. "Mum, are we done?"

"Not quite. What's *bollocks,* in French?"

"Charming. You'll wake Dylan." Billie brushed past but sensed Mum following her into the kitchen, where they faced each other like a pair of alley cats, neither giving an inch. Billie bluffed for a while but when Mum mentioned *your dad turning in his grave,* Billie felt something crack apart inside and she turned away. She leaned her forehead against the back window, looking into the dark garden beyond and wiping tears. Her confession dribbled out.

"I was at Callum's, ok? Callum Xavier. He's in a different school, same exams."

"The skateboarder at the bus stop? I'm not stupid. Why not just tell me, like an adult?"

"Because he's sort of my boyfriend and you probably won't like him."

"Why, is he a serial killer?"

"He's just… different. Mum, give me a break, for once."

"Where were his parents while all this was going on?"

"All *what*? Cal's dad was there. He's a designer. Divorced but not from reality."

"What's that supposed to mean?"

Billie examined a fingernail. "Some parents are more laid back."

"Perhaps because their kids are less sneaky about what's going on."

"I'm not a kid and nothing is *going on*. Give me a break! We were downstairs in the rock garden. We had food, listened to music. I was tired from revising. I nodded off."

"What did you eat, sleeping pills?"

"*Momo*. They're very eclectic. Not like us, if you know where I'm coming from."

"Venus?"

"You can talk, Planet Quilt; I'm going to bed."

"Not so fast. I want a promise, a guarantee. You will not disappear again, OK?"

"*Guarantee?* I'm not some electric fridge. I'm a *holistic being*."

"You're a dirty stop-out."

Billie closed her eyes and fought an urge to punch the window. "I *knew* it, I knew you'd give me a hard time. You keeping saying we should talk like adults. But why should I, if I get this crap? Mum, just because you're a Catholic, doesn't mean everyone else is a sinner."

"Maybe not. But you *are* unreliable. I've never even met your sort-of-boyfriend. "

"Fine, I'll invite him for tea. Then you can ask how many kids he's chopped up."

"Maybe you should, and I won't. Billie, love, I'm your mum. I worry. It's my job."

Billie turned away, gazing at her own reflection in the window. Her face was puffy. She refocused on the garden, tried to picture Callum sitting out there some sunny afternoon sipping Earl Grey, listening to Mrs Kean babble about quilts. *Go with the flow, babe.*

Chapter 34

The days were worst; so long and hot. Dudu felt as though he were sitting in a furnace, not a freight wagon. He sipped water and looked across the scrubby savannah, his bones aching from the endless jolting – up and down, *clacketty-clack* – and hunger gnawing his guts. The train rattled across the land, hour after hour, sometimes on a ridge, sometimes through dense forest, sometimes on a plain. The river would curl away from the silver glinting track but always return, as though it could not bear to separate from its friend; they too were travel companions, like him, Kilanda, and Bap Bomoy. Sometimes the water was so close they shouted to men paddling pirogues and watched clever birds dive for fish; sometimes it was far away, just a gleaming thread in a vast carpet of green and brown.

They passed a train carriage turned upside down in a ditch, all bent and battered, its windows long gone, the blue and yellow paint scratched and faded. Once, it had been full of passengers riding to far-off places where their family and friends would hug and kiss them.

Bap looked sad. "This line was part of the National Route. That means two thousand, six hundred and fifty-five kilometres of rail, river and rail from Lubumbashi to Ilebo to Kinshasa to Matadi. But look, boys! Derailment and death! This rolling stock has not been renewed since independence, forty years ago. Do you know about rolling stock? Do you know what *independence* means?"

Dudu shook his head.

"Do you know how to shut up?" Kilanda said. Bap looked

worried and said nothing.

"What's *indepep*… that big word, Bap?" Dudu asked, and Kilanda rolled his eyes.

Bap explained, about the trains first. He seemed a nice man even if his stories were sometimes confusing. He was helpful and wise, like a nice uncle, a grown-up you could trust. Dudu wondered how it would be to wear a school uniform, attend Bap's class.

The evenings were cooler. They would sometimes stop near a village and sit in the wagon listening to men laughing and bottles chinking to loud music. They watched the slow silhouettes of engineers with flashlights walking alongside the train, *tap-tap*. Bap explained. *Calibrating the wheels*. On their second evening, the train stopped for a long time.

"Probably because a romantic liaison is occurring," Bap said, "between our drivers and their local sweethearts." Dudu looked at Kilanda, who did not seem to understand either.

Later that night, a large spotted beast with round ears – *a leopard or hyena,* Kilanda reckoned – stood on its hind legs at the wagon door, sniffing the air. Bap threw a pebble and the creature vanished into the darkness. Even so, Kilanda drew a pistol and aimed at the gap.

"It's bushmeat. If it comes back."

"Yes please, very tasty," Bap chuckled. "Bushmeat with *fufu*."

"And fried plantain," said Dudu.

"And *pilipili*," said Kilanda.

"I'll summon the waiter," said Bap, clicking his fingers at the darkness. His joke made them laugh, even though they were scared. They took turns ordering invisible food for an imaginary feast: peas and nuts, pumpkin and *pondu, lituma,* okra, hot pepper soup, *tshitekutaku, mwambe* chicken in peanut sauce, mushrooms, goat meat with rice, *ndakala* fried fish. Their bellies were groaning. They sucked pebbles and Bap said, "Delicious, gentlemen! Now we will retire." He curled in a corner and was soon wheezing away.

Dudu lay with his head on his satchel. He dreamed of Tata catching a fish that flopped and gasped, unable to believe its bad luck. Tata cooked and sliced it. They chewed and chatted, mostly about Nana Kima.

Dudu woke in a cold sweat at dawn and remembered what Pastor Precious had said, about bartering with Satan, about swapping food for Nana's soul.

The train had not moved. Kilanda hopped off and walked into the bush to hunt. Dudu followed but was soon sent back. "Two feet are quieter, Dudu; go read your picture book."

"But what if we leave without you?"

"If I can catch breakfast, I can catch a train. Get lost."

Dudu went back towards the train, kicking stones. He sat on a rock and gazed at his MONUC boots, thinking about that Major and the other soldier. *What if they're dead? Did Satan visit Kilanda in a dream and swap food for their souls?* He watched Kilanda padding through the bush, like a hunter. Bap approached, sat on the rock, and said, "Two men in a burning house must not stop to argue."

Kilanda returned with a small monkey and a snake he had caught with a forked stick. "I saw an okapi but it was too fast," he said. "Let's make a fire and cook the snake."

Dudu gathered dead twigs. Kilanda skinned the snake by standing on the tip of tail, stretching it up straight and cutting carefully along the belly. Bap watched closely and chuckled.

"My dear wife Malaika was a good cook, but she never fed me snake. We had champagne at our wedding, you know. She had rich relatives, but that was then."

Kilanda stood wiping his hands. "Where is she now?"

"My wife jumped in the river. A lesson to us all."

A whistle blew, down the track. The train lurched forward

a few yards, stopped with a squeak and lurched again. Dudu and Kilanda hopped aboard and helped Bap to clamber up. The train rumbled on and Dudu squatted at the door, gazing back at the unlit fire. *What a waste.* A hawk flew from a tree beside the track and soared alongside the train, eyeing the bloodied snake in Kilanda's hand; he cut a piece of meat and threw it. The hawk caught the meat mid-air and circled away. They watched it land, wings flapping as it settled to feast. The train clanked faster and soon the hungry bird was just a blur of grey and white in the distance.

They roared on at full speed, hour after scorching hour. Kilanda spread the map. "Are we going north-west, brainbox?" Dudu checked the map and said, "Think so."

Bap pointed at rivers sparkling in the distance. "Look! There's the Lombelo, the Lekedi, and the Lutshuadi. They're going to Ilebo like us. We'll be there soon, my friends."

"So will MONUC," said Kilanda. "And they're not my friends."

At dusk, the train stopped outside a village and some kids trotted alongside to sell snacks to whoever was inside the open wagons. Kilanda hopped out, waving money before their eager eyes. He bought boiled eggs, sardines, *kwanga,* chocolate bars, fried peanuts, biscuits and even batteries for his CD player. As the train moved on, he laid the food on a sack like a banquet and Bap explained something called *the importance of good nutrition.* They drank *sucrés* until their bellies bulged. Kilanda put his headphones on the floor and turned the volume up. He stood clutching an empty bottle like a microphone, swaying his hips.

"Hear that music? It's party time, Dudu! Koffi Olomide, *c'est moi.* You two are the Koffiettes, so get up and dance, ladies."

"We'll try our best; come Dudu." Bap rose to his feet, burped and said, "Pardon me."

Dudu and Bap tried to dance like glamour girls, wiggling their bottoms around the juddering wagon. Kilanda mocked them. "No! This is how to dance like a Kinshasa *sapeur!*"

"Like a what?" Dudu copied him, trying to master the moves: *left, right, back...*

Bap nudged him. "A *sapeur* is a cool fellow, one who dresses very well."

"Quiet! Pay attention," said Kilanda, "because when I'm rich, I'll need dancers."

They danced until they could dance no more and flopped to rest cross-legged against the rattling walls of the boxcar, Bap sitting between Dudu and Kilanda with his bony arms across their shoulders. "A word of advice, boys. Did you know that our famous pop star Koffi Olomide has a bachelor's degree in Economics, and a master's in Mathematics from the University of Paris? That's why he's rich."

"He's got *what?*" Kilanda said, looking surprised, but Bap ignored the question.

"And now, boys, if you will permit, I will sing. I only know one composition, entitled 'Malaika', which means 'My Angel'. I will dedicate it to my wife, who is watching over me."

The sun poured gold into the Lulua River as Bap held an empty bottle and gazed at the horizon. His song was slow and sweet, perhaps the saddest Dudu had ever heard.

> *Malaika, nakupenda Malaika.*
> *Nami nifanyeje, kijana mwenzio,*
> *Angel, I love you Angel.*
> *And me, what should I do, my love?*

Bap sang that he wished to be with Malaika but life had torn them apart, that he dreamed of her at night. Dudu listened intently and the song made him think about how Mama must have felt after Tata died; he thought about Ginelle too. How he longed to be with her, how she had walked away from his bus wiping dust from her eye. Now he wished they had kissed. He had been proud, too jealous, too stupid. Would he ever get another chance? Bap finished the song, wiping his eyes. Dudu swallowed hard as if he had a pebble in his throat.

"So," Kilanda said, chewing gum, "why did she jump in the river, your wife?"

Bap shrugged. "She lost hope. I was a schoolteacher, I had a class of thirty."

"It was twenty-eight last time," Kilanda said, sounding bored. "Why did she jump?"

"Because one of my former pupils, Destin, accused me of spying for the invaders."

"So what? That stuff happens all the time. Some *kadogo* even accused me, once."

"I had not spied! My protests fell on deaf ears. Destin was a *kadogo*, too."

"I know all about that. Two years, all over the place. That front line kept changing."

"Destin came back from the front and decided to give his teacher a lesson."

"Half the time, you don't even know who is shooting. You just shoot back."

"My two children went missing. Nathalie and Trésor. I searched everywhere."

"War is stupid," Kilanda said. "Did you find your kids?"

"Yes, I found them next day; they were waiting in my schoolroom at their usual places, two desks near the front, gazing at me with their pencils in their mouths. They were always proud of Tata, their teacher. Except that day, they were not my children anymore."

"They'd enlisted? They were *kadogos* too, like that Destin?"

"No. They were just heads," said Bap, and Dudu shivered as if a ghost had come to listen. But Bap could say no more. Instead, he wept into his knuckles and Dudu looked away.

The train lurched into a bend on a big river shimmering north to Ilebo, and the town twinkled in the black distance, a slumbering beast that would wake in a few hours.

Chapter 35

Frank squatted in the hall of his flat, looking at his rucksack, packed and ready; it slouched by the door like a dog hoping for walkies. He counted on fingers the days since his visit to MO-NUC. Still no word on a flight east; *has busy Alphonse forgotten?* He thumbed an SMS and got a reply: *Any day, be ready, Al.*

Frank paced the rooms, bored witless, eventually settling on the stinky sofa. He found a tatty paperback novel stuffed down the side and skimmed a few pages – crack commando Chuck Stern was skimming tropical treetops in his helicopter. How many forms had Chuck filled in? The book did not say. Frank tossed it aside and opened his laptop to check his worksheets for the next seminar, adding a few notes, lessons learned from Kinshasa. He owed Ruth an email but the link was down, as ever. He should probably write to Billie, ask if she needed help with French homework, ask her about child-minding Audrey. Or Andrea? It seemed only yesterday that Billie had been a kid, now this. *Money for old rope,* Ruth had said, and company for Dylan. He closed his laptop and went onto the balcony for a smoke.

He dialled his mother on his mobile but the connection failed. He went back inside and tugged the satellite phone from deep in his rucksack. The line was perfect and so it should be, at the price. Mum sounded pleased but also puzzled that he would bother phoning.

"So," he said, changing the subject, "what you been up to?"

"I was in the garden shed. Rooting through your dad's angling gear."

"You should give those rods to charity; he can't fish in

heaven."

"Perhaps I will. Perhaps you can help me clear out when you next visit."

She was fishing; who could blame her? "I'll talk to Ru," he said. "How's Gripturn?"

Frank got the gossip from home and tried to match names and faces, but they soon blurred into one, a sea of memories that made his head spin. His mother seemed to sense it.

"Anyway, Francis, I'll not waste your money, this call must be costing a bomb. When will I see you lot up north? Before the baby?" She paused, probably for effect. "Or after?"

"Depends on Ruth," he said, watching the hazy river. Most things did.

"Am I boring you?"

"No, I'm just a bit… restless."

"Makes a change. How many countries is it now?"

"Ninety-nine."

"My God, Francis. You're lucky she doesn't divorce you."

"I'm lucky full stop. I had a wonderful mother."

"No need to be sarcastic, son. And be careful of the water. I saw a documentary."

He listened, watching the tropical river and listening to advice about not swimming in it. They said goodbye and he went to his desk, something stirring in the back of his mind as he checked his notes from the USAID briefing. He flipped the ring-bound pages until he found three scribbled words: *Swim? Cercle Sportif.* Alberto had mentioned it. And why the hell not?

He soon found the sports club, nestled in a leafy lane ten minutes' walk from his block. A muscle-bound fellow in a T-shirt offered a tour of Cercle Sportif's rather dilapidated facilities. The weights room was a sight for sore biceps and the bushy privets needed a trim but when he saw the outdoor pool, Frank could only gawp. The water shimmered long and wide; most of the sunloungers were empty; diligent waiters attended women in bikinis; kids leapt from a springboard and a young guy with bulging calves padded past on splayed toes; his tattoo said US *Marine Corps – Semper Fidelis*. Two coltish girls giggled and, best of all, there was not a pastor in sight. Only Satan, sunbathing all alone, tanned and topless.

"I'll enlist," Frank said, and strode back to reception to pay up and sign in.

He undressed in a vintage wooden cabin that had seen better bodies. He lowered himself into the cool pool and swam lazy laps listening to Nancy Sinatra and her famous father crooning from speakers in the palm trees. Then he went and spoiled it all by trying something stupid like a flip turn. Stinging foam shot up his nostrils. He hauled himself out and tottered back to his sunlounger to read his tatty paperback, one eye on *Le Snack Bar*. He was munching a sandwich and parachuting out of a Special Forces chopper with commando Chuck Stern, when his phone rang. He squinted at the screen. Maybe it was Alphonse, with news? Fat chance. It was Claude, with questions. "Hello, Frank, what are you doing?"

He turned another page. "Top secret."

"You want to meet that priest? I'm going over that way, later today."

"No thanks. I'm at Cercle Sportif, relaxing while I can. It's called downtime."

"You should come. Yom is different. I told you. He's a real priest."

"I'll bet."

"He works with street kids. Ten years. We can visit his centre and meet some."

"Has this priest got a nasty ulcer on his leg, by any chance, from all that sorcery?"

"Frank, you're too prejudiced; I thought you said travel broadens the mind?"

"So does reading," Frank said, beginning to wish he had never asked about street kids.

"I'll pick you up at two, OK?"

There was something in Claude's voice and sunburn on Frank's knees. "Two-thirty."

"Two-fifteen. The clock is God, Frank."

At 4 p.m., after a bumpy ride to a dodgy neighbourhood, they parked in a winding alley hardly big enough. Frank watched from the back seat as a sunken-eyed vagrant urinated at a pitted wall; golden droplets bounced onto the man's shoes. A street kid stood inhaling solvents from a plastic bag. Claude pointed to a sign pinned to high black gates.

"There it is. Centre Tosalisa."

"Nice neighbourhood. I'm so glad you brought me."

"*Tosalisa* means *let's help*. That's how we say it in Lingala."

"Fascinating." Frank checked his watch. "How do you say, *Yom is half an hour late?*"

"He'll arrive soon. He's got a problem with his car. "

"Not to mention his clock. God is watching, by the way. Why is he called *Yom?*"

"Short for Guillaume."

"Guillaume means William. Maybe I should call him Liam. *Father Liam*."

"Just call him Yom. He's from Strasbourg, did I tell you?"

"No, but I've been there. Plum tart, Gewürztraminer wine and a weird dialect."

"He speaks good English too. He'll be here soon."

"If he's not, I won't be. I should've stayed at the pool; this is a waste of time."

They sat in silence, windows down. Three inquisitive kids swaggered up. Their cross-eyed leader walked alongside the car, leaned in and screamed at Frank's face, "MONUC!"

Frank recoiled, ears ringing. Claude popped his door and stepped out, "Hey, get lost!"

The kids backed off, but the loudmouth was yapping at Claude and raising his hands to his head, making horns with his fingers. "*Ndoki!*" They turned and ran, whooping. Claude stepped back into the car. Frank watched, tinnitus hissing in his head. "What was all that?"

"*Ndoki* means *witch;* he told me sorcerers live in the Centre and we should leave."

"Oddly enough, I agree," Frank squirmed in his seat. "My back feels like it's on fire."

"Frank, five more minutes, please. I told Yom. He said he would be coming back."

"So did Jesus." Frank shut his eyes, dreaming of cool calamine lotion. "By the way, do you know where I'd really like to go? That stadium where Ali fought George Foreman."

"Boxing? I don't like it. Anyway, we're on the wrong side of town."

"Thanks for being so hospitable. Perhaps some other time." Frank settled himself back in his seat and was soon floating like a butterfly in the African afternoon.

The sound of noisy kids roused him. He opened an eye and saw the same boys badgering a skinny white nerd coming up the alley in his Scoutmaster shorts and a T-shirt with big letters and a hyphen screen-printed across the front: PRAG–. Frank looked closer. PRAG what? A bright yellow Walkman sagged from the nerd's belt. He might as well have worn a placard: *I'm a tourist, mug me.* He approached the jeep, flashing his goofy *where-can-I-buy-postcards* grin and tapped the driver's window. Claude jerked awake and said, "Yom!"

"Sorry to keep you waiting, gentlemen, the Beetle broke down. It's Frank, yes?"

Frank climbed out and shook hands; nerdy Yom had a bouncer's grip and gestured to the gates, which swung open as if by magic. "Shall we? Claude's told me about your work."

"Likewise, Father."

The real priest gave him a real smile. "Just call me *Yom*, if you don't mind?"

He walked ahead and Frank saw, printed on the back of his T-shirt, six big letters precede by a hyphen: –MATISM.

There was just enough space for the letters and, presumably, that was the point. He turned to Claude and pointed. "Cool shirt! PRAG–MATISM. Get it?"

Claude gave him a look as if to say, *five minutes ago you wanted to go home.*

Frank entered the well-swept courtyard and watched a small army of barefoot boys engulf the priest. Yom slapped high fives. "*Mbóte sango ya pokwa?*"

One of the boys yelled back, "*Matondi mingi, tozali malamu. Oye sima,* Yom!"

Claude turned to Frank and offered a translation. "We're fine but you're late."

Centre Tosalisa was more utilitarian than utopian. Four breeze-block huts flanked the yard; an iron pump dripped water into a rusty trough; teenagers sat on steps in sunglasses and bandanas, too cool to fuss, some nursing guitars. Yom said, "Come and see inside."

Frank and Claude followed him into the nearest hut; it contained sturdy bunk beds and benches. Five boys crouched on a concrete floor playing cards under the neon strip light, their dealer as quick as a Vegas veteran. Yom spoke and four of them left, good as gold. Only the smallest stayed, to gawp at Frank. "They love poker," Yom said, "until someone cheats."

"Then what, pistols at dawn?" Frank glanced around. Faded clothes sprouted from plastic bags, one to each bed. A crucifix hung askew on the wall. Yom chuckled.

"Razor blades at midnight, actually. Take a seat. I have no office, sorry."

"Razor blades?" Frank sat on a bench and the small boy squatted at his feet, all smiles.

"They're pretty wild when they arrive," Yom said. "This is a halfway house, a place they can sort themselves out, learn to read and write. If they're under twelve we try to rehabilitate them with their families; but if they're older, it's hard for them to adapt. I have two local staff who sleep over, cook, clean and teach. My religious order pays them." Yom moved to a window, sharing a joke with boys beyond. The kid snuggling at Frank's feet had eyes the colour of conkers and a heart-breaking smile. Frank smiled back. "Are they orphans, Yom?"

"Some, yes. But most are just surplus to requirements. Look at this." He turned from the window, dangling from his fingers a small bundle of rags bound with twine. "Another fetish." He passed it to Frank; the thing resembled a half-finished rag doll. Spooky, though.

Yom sighed. "Seems it came over the wall this morning. Our third this week."

Claude shifted position and said, "You should burn it and let them see."

"But if I do, it means the fetish has power. I'll bin it. Least said, soonest mended."

Frank jerked a thumb towards the street. "The kids who were pestering you earlier, outside? They seemed scared of this place. One told us, *ndoki*. Would they make a fetish?"

The boy at Frank's feet looked worried, and Yom said, "Maybe. Some call this place *Centre des Sorciers*. But, maybe one of ours made it. You never know."

"Do you ask?" Frank said, passing the fetish back.

"They'd never admit, even if I did. Watch this." Yom caressed the head of the boy at Frank's feet. "*Mbóte Kadima. Nazali na motuna ya muke pona yo. Basi bafunda yo ndoki?*"

The boy shook his head and spoke quietly, eyeing the concrete. "*Te Yom, kasi nayebi mutu moko oyo bafunda ete aza ndoki.*" He stood up, hopped on a bench and slithered through the open window. Yom smiled into sunlight, his wispy beard lit like golden moss.

Frank glanced across the room for a translation and Claude said, "Yom asked Kadima if he had ever been accused of sorcery. Kadima told him *of course not, but I know who was.*"

Frank looked at Yom. "And?"

The priest laughed. "Kadima is lying, of course. He arrived six months ago with a broken arm and a black eye, after an exorcism. Anyway, Frank, do you like rumba?"

"Is that a card game?"

"No, it's Congolese music. Want to hear our house band? Self-taught, very good."

"Let's rumba," Frank stood up, but when he took a step, his feet seemed glued to the floor and he had to lunge for the nearest bunk to avoid falling. He looked down; his shoelaces had been tied together. Claude tittered and Yom offered a goofy grin from the doorway. "That's one of their favourite tricks. Sorry, I should've warned you."

Frank looked at the open window. A row of sweet little faces smiled in. *Bienvenue!*

Chapter 36

Frank stood in the yard of Centre Tosalisa, watching the young musicians tune their guitars, tap their drums and practise their vocal harmonies. Some of the lads were short and solid, others tall and skinny; their ages probably ranged from early-to late-twenties. They had no uniform dress code but bags of style, each in their own way. Some sported spotless tracksuits and trainers, others preferred pressed chinos, office shirts and bright ties. One lad appeared to have stepped from a beach in his Hawaiian top and board shorts. The bass player wore his hair shaved up the sides with dreadlocks on top; his head resembled a pineapple. The drummer held up a shard of mirror, carefully tilting his grey homburg hat, just so. What they all had in common, however, was a certain quiet charisma; born cocky. They looked like a team of clever accountants infiltrated by a street gang. He needed a camera. *Stolen; damn.*

"These fellows were my original intake," Yom said, beaming. "They were the reason I started this centre. I used to drive around giving food to street kids at night. But some needed medical help. You see Jo-Jo, wearing the red top? He lived rough for five years; when we met he was half-starved with wounds full of maggots. You see Mamba, in the blue? His uncle scalded him in an exorcism, serious burns. I took them both to a home for abandoned children, where Sister Marceline's nuns patched them up. I lobbied my order in Belgium for funds, built this place. Jo-Jo and Mamba were the first to move in. We would drive around at night looking for kids in trouble. With Jo-Jo and Mamba on board, it was easier for me. Over the years, the others came to live here. They made these instruments, taught themselves how to play, formed this band, Orchestra Tosalisa. They won a talent contest. Most have moved out now, have jobs, live with friends, but they come back to practise and help out. They know about life on the street so they liaise with these younger ones, help them find their feet. Role models, you see?"

"Rock 'n' roll models," Frank suggested. Yom groaned.

The musicians gathered in neat rows on a flight of steps and the young residents sat on the ground to watch. The guitarists started first, fingerpicking fast runs that whirled around the yard like leaves in the wind. The big acoustic bassline came next, plinking and bobbing. Finally, the singers added sweet harmonies on top and Frank could only stare, mesmerised.

"Wow. These guys are good, Yom."

"Told you. They wrote this one themselves, 'Enfant dit Sorcier'. It's about a pastor who accused them of sorcery. The chorus goes, *I'm not a witch, just a kid like any other*. Listen."

Frank listened. It seemed inconceivable that such miserable lives could produce such uplifting music. He watched Jo-Jo in the red top, arms out and head flung back, laughing at the sky, singing of his triumph over adversity as he ducked and preened before his grinning audience. Jo-Jo veered off to the right, spinning like a dervish, punching the air. The song took a left turn and Mamba took centre stage. The audience clapped along; someone whistled. It was small wonder, that music had inspired poets from the dawn of time and that drummers had often led troops into battle. This was more than a band, with more than a song. It was a steam train of emotion at full throttle, sparking tears of passion. Frank's eyes brimmed.

"Yom, seriously, you've done an incredible job. These guys… should be on MTV."

"I could certainly use some PR, to impress my donors. Could you send a journalist?"

"I'll put the word out. My God, they're talented."

Yom turned. "And yet you don't believe in God, only travel, or so I hear."

"Claude's been gossiping. What I meant was, I don't buy some old guy in a white beard."

"You don't believe in Santa? *Le Père Noël?* That's a shame."

"Religion, heaven and hell, miracles, all that… stuff."

"Look around, Frank. Every boy in this centre is a walking miracle. And trust me, they've been through hell outside." Yom stood bobbing to the beat, clapping his hands.

"Sure, but if someone up there was watching over them, they wouldn't have to."

"Someone with a white beard sitting on a cloud, Frank?"

"What do you think? You're the priest."

"I think God is the best we can be."

Frank mulled it over. "I like your theory; pity so many zealots don't practise it."

"It's not my theory. The idea goes way back. You'll find it in Krishna, karma yoga."

God is the best we can be. It was an interesting definition, a good quotation, especially from a Catholic priest. Frank felt something stirring in his veins. A story, maybe.

"Tell you what, Yom. I have a friend in London, subeditor on a big newspaper. He might take a story, from me. But I'd need photos; an interview with you and the lads."

"Which newspaper?"

"*Perspective.*"

"Oh-la-la."

"I'll try my best," Frank said. "But don't tell the Congolese Ministry of Information."

It was almost dusk when he left with Claude in the jeep, bouncing down the alley under an orange sky smeared with translucent clouds of silver and grey like mother of pearl.

"Glad you came, Frank?"

"Top band. Yom even promised to show me the famous boxing stadium."

"Saves me the trip. I told you Yom is decent. My favourite priest, actually."

"Why doesn't he wear a clerical collar?"

"Ask him."

"Maybe I will." Frank tapped his fingers and hummed a catchy tune. *I am not a witch.*

He hopped out at his local supermarket and pushed a trolley down a narrow aisle jammed with cardboard boxes and three staff stacking tins, chatting away, taking their time. He tried to pass. No chance. He turned his trolley around and went the other way.

Shopping was a pain because no items carried price stickers, presumably since inflation made it a waste of time. Instead, each product bore a sticker with a five-digit code that you cross-checked against a price sheet at the end the aisle. Still, at least you could pay in US dollars. He bought tortellini, canned tomatoes and two disposable cameras. The checkout girl scrutinised his cash. "Mister, some of your dollars are *big face,* some are *small face.*"

He emerged lugging plastic bags and a crew of street kids lined up to salute him, *Papa, can we help?* He gave one lad some stuff to carry to the car. Halfway across the crowded pavement the kid froze mid-step, put down the bag and stood erect, hands by his sides. The other pedestrians did the same, as though paralysed by nerve gas. The cars zooming past slowed to a crawl and stopped. Solemn music filled the air and Frank stood watching the national flag of Congo flutter down its pole across the street. He glanced around at the loyal citizens of all shapes and sizes in their smart suits, bright robes and ragged shorts. It seemed bizarre. Only in a country whose leaders had guzzled resources for decades would they feel obliged to pay their daily respects. *Perhaps there really was a nerve gas, called power?* Yes, it was invisible, deadly and reeked of contempt. He spotted a poster on a wall, advertising the demon-busting services of PASTOR ZUHENA, WARRIOR OF GOD. It showed a woman in a cleric's collar, black beret and army fatigues brandishing a crucifix under a halo of yellow fire. She looked bonkers, but no doubt this was the best she could be and she had worked hard along the way. His phone beeped. *Got u a flight, pls. confirm? Al.*

The music stopped, he trotted to the jeep, tipped the helpful street kid and asked a dozing Claude to drop him up the boulevard at an Internet café near his flat. "Asap, please."

"Why at the café? Yossef told me you would have Internet in your flat."

"And new furniture too, right?"

In the Internet place, Frank sat on a wobbly stool and stared at a dusty screen. Alphonse's email detailed an itinerary for MONUC flights to Kisangani, Goma, Bukavu and back. The next email down was a reply – better late than never – from the Congolese rebels.

> *Dear Mr Kean Frank,*
> *Thank you for your recent correspondence by*
> *electronical mail requesting to visit our territory of the*
> *Rassemblement Congolais pour la Démocratie, to train*
> *these journalists.*
> *Too often they lack professional and seek only scandal,*
> *rumour and denigration; too few seek truth, so crucial to*
> *the goals of RCD.*
> *Therefore, I welcome you with cordial and impatience.*
> *Sincerely,*
> *Dr Kimenyi Hitimana, RCD-Goma.*
> *Reply to: rebels2002@yahoo.fr*

He went to the front desk, bought a cold Primus and sipped it eagerly, chuckling to himself until he recalled something Jerome Braddock has told him, that first morning.

They'll have you all right.

Whatever. There was one more task to complete. Frank went back to the computer and wrote to his friend at *Perspective,* offering a photo feature on child witches, so-called.

Dear Saul, long time no beer...

Chapter 37

Silvery sunbeams tickled Dudu's face at dawn. He raised his head from his satchel and squinted across the clanking train at Kilanda, who was perched at the open door with his pistol raised pretending to shoot something outside: *boom!* There was no sign of Bap Bomoy, just chalky scrawl on the steel floor: *Adieu, mes amis!* The elegant handwriting suggested Bap had been accustomed to such tasks, as a schoolteacher. Dudu sat up. "He's gone?"

Kilanda turned and said, "Maybe he jumped into a river, a lesson to us all." The train trundled past glittering water, just yards away, close enough for them to jump in. He pointed his pistol into the distance. "There's Ilebo dock, see? Mouth of the Kasai. It's time you and me split up. I'm taking the first barge downriver." He wrapped his pistol and dagger in a sack.

Dudu stood beside him, looking along the brown river towards hazy, grey Ilebo. The town seemed bigger than Lukamba and would be full of *shegués* ready to slit your throat for a *sucré*. There would be Blue Hats too, big soldiers ready to ask difficult questions about Major Monuc and lock you up. He listened to the faint buzz of trucks and motorbikes. It would be difficult to get by without Kilanda the clever *kadogo*. "*Split up?* What about me?" Dudu said.

Kilanda shrugged and leaned out of the door, watching the track. "You're staying in Ilebo."

"What if the Blue Hats lock me up?"

"Just tell them what happened. I'm the one they're looking for, not you."

"I don't know anyone in Ilebo. I want to come with you."

"I'm faster alone. I helped you enough, already."

"I helped you read the map."

"Keep it."

"You can't just leave me!"

"Says who?"

Dudu sank to his heels and wept for the first time since he had left Mavuku. He listened to the wheels, *clacketty-clack,* taking him to a strange town. He thought about nasty Moses and Pastor Precious, about Mama and Emile. He pictured Ginelle filling her bidon. How had he ended up here? He heard a sharp click and looked into the barrel of a pistol, the one Kilanda was pointing at him. Dudu wiped his eyes. "Are you going to shoot me?" He gazed at the gun and waited for an answer; he did not feel scared, just very tired. Perhaps this long journey, which Nana Kima had predicted on her deathbed, would soon be over and he would he meet her in heaven. Or would he burn in hell? Perhaps Kilanda was planning to kill him, steal his satchel, kick his body off the train. He thought about Tata's bones, scavenged by vultures and bleached by the merciless sun. The train's brakes squealed like a pig. The wagon juddered and rocked, slowing down. He gazed into Kilanda's snake eyes. "What are you going to do?"

"Shoot you in the head, if you don't stop crying like a baby. Grab your bag."

"Can I come with you?"

"You can go to hell, for all I care. And you will, if you slow me down. Got it?"

Dudu nodded. Kilanda dropped from the wagon like a rock off a cliff. Dudu followed.

He trotted alongside the track, his satchel heavy with the pistol and his heart pounding when he saw, among the knots of people carrying bundles and bags along the dock, three soldiers with pale blue berets sitting on their heads like slugs. Kilanda stopped. Dudu offered his battered cap. Kilanda put it on and tugged the peak low. They slipped through the hustle and bustle, straight past the Dirty Blue Hat Bastards who were laughing because MONUC had sold Congo to Rwanda and they had all got rich. Kilanda elbowed Dudu in the ribs and said, "Maybe I won't shoot you, after all." He gave the hat back and Dudu put it on.

Boats bobbed at the quayside; some big, some small. Fishermen laid their stinky nets out to dry. A Congolese soldier stood with a clipboard, checking a pile of cartons on a wooden pallet. People were buying tickets at a kiosk. Kilanda pointed to a moored barge. "There's our ride."

The barge was big; about a hundred metres long and fifty wide. It sat low in the water like a lot of big rusty matchboxes bolted together, end to end. The wheelhouse rose high at the back and passengers were moving around the deck with their baggage, erecting tarpaulin shelters, securing their pigs and goats, filling braziers for the trip. Kilanda pointed to a sign: *Departs: 06.00. Last stop: Bandundu.* Dudu sighed. "Bandundu? That's a long way."

"So stay in Ilebo."

"No, I'll come. But we need to buy tickets."

"Tickets?"

"Otherwise, how do we get on?" Dudu said. Kilanda rolled his eyes and sat on a bollard, watching the barge. Perhaps he did not know the answer. Perhaps he wanted to shoot someone in the head. Dudu watched ants racing to a tiny hole, carrying bits of a dead fly. Some strayed too far from the nest and got lost. "What's Bandundu like?" Dudu said.

"We'll find out in a few days. But we're not buying tickets. We need money for supplies."

"Supplies?" Dudu said, and got a punch in the arm that made him wince.

They walked uptown and Kilanda exchanged some of his stolen dollars for francs, with a jolly lady whose jokes did not make him laugh. He bought two pairs of mirror sunglasses from a man wearing ten pairs on his head, sparkling like a

crown. Next he tried on several caps, telling the stall owner, "Light blue is bad luck." He bought a knapsack, crouched
in the shadows and stuffed his pistols, dagger and clip of AK
bullets inside it. The two raffia mats he bought for sleeping
on reminded Dudu of Nana Kima; she was wrapped in one
just like these, in cold soil. Kilanda bought soap and a plastic
bucket. "Done. Let's eat."

They went to a café and sat chewing goat brochettes and
watching soccer on TV. Kilanda licked his fingers and said,
"Arsenal or Chelsea?" Dudu shrugged, wishing he could be
like this tough *kadogo* with the milky eye and lopsided face
who did whatever he pleased and went wherever he wanted,
like the grey cat that came wandering to their table, tail in
the air.

The cat approached Kilanda for scraps. He chased it. "Get
lost." It circled towards Dudu.

"Get lost," Dudu said, but the cat stayed. At least it was
not a black one.

After they had eaten, they walked back to the dock carrying their supplies. Kilanda chose a spot alongside a white
building with black patches of mildew and a good view of
the barge. They settled on their raffia mats and lay down to
doze and wait, listening to the rumbling of the town and the
lapping of water at the quay.

It was dark when Dudu felt a wiry hand shaking his arm and
heard Kilanda whispering in his ear, "Get up, baby, and follow me."

Chapter 38

The UN's departure lounge in Kinshasa was a Portakabin with maps on the walls. The tiny snack bar offered lukewarm coffee and overpriced cheese rolls in sweaty cling film. Frank stood before a map, plotting today's trip: *Kinshasa to Kisangani, about nine hundred and seventy miles, then Kisangani to Goma, four hundred miles?* Yes, depending on stops and acts of Satan. He shouldered his rucksack and walked outside.

He stood in blinding sunshine, squinting at the other passengers, about fifty in all, some chatting in groups. Two stocky black women crouched beside scuffed suitcases, attaching Red Cross tags. A silver-haired man in a linen suit was frowning at a document in his freckled fist like there would be hell to pay, but not by him. A walkie-talkie crackled, someone gave the nod and Frank walked with the others across tarmac towards a gleaming white jet with UN painted on the side in black letters, six feet deep.

He chose a window seat and they were soon up and away, no fuss, no fixed grins from the cabin crew and no wailing kids. The plane followed the Congo north-east but the river soon vanished below cloud and Frank opened his tatty commando novel.

The plane stopped briefly in Mbandaka, four hundred and fifty miles upcountry. Some passengers got off and new ones got on, taking their time choosing places. The plane rose, banked east to Kisangani and Frank dozed until his ears popped, descending for Simi-Simi Airport.

Things were different in the rebel zone; he sensed it right away, walking down the steps of the aircraft. Even the air seemed heavier, too humid. The airport looked ramshackle, pitted with bullet holes and surrounded by banana trees, like the ruins in the *Jungle Book* cartoon, engulfed by the forest, where the party goes on, no matter what. Sullen-faced soldiers stared from a dented jeep, weapons ready. In the run-down terminal a yawning official flicked through Frank's passport and nudged it to his weasel-faced colleague who peeped in and passed it back. There was no inky stamp, just their indelible gaze of suspicion. "You travel a lot, Mr Kean, so many visas and residence permits. Except the sort we require."

Frank licked a fingertip, turned pages. "Actually, I have a visa. Got it from your embassy in London. Quite a trek, that was too. Just give me a moment and I'll—"

"Our *embassy in London*? How do you mean?"

Frank flipped a few more pages. Should he tell them that Congolese embassy, in swish Belgravia, no longer existed; it was now a building site populated by clueless Cockney navvies? That he had sought advice in a nearby consulate and been sent to what looked like a crack house in suburban Golders Green? How the embassy's front garden was overgrown, the filthy net curtains drooped and the threadbare carpet inside was pitted with cigarette burns? How he had paid over forty pounds on taxis and three hundred and fifty for the visa? Maybe not.

"Here it is, you see?" Frank held open the correct page, for them to see.

"Mr Kean, this visa is for the Democratic Republic of Congo, which means it is not valid here."

Frank gawped across the counter. "Not valid? Why?"

"Because you are now in the territory of the Rally for Congolese Democracy. And it vexes us, considerably, that the so-called *Congolese embassy in London* presumes to issue visas and expects us to accept them. So, we do not."

"Mr Kean," asked the other official, leaning in, "how much

did you give them for this so-called visa?"

"Three hundred and fifty pounds, cash."

They wobbled their heads like wooden ducks in a shooting gallery. Perhaps they expected a bribe? Frank glanced at the adjacent queue. The two Red Cross women were through, no problem. The crabby guy in the linen jacket, too. "Do *they* have visas?" Frank said.

"Mr Kean." It sounded infectious, just as it had, back in Kinshasa, at Min-Info, on the other side of the ideological divide. Frank waited in silence. "Why are you here?"

"I'm on my way to Goma. To train journalists. Sir."

Their eyes lit up as though he had been nabbed rolling barrels of treason and plot under their desk. "To train *journalists*? But do you have our *permission*, Mr Kean?" Frank extracted Dr Hitimana's email from a pocket. They read it avidly, seemed vaguely disappointed. One of them initialled it and handed it back to Frank. They craned their necks at the person behind him. Frank stayed put, fearing the worst. Their sudden indifference suggested he no longer existed. They clearly resented the Kinshasa government making money and stamping pages, but had Dr Hitimana's endorsement cut no mustard? Was there a communication problem, within the RCD?

"You're free to go, Mr Kean. Enjoy your stay."

"What about a visa?"

"Move along, Goma departs soon." The official in the baggy jacket dismissed him with a flick of the hand.

He walked outside and sat on a crumbling wall facing the runway. Two raggedy crows were fighting over a worm beneath an old Sikorsky helicopter that squatted before him like some huge, grey, arthritic grasshopper, its rotor blades drooping and rivets rusty.

A few more passengers emerged from the transit area and stood nearby, one of them perusing her passport in detail, equally puzzled by the look of it. Two pilots in crinkly green jumpsuits ambled towards the helicopter, a pair of sky princes oozing cool. They kicked its tyres and climbed the ladder. The engines were soon whining. A skinny white lad strode across the tarmac next, tall with olive skin but blonde hair and Scandinavian cheekbones. He had a big Canon camera in his hand and a MONUC ID card hanging on a cord around his neck. He nodded at Frank and squatted nearby, lean of limb, plucking a blade of grass to chew. "Immigration on your ass, huh?"

"Something like that," Frank said.

"Just remember the president lives in Kin, rebels live here. *Kabila bad*, RCD *good*."

"Thanks for the tip. Nice camera."

"This? Cost a frickin' fortune. But, in the store, back home, I'm like, *whatever*. Because you would not *believe* how much money I make. Seventy-two thousand dollars a year and I'm, like, twenty-three years old? Bought this too. Take a peep." He offered a shiny white gadget, small and slim. "It's called an iPod. Tons of tunes!" Frank took a peep, but his gaze wandered to the lad's ID photo, in which he looked about twelve.

"Nice," Frank said, giving back the shiny white thing. "What do you do at MONUC?"

"Logistics, upcountry." The youngster nodded at the helicopter. "Seen the piece of shit they gave us for Goma? Same every time and I swear one of those Russian pilots is frickin' tipsy, but I'm like, *whatever*." He offered a firm handshake. "Hey, I'm Matt, but don't ask my second name, you won't be able to say it. I'm half-Brazilian, half-Icelandic. I never saw you up here before. New, huh?"

"This is my first visit. Frank Kean by the way, easy-peasy."

Two white herons sailed overhead, boxy as bombers. Matt stood and raised his camera, twisting at the hips. Frank wondered about the camera, but mostly the salary. "So, Matt, how's MONUC doing? A Congolese friend of mine says it can't stop the war."

"MONUC? Dad got me in, through his college buddy." Matt shaded his eyes. "Sunbird, in the tree, see it?"

They sat in silence for a bit, Frank trying to spot the

sunbird, whatever that was, and Matt wiping his lens with a tiny green cloth, teasing its cap back on with nimble fingers. "Hey Frank, careful here in the east. Things change fast. When are you back in Kin?"

"Six weeks or so. After my seminars. Goma, Bukavu and Kisangani."

"Great. So you'll still be around. We're organising some R & R. Namibia, this time. My boss Alphonse likes seafood."

"I met him in Kinshasa. Sounds a fun trip, but—"

"But what? Quad bikes in the desert. Can't be beat."

Frank raised his left hand, to show his wedding band. "Married, new baby coming. I should get back to the UK."

Matt shrugged. "Bummer. I mean, congratulations."

A pilot in sunglasses leaned from the chopper, beckoning them to board. They climbed up the steps after the other passengers and shunted their bags under webbing tied to karabiners. Frank squeezed into a bucket seat. *Jesus, the noise.* He recalled a ride in a Chinook, swooping low over Croatia on some British Army press jaunt years ago, but he had forgotten this head-splitting, metallic roar. He cupped his hands over his ears; savvy Matt pulled on chunky ear defenders of tough red plastic, poking underneath them white earbuds connected to his shiny white gadget. He sat alongside, grinning. "Say your prayers, Frank!"

The helicopter wobbled upwards. Palm trees vanished under scuffed portholes. The rattling beast tipped sideways to reveal a ring of thatched huts and then lurched level, screaming away to Goma. The woman on Frank's left opened a pristine guidebook about DRC. Frank thumbed his battered novel; crack commando Chuck Stern was trapped in a Russian submarine, and his code name was Dmitri.

Chapter 39

"I'm still half-asleep. Why do I have to come to Richmond Park?" Billie said, from the passenger seat of the Mondeo.

Ruth stopped en route, on Tudor Way. "So you can bond with Aubrey."

"Bond. James Bond," Dylan said, from behind.

"Do I get paid for today as well?" Billie said, with a theatrical yawn.

"No." Ruth stepped from the car and walked to the ATM. An empty Coke can rolled along the pavement, probably dumped by the usual suspects – five teenagers on a low wall, hoods up and heels dangling. They looked increasingly surly these days, as if they had realised there was more to life than Game Boy. She sensed them watching as she withdrew her cash and retreated. Safely back in the car, she noticed one of the lads raising a thumb at Billie, who nodded at him.

"Friends of yours?" Ruth said.

"Not really. But they know Callum, so I suppose—"

"*Hole-in-the-Wall-Gang,*" Dylan said, "that's what Daddy calls them."

Ruth drove into Richmond Park and found an empty spot next to a Land Rover with its bonnet up. Two excited Labradors – one brown, one white –swirled in the back like a pint of Guinness; a whiskered and well-spoken gent in a deerstalker stood alongside the car, arguing with a bored-looking lady in a Hermès headscarf.

Ruth donned a sweater and anorak. Billie hunched against

the breeze in her T-shirt and declined the offer of a fleecy top. Dylan checked his knapsack: torch, compass, binoculars, map and water bottle. "No ice pick?" quipped Billie. Ruth crouched to tie Dylan's boots. "Double bows," he said. Tyres crunched nearby.

Pippa Price slid out of her Range Rover in corduroys and a Barbour jacket, followed by a grinning Aubrey in red gaiters and a cute bonnet with earflaps. They stood side by side surveying the great sweep of sloping land, and Pippa said, "Gosh. Splendid idea, Ruth! Which way?"

Dylan brandished his battered map. "Follow me."

They walked up Dark Hill, through a clutch of sturdy oaks, to the clearing at Corretts Copse. "I brought my camera. Will the deer be rutting?" Pippa asked.

"Only in autumn, when the sap is rising," said Dylan and Ruth winked at him.

"You're regulars, I take it?" Pippa said. Ruth nodded. Billie shook her head.

Civilisation faded fast. They walked single file along a path through snagging bracken, deeper and deeper into one of London's best-kept secrets. Ruth paused to read aloud from a rather weather-worn information placard. "Two and a half thousand acres of wilderness. Acidic grassland. A fragile habitat for six hundred deer, foxes and fungi, it says here. Not to mention creepy crawlies, so let's hope we see some. Oh, it forgot to mention that King Henry VIII came here to hunt." She stood aside for a bobble-hatted jogger.

"Hunt what?" said Pippa.

"Catholics probably," Billie muttered. Ruth let that pass, and the jogger.

They walked uphill, from bracken into damp grass with a nutty smell. Ruth spotted two Purple Hairstreak butterflies in a corkscrew ballet. Dylan pointed out a parasol mushroom, six inches tall, creamy white. "Look! Poisonous, Daddy says."

"And how is Daddy?" Pippa said, turning to Ruth.

"Riding around Congo in a helicopter." Ruth updated her as best she could, eyeing the sky. She nudged her son. "Kestrel, Dylan, over there. Remember how she finds food?"

They watched the hovering hawk. "Yup. X-ray eyes. Grabs it with her sharp talents."

Aubrey looked puzzled, so Ruth explained. "A hawk like that can see ultraviolet light in the pee of a mouse. The fresher the better, like a map, criss-crossing a field. She tracks the brightest light, spots the mouse and dives: *gotcha!*" The kestrel flew off and Aubrey frowned. "But, how do you know, Mrs Kean?"

"They interviewed one on Animal Planet," said Billie. Aubrey laughed and trotted to her side. Ruth hung back with Pippa, who said, "Bonding! So far so good!"

At Spankers Hill Wood they turned left for Leg-of-Mutton Pond and stopped to inspect a blackened tree, scorched by lightning. Ruth poured milky coffee from her bashed-up Thermos. The kids sucked on cartons of pear juice. Dylan wiped his mouth on his sleeve and Ruth passed him a paper napkin, good quality, super absorbent with a floral motif. Cost a bit too; IKEA, top of the range. Dylan took it and said to Aubrey, "We don't usually bring these ones."

They walked on, Billie marshalling the two kids. The sight of the three of them holding hands put a spring in Ruth's step. *Soon, I'll have three of my own.*

"So how did you meet Frank?" Pippa asked, as if reading her state of mind.

"I was a single parent," Ruth said, "working for a dentist in London, mid-'90s. Billie and I had moved up from Wales; she was about ten. We stumbled across an anti-Thatcher demo in Trafalgar Square and this radio journalist starts chatting me up. A week later, he's sitting in the dental surgery, telling me the unions have no chance. He was right, but he wasn't really a journalist. He was a trainer, heading off to Hungary, back soon. I fell for it, like a silly bugger. Story of my life ever since."

"Quite romantic, actually. You seem to cope well with the separation."

"Absence makes the cash grow bigger. How do you cope with China?"

Pippa seemed bemused. "Well, if they would devalue their currency…"

"I mean your *husband* in China. At least, that's what Aubrey told Dylan."

"Ah, *Daddy* is quite the slippery slope. Let's leave it at that. Which way?"

They plodded up to King Henry's Mound and, waiting behind other walkers to peep through a gap in a holly hedge at St Paul's Cathedral ten miles east, Ruth found herself wondering why Pippa was so cagey about Mr Price. *Are they heading for a divorce?* Wren's famous white dome sat in the distance like half a peeled onion. Ruth pointed at the gap. "Protected view, this, since 1710. Your turn, go on."

Pippa stood peering through the hedge. "Frightfully competent, aren't you?"

"Not really. I just like to walk; it blows away the cobwebs, clears the mind."

"Indeed. I prefer the City from a distance!" Pippa turned, grinning, and Ruth grinned too. *Perhaps we'll be mates after all.* Aubrey stood tugging hard on her arm, head back and mouth open like a chick expecting a worm. "Mrs Kean, where next?"

Dylan checked his trusty map. "That way, south-east. Lunch in half an hour."

"Aye aye, sir." Billie led the way, shoulders hunched, pale as a ghost.

They walked in silence until Ruth noticed a butterfly settling on Aubrey's coat, its wings dusty red-gold with dark tips. "Wow. This is an Essex Skipper."

"I could pin it to my cork-board," whispered Aubrey,

wide-eyed.

Ruth shook her head. "Best not. They're quite rare." The butterfly spiralled away, as if sensing danger and Pippa said, "Beautiful. I do so adore the countryside."

"Did you grow up in a town?" Ruth climbed carefully over a fallen tree trunk.

"Not quite," Pippa said. "I was more of a Berkshire *gel*. Boarding school then off to the LSE, where I somehow scraped a third; friend of Daddy's placed me in a merchant bank, mainly to fetch the cappuccinos; dogsbody in a nice frock, you might say. I worked my way up, noticed the glass ceiling and *woke* up. I branched out, got my MBA and now I'm a consultant to the same arrogant oiks who used to say, *Pips darlin' where's me bladdy mocha?* I make pots more these days. Money, that is."

She was hitting her stride, braying like Lady Muck, about *risk management*. Ruth tried to keep up but after ten minutes of *credit risk* and *market risk, volatility, Basel Accords, liquidity* and the *hedgehog irrelevance proposition*, she declared herself lost, up the creek without a pension. "*Hedging*," tittered Pippa, "as in fund."

A big Doberman bounced from bracken, a black and bony silhouette, sniffing and grinning, darting left and right. Its owner – a stubble-jawed man in a camouflage jacket – gave Pippa a hungry look and clicked his teeth.

Half an hour later, Dylan called a halt for lunch. Ruth unpacked foil-wrapped cheese and watercress sandwiches, boxes of beetroot and cranberry salad, chilli chips, biscuits, bananas, more coffee and juice. Pippa contributed a tube of Smarties, which proved equally popular. Replenished, they strolled down the lush pasture of Flying Field. The deer – conspicuous by their absence so far – would be up ahead.

Aubrey took Ruth's hand. "Mrs Kean, do you know any more jokes?"

"Well, I once met a monkey in the jungle. He was holding a banana and a can opener. So I said, *you don't need that to peel a banana.* The monkey replied, *it's for my tin of custard.*" Aubrey shrieked in delight and ran to tell Dylan, who did not.

"I like your Welsh lilt, Ruth," Pippa said. "Coal mines and sooty valleys?"

"No, I'm from the coast," Ruth replied breezily, but the question snagged like a loose stitch – pull it and everything would unravel. "Actually, I went to boarding school, like you. We were quite well off from Dad's furniture business. But I was allowed only one phone call per week. Talk about deprivation! No wonder I played up. One time, a gang of us put boot polish on the door handles; April Fool."

"Good stuff!" said Pippa and they chuckled along, swapping dormitory japes. But Ruth's mood soon darkened. *If we're here to bond, Pippa might as well hear some bad stuff. Perhaps she'll open up a bit more, too?*

"Dad had this car, a big shiny Jag," Ruth said. "He liked driving to the races, having a flutter; liked a drink, too, so Mum would drive back. The Jag broke down on their way home from Kempton. Mum parked on the hard shoulder and stepped into the path of a bus; died on the spot. After the funeral Dad went on a bender, first of many. Took me out of boarding school; too costly with the business sliding. He would get rat-arsed and tell me it was all his fault. As if I didn't bloody know."

"Good God."

"We'll get to Him later. Anyway, my state school felt more like Mars, and all that booze at home made it easy to make the wrong friends. I went from jolly hockey sticks to juvenile delinquent in six months. One of Dad's delivery men knocked me up on a pint of snakebite. Dad fetched a shotgun and I left home at seventeen."

"Billie's father is a *delivery man?*"

Ruth straddled a wooden stile. "No, I had an abortion, God forgive me. Then I spent two years on the dole, surfing in Swansea, drinking the Mumbles Mile. Slept on the beach at lot. Moved to Cardiff eventually, crashing on sofas until I got myself sorted."

"Is that where you met…?"

"Eventually, yes. I was pulling pints in a jazz pub and wearing a low-cut top, because tits means tips. Some horny dentist asks me to be his receptionist and the next thing I know, I'm studying to be a dental nurse, three days a week. Kept up the bar work, mind; tidy money and I liked the craic. That's where I met Max Estephane."

"Exotic name," said Pippa. Ruth nodded and put a finger to her lips. She pointed to a clearing; a dozen red deer were sitting low in the grass, almost invisible, spiky antlers in a row, like leafless bushes. Dylan and Aubrey had spotted them too and trotted ahead. A beautiful fallow buck rose from nearby, head down and chewing, its rear end towards the children. "Careful, Dylan, not too close," Ruth said. She glanced at Billie who was texting on her phone, bored shitless probably.

Ruth leaned against an oak for a breather. She gazed up through dark green foliage, watching fluffy clouds soar over. The dappling light flashed like a strobe and made her woozy. The sun shimmered like a giant orange, inching towards the fuzzy horizon, the west of England, with Wales beyond, where her crazy years had been and gone, up in smoke. Pippa lit a Dunhill and folded her arms, puffing away.

"So, Billie's father? Good-looking I'd expect, judging by Billie's bones. I do love her coppery skin. Max Estephane was black, one assumes?"

Ruth nodded. "His family was from St Lucia originally; he looked like Sidney Poitier; six foot three. Great dancer too, debonair like Fred Astaire."

"Gosh, lucky you."

Ruth winked, accentuating the positive while she could. "Max grew up in Bristol, bit of a drifter who loved music. The band he was managing came to play The Treble Clef, where I worked, and went down a storm; not your usual jazz buffs in black berets. They wore American retro and had real tunes, jive and rockabilly. We'd shove the tables back for a bop. Do you like jive, Pippa?" Ruth wondered if her posh new friend would invite her to Covent Garden, some sparkly evening.

"Gracious, no. Opera usually. Jazz less so, but I'm partial to *Kind of Blue*."

"*Modal yodel*, Max called that. I can't remember why. Where was I?"

"Falling in love."

"Too right. The band got a regular slot, ram-jam every week. They would drive over from Bristol in this old Cadillac with their name on the side: Soda Pop."

"Clever marketing! I like it. So when did you capitalise on your assets?"

"After the greedy landlord increased his door price on the sly. Max found out, demanded a higher cut and all hell broke loose. I'm behind the bar in my peroxide curls and Wonderbra, polishing glasses and I yell, *split the difference!* So, they did."

"Excellent intervention!" Pippa exhaled smoke, coughing enthusiasm. "The band realised low risk meant low returns and they should try not to cap their upside, while securing a guaranteed portion. It's known as a limited downside, flexible upside strategy. Third party brokered a decent deal. This means you, Ruth."

"Really? Perhaps that's why Max invited me out." She glanced at Dylan and Aubrey crouching in the grass to watch the fallow buck graze ten metres away. Most of the herd sat motionless as if posing for an oil painting but now and then a head would slowly rotate, antlers like radar, checking. "Careful, kids!" Ruth said.

Pippa took a small camera from her Barbour jacket. "Don't worry. Deer are shy. They'll run away, which means I should snap that pretty picture while I can."

"Actually, Pippa, they can be quite territorial."

"And where was your first date, with the handsome Mr Estephane?"

Ruth chuckled at the memory. "We went to a Bristol warehouse full of Americana, bowling shirts and Levi's. That stuff was gold dust back then. Max bought me two pair of 501s. Soon I was taking orders for my mates and when Soda Pop split, I told Max to try the rag trade; buy in Bristol, sell in Wales. Why not? Six months later, we had our first shop, Soda Pop. That was my idea too. We got rich. And got married in Vegas by a preacher dressed as Elvis. Cost six hundred dollars."

Ruth's smile soon cracked, because she could not hide her feelings like a poker player or a politician; she pasted them on the billboard of her face, for the world to see. Pippa stubbed the Dunhill underfoot. "So what went wrong?"

"Everything. We grew too fast – four shops in two years. I gave up my dental studies, to be a roving manager. We got a cheap mortgage on a big old house, started doing it up. I got pregnant. Next thing I know, Max meets some out-of-work chef and wants to open an American diner – Soda Pop Bar – with chrome stools and a bloody Pontiac coming out of the wall; we made a mint on burgers and apple pie. Ask Billie, she remembers, just. But success spoiled things. Well, spoiled Max."

"How so?" Pippa moved away to click her pretty kid. "Photo, Aubs?"

Ruth followed. "Well, there I am, a multitasking mum while Max is out having fun and meeting cocky DJs with big ideas and empty pockets. We're talking 1988, Summer of Love; he's promoting raves, making money and popping pills. In 1990 we go to Glastonbury. I take Billie to watch Punch and Judy. We come back to our tent and Max is high as a kite, shagging my best friend. That's when I realised."

"Realised what?" said Pippa, snapping Aubrey and the herd of deer.

"You can't change strong people, especially when they're weak. I moved out of the house. Billie was five and old enough to notice Max sinking. I'd seen my dad on binges as a kid and didn't want her going through that, as well as a divorce."

"Mummy, look!" Dylan called from the knee-deep bracken. He was edging towards a young deer near the big buck and Ruth called out, "Stop there, Dyl."

"Gosh, a little one!" Pippa said. "Move closer, Aubs, a snap for Mummy?"

"Bad idea," Ruth added. "A startled stag is dangerous. Dylan, back, now!"

Pippa strode on, camera ready. "Forward Aubs, don't worry, they're shy."

"Pippa, I'm not sure—" Ruth broke off, as Aubrey stomped forward, cracking bracken. The young deer bolted. The big stag shuddered and raised its head, nostrils flared, silken neck bristling, brown eyes like pools of mud. The spiky antlers dipped, sweeping through air just metres from the two children. The strong legs quivered and flexed, ready, and Ruth said, "Oh, God. Dylan, walk away! Now!"

The deer charged, leaping sideways, high and mighty, tossing its head. Dylan toppled back, landing with a crunch. Aubrey squealed and the camera clicked.

"Perfect!" said Pippa. "I got it, mid-dash."

Ruth ran to Dylan's side, hauled him up and brushed him down, her heart pounding as she pulled grass from his hair. His face was drained of colour. The deer trotted away but turned to survey them, perfect as a picture postcard. Pippa clicked again. Billie was still texting, oblivious. Ruth hugged her son, "Are you OK, love?"

Dylan nodded but his blue eyes were glazed with tears. "It jumped at us!"

"Because you scared it, Dyl. This is their home, not ours." She spared him the gory talk of losing an eye or having his belly punctured by antlers. She looked to the crest of the hill. The stag's jagged crown forked into blue sky. The deer trotted off.

"And after you left Max?" Pippa said, but Ruth ignored her and led Dylan away.

She had let her guard down, been sidetracked by ancient strife. She felt a kick in her belly, a warning from her unborn baby that the future was more important. Next she felt a surge of resentment – *Max, leave us alone please.* The wind was up and Dylan was shivering. She yanked his fleece from his knapsack. "Put this on."

Aubrey approached, ruddy-faced. "Did you see that deer jump, Mrs Kean?"

"Yes, Aubrey. But remember, it's a wild animal; not cute like Bambi."

"Indeed," said Pippa. "The real thing is far more… majestic, somehow."

Ruth stared. How could a *Berkshire gel* be so blind to danger in the countryside? She let Pippa go ahead to chat with Aubrey, the pair of them gushing like greenhorns. Dylan still seemed pale and dazed, almost in shock. Ruth took his hand and pointed to a rare Double Line moth, which raised his spirits. They walked on and Billie caught up, beaming. "Cal's dad might lend us his van for Glasto!"

"Some childminder you are." Ruth trudged down the path towards Robin Hood gate, watching long-legged Pippa yapping to Aubrey a few yards in front. Ruth's gaze burrowed into the back of that clever head, trying to fathom the contents.

Maybe Pippa's job was not so much to manage risk as to exploit it for her own gain? She didn't really *avoid* risk at all; she *thrived* on it, *enjoyed* it and got rich in the meantime? Her private life too, it seemed – the risk of a new home far from her office; of marriage to an absent and slippery husband; of parking her kid with a family she hardly knew; of *one more photo*. In some ways she seemed oblivious to risk, or at least the sort that could hurt a child. Awkward questions flooded Ruth's head: *is Pippa one of life's gamblers, just like my dad? If so, does she ever lose?*

Pippa turned, all smiles. "I hope we didn't overdo it, you being preggers."

"I'm not sick," Ruth replied. "I'm having a baby. Fresh air will do us good."

They walked the last hundred yards together through

ancient oaks, down Dark Hill to the car park. "And so, Ruth, what happened after you left Max?" Pippa seemed keen for a grand finale, the flip side of the upside-downside flexible how's-your-father. Ruth fumbled in her pocket, tossed the car keys to Dylan and told him to run on. He scooted off with Aubrey in pursuit. Billie was shuffling after them, talking into her phone and hunched like a crone, the heels of her baseball boots all muddy. When Ruth finally replied to Pippa's question, her voice cracked.

"What happened, is that Billie found her dad hanging by a rope, covered in snow, with a blue tongue, when she was seven years old. Can we leave it at that?"

Pippa gawped, linked arms like a best friend and Ruth tried not to cry.

Chapter 40

Frank loosened his safety belt and twisted around to peep through the helicopter's porthole at the rainforest a few thousand feet below. He glimpsed tiny clearings and wisps of smoke. Forest stretched to the horizon like broccoli. Matt yelled from the next porthole along, "Congo Basin, Frank, one and a half million squares miles!"

The river wound across it, draining rainfall and meltwater from the heart of Africa, a sucking, slumbering snake, oozy and brown, drunk on nutrients. Frank was getting a crick in his neck and turned back. The woman to his left was still reading a DRC guidebook. Frank cocked an eye at the open page like a cheat in a high school exam, and read:

> **Size:** *World's 2nd largest river by volume. 3000 miles of navigable waterway punctuated by ferocious cataracts.* EG. *Gates of Hell – a foaming chasm 75 miles long. Power: Livingstone Falls boasts as much hydroelectric potential as all* USA's *rivers combined.*

So, Africa was full of potential, as if we didn't know. The woman with the book glanced at Frank. He looked at the luggage under the net on the floor. Only an hour to go.

Eventually, the tone of the engine changed and the Sikorsky dipped to reveal a silky Lake Kivu below. Mud shacks clustered like mushrooms on the hilltops. The city of Goma appeared to be partially smothered under fresh black tarmac but as the pilot flew lower, its pitted surface suggested an ogre had emptied a giant bucket of cinders on the hapless place. Matt pointed at a volcano in the distance. "Mount Nyiragongo! She blew a few months back, lava reached downtown! You'll see where it stopped, a high wall of it, two metres deep!"

Frank angled himself for a better view. The volcano looked Disney-cute; high, steep and harmless. Not dangerous and deadly. "Saw it on the TV!" he yelled back. "Bad news!"

Matt nodded. "Forty-five dead, four hundred thousand displaced! The lava ran a thousand metres wide!"

The chopper banked and Frank glimpsed hundreds of plastic sheets flapping like bluebirds across the extraterrestrial landscape, courtesy of the UN. Matt pointed, dipping his head at the sunlit porthole. Frank noticed hairs on his chin, pale and fluffy, childlike.

"UN stood and watched the Rwanda genocide, Frank! Because we had no real mandate! But when the killers escaped across the border into Goma, we raised a million dollars per day to help build their camps and protect them from cholera! How frickin' insane is that?!"

Twenty feet from touchdown, Frank saw barefoot kids scurrying up, to lean into the rushing downdraft. They lurched like zombies on the flattened grass, shut their eyes tight and spread their arms like skydivers; it looked like fun and they probably deserved to have some. Frank extricated his rucksack from the pile under the webbing and followed the other passengers down the helicopter's steps. The engines wheezed farewell, a pilot raised a thumb.

The officials at the RCD office in Goma seemed friendlier than their colleagues back in Kisangani; even the tough-looking security guy in a leather coat gave Frank a nod. An affable fellow in a dogtooth sports jacket peeped in Frank's passport. He did not ask why Mr Kean was here. He handed it back. "Good luck with your seminar." He already knew.

Matt vanished into a UN jeep and Frank straddled the back of a bumpy motorbike into town, getting a better look at what was probably the strangest place he had ever been. Goma resembled something out of a sci-fi movie, a frontier settlement on a new planet of petrified lava punctured by the roofs of submerged buildings. Half-melted cars lay upside down, frozen in rock. The street level rose and fell, depending how the lava had cooled. People scuttled about like ants busy rebuilding a damaged nest. Kids pushed bulging sacks on huge bicycles made entirely of wood, even the wheels. Elderly men sat hunched beside old photocopiers, behind typewriters or wonky-looking scales. They offered to print, write, weigh whatever you wanted; anything to eke a living. It seemed that, despite horrendous odds, this town had refused to roll over and fry. It was more than three months since the eruption but a dusty haze hung still, coating Frank's throat and nostrils. The motorbike bumped, wobbling.

Frank's skilful driver wove through the traffic and pointed a wizened finger, yelling back over his shoulder, "My house was there, see? We had to leave. The lava stopped fifty metres away! I watched our bricks explode, *pouff!* I will build a new home, but not here!"

They left the busy streets and bounced up a quieter lane overlooking Lake Kivu, to a small hotel *much appreciated among foreign visitors,* according to the driver. Frank climbed off the pillion seat and opened his wallet. The driver shook his head. "Blue money not good."

"What do you mean, *not good?*"

"Blue money is from Kinshasa. Here we use red money, like this. Everybody." He pulled a wad of mucky scarlet banknotes from his denim shorts. Every note was fifty francs; tattered, torn, ancient. There were no blue one hundred franc notes. Frank offered crisp US dollars. "How about green?"

The driver smiled. *That'll do nicely.*

The hotel was small but swish. Frank stood in the lobby, musing on the sudden change in his surroundings – he had stepped from scenes of Biblical devastation into a brochure for the Côte d'Azur. He was given a room with a view and flopped into a wicker chair on a terrace to rest his bones after the juddering motorbike ride and three hours in a screaming bucket, his ears still ringing from the Sikorsky symphony. He sipped a chilled Pepsi from the minibar and spent ten minutes watching stick men paddle dugout canoes across vast, limpid water. A cormorant sat preening itself on a rock, its silhouette an oily question mark. Time for a swim? Frank unpacked his rucksack and tugged on his swimming shorts, lowered himself over the low balcony and slithered down mossy steps into warm water; it had a faint aroma of... eggs? He swam out a bit, nice and easy, turning to observe the hotel, get his bearings. He spotted a bald, obese white fellow in a Hawaiian shirt sitting among the rocks, browsing a book. Frank nodded *hello*. The man closed his book and yelled.

"Hey there, buddy, yew sure that's a good idea?"

His accent was Texan, perhaps, and broad as a cowboy's shoulders. Frank replied, short of breath. "You should... try it!" But something was wrong; his body felt heavier by the second, his heart pounding, some invisible force pulling him from below despite his best efforts to stay afloat. He tried harder, gasping and splashing. *Jesus, is this a heart attack?*

The fat man grinned from his perch in the rocks. "Now you're feeling it, ah reckun?"

Frank swam with lunging strokes for the mossy steps; the water seemed as thick as molasses. He climbed out, eyes stinging and chest heaving. *What the hell was that about?* The friendly stranger waddled through the rocks, book tucked underarm, and said, "Me, ah don't *never* swim in there; too much methane. Yew are in *volcano* country. And that's a fact."

Frank glared at the lake, far and wide. *Methane?* No wonder it smelled of eggs. "Thanks for the tip. Thought I was having some kind of seizure. You staying in the hotel?"

"I own it. You're in room six. Ah don't suppose yew play backgammon?"

They dined together two hours later on the main terrace. The manager's name was Marc; a Belgian, go figure. He recommended a local fixer, Cedric. He also recommended his hotel's conference room for Frank's seminar. They played backgammon over coffee and he recommended that Frank should never use an opening 4-1 with a 13-8. "Else you'll drift into untenable poe-sitions, like now." He swept pieces from the board. "I win. You lose. Another game, champ?"

"Why not?" said Frank, and asked about the peace talks. "Will they help, Marc?"

"Yew gotta be kidding me."

Frank asked about that Texas accent.

"Well, ah spent twelve months in Austin," said Marc, pronouncing it *Ow-steen*.

"You mean twelve *years?*" said Frank. Marc shook his head. *Months.* That was a fact.

In the Gospel According to Marc, the manager had seen it, been it and done it. He had watched a teenage Stevie Ray Vaughan play at Antone's blues club on 6th Street; he had bred St Bernard dogs in the Austrian Alps; fought as a mercenary in Bosnia. Frank listened as the night grew long and the tales grew tall. He watched Marc's pieces fly and said, "Wow." He did not say that Marc reminded him of his driving instructor, back home in Gripturn. Frank had been sixteen and his instructor, Norman, that anaemic beanpole with a comb-over, had been a retired test driver for Formula 1 and an ex-member of the SAS. The memory lingered. There was something about driving instructors. There was something about Marc.

They sipped cognac at midnight, on the house. Eventually, Frank checked his watch and said, "Yikes, time to hit the hay." He was back in room number six before Marc could *il-lu-minate* him further about his lonesome years ropin' mustangs on the wild *prair-ie*.

Chapter 41

How did Kilanda get so smart? Dudu sat at the back of the barge watching the water ripple a V-shape. The sun rose and Ilebo shrank to a hazy blur in white fog; the black cranes on the dockside looked like burnt matchsticks. *Perhaps the* Mai-Mai *taught him?*

Kilanda nudged his elbow. "Let's explore this dump."

Dudu followed the clever *kadogo* along the edge of the barge towards the main deck. There was no guardrail and most of the passengers seemed as sure-footed as goats, strolling about, squeezing through gaps. The barge had become a floating village crammed with families and animals, trucks and timber. The mud-coloured river flowed straight to the horizon and, on the distant bank, woodsmoke curled in wisps above a village. Children perched in trees and waved. Some were too busy carrying yellow bidons, just like in Mavuku.

Kilanda showed his map to a man in a singlet sitting in a wicker chair. "Hey mister, it's two hundred and fifty miles to Bandundu, how long will that take?"

The man squinted at the map. "Two weeks, unless we hit a sandbank. But Captain Clemens is clever and *Romleon* is a strong boat. Good map, son. You got this from MONUC."

Kilanda quickly folded it away. "Mind your own business."

They walked on, worming down the crowded deck until they spotted a fellow approaching, checking people's tickets. Kilanda pulled Dudu under a sagging shelter and pretended to help a woman struggling to secure it. They tugged her sheet of tarpaulin over a bamboo frame. "Perfect," she said, "this will keep out the rain!" They walked on and Kilanda muttered, "That's what she thinks."

Dudu paused to look at pigs and goats, tied up. Kilanda pointed. "Tasty brochettes!" "Do you know about Noah?" Dudu said. "Noah filled a ship with animals."

"Never mind them," said Kilanda, pointing. "There's the captain. On the bridge."

A handsome fellow in a white shirt was leaning from the wheelhouse to watch the water. He wore binoculars and was calling to other men who stood plunging long wooden poles, painted blue and white, straight down into the water from the edge of the barge. After pulling the poles up, they shouted up to the captain to tell him how deep the water was. Theirs seemed an important job; Dudu imagined himself doing it and the captain saying later, on the bridge, *Good work, Dudu, now take my binoculars and steer the barge; I need rest.*

The stink of bushmeat distracted Dudu and he turned to watch an old lady in a headscarf, who was roasting a monkey on a brazier, scraping the fur with a knife. Another monkey sat tied up, its white face as round as a clock, the pale brown eyes watching. Kilanda crouched nearby and said, "You're next, my friend." The monkey snarled, baring sharp fangs; it seemed to understand. Dudu considered this a cruel joke from his *kadogo* companion.

They moved on, stepping around a man fixing a radio, and another who was making a chessboard from a piece of card, carefully inking the black squares with a marker pen, watched by a tiny boy who pointed and said, *you missed one, Tata.* A woman sat braiding a young girl's hair in bright ribbons; a fat puppy chewed its leash and a man in a black hat stood with an anxious regard, clutching a big old Bible.

"I'm your pastor," he said to Dudu, with a wrinkly smile. "Will you join us to pray for a safe journey?" The pastor looked disappointed when Dudu shook his head and edged past.

A little pirogue came floating towards the barge and the wiry fellow paddling it shouted to Kilanda and threw a tattered rope. Kilanda tied the rope to a post; it tightened and the pirogue swung alongside. Dudu spotted woven baskets inside, full of food – smoked fish and *kwanga,* bananas and mangoes; Kilanda greeted the man, waving stolen money. "Me first!"

They ate a fine breakfast while watching the river, and Dudu asked, "Did they give you good food in the *Mai-Mai?*" Kilanda chewed a chunk of smoked fish and shook his head. "The only decent meal I got was at my initiation. The rest of the time it was bugs and *boma.* I ate so many of those snakes, someone told me I *looked* like one. Do I look like a snake?"

"A bit." Dudu spat a fish bone into the swirling water. Kilanda laughed and sat back, telling stories from his militia days. He sat gesturing, making faces, repeating the best bits. "Now a question, Dudu: if your commander says to chop a fellow up, where do you start?"

Dudu shrugged and Kilanda said, "You start with their feet, otherwise they kick you."

"Pastor Precious got kicked when Cyril poured hot water on Emile's leg."

"Anyway, for my initiation, the *Mai-Mai* took me into the forest. They wore pointed hats made from shells and leopard skin. I was naked. They placed a machete blade flat on my chest and hit it with a bamboo stick, four or five times. They rubbed water on me, lit a fire and danced about, singing, '*Mai! Mai! Lumumba! You are invincible! You are Mai-Mai, summoned by our ancestors to save our country!*' Afterwards, we cooked a whole goat and drank banana beer. That was it. We smoked some stuff and I was ready for the front line."

"Did they cut your finger? Mix your blood and say, *now we are brothers?*"

Kilanda bit into a mango, its juice dribbling. "No. I saw that on TV. Crocodile!"

Dudu spun round. The crocodile was lazing on the river-bank, grey and still like a dead tree. The hippos were easier to

257

spot, bobbing past in the water with snouts all pink and brown, but Dudu got bored of counting them and went for another walk around the barge, hunting for something to carve with Tata's penknife. He found three bits of wood and settled in a corner, remembering Tata's advice: *Don't just look at the wood, Dudu, listen to it.* The wood was soft, the blade was sharp and soon he had carved a collection of animals, like Noah's. The hippo looked OK but his crocodile resembled a canoe. He dropped them in his satchel and noticed a worried-looking fellow watching, as if the little crocodile might bite.

The barge moored before dark. "Because night navigation is treacherous," Kilanda said. They slept on their raffia mats, swatting bugs and listening to a monkey shriek in the bush. They heard the splashes of butterfly fish, killifish and goliath fish jumping for insects.

At dawn, rain tinkled from black clouds that blocked the sun; the air seemed sticky and hard to breathe; it pressed on Dudu's chest like a shirt that was too tight. Soon, the sky flashed and cracked and rain hammered down until the deck boomed like a thousand drums.

Dudu noticed how the tied-up animals reacted in different ways to the storm. The goats bleated and hopped but the mottled pig stood quietly watching, as rain cascaded from the tip of its snout like water from a jug. The rain swamped the tarpaulin canopies and soaked the people beneath. Kilanda wore his plastic bucket tipped back on his head like a hat; he stood there laughing at them. "I knew it!" But he did not know where to find a second bucket.

Most passengers seemed to realise it was pointless trying to stay dry and emerged from their wet shelters to continue with their chores. Women filled steel tubs with rainwater and scrubbed their laundry, elbows deep in frothy bubbles.

Giggling men stripped down to their underpants; they soaped up and wandered about like demons who had strayed from the forest; tiny kids crept from hiding places to stand open-mouthed under the roaring sky.

The storm lasted most of the day and night, stopping and starting again; it ended with a final flicker of lightning twenty-four hours later. The sun peeped pink through pale grey clouds, as though checking if it was safe to rise and, when it did, Dudu and Kilanda climbed onto a dripping ledge and looked down the barge at a long, glistening jumble of tarpaulin, bedraggled animals, bamboo poles, and passengers putting their lives back in order.

Two days of sunshine followed, brightening everyone's spirits until they spotted a huge barge stranded on a sandbank. This bigger barge was laden with dozens of huge tree trunks, thirty metres long, three metres wide and sawn at the ends; they were stacked three deep and worried-looking people peered out, like rats in holes, from the gaps between them. Captain Clemens leaned out of his wheelhouse window, looking through his binoculars. He blasted his horn and the *Romleon* changed course, drifting closer.

A man in a blue hat leaned from wheelhouse of the stranded barge. He had a little grey beard and shouted anxiously, "I've been stuck here two weeks! Supplies are low! It's a scandal, my friend, these channels were not dredged for years; where does my river tax go?"

Captain Clemens shouted encouragement as the *Romleon* nudged alongside, trying to dislodge the other barge from the sandbank. The men with long sticks yelled advice and passengers leaned from the edge to watch. After an hour of roaring engines, black smoke and churning water, Captain Clemens yelled, "I'm using too much fuel! Good luck, my friend!"

The *Romleon* sailed away and soon the big stranded barge looked like a little toy in the distance; its gigantic logs resembled pencils and a toothless old man standing beside Dudu at the rail said in a loud, mournful voice, "This river eats its children."

The sad-eyed pastor was standing nearby. "We'll ask God to send angels to their rescue."

"You should ask President Kabila to dredge the river," the old man said. The pastor ignored him and turned to Dudu and Kilanda. "You boys will join my prayer service."

Dudu shook his head and Kilanda said, "*Longwa kuna.*"

The pastor looked shocked and scuttled away. The old man gave Kilanda a gummy grin but some of other passengers were murmuring and gesturing at Kilanda with long faces. Dudu took him aside. "Did you just tell him, *go to hell?* That wasn't smart, *kadogo.*"

Kilanda flicked a finger in Dudu's ear. "If I want advice, I'll ask. You stink, by the way."

They were washing their T-shirts in Kilanda's plastic bucket when they heard men singing, but not from the pastor's prayer service. The songs came from militia in a rubber dinghy, cruising up the river. One soldier was clutching the scarlet cone of a small missile, like a microphone. He stood erect singing, *Hold tight, we will die for our Congo!* He looked about fifteen. Some of the barge passengers cheered but Dudu just watched, thinking about the militia who took Tata into the bush. Kilanda seemed uneasy. "That was our song, once."

Late afternoon, Captain Clemens stopped the barge at Kota, a riverside village of muddy paths and market stalls. Dudu went with Kilanda and some others for supplies. They stopped at a table stacked with watermelons, sliced open, red and juicy. "Wow," Dudu said.

Kilanda beckoned him. "Never mind those. Come and see this."

They walked to a wretched-looking man kneeling bare-chested, his hands in the air, pleading for mercy. The young soldiers from the dinghy stood in a half circle around him. "Yes, yes," one replied, sounding bored with the fuss, "but you've been caught before."

The man blubbered something about his losing his land. "I have nothing left. Please?"

"He's a thief!" someone yelled from the crowd and others muttered, *yes, yes*.

The soldier drew a pistol and shot the man. POP! A red hole appeared in the man's chest. The other soldiers emptied their pistols into him – POP, POP! The man jerked and jiggled in the dirt, leaking blood and bits. Some people covered their ears but none covered their eyes. The firing stopped. The leader slid his pistol into a holster, fastening the brass button.

"Citizens!" he said. "President Kabila will not tolerate thieves! Leave this body here for two days. If anyone moves it, they will be very sorry when we return. Now, disperse!"

The crowd melted away and Dudu noticed two *mindele* standing wide-eyed. The man wore baggy shorts and his knees were pale pink like a piglet. His mouth hung open. The woman's blonde hair had dark streaks, like a half-painted door. Kilanda walked around the body, all bloody and torn. He pointed back to the market. "Let's go and buy a watermelon."

Back on the barge, they sucked melon and listened to the gossip. Some passengers said it was *wrong to kill* but others said, *no smoke without fire*. Most just sat waiting to depart.

The solemn mood lifted when a happy-looking fellow shouted from the wheelhouse window, "I am First Mate Samuel and I have good news! Our captain's wife has just had a baby, back in Ilebo! We will stop here tonight and celebrate, I will distribute the beer!"

The passengers cheered and one man threw his cap in the air; it landed in the darkening water and his friends teased him. Samuel and some of the crew waddled about the barge with crates of beer for the grown-ups. Kilanda managed to grab three bottles. Music blasted from speakers and women danced, their bottoms pumping, their men shunting behind, clapping. Kilanda offered Dudu some beer. "No thanks," Dudu said; the smell reminded him of Moses.

Kilanda quickly drank all three bottles as if he were worried someone might steal them, then wandered off to find more. He was gone quite a while. Dudu sat watching fish splash in the darkness. After a while he heard a pistol fire: *POP!* Kilanda was standing a few yards away, shooting at a bottle floating by. Women shrieked. Dudu moved quickly along the barge and pulled his friend into the shadows under a tarpaulin canopy. "You're crazy!"

Kilanda burped, offering the pistol. "Target practice. Try!" Dudu took the pistol, shoved it into Kilanda's knapsack and fastened the straps tight. "Don't be stupid!" Kilanda closed his eyes and sang, *I will die for my beloved Congo!*

The worried faces turned away. The dancing resumed and Dudu watched the bottle bobbing along the calm Kasai. There were no fish jumping; they were not stupid.

Dudu sat listening to Kilanda's song, wondering about the words. If this *kadogo* was ready to die for his beloved Congo, why had he left the militia, the *Mai-Mai*? Why had he not applauded the soldiers in the dinghy, earlier in the day? And if he wanted to travel fast and avoid trouble, as he had said in the train, why shoot at a plastic bottle? The more Dudu considered it, the more he realised that Kilanda was just as good at causing problems as he was at solving them. So now, perhaps the real question was, *which came first?* Like Tata's tricky riddle about the chicken and the egg, any answer seemed right and wrong. He was still thinking about it when three men with muscles appeared from the gloom; the first man shoved a sack over Kilanda's sleepy head and the second said, "Captain wants to meet him."

The third man smiled, held up a dusty sack said to Dudu, "You too."

Chapter 42

Dudu stumbled up steep steps to the wheelhouse. The sack over his head smelled musty and someone was jabbing him in the back with a finger – *hurry, shegué!* He slipped, scraped his left shin and got a sharp kick in the bottom. Ahead, a door slid with a loud squeak, the sack was yanked off and he stood blinking at white walls and dark beams. Maps and charts lay on a polished table and a brass bell dangled from a hook. A wooden mask caught his eye – yellow feathers for hair and shiny cowrie shells for eyes. It was a good one, well made.

The wheelhouse had a nice smell – like fresh paint – but the anxious-looking, black-suited pastor was perched in a corner, watching like a crow. Captain Clemens stood opposite with his arms folded and a serious expression. He looked tired from watching the river, every day. He did not say, *Good work, Dudu.* What he said was, "Gentlemen, show me your tickets."

"We lost them," Kilanda said, blowing bits of sacking from his mouth. Samuel the first mate looked at the captain and grunted, "A likely story." The pastor pointed at Kilanda. "This is the same one who blasphemed!"

One of men unfastened Kilanda's knapsack and pulled out the two pistols, the dagger and the AK clip. He spread them on the table. The captain rubbed his chin.

"Quite a collection. Where did you get these?"

"I was *Mai-Mai*," Kilanda said. "What if someone steals my bucket, from the deck?"

The captain turned to Dudu. "How did you lads get on my barge without a ticket?"

Dudu glanced at Kilanda, whose expression seemed to say, *they can't prove it.* But the captain raised an eyebrow as if to say, *we can throw you overboard.*

"With a plank of wood, sir," Dudu said. "When it was dark. In Ilebo, sir."

The captain stared. "Honest *and* polite? What's in your satchel, *hand grenades, sir?*"

Dudu opened his satchel and took out the picture book and carvings. The sad-eyed pastor swooped to grab the little Power Figure and cried, "Fetishes!"

The captain picked up the little wooden hippo. "Not bad, this. Who taught you, son?"

"My tata had a workshop. He worked as a carpenter."

"*Nswendwe,* actually," added Kilanda.

The pastor made the sign of Jesus Cross. "Captain, you must burn these fetishes."

Captain Clemens placed the carvings carefully on a ledge. "Maybe later."

"Now, Captain! *Shegués* bring trouble, every time!"

First Mate Samuel stuffed Dudu's book back into the satchel and the captain sighed. "Do what you must, Sam."

"In the forest, Captain?" said Samuel. The captain nodded and went to his map table.

The pastor stood before Dudu and made the sign of Jesus Cross. "God forgive you."

"*Longwa kuna,*" Dudu said, and someone slapped him across the back of the head.

They shoved him out of the wheelhouse, down the steep steps and across a gangplank. He stumbled along the slippery bank and heard Kilanda behind him, cursing at the men. "Stop pushing!"

The men led them up a slope towards trees. Dudu asked why but received no reply. He glanced back. Kilanda was struggling to free himself from the man gripping his arm. The lamps of the barge shone like glow-worms. He could no longer hear the passengers' songs.

They went deeper into the buzzing forest. Samuel was carrying one of the MONUC pistols, sliding out the clip and checking the bullets. He snapped it back in, stopped under a baobab tree and said to Kilanda, "So, *shegué*, you think it's fun to scare our passengers, with this?"

Kilanda stood humming a tune that Dudu recognised. *Brothers, we will surely die...*

Samuel seemed puzzled. "I suppose the *Mai-Mai* told you bullets can't hurt, yes? Nothing to say, *shegué?*"

"You gave me beer, I got drunk," said Kilanda. "Pull the trigger, if you know how."

"Good idea." Samuel aimed at Kilanda's temple and squeezed the trigger until it clicked. Kilanda flinched, his chest rising and falling. Samuel cursed and tried again. *Click.* Kilanda gave a little whimper; he sounded like Uncle Moses kissing Mama in the dark.

Dudu thought about home. About dying, here, tonight. His bones would be picked clean like Tata's. His knees were wobbling and hot pee trickled down his leg.

"Let me try," said one of the men, aiming the second pistol. *Click.* Kilanda jerked his head aside. Dudu spotted tears dribbling down the *kadogo's* face. Kilanda would die any second, dance in the dirt, cut apart by bullets, red and mushy like a watermelon. Then it would be his turn. Dudu wiped his tears and stared at Samuel. "Please, sir?"

"What?"

"We're sorry. Don't kill us."

"And waste ammunition?" Samuel was grinning and brandishing a cartridge of bullets. So that was it. The pistol was not loaded. He poked Kilanda. "Still think guns are funny?"

Kilanda shook his head. Samuel booted him hard in the bottom. "Get out of my sight, the pair of you!"

Dudu raced along the path with jeers ringing in his ears: *Run for your life, shegué!* He scrambled up a slope and stopped at a road with traffic rumbling in both directions. Kilanda ambled up eventually, chewing a blade of grass, as if out for a stroll. But surely this *kadogo* would run out of luck, one day. He reached the road and spat in the dirt. "Thanks for waiting, *mon ami*."

"They could have shot us!"

"Who cares? We're *shegués*. And you're a sorcerer, didn't you hear?"

"I'm not a *shegué*! I'm not a sorcerer! I don't want to get shot. Do you?"

"By those guys? They've got the guns, but no guts. Looks like you peed your pants."

"So what?"

"You better go back to the barge. Fetch my bucket and wash, stinky *shegué*."

"I'm not going back. You go for your stupid bucket."

"Just kidding. I was getting seasick anyway. We'll go by road."

"Go where?" Dudu tugged at his damp shorts.

Kilanda looked left and right at passing trucks. "Kinshasa."

"*Kinshasa?* No, too far. Why go there?"

"Find my brother Luc. Yeah, why not? I've always wanted to see Kin la Belle."

"You're crazy."

Kilanda was gesturing at drivers to stop. "At least I've got dry pants. See you around."

Chapter 43

Frank's fixer, Cedric, turned up next morning dressed like a park ranger; he stood in the hotel reception with a toothpick in the corner of his mouth, his arms folded, listening. Frank paid him half the daily fee upfront and outlined his plans. First, they would tour radio stations, recruit journalists. Second, they would source supplies – folders, marker pens. Third, photocopy worksheets. Cedric shook his head. "First, you change money. I want red money."

"Sorry, I forgot," Frank said. Cedric gave him a look, which Frank would not forget.

They rode a Suzuki motorbike to a dimly lit arcade where they exchanged two hundred dollars for several bricks of faded Congolese banknotes, scarlet and stinky, in a plastic bag. Frank shook hands with the taciturn Greek manager and tucked the bag under his arm. Cedric emerged from the shadows twirling his toothpick. "Not so fast; check every pile." They stood together under a naked bulb, thumbing the musty wads of cash. It took a good ten minutes but they found several duds; the Greek swapped these for kosher ones and said, "Come back soon."

Frank climbed onto the back of the Suzuki. "Thanks, Cedric. Now the radio stations."

Cedric shook his head. "Now the RCD. To pay your respects, tell them you're here."

Riding across town, Frank protested. "But I met the RCD at Kisangani; at Goma heliport too; they know I'm here!" Cedric drove on and sure enough, when Frank strode into the local RCD office ten minutes later, the soldier at reception had never heard of Mr Kean, but an eager-eyed fellow in a suit read his copy of Dr Hitimana's email and said, "I'll follow up."

Frank spent the next three days razzing around radio stations; his favourite trip was to the one perched on a steep hill with spectacular views of Lake Kivu and the gentle slopes of Rwanda just down the coast. The place looked serene, heaven on earth. He suggested a quick ride over the border, perhaps once the seminar was ready, to visit his hundredth country. Cedric advised against it. "Border guards can be tricky. I had problems there recently. Some Dutchmen too, they were diplomats, VIPs. You're not." Cedric managed a smile even so, exuding the cautious optimism of one who sensed life might get better some day, if only because it could not get much worse. Frank asked him about the Hutu refugees in '94, about cholera, molten lava. Cedric twirled his toothpick and said, "Bad."

They were buying marker pens and jotters from a kiosk, around noon on Sunday, when a sharp BOOM echoed up the narrow street, followed by distant screams. People were pointing, running, looking worried. Frank heard police sirens. He paid the kiosk owner, stuffed his purchases in a bag and said to Cedric, "Whatever that was, it's news; let's go and see." Cedric strolled to his motorcycle. Frank hopped aboard and, as they sped in the opposite direction, the driver yelled something over his shoulder about *avoiding trouble*.

That night, Frank sat in his hotel room watching a report on Goma TV. The bang had been a grenade attack on a local Catholic church – three dead, some priests wounded, culprits unknown. CNN and BBC ran the story too. Time to phone home. Frank dialled Ruth on his mobile, no luck. He took his sat-phone onto the balcony, got her clear as a bell.

He reassured her that he was fine, watching cormorants dive into Lake Kivu, actually. She told him to stay away from the Catholic church, which was ironic, coming from her. "No problem, Ruth, " he replied.

"What about your seminar, can't you cancel it?" she said, and he chuckled.

The conference room overlooked the hotel car park and offered a great view of the lake. On Monday morning, ten journalists arrived at 9 a.m. sharp to fill in their folded name tags. Most kept their introductions brief except for Yves, who told a meandering tale of diplomas gained and opportunities missed; meals too, by the look of it – the guy was skin and bone. Someone mentioned the grenade attack. Most of them had already reported on it, but none seemed too surprised about folks getting blown to bits on a Sunday afternoon.

Ekanga with silver hair spoke next; he had a deep voice and dusty shoes. "Welcome to Goma, Mr Frank. I'm a reporter, fifty-two years old. This morning, I have just walked seven kilometres from my home to attend this seminar, and tonight I will walk back. Because, personally, I never had journalism training."

"I'm honoured," Frank said, "but… you could take a taxi; our per diem will cover it."

"I'd rather walk and save the money," Ekanga said, deadpan, and probably dead tired.

Next up, Yohali, whose spectacular orange headscarf was tied like a piece of sculpture. She spoke as if the walls were listening. "They will not let us be real journalists."

"*They?*" Frank asked, as a convoy of jeeps roared into the car park. Dust buffeted the windows and the vehicles distracted all of the journalists except Cherubin, the debonair presenter in a grey cravat, who said, "Does the Queen of England tell journalists what to do?"

"Well…" Frank said, but stopped, because the others were

not listening; the mood had changed. The conference room's door swung open and a solemn-faced soldier strode in, carrying a rocket launcher with a red cone protruding from the end. Next came several older men in suits, and three young soldiers armed to the teeth; about ten visitors in all. Frank stepped forward, smiling. "Gentlemen! Wrong room, I think? This is a journalism seminar."

A tall man in a dove-grey suit entered and offered a firm handshake. "Hello, Frank, thank you for your electronical mail. Welcome to the territory of the RCD!" He was film-star handsome with citrus cologne and a steady gaze. "Dr Hitimana?" Frank suggested, and the visitor nodded, all smiles, *C'est moi.* "I'm here to launch our seminar, if you agree?"

Frank smiled back, and considered his options. *Our* seminar? Dr Hitimana had the air of a man accustomed to getting his own way, and / or getting you out of the way, but Frank recalled advice from Hector Harris back at HQ: *don't be co-opted.* The canny Scot had clearly meant at times like this, but how? Should Frank refuse the VIP's request, and see three seminars go belly-up in east Congo? Alberto Rossi at USAID would be very displeased and Misti Puffer would have a duck egg. Some more recent advice echoed too: *avoid trouble.*

"Launch the seminar? What a good idea. Please do!" Frank replied.

Fingers clicked and two soldiers rearranged the semicircle of chairs into neat rows. Six more men entered the room wearing bush vests with PRESS logos. They carried TV cameras, lights, and microphones on boom poles. A photographer in a red bandana followed, then a soldier in sunglasses checking a cassette recorder, and finally a nervous shrimp of a woman in a business suit, clutching a pen and a ring-bound jotter. The TV lights fizzed hot and bright. Dr Hitimana moved behind the front desk and beckoned Frank. Everyone present stood erect to sing a patriotic anthem. Dr Hitimana gave a speech about *democracy, free media and objective reporting.* He replied solemnly to easy questions from the TV reporters, the radio fellow in fatigues and the jittery shrimp with the jotter. Frank's journalists watched from the sidelines like a bored b-team. Only one of them, reedy Raputo in his pinstriped jacket, seemed happy, and overly keen to establish his presence with unctuous queries.

Invited to speak, Frank thanked Dr Hitimana for his co-operation and posed for press photos. He slipped his disposable camera to Yohali in the headscarf and requested snaps for home. The various visitors trooped out forty minutes after they had arrived and Dr Hitimana clasped Frank's hand like a munificent uncle. "I'll be back on Friday to officially…"

"… close the seminar?" Frank concluded, "and perhaps award the diplomas?"

Dr Hitimana beamed and turned on his heel. Frank watched from the window, as the VIPs and press posse vanished in their roaring jeeps amid swirling plumes of volcanic dust.

"And finally," said Yohali, returning Frank's camera with a smirk, "can we start?"

Chapter 44

Monday night, sprawled on his bed after dinner, Frank watched the local news on TV. The first item was yesterday's grenade attack, culprits still unknown. The second item was the Unicorn seminar. The glamorous presenter explained that the RCD had organised the journalism training after detailed discussions with the US government, which was news to Frank. The item lasted ten minutes and consisted mainly of Dr Hitimana citing the importance of objective reporting and how anyone with a different agenda would never subvert this noble goal. Frank glimpsed himself onscreen; among all those black faces he looked anaemic, his ridiculous blonde curls shining under the dazzling lights; he resembled a ghost wearing a Georgian-era wig. The caption below identified him as *Frank Trainer*. A reporter asked, "Mr Frank, and now, please tell our viewers, what are you doing here?"

"Training journalists. I'm grateful to Dr Hitimana for his help."

"But please tell our viewers, what is America's intention in Congo?"

"May I suggest you ask President Bush?"

When it was over, he watched the ceiling fan whirr its disapproval. New questions arose. Had he sounded like a foreign smart-arse? Were the RCD vainglorious busybodies with a siege mentality and maverick DNA? He recalled his fixer Cedric's analysis, which sounded about right: the RCD were no worse than the government in Kinshasa or the nine foreign armies that carved up Congo in the '90s. There had been lies, double-dealing and atrocities all round. He listened to the lake below his window, licking the lava shore, now and forever.

He went onto his balcony. The rocks below glistened wet and black in the moonlight, like basking seals. Compared to the view from his Kinshasa balcony, this made a pleasant change. He remembered something else, from school, a line from Chaucer's *Canterbury Tales* about *grisly rokkes blake*, a *foul confusioun?* Yes, rocks that wrecked ships and caused men to drown, in "The Franklin's Tale," where a lovesick wife wonders why a perfect God would allow people to suffer. That was a good question too; universal, eternal even? Frank lit a cigarette and blew a perfect ring of smoke at the endless heavens. He would ask that priest, Yom, back in Kin, on their trip to the boxing stadium. Rumble in the Jungle. If they ever went.

The week flew by. The journalists dubbed their hypothetical news station Goma 24 and hit their hourly deadlines. But they argued so fiercely that, sometimes, Frank thought they were going to hit each other. They seemed keener than most of the journalists he had met in Kinshasa, perhaps because, up here in the sticks, training was less frequent and considered more precious. The women proved especially adept and eager to learn, churning out their vox pops, despatches, bulletins and round-table debates. The grenade attack offered plenty of scope – some went to interview grieving families, others to a hospital to check on the wounded. Loyal Raputo raced to rebel HQ for daily updates from Dr Hitimana, and the presenters in the seminar room used a press release from UN boss Kofi Annan in their mock bulletins. He had told the world the grenade attack *compounded the grief and sorrow of Goma.* It was a good line to head a bulletin, but someone got his title wrong and the despatches from the hospital were often wildly exaggerated; the number of dead rose by the hour, fuelled by all manner of conspiracy theories. Frank told his trainees to stick to facts and suggested a refresher session on ethics, the rights and responsibilities of a free press. But they seemed uneasy and he felt as if he were holding a tiger by the tail. The growling soon began.

"Our hands are tied," said Cherubin, adjusting his cravat.

"Only because you spread gossip about the RCD," said Raputo.

"You two are as bad as each other," said Yohali, inspecting her calloused heel.

Frank intervened. "As journalists, we must be careful what we broadcast."

"Not tell the truth, you mean?" said Cherubin, palms upturned.

"Truth is often a matter of perspective. Don't forget that."

"What about grenades in churches, people dying, bodies disappearing?"

"We must try to establish the facts from different sources."

Yohali yawned. "Can we talk about something else? I'm bored of bombs."

"It was a grenade, stick to the facts," Raputo said.

Frank stood at the window and looked at the lake, watching small boys paddle a canoe. "Do you report on street kids?" he said, over his shoulder. "It's an interesting subject."

"Is it?"

"Sure. Are they ever accused of sorcery? How do they feel? Do they get hurt in exorcisms?" He turned to face the group. They gawped in silence. It had been a long day.

On Friday, the RCD returned, as promised, and laid on a buffet, which was decent of them. Dr Hitimana gave a short speech, followed by a long one, about objectivity. The journalists lined up for their diplomas. They gobbled the free grub like veteran liggers. Dr Hitimana took Frank aside and stood munching snacks. "Frank, a little bird tells me you have been discussing press freedom, specifically in relation to journalists in our territory?"

"Well yes, just as back home in the UK, it's always up for debate. That's democracy."

Dr Hitimana's fingers formed a pincer on Frank's wrist, like a warm handcuff. "Have you ever heard of *mokele-mbembe?*"

Frank shook his head, munching a cheese straw. "Congolese singer?"

Dr Hitimana smiled. "No, in fact it means, *one that stops the flow of rivers.*"

"You mean, like a dam? Or those green plants? Hydrangea? Water hyacinth?"

"Actually, it was a sauropod, a dinosaur that once lived in our Likouala region. French priests discovered its footprint in 1776."

"Wow. I never heard about that. But why do you ask?"

"Because some say a political species of dinosaur exists still, in Kinshasa, and here in the east. But, I assure you, I wish for progress. Fair play, as in cricket. This is why I am so gratified to learn that our journalists enjoyed the seminar, and why I am here to support you."

"Perhaps *they* need your support, too. But thank you; I tried my best, like them."

"You did well. But in Congo, if you are too modest you go hungry. So eat up, you are my guest. And if I can assist you in future, please ask. These are difficult times for us all."

The celebrations wound down and the VIPs left in their jeeps. Yohali stood beside Frank and said, "If we report objectively, after you go, they'll probably lock us up." She examined her Unicorn diploma at arm's length. "But, this is nice, thank you."

Back at the hotel, Frank sat out under a cobalt sky, catching voices and laughter from fishermen on the lake; they seemed happy enough with life in Goma, cracking funnies in the dark. But Yohali's gloomy prediction echoed in his head and made him wonder. *Am I doing any good, here? Am I swimming or sinking? Is this the best Frank Trainer can be?*

He spotted Marc, the baldy and opinionated Belgian manager, waddling across the dining terrace towards him, clutching his backgammon board. Marc was wearing a bright pink polo shirt with a big NASA logo, and Frank had a feeling he would soon find out why.

Chapter 45

It was hard to know sometimes whether Kilanda was telling the truth or making things up. *My brother is rich. Our troubles will be over. Trust me, Dudu.*

They were sitting in the back of a truck roaring along a bumpy road, under tall trees and a full moon. Dudu's face was coated with dust. The silver light glinted on a fat black beetle trying to climb up a bulging sack; each time the truck hit a bump the beetle would slip down but try again. Kilanda squashed it with his boot. He would squash stories as well, if they were not about himself or his rich brother. Dudu tried again. "Uncle Moses got rich too. In the militia. He shot ten men. And a girl. He's a bad—"

"You already told me that one," Kilanda interrupted. "Anyway, never mind about your nasty uncle, I got an idea, listen: you can carve wood, make things in Kinshasa; *mindele* buy that junk. My brother will help, he's in business. *Lucky Luc*, they call him."

Dudu sat back, wondering what to say. "It's not junk. Why do they call him *Lucky*?"

"Because he probably is. That's how he signed his letter, anyway."

"What letter?"

"You don't listen. He sent one before the war. My sister read it to me."

The brakes hissed and the truck slowed to a stop. Dudu peeped through wooden slats on the side. A woman wobbled towards the driver's cab wearing a low top that showed most of her chest. She was chewing gum and her long red fingernails reached for the door. It swung open and she climbed up in her shiny shoes, nimble as a goat. She smiled at the driver. Dudu knelt up to look in on them, through the dusty glass at the back of the cab. The lights on the dashboard glowed yellow and blue and the driver lay on his back, pulling his pants down. The girl hitched up her short skirt and squatted above him like she wanted to pee. She lowered herself onto the driver; he pulled at her top and leaned forward to chew at her breasts. She held his neck – *easy, baby.* She moved slowly to the music on the radio. The glass got foggy and Kilanda said, "She's a *pute* and he hasn't got a gun."

"How do you know?"

"If you've got a gun you don't pay. You just do it. Ever done it, Dudu?"

"I've done kissing." He wished it were true. Kilanda cupped a hand at the window. "If you've got *Slim, Henry IV*, you should do it with a virgin. That stops *Slim*. If you're in the departure lounge, as they say. You just do it with a virgin and she will cure you."

Dudu wondered if Old Koosie was dead by now, back home. "How do you know?"

"My commander had *Slim*. We had to find virgins."

After a while the girl hopped from the cab and tottered into the dark, tugging at her skirt. Dudu watched her hips go left, right. "Quite a wiggly bottom."

"The bigger the better," said Kilanda, curling back into his corner.

Dudu craned his neck, to see the distant lights of a town. "Where are we?"

"Somewhere different," Kilanda said, one hand burrowing into his shorts. "Shut up and go to sleep."

The brakes hissed and their truck lumbered into the night. Bugs buzzed from silvery trees by the road; the howls of dogs filled the cool air and the engine growled back. Dudu sat wondering how long it would take to reach Kinshasa in trucks that bounced and rolled.

They passed their days in clouds of dust under a blinding sun. They washed at standpipes or in streams beside the road, bought bananas from wiry men, and *Kin 7 Jours* from a gap-toothed lady who told them it was the *tastiest, longest lasting, king of* kwanga. They took whatever rides they could, sometimes with fifty people on a truck and the wind in their faces. The road stretched straight or curled like a river. Kilanda would give some drivers money from his boot, if they asked. Dudu would spread the MONUC map. "Kinshasa, see?"

Kilanda's reply was always the same. "In the south-west, are we going south-west?"

"Yes. We just passed Mushuni, see? Kenge is next, and this river is the Wamba."

"You read pretty good."

"Tata taught me." Dudu shaded his eyes to watch tiny bright blobs in the distance – people working the land, clearing it for crops, a great triangle of dark smoke rising to the sky.

He sat with Kilanda for five hours at a busy junction with a dozen other travellers but few trucks stopped. By dusk, they were thirsty and irritable; a man in a black shirt approached with a Bible under his arm and asked, "Boys, would you like to meet Jesus?"

"No, would you?" said Kilanda, fanning himself with his cap. The man walked on and Kilanda stared with a weary look. "Pastors! I swear, Dudu, if I had my pistol…"

Next came a man selling electric plugs. He wore electric cables around his neck, like white plastic snakes. He was with a bow-legged boy selling scratch cards. A truck of chanting soldiers trundled by. Kilanda watched and Dudu said, "Maybe we should join the militia."

"Not me. I had enough of being a *Simba*. That's what we called ourselves – *Lions*."

"Why did you leave?"

"They left me." Kilanda sat picking his nose. He watched

the truck until it vanished around a bend. He rolled up one leg of his pants to reveal an ugly scar, like melted skin. "See this? Shrapnel in and out. I spend two days drinking rain-water and eating ants. My unit had moved on. I remember sitting by a road, just like this. I woke up in a hospital for *kadogos*. Imagine that! *Mindele* doctors, free food. All you had to do was draw pictures, for them."

"Pictures of what?"

"The war. Some *mundele* lady with grey hair looked at mine and started crying."

"Why?"

"Who knows. Then she said *we're hoping to reintegrate you.*"

"What's that?"

"It means you've used too many red crayons." Kilanda pointed at a big truck with gold letters on the window. *Only God Can Judge Me.* "Our ride," he said, "if we're quick."

They trotted to meet the truck and Kilanda made a big sign of Jesus Cross for the driver to see. The truck stopped and he beckoned them aboard. They climbed into his cab and the brakes sighed a welcome. The people still waiting outside looked a bit angry. Kilanda smiled and waved, "See, Dudu? You have to be quick like me, not thick like them."

The driver wore a Jesus Cross on a leather cord. His tattoo was of an angel and his cab was decorated with tiny pictures in frames, mostly of Jesus Cross and Mother Mary.

"Welcome, brothers, I'm Thomas!" He gave them a small plastic bottle. "Holy water, please dab your fingers and bless yourselves for a safe journey." Kilanda pretended to do so and passed the bottle to Dudu. The engine roared. The dusty windscreen was covered in dead bugs and Thomas said, "Off we go, young pilgrims! But, tell me, what have you done for Our Lord, lately?"

Kilanda told Thomas how their barge had been stuck on a sandbank for three weeks, that the river had eaten all its children except them, and that they were going to Kinshasa, where they would thank Jesus by collecting money. They would build a wooden church that Dudu had seen, in a holy vision, while swimming across a river of snapping crocodiles, at midnight.

"This is unbelievable!" said Thomas and Dudu nodded, because it was. Kilanda continued talking. His voice sounded more like a spell, making you believe any fib he told. Perhaps this did not even matter, because at least life with the resourceful *kadogo* was not boring, like it had been in Mavuku sometimes. But the catch, the tricky bit, was that Kilanda was two people, not one. He could tell you the truth, or the right thing to do just in time to avoid problems. But he also wove strange lies from thin air, often did the wrong things and got you into trouble.

"Astonishing!" said Thomas, and spoke about how important it was to spread the good news, like Joan the Baptist; to be brave like Joan in the Whale, who got swallowed; to listen to the voices in our head, like Joan of the Ark, who was probably Noah's sister. "Not that we should fear death, my young fellows, because if we are pure we will go to heaven. Do you know how?"

Dudu shrugged and Thomas explained: *no alcohol, no tobacco and no fornication with beasts*. It turned out Thomas had been quite a big sinner, once upon a time, but not anymore. Dudu watched the miles roll beneath the truck and said, "When will we reach Kinshasa, Thomas?"

"In three days! You shall be delivered, join my church and tell your incredible story to my congregation. They will welcome you as special guests. This is destiny."

Kilanda said, "No thanks. Actually, I made it all up. We're *kadogos* and murderers. Have you got any whisky?"

The truck screeched to a stop and Thomas ordered them out. They clambered down and watched from the roadside. He sprinkled holy water on the empty seats, slammed the door and drove off without waving. Dudu said to Kilanda, "You blew it. Thomas was nice."

"He was nuts. Three more days of that? Not me. Anyway, time to stretch our legs."

They walked along the darkening road, and rinsed their faces at a bubbling stream. Further up, they came to a neon-lit yard with minibuses parked outside a busy little café. Dudu peeped through the door at noisy men watching soccer on TV. Kilanda said, "Juventus." The waitress in a white apron said, "Out, *shegué!*" They retreated to the yard.

It was time to sleep. They searched the bins and squashed cardboard cartons for beds. Dudu found a wooden pallet and set it diagonally against a wall to make a sloping roof. Kilanda clicked his teeth. "Hey kid, you're learning." They sat cross-legged for a bit and Kilanda boasted about *Lucky Luc* getting rich in Kinshasa, and how he would too, one of these days.

Dudu drifted off to sleep and dreamed of fishing with Tata. A crocodile tried to gobble them. The sound of hissing brakes woke him up and he wondered if he was lying in a truck, but when the morning fog kissed his eyelids he was lying in the yard and feeling cold.

Around noon, a man brought supplies to the café and agreed to let them ride in the back of his truck, for some money from Kilanda's boot. His neatly pressed red shirt bore white words above the pocket: *Eddie's Bowling – Go Tenpin.* He looked at Kilanda's map. "So tell me, boys, how many days have you been travelling?"

Dudu counted fingers. "Let's see. We spent three days on the train, and it's six days since we got kicked off the barge. So, nine or ten. I think." Kilanda trod on his toe: *be quiet.*

The driver pointed to the wrinkled map. "We're on the R214 south. I can drop you at the N1 turn; Kin is two hundred kilometres due west of that. Easy, unless you get kicked off my truck." He folded the map and slapped it against Kilanda's chest. "I'm Eddie. You boys are trouble. But so was I, at your age. So climb aboard. No shitting in the back, I had enough of that; if you need to do your business, tap on my roof, and I'll stop. Got it?" They nodded and clambered over the tailgate to sit between crates of empty bottles that tinkled like raindrops, as the truck rumbled up a hill. "I'll pee in these," Kilanda said, "he doesn't know what trouble is."

The road uncurled behind them like a snake; villages whizzed by and Dudu saw a woman pounding manioc with a wooden pole – *dub dub* – just like Mama would. A small girl placed a rotten banana in the road and stood to watch a passing motorbike mash it flat. After a few more miles, Eddie stopped to let an old, barefoot man and a young boy of five or six climb into the back of his truck. The man sat staring at his gnarled feet. The young boy had a dirty bandage on his head. Dudu asked him why and the boy said, "Because it hurts."

A few hours later, they reached Mayamba near the N1 turn. Eddie told them *good luck* and drove away, waving. They wobbled to a garage to buy food. Kilanda spread the map on the ground and said, "Kin is two hundred kilometres due west of here. Easy." He sounded like Eddie.

"Where did you get that?" The new voice came from above, deep and serious, like God. They looked up to see a pink-faced soldier in a pale blue beret, standing over them.

"Oh, this?" Kilanda folded the map and stood up. "I found it."

The soldier smiled. "Of course you did. But it's UN property. So give it to me."

"Why, so you can sell it to the Rwandese?"

The soldier laughed. "What?"

"*Bateki mboka.* MONUC *eteki mboka.* You sell our country. It's not funny."

Dudu stood wondering whether to run while he could. He looked at Kilanda with his clothes all mucky and his face full of quiet rage, glaring at this soldier with the walkie-talkie and pistol on his belt and a little flag of red, white and blue sewn on his nice clean uniform. Cars and trucks rumbled up the road, taking the N1 turn, all going to Kinshasa, a place that suddenly seemed farther away than ever. The soldier folded his arms. "*Bateki...* what?"

Kilanda's chest rose and fell. "So, you came all the way to the Congo to worry about UN property, is that it?"

"I'm worried about lots of things, including your country."

"There's a barge on the river Kasai."

"And?"

"A barge named *Romleon*, it will be docking in Bandundu in a week; the first mate is called Samuel and he stole two MONUC pistols."

"Also a dagger," said Dudu. The soldier looked confused to hear it.

"So, Blue Hat, get on your MONUC radio," Kilanda said, "and get promoted."

The soldier unfolded his arms. They looked big and strong enough to turn you upside down and shake the dust from your pockets. But he just scratched his nose. "Is this a joke?"

"It's Congo," said Kilanda. "Need a map?" He offered it. The soldier reached but Kilanda let the map drop to the ground and said, "Oh, sorry about that." He strode away, hitching up his pants to reveal his stolen MONUC boots. *See these?* Dudu copied him and glanced back. The soldier had the map and was tapping it into his palm, watching them go.

Chapter 46

From a few hundred feet above, Bukavu resembled a holiday postcard. Elegant fingers of land protruded into the southern end of Lake Kivu, like a giant hand dipping into dark blue water. Tin roofs glinted on ranks of red-brown buildings that jostled for space on pea-green slopes. The town had a sleepy charm and looked very inviting.

The shuddering Sikorsky flattened a small field of lush grass and Frank disembarked to a welcome blast of rural air – no fumes, no dust. UN Land Cruisers, local taxis and motorcycles sat in a line, beyond the chicken wire fence, ready to roll. Frank noticed a tall Congolese man in a suit, standing with his hands behind his back, gazing through the wire.

The RCD office at the heliport consisted of a large grey tent containing a trestle table with a khaki blanket. Frank stood in line. The place resembled a movie set for a court martial. The young immigration officer wore a pork-pie hat and wrap-around shades. He pointed at the sunglasses hanging from Frank's shirt pocket. "Ray-Bans. Where from?"

"Duty-free," said Frank, "Heathrow Airport, I think. Bought them a long time ago."

"Perhaps you'll bring me some, when you come to do your next seminar?" He dipped his head, winked over his cheap wraparounds and Frank said, "Sure, why not." He walked out into a yard of eager teenagers straddling their dented motorbikes. He was negotiating his fare into town when he felt a tug at his elbow. "Not necessary, Mr Kean; this way, if you please?" It was the tall fellow he had noticed watching through the wire, all smiles now. "My name is Ngabo. You will be more comfortable with me." Ngabo gestured to a beat-up Nissan, its side door already open. Whoever he was, at least he had a car. He also had a point.

The long road into town resembled a bobsleigh track carved from red clay. Ngabo sat up front, clutching his old briefcase like it contained a nuclear code. The bear of a driver seemed intent on breaking the sound barrier. Frank bounced around in the back watching trees fly past, and listening to his silver-haired saviour. It was quite a story.

Official version: Ngabo was a retired member of the local Journalists' Union who, in a spontaneous gesture of fraternal solidarity, had taken it upon himself to meet the Unicorn trainer. *Conspiracy theory:* Ngabo was an RCD chaperone whom the rebels had sent to keep tabs on Frank. "As regards accommodation," Ngabo said, "assuming you have no prior arrangement, I know of a small guesthouse, central, well appointed. The Eternal Light."

"Thank you, The Eternal Light sounds promising, as long as they turn it off at bedtime," Frank said.

Ngabo gave a Gallic shrug and said to his driver, "I think this is English humour." The driver crouched at his steering wheel, as if he thought this was an Italian sports car.

Ngabo chatted on about his work, his hopes for the Unicorn seminar and how keen he would be to assist in any way. He seemed quite the gentleman, and did not mention money; but his frayed collar indicated that a fixer's fee might not go amiss. And who better for a fixer, than a fixer from the rebels' cosy nest, if this was the case? Only time would tell.

They agreed on a deal with an unspoken sub-clause: Frank would assume that Ngabo had come on behalf of the Journalist's Union, unless and until his behaviour indicated otherwise. He pictured Dr Hitimana preening himself on their entente cordiale, and that priest Yom wearing an old T-shirt that spelled it out in black and yellow: PRAG–MATISM.

He watched the citizens of Bukavu walking up their steep, busy streets. He watched kids lugging plastic jerry cans on those huge wooden bicycles, like in Goma. Ngabo told him the word was *chukudu*. And as for street kids, those little beggars were *maibobo*.

The Nissan spun up a slope, into a sunny courtyard with a big crucifix draped in pink ribbons outside a freshly painted hotel. Inside, however, The Eternal Light was a poky place of dark wood and shadowy corners. Frank signed the ledger under the keen eye of a rather fussy young manager in a buttoned-up waistcoat, who insisted that he fill in the box marked *Religion*. Frank scribbled *Boeing 747* and said to Ngabo. "Back in five, buy you a beer?" Ngabo grinned like a kid at Christmas and Frank tailed the manager upstairs, rucksack slung.

Frank's room lay at the narrow end of a passage and contained a bed and a bucket of cold water. "Just in case," the manager explained. Frank glanced around. In terms of ratings, the hotel was not so much one star, as minus three. He read a framed notice in bold font.

> *This is a House of God. No entry after 22:00.*
> *No alcohol, no smoking, no opposite of sex.*
> *Peace & quiet always. Thank you, I am your Manager.*

A gruesome crucifix hung nearby, lest ye forget the CEO.

Frank dumped his rucksack and followed the shiny waistcoat downstairs to a sunny room that contained twelve desks and chairs arranged in a semicircle. *What a coincidence.*

"Is there a problem?" Ngabo said.

"Absolutely not." Frank went back to the reception, handed the young manager a hundred dollar deposit and strolled downtown with Ngabo, who knew just the place for that beer.

The Victory Café was small but with bright décor. A few youths in tracksuits sat in attentive silence, watching a soap opera on TV; the screen showed a priest yelling at a scared-looking boy. As Frank passed the bar, one of the young women perched on stools giggled at his Harpo Marx hairstyle, as if it were a wig she would never wear.

Ngabo chose a corner table and ordered beers. He took a sheet of paper from his old briefcase. "I've selected the journalists for your seminar. Here are their names and stations."

Frank read the list, with growing unease. "Thanks, but *five* military reporters? I'm not here to train soldiers. I want more journalists from commercial stations. I'll visit some."

Ngabo pursed his lips in sulky compliance and gazed at the TV. Frank sipped his beer and sat back to watch the soap. The actors were doing their best but lacked credibility; too melodramatic. Someone had died, onscreen. They blamed the kid. Frank passed the sheet back to Ngabo. "I met Dr Hitimana, he seemed to like how I handled the Goma seminar."

"I know."

"We discussed Bukavu. He's was quite a gentleman, seems very bright too."

"He has a PhD in geology. But he has political aspirations. You'll see."

"He mentioned *mokele-mbembe,* real and metaphorical, if you get my drift."

Ngabo's eyes popped. "*The dinosaur?* Is that what he called me?" The genteel insouciance was gone; Ngabo looked troubled, confused by events and loyalties, or perhaps by his job. Frank thought about the other helpers he had met. Ngabo was not like Claude in Kinshasa, the city kid with his life ahead of him; or Cedric in Goma, a tough cookie in a tough place. Ngabo was jaded, his best years gone and his future all uphill, here in sleepy Bukavu.

"You misunderstand, Ngabo. Dr Hitimana never mentioned you. He was talking in general terms, about challenges he faces. That was my interpretation. You could ask him?"

Ngabo looked as though he would rather invite Dracula to dinner. "That won't be necessary. But thank you. Politics is a puzzle, especially here. You never quite know…"

"Tell me this: if Dr Hitimana supports my training, wants

accurate reporting and balanced news, why do some reporters in Goma say they cannot broadcast a vox pop until the RCD checks it? Are their hands so tied? And how is it in Bukavu, off the record, *entre nous?*"

Ngabo leaned closer. "We can't really tell the truth. But we can survive."

"What happens if you quote a source who disagrees with the official line?"

Ngabo winced but would not be drawn. Perhaps that was one of his Frequently Avoided Questions. Instead, he studied the table like he was deaf in that ear and Frank studied his profile against the amber decor. The bushy eyebrows looked like some prehistoric caterpillar trapped in resin; the deep creases around his eyes suggested laughter, long ago. The drooping bags hinted at sleepless nights. Frank noticed rain clouds buffeting the hills beyond the café and a long line of soldiers in green gumboots striding past in single file, one metre apart, perfectly spaced. They were tall and skinny; classic Tutsi? "I thought Rwanda had agreed to pull out of DRC," he said. Ngabo sipped his beer and watched the TV.

Frank let the subject drop, weary with the byzantine politics of the Great Lakes region, and rather wishing he were somewhere else. *Ninety-nine countries; visit one more, such as Namibia, and I can join the Travelers' Century Club.* He thought about Alphonse at MONUC raving about *quad bikes and shrimps.* If only...

Chapter 47

Warm rain from a black sky. Dudu perched on a tree stump by the roadside, gazing up as the drops trickled across his face. Kilanda was walking about, kicking stones and yapping about starting a business in Kinshasa, a workshop. Dudu would carve and he would distribute. They would split the income. He seemed to have forgotten that tools cost money and you had to sell before you could earn. A huge truck rumbled out of the darkness, brakes hissing and lights flashing. The crowd of people waiting at the N1 turn for Kinshasa reached for their bags and wobbled forward to meet it. Their big bags and little kids slowed them down, so Dudu and Kilanda trotted ahead, easily winning the race. The door on the driver's cab had a lion's face painted on it. A hand came through the open window. Kilanda hopped onto the step and offered money. The fingers wiggled: *more, please.*

Dudu ran to the rear and climbed over the rusty tailgate, worming his way through sleepy-faced passengers huddled together; wrinkly men, irritable teenagers and tired-looking women with babies strapped to their backs in shawls. One of the kids had a runny nose.

Dudu stepped onto a big wooden crate and helped Kilanda up. They sat cross-legged on top of the crate, watching the sky flare with distant lightning and waiting for thunder that never came. The truck rumbled on and some of the men started chatting in the shadows. One spoke of *more trouble in South Kivu;* the others nodded, *what's new?* Someone asked about Juventus and they were soon teasing each other about tactics. But most of the passengers had little to say and hunched together under the pattering drizzle, eager to reach their destination, whatever it might be. A white MONUC jeep zoomed past and Dudu watched its red lights shrink to tiny dots. A man sitting beside him said, "MONUC *eteki mboka*." Kilanda nodded in agreement, and Dudu said, "If the Blue Hats sell Congo, why did you give them our map?"

"Because that soldier was a busybody; I lose today, I win tomorrow. Tactics, Dudu, tactics."

The truck entered a small and lively town with big colour-ed hoardings: *Boutique Gracia, Kerrygold, Philips*. The driver stopped near a café and the smell of fried meat made Dudu's tummy grumble. Passengers disembarked, lugging their bags and kids. The truck drove into the night, with more space in the back now. Kilanda found a roll of tarpaulin and Dudu helped him stretch it between crates; it stank of stale rainwa-ter but made a good roof. They lay beneath it, back-to-back for warmth, listening to the grinding axle.

At dawn, the driver parked in a yard and they swapped to a truck carrying sacks of peanuts lashed together with rope and bulg-ing over the tailgate like too much *fufu* in a pot. Kilanda poked a hole in a sack and some nuts fell out. Dudu sat watching the road curl ahead, popping those shells and chewing until his belly was full. This truck did not cough or growl, it purred like a lazy cat even though the road was bumpy. The driver went for hours without stopping. They stood peeing from the side, spraying the bushes by the road. Kilanda giggled like a kid but the wind changed direction and Dudu pointed, "Wet your pants?" They wrestled each other for fun, until two men pulled them apart.

They got off the truck twenty-five miles from Kinshasa and sat by the road until a Toyota pickup stopped for them. It reminded Dudu of the ones in Banza's yard, so he looked carefully, just in case Moses or that nasty Pastor Precious were inside. Shiny gold letters spelled MIKEY DREAD across the driver's windscreen, and he jabbed a thumb: *hop in the back!* Mikey's dusty hair sprouted in clumps as if strange vegetables were growing from his head. Music boomed from the cab and, as he drove along, Mikey yelled the names of the singers through the back window of the cab, where the glass was badly cracked. "Burning Spear! Dennis Brown!" Sometimes he yelled the words of the songs too. "Barrington! *Broader than Broadway!*"

Mikey stopped to buy goat brochettes at a roadside café and they sat together at a table chewing the warm meat. He had bloodshot eyes and smelled of *diamba*, like the stuff in the cigarette Dudu had smoked with Major Monuc, that made your head wobble. But Mikey did not say *come with me.*

He sucked the meat off his skewer and said in his sing-song voice, "Rasta spent most of de war in Brussels in Matongé district, with me bredren. Went to Atomium. Got wicked tunes, me blood. And you best listen up else it's pearl before de swine."

Kilanda asked about Kinshasa. Mikey frowned and shook his head. His hair danced on top. "Town be full with dem *shegués,* like you. Chop a man up for his cardboard bed."

"We're not *shegués,*" said Dudu, chewing.

"What is you, businessmen?"

"Soon," said Kilanda. His face looked fat and tight from no sleep, as if someone had put a bicycle pump in his ear and pushed the handle. Mikey wagged a greasy skewer. "Lissen, mon. When we get in Kin, don't be easy meat. Be cool, strictly irie? Seen."

Kilanda nodded. He understood. Dudu bit a brochette and said, "What's easy meat?"

"Sometink you must not be. Now eat up and let us go,

before darkness don come."

They drove past a huge lake that glistened and swirled to the horizon, gold and pink where the sun slipped away. Mikey pointed. "River Congo!" The gaps between villages became shorter. Soon there were no gaps, just houses and big buildings, all the way.

When darkness don come, Mikey shouted, "Kinshasa la Belle!" The big city beeped and glowed like a mighty robot monster, ready to gobble them up. The singer on Mikey's wicked tape sang, *This Christmas bring back the love.*

"Is it Christmas?" said Dudu, and Kilanda shrugged.

At a roadblock, a little soldier with rolled-up sleeves walked around the Toyota looking at the scrap iron in the back. He asked questions and listened carefully to Mikey boasting about Belgium, chewing a matchstick and staring at the bag of tapes. When Mikey had finished, the soldier leaned in the window and said, "While you were in Matongé, I was in the bush. So give me those tapes for patriotic motivation." He pointed a scabby finger at the bag. *Those, give, now.* Mikey groaned and passed the bag through the window. The soldier said, "One love." He strolled away, looking at the wicked tapes, bow-legged with a fat pistol low on his thigh. More soldiers came to peep in the bag too and were soon smiling. Mikey drove on but did not shout from his window anymore. He poked the buttons on his radio but did not find any wicked music. He howled like a baby and Kilanda laughed.

They hopped over the tailgate at a junction. Mikey leaned out to say goodbye and his eyes looked red from weeping. He bumped knuckles with Kilanda and said, "Don't be easy meat, like me." He bumped knuckles with Dudu and said, "Be iron like a lion in Zion." They watched his little pickup truck vanish into the city and Kilanda said, "We made it, Simba."

Dudu smiled because he liked being called a *lion*, although he did not much feel like one. He felt tired. Grime clung to his face and his hair; his stinky clothes hung limp. He watched the snarling traffic and was relieved to have finished travelling. He looked at the big buildings and a stump-toothed beggar on the boulevard, whose bare leg was twisted like little Emile's. How many days had passed, since Mama had said *goodbye* in Mavuku? It no longer mattered. Tonight he would get clean and sleep at Lucky Luc's house, somewhere here in Kinshasa la Belle. He turned to Kilanda and asked, "So, where does your brother live?"

"In a cemetery," Kilanda said, picking his nose.

Chapter 48

No water, no soap? Frank left the bathroom and went up the gloomy corridor of The Eternal Light guesthouse, back to his room. He dug a stub of Palmolive from his bag and returned, hauling his sloshing bucket. He could not complain, really. If Congo were a fully functional country, it would not need guys like him. He dipped a toe into the cold water.

Ten minutes later, clean and dry, Frank lay in bed with a mosquito buzzing above, the clever bugger biding its time. He thought about theory and practice: in theory he was here to help, but in practice would he make any difference? Sure, he was earning money and paying bills back home, but what about Congo, its people, its future? The mosquito made a pass, *I'm glad you came.* Frank reached for his anti-bug aerosol and sprayed a reply. *Sod off.*

He woke around 4 a.m. to the sound of a woman howling in ecstasy for all to envy. He sat up to sip water. Good luck to the lovers. Then again, what about the framed notice on his wall. *Peace and quiet at all times?* He buried his head in the pillow. They were still at it. Maybe it wasn't sex; maybe she was being murdered? He got up and crept down the steep steps to reception. A security guard was sleeping in an armchair, head back and gob open, rifle across his lap. Frank tracked the howls down a corridor and nudged a door. He stood in his T-shirt and shorts, watching a tearful young woman in a headscarf, white blouse and long skirt. She was pacing the kitchen and shrieking at the ceiling. She looked demented.

"YES! YES! That's why I LOVE you Jesus. I ADORE you! My GOD! YES!"

"Excuse me," Frank said, "but may I ask what you're doing?"

The woman froze. Her face creased into a beautiful smile. "I'm praying."

"In the middle of the night?"

She was off again, arms waving. "YES! JESUS! You are everywhere!"

Frank entered. "If Jesus is *everywhere,* he's in this kitchen. No need to shout."

"Lord, I will REJOICE in your presence!"

"You'll wake the dead."

She beamed at him. "But this is how I pray. Every morning."

Frank did not beam back. "There's a sign in my room: *peace and quiet.*"

She stared at his pink knees, tilted her head and flashed a flirtatious smile, part saint and part courtesan. "As I said, this is how I pray."

He circled the table. "I cannot sleep. Should I complain to the manager?"

The girl stood her ground, fists up, ready for a scrap. "Get out! Leave me alone!"

Frank stared. She did look quite mad, with him especially. He stumbled back upstairs and lay awake, while she howled on, for ten minutes, louder too, as if to spite him? At 4.30 a.m., some heaven-bound cockerel added its doodle-doo. Next, a tinny radio blasted breakfast news and zinging guitars. He was still awake at seven and shuffled down to breakfast, light-headed and ready for trouble, preferably with the manager, who listened, clearly perplexed.

"Mr Kean, did you say *soft in the head?*"

"Yes. It means she's mad. And by the way, about your *rules*, that sign in my room?"

"She is not mad. This is a House of God. Her devotion

brings us blessings."

"I didn't come here for blessings. I came for *peace and quiet*, like it says upstairs."

The desk phone rang and the manager took the call, glaring. Frank took a seat and sawed at a rubbery omelette. A happy waiter in clicking heels brought coffee. The manager vanished and Frank heard a croaky voice from across the room. "Sir, that was unwise. The girl you insulted is his sister. Very devout." The accent was European. Whoever it belonged to sounded intelligent but also rather too sure of herself. A retired headmistress?

Frank swivelled in his chair and looked at a stern-faced white woman sitting in the shadows, her grey hair tied back. A tarnished silver cross of gothic design hung from her neck. Perhaps she was here to hunt Congolese vampires. Frank shoved his plate aside and lit a cigarette. "Thanks for the advice, but I don't care if she's Mother Teresa. Rules are rules."

The woman gave a theatrical cough. "Sir, smoking is not allowed."

"I'm Rastafarian," Frank said, puffing at the ceiling, "and I'm very devout."

When Ngabo turned up they toured the town, pitching the Unicorn seminar to journalists and managers at local radio stations, most of which were home-grown and seemed to be run on a shoestring. The plusher stations were faith-based with religious support, mostly American. Frank chatted with chief editors in ties and deputy dudes in tracksuits. They were full of ideas and scared to implement them. "Community issues? We must be *very* discreet about those," said Dominic, boss of Sunrise FM, with his black Stetson tipped back.

Frank sat forward. "Ngabo tells me the new traffic regulation is not popular. My trainees could do a vox pop before it's implemented." He watched the eyebrows rise.

Striding back to the beat-up Nissan, Frank said to Ngabo, "I knew it. My seminar won't make any difference. USAID is wasting its money in east Congo."

Ngabo trotted to keep up. "Wrong. Journalists are keen to learn new theory."

"Theory, exactly, but can they *practise* it? That's the question. Guess the answer."

"You judge us too harshly. Our city is perhaps the most hostile of all, towards the RCD. Many brave journalists have spoken out, some were sent to jail. Priests, bishops, activists from civil society, many have also voiced their opposition to the Rwandese presence. We have learned our lesson the hard way. I told you: we survive, but we cannot tell the truth."

"Because of the RCD? With Rwanda supporting them, I suppose, Little Big Bother?"

Ngabo nodded. "Some who dared to complain have perished."

"Like in the grenade attack, last week in Goma. What was all that about?"

"Let us focus on your seminar. That's why you came."

"Sure, and why did you come? How did you know what time I'd land, yesterday?"

Ngabo opened the car door. "Because I'm a journalist. Or I was. And I want to help."

"Good, let's do my worksheets." Frank climbed aboard and they drove to a kiosk with a juddering photocopier. Next, they scoured the town for a whiteboard to rent; last, he bought pens, folders and ring-bound jotters. It was a boring routine now, especially as it would do little good, but Ngabo looked intrigued, eyeing the freebies. "Lucky trainees. May I sit in, for the seminar?"

Frank wondered what to say. *Is Ngabo short of stationery? Does he miss journalism? Is he playing for two teams?* Frank draped an arm around his ageing fixer as they walked up hill. "Sure, join us." He spotted a camera shop and handed in his

298

cheap disposable, with the Goma shots. The owner promised prints in two days. Ngabo beamed. "A successful day!"

It was dark when Frank got back to the guesthouse, and the shadowy corners of The Eternal Light gave him the creeps. He went to see the seminar room, just to be sure the white-board would fit. He noticed the twelve desks and chairs had gone. The room contained three sofas and a coffee table. The young manager appeared, thumbs tucked in his waistcoat.

"Change of plan, Mr Kean. You'll hold your seminar in a different room. Follow me."

He led Frank to a poky brick-lined basement, hardly big enough for six people. It reeked of damp and the naked bulb flickered yellow. It resembled your average torture chamber. Frank blinked first. "No way. Ngabo reserved the room up-stairs. I paid a deposit."

"Sorry, the general manager and his associates need the room upstairs, from Tuesday."

"Tuesday? That's when my seminar starts. Wait, aren't *you* the manager?"

"Only at weekends."

"It's Sunday evening."

"Your seminar starts on Tuesday. I'm not the manager on weekdays." He raised a hand to scratch his mouth. *Why, because we often try to hide the source of our lie?* Frank backed into the bricks. "You accepted my deposit yesterday, Saturday. What changed?"

"I'm sorry. The general manager's decision is final."

"May I speak with him?"

"I'm sorry, he is travelling." The weekend manager scratched his neck. Frank had forgotten what that gesture meant, but he had not forgotten the young woman in the headscarf and white blouse. He glimpsed her peeping round the door of the bat-cave, humming a sweet little hymn. *She's his sister, very devout.* Perhaps this was payback. Yes, he saw it now, written all over their pious faces. He spotted a crucifix on the wall, draped in ribbons. Jesus.

"Tell you what," Frank said, with a sigh, "why don't I just move out?"

The weekend manager looked worried. "No, sir. I believe your young students will be happy and very comfortable in here. We have staged many seminars in this room."

"My *students*, as you call them, are professional journalists. I'll try another hotel."

"Sir, I ordered food for fourteen people, including Ngabo and yourself, for five days."

"Eat it. *Bon appétit!* And please prepare my bill while I pack. You can deduct my room fee from my deposit. I'll take the difference in francs. Now, if I can just squeeze past?"

"No sir, please sir…"

"Try *yes sir*," Frank growled and slipped under the brick arch, past the smirking saint.

He tramped up to his room. Flung back the door. Booted the empty water bucket and stuffed his clothes into his rucksack, cursing the place and everyone in it. He phoned Ngabo, and told him the good news. "Sorry, Ngabo, but we need to find a new place for my seminar, and soon. It's Sunday. I've got twelve journalists coming Tuesday morning."

Down the line, he heard crockery clinking, someone washing dishes. Next came a long sigh, Ngabo racking his brains. "Frank, it's 9 p.m. This is *very* short notice."

"I also need a place to sleep. Do you know another hotel, preferably pagan?"

"I suppose the Sisters of Redemption might help."

Nuns? Frank groaned, head in hand. "Perfect. Please redeem me, if you can."

Chapter 49

Some couples thrive on disagreement; it's like a glue that binds them. As far as Ruth could tell, her boss was stuck fast. Simon looked happy and sad, like a loyal dog chained outside a supermarket, hoping for the best. By now, home time, Simon should have looked pleased, ready for golf or whatever. Instead, he lingered in the lobby, watching a TV trailer for *Big Brother*. Purple Jane was grinning like a gargoyle. "New series, starts tonight!"

Simon sighed. "Lucky you. The last time I wanted to see this show, Cade changed channels and we watched a documentary about Darfur. Laugh a minute, that was."

Ruth murmured her condolences and glanced at her watch. *6.10 p.m.* She changed out of her scrubs and went back to the surgery to check the autoclave. Simon came in to wash his hands at the washbasin, gazing at the silver-framed colour photo of himself and Cade astride their mountain bikes. "Funny how life turns out," he said, with no trace of a smile. He slung the towel on its hook and reached for his bag. "I suppose you'll watch *Big Brother*, too?"

"Not me, Simon. I can't stand it. Plus, the boyfriend is coming to dinner."

"Does Frank know?" Simon smiled at last, sniffing for trouble in someone else's life.

Ruth drove home listening to Sheryl Crow singing "If It Makes You Happy". She hit a tailback halfway and sat watching a mother push a buggy uphill. *That'll be me, soon.* She changed the CD to Dire Straits, that song about Guitar George, for a bit of swing.

As it turned out, Billie's boyfriend Callum knew a few chords too. Ruth arrived home, and found him perched on the sofa strumming the dusty guitar Frank never learned to play. Callum was good-looking with broody, intelligent eyes, like that Beatle who died in Munich in the '60s, Stuart someone. *Or was it Hamburg?* Dylan was squatting at Callum's feet and Aubrey was sitting in an armchair, her head in a book and her legs in white tights. Billie did the introductions, on her best behaviour, sweet as a nut. "Mum, Callum. Callum, Mum."

The sitting room reeked of patchouli oil. Ruth sat making polite chat. Callum was quiet but not shy, confident with his answers as though it would only be a matter of time before the world agreed. Billie chewed a fingernail, bug-eyed, like her life depended on his replies. She cut in, breathless. "Oh, and Mum, Callum wrote a song. It's so *am-azing.*"

"And he can juggle apples, like this," said Dylan, jerking his empty hands up and down with grim concentration. "Mummy, can you juggle?"

"Activities, yes; apples, no. And by the way, where did you find Daddy's guitar?"

"Under your bed."

"Do you have permission to root in my room?" Ruth said and Dylan shrugged.

"Music, maestro," said Billie. Callum twisted the tuning pegs, wincing as they creaked. Eventually satisfied, he slowly plucked the strings and sang, rather well.

You don't listen to a word I say,
You just smile, Open File, and slowly drift away

Ruth folded her arms. She pictured Frank at his desk, writing endless reports, job applications and training proposals. She watched the nimble fingers slither up the guitar.

I wouldn't mind, and I shouldn't mind but I don't think it's fair,
Because there's lot of places we could go, and people we could share.

She sat there, gobsmacked. Callum had nailed her life without even trying. Yes, the world was full of new places, interesting people. But that was Frank's job, not hers. The song ended on a haunting chord, Ruth applauded and went out to the kitchen, humming the tune; she knew a hit when she heard one. It needed a middle eight though, as Max used to say, but still, Callum was talented, Billie was in love and yes, it would end in tears. She was grating Parmesan cheese when The Boyfriend came mooching around the kitchen, humming his song. He sat on the nearest stool and said, "So, what's it like being a dental nurse?"

"Better than being a barmaid. Could you pass me the pepper, please?"

Callum passed her the grinder. Ruth heard feet thumping above and whoops of laughter from Aubrey. She walked into the hall and shouted, "Billie, what's going on?"

"Playing crocodiles, why?" Billie's muffled reply suggested she was inside one. Ruth returned to the kitchen and Callum said, "I have a psychological problem with dentists."

"Only because you don't understand the process, why-we-do-what-we-do." Ruth turned away to fill a saucepan with water and set it to boil. When she turned back Callum was juggling three of her best apples, his head tilted and mouth open, as if he were planning to swallow one. She wanted to say, *if you drop them, they will bruise,* but instead she said, "Very impressive, Callum; perhaps you should join a circus."

Callum grinned, juggling faster. "Wanted to... as a kid... after a row at home."

"Me too. Parents, eh?"

"Sure. Why did Billie's dad ... commit suicide?"

Ruth stared through the spinning apples. "I beg your pardon?"

"Just curious… about the …psychology… of it."

"With all respect, Callum, what happened to Max is none of your business."

Callum deftly caught the whirling apples, "Sorry, I didn't mean to pry. Hey, want to see a Reverse Three Ball?" He flipped the apples, yapping about some ancient row with his father, whom he referred to as *Jay*, and Ruth wondered how he could juggle *and* talk.

"You'll bruise the fruit, Callum, if you drop them."

"Like this?" Callum feinted a fumble, and it startled her. He laughed, caught the apples and placed them back in their bowl, caressing each one. "I love you to the *core*."

No wonder Billie was smitten. The doorbell rang and Ruth said, "Excuse me."

Walking down the hall she heard Pippa outside, *Yes, darling, I fully intend to ask.* She opened the door and Pippa stepped into the house wearing chamois leather slacks and a black blouse with studded cuffs. She smelled like a flower shop and moved like a catwalk diva. Ruth stood in a pinafore, feeling like Mrs Mop. Aubrey appeared looking fed up.

"But Mummy, I'll miss supper. *They're* having pasta."

Pippa checked her hair in the mirror. "Ah, bad luck. But what if I told you Uncle P has sent a car and invited us to dine somewhere special? Let's away, Aubs, come now!"

Aubrey sighed, resigned to her fate. "Bye-bye, Mrs Kean, wish I could stay longer."

Ruth ruffled the girl's cute blonde curls. "Maybe you will, next time."

"Actually, Ruth, might I have a word?" Pippa said. They stepped outside and walked down the path to the gate; Pippa was warbling about *a weekend away, business retreat in Frankfurt, might Aubrey stay with you?* Ruth was only half-listening because of the gleaming black car parked nearby, lights on and engine purring. She watched Aubrey trot towards it. A rear door opened as if by magic and Pippa finished her pitch. "What say you?"

"Certainly. No problem at all, Pippa. Dylan will be thrilled. When did you say?"

"In two weeks?" Pippa grinned. "And *here*... is the financial damage so far."

Ruth received an unsealed envelope made of good quality paper. She peeped inside at a slim wad of banknotes, the edges razor sharp. Pippa urged her to count the cash but she tucked it into her pinafore, like a washerwoman with a Christmas bonus. "Thanks, Pippa."

"And how is your wanderlust husband doing? Off somewhere warm, I dare say?"

"Bukavu, wherever that is," Ruth said, waving at the car. Aubrey waved back.

Pippa turned and cut smartly across the verge, hurrying to meet Uncle P, whoever he was. Ruth watched the high heels sink into glistening grass. This time, a driver wearing a peaked cap and gloves stepped out to open the rear door. Ruth stared. *Who on earth would send a chauffeur-driven limo?* She watched the car glide away like a well-kept secret.

Halfway along her garden path, she heard tapping from the guest room window and looked up. It was Billie, chewing on an apple, and rubbing finger and thumb in the air: *money?* Ruth nodded. *You got it.*

Chapter 50

The Sisters of Redemption occupied a large two-storey house overlooking one of Bukavu's quiet inlets. A stooping nun showed Frank into a spacious dormitory and played the silver beam of her flashlight into the gloom, revealing six empty beds, sheets neatly tucked. "We turn the generator off early. Come to see our conference room."

She led Frank down a sloping garden path to an annex. Frank nudged his fixer, and whispered, "What's her name again?" Ngabo leaned closer. "Sister Safi; the boss."

They entered the annex. It had decent desks, a wide blackboard and a spectacular view of Lake Kivu twinkling under moonlight. The place smelled of fresh concrete reminding Frank of his dad, long ago. Building an extension? Yes. Frank stepped outside and watched a white cat, rolling amid rosebushes, belly up for a tickle.

"His name is Aloysius, *he's* the boss," Sister Safi said, with a discreet glance at Ngabo. "And now, Mr Kean, regarding our terms. I hope you'll find them reasonable…"

Frank listened, watching the cat. The terms sounded ideal, far better than those offered by the Zealots of Eternal Darkness. He opened his wallet, peeled a pile of dollars, and added twenty extra. "Treats for the boss," he said. Sister Safi had that classic nun gaze: clear-eyed and vaguely disappointed, as if she knew all his sins or could probably guess. But she smiled eventually, shook his hand, then turned and disappeared into the night with Aloysius hopping behind her like a furry ghost, tail aloft and meowing, *Hey, I want a word.*

Frank walked with his fixer to the gate. "You're a saint,

Ngabo. Just one more—"

"Don't worry, I'll call your trainees, explain where to find you. Goodnight, pagan."

By midnight, Frank was curled in bed with a large white cat purring at his feet.

He spent Monday morning sorting his photocopied documents and preparing the seminar room. The dusty concrete floor needed a wash. Sister Safi brought him a mop and bucket. Aloysius came to spray his territory, tail up and eyes glazed. When their jobs were done, man and cat lunched together on the terrace, fried fish and *fufu; meow*. The houseboy scooted around in a panic even though Frank was the only guest. Monday afternoon, Frank relaxed on the terrace, reading local newspapers, snipping articles.

Tuesday morning, the first of the seminar, Ngabo arrived early wearing a white shirt, paisley tie, and shiny shoes. Frank stood with him in the lush garden watching whitecaps in the bay. The cat rolled amid roses, exposing a metre of its furry belly. Could life get any better?

"Great place," Frank sighed. "Thanks, Ngabo. When I said *saint*, I meant genius."

"Some journalists say I'm history." Ngabo glanced up the slope. A bell was ringing at the gate, the security man sliding back bolts for someone outside. "Here they come."

Down the slope they came, in their bright frocks and smart suits, headscarves and waistcoats. Frank counted ten journalists in all. *Two missing? Even so, we're lucky to have a room.* He stood at the door of the annex, shaking hands as they entered. The older men bumped heads with Ngabo, buddies from way back; two young women gave him a deferential nod. The journalists stared at the arc of desks and chose their seats; some smiled as they inspected the freebies, but others seemed wary. Of bribes?

Frank perched at the front, wondering which of his trainees would be the keen hack, the clown, or the lazy cynic. Or perhaps they would all be diligent and keen to learn, about theory if not practice. Ngabo settled at the back and sat arranging his pens, grinning like a Bukavu cat. Frank felt bad about having suspected his fixer of collusion, of running with both hare and hounds. No, Ngabo was decent, eager and efficient, no flunkey. Frank checked his watch, 08:59. Perfect timing. All's well that ends well and it was time to start. All eyes were on him, every jotter was open, every pencil poised. Should anyone drop a pin, he would hear it.

Instead, he heard the bell ring at the front gate. He went to a window and watched the security guard sliding back the bolts. The gate swung open and a couple of soldiers sauntered in, swinging their briefcases. Probably the two military reporters, as agreed, and better than five.

Frank watched as four more men trotted down the slope in khaki vests with PRESS logos. They carried TV cameras and microphones; one of them was yapping into a phone. Next came a teenage soldier carrying a rocket launcher with a red-coned missile, then three fellows in suits flanked by a tough-looking dude in a leather hat and wraparound sunglasses. He looked familiar. *The guy from the heliport?* Finally, Dr Hitimana strolled down in a cream trench coat, tails flapping in the breeze. He spotted Frank and waved. Frank waved back, retreated from the window, closed his eyes and gently headbutted the blackboard three times.

Chapter 51

A loud banging noise woke Dudu up. He lay on his back in dazzling sunlight. A security guard was standing over him, whacking a black truncheon into steel shutters.

"*Bonjour, shegué,* go!" The guard grinned, his teeth brown and cracked. Dudu sat up and looked along the litter-strewn pavement. Kilanda stood nearby, yawning.

They walked to the main street and bought little bananas from a man with a squeaky trolley, and some plastic bags of water from a *shegué* with a withered leg. Kilanda glanced, left and right, as if he were expecting Lucky Luc to stroll up any minute. The city bubbled with vehicles; Dudu watched lurching trucks cough their thick black smoke; motorbikes went buzzing past, busy as bees. Some drivers wore fine clothes, some just T-shirts and shorts. But they all beeped their horns if they had to slow down, because they were in a hurry and anyone else was a nuisance, especially two *shegués*. Police in white gloves stood in concrete boxes above the traffic, whistling and waving. A line of schoolgirls in smart black and white uniforms crossed the road. The tallest of them gave Dudu a nasty look to show she did not like stinky boys; her bossy air reminded him of Ginelle, who would probably give him some advice if she were here. A woman in a pink dress tossed her head, laughing into her phone; perhaps someone had told her a joke. A white UN jeep zoomed by and Dudu wondered about Major Monuc and that other solider lying on his tummy in a forest.

"Why the long face?" Kilanda said, chewing banana.

"You told me *Lucky Luc has a big house.*"

"No, I said *he will one day*. Last I heard, he lived in some old cemetery, growing vegetables to sell. Did you know, old bones make the soil good?"

"You don't even know which cemetery."

"Stop complaining. I'll find him."

"You've been saying that for the last three days, since the moment we arrived. We could walk three weeks and not find him. Kinshasa is too big."

"So go back to your little village."

Kilanda peeled another banana and strolled away. Dudu did not follow this time; he sat on a wall instead and wondered about the *kadogo's* big ideas, all those promises that changed like the wind. He thought about Mavuku. *I can't go back there yet*. So, what to do?

A mean-looking *shegué* walked up, snatched Dudu's hat and said, "Nice. Thanks." A bigger boy trotted up and grabbed Dudu's leather satchel. Dudu yanked it back and ran after Kilanda, calling for help. Kilanda turned, still chewing banana; the two troublemakers stopped in their tracks and stared at the *kadogo* with the lop-sided face and fearless gaze.

Dudu followed Kilanda across the street into a busy market where loud music pumped into their ears and all those bolts of bright fabric made Dudu's head swim. Steel pots and pans shone in the sun and wooden spoons dangled from string like Tata's sun-bleached bones.

"That *shegué* took my hat," he said. The fear and anger in his tummy made him feel sick, but Kilanda the *kadogo* just wandered about, cool as you like, admiring the Adidas tracksuits and chunky headphones that looked like huge beetles. He stopped at some hats and shoved a pale blue one on Dudu's head. "Suits you. Just like Major Monuc, remember him?"

Dudu swiped the hat off and put it back. He spotted a row of soldier dolls dressed in uniform, like the militia who had taken Tata. There was even a pastor doll. A real pastor in a round collar tapped Dudu's arm and he jumped in fright, but the pastor just said, "Sorry, may I squeeze by?" Dudu moved aside and watched him, feeling queasy.

Kilanda pointed to a belt with a golden clasp. "Know that logo, Dudu?" Dudu peered at the buckle made from two letters linked together: *D & G*. "No idea," he said.

Kilanda reached up to touch the buckle. "*Dolce & Gabbana*. The best, and I'm going to have a belt like this, some day. After I get rich. What's up, you OK?"

Dudu puked bananas and Kilanda howled. "Jesus, not on my boots!"

By noon they were sitting at the edge of a dusty field, scanning higgledy-piggledy headstones and wooden crosses. Two women placed flowers at a hump of earth, dabbing their eyes and Kilanda said, "Oh well, it's not this one either."

Mid-afternoon they heard music coming from a well-swept yard and paused to peep up it. Three pretty girls in tight tops were grinding their bottoms to a tune from a radio. Kilanda pointed. "See those beauties? They're practising *ndombolo*." A man in a Rasta bonnet leaned from a doorway, observing the strangers. Kilanda shunted his hips to show he was enjoying the music but the man just laughed and shouted, "Got arthritis, *shegué?*"

Kilanda walked away. "Ever seen such beauties, Dudu? Luc will find one for me."

"If you find Luc."

They wandered streets until dusk, avoiding gangs of *shegués* and looking for a quiet place to sleep. They bought dried fish and crouched in an alley to gobble it down like starved rats. They did not sit at a table in a big house. "Because you don't listen," Kilanda said.

Next morning, they got a lucky break and Dudu spotted it

first. He stood outside the alley and pointed across the road, through a swarm of beeping motorbikes. "I'll ask in there." Seven open coffins stood against the wall across the street, like doors into the next world.

Kilanda seemed confused. Dudu led him through traffic. "Trust me, a carpenter will know." They entered the carpenter's workshop; it smelled of sawdust and glue, like Tata's long ago. The fellow inside took off his spectacles, rubbing them on a cloth and listening to Dudu's questions, then he scribbled a list of local cemeteries on a pad and tore out the page. Kilanda nuzzled beside Dudu. "Read it out, smarty-pants, maybe I'll remember the name."

"Boboto Cemetery?" said Dudu. Kilanda shook his head, gazing at the coffins. Dudu read on. "Kasa-Vubu, Kintambo, Kimbanseke, Gombé, Benseke, Downtown or Tsieme?"

Kilanda frowned. "Actually, I think it was the first one. Where's Boboto?"

The carpenter drew a little map and Dudu thanked him, but Kilanda was silent, more interested in the shiny coffins, running a finger inside them, up and down. "Let me guess, Kilanda; after you get rich, you'll have one just like that?" Dudu said, and walked outside.

Kilanda came out and snatched the little map. "*I'll* find my brother, not *you*, ок?"

"Boboto is five miles," Dudu said. Kilanda stood checking the map, glancing along the street, left and right. Dudu turned the map right side up and pointed ahead. *That way.*

They trudged a busy boulevard where *shegués* perched like crows on a wall, sucking at bags of glue and glaring from under their puffed-up eyelids as smooth as pebbles.

At a restaurant terrace, well-dressed men sat with pretty ladies in fine robes, nibbling food. Dudu walked on and stood at some waste ground where grass grew in clumps. A misshapen football sailed through the air and boys ran like nervous goats, jostling to be first.

The sun was high and hot; the pavement seemed to melt underfoot. Dudu noticed a young *shegué* curled on the ground with his knees to his chest and wearing only a baggy T-shirt. The boy looked puzzled, somehow, more dead than alive, gazing solemnly into the distance. A fly landed on his scabby head, rubbing its front legs together as if hatching a plan.

Dudu checked the map again. It led them up a quiet lane with high walls and big houses. At a top-floor window, a bored-looking woman stood cradling a baby next to a vase of white flowers. A fierce-sounding dog snapped at Dudu's heels through a gap under a gate.

After two hours of tramping about, usually in the wrong direction, they stopped for another rest, squatting against a kiosk that sold scratch cards. Dudu watched cellophane wrappers glitter in the gutter and thought about Banza's wife back in Mavuku, the village phone lady who was getting rich. *Like Lucky Luc, if we ever find him.* A boy ambled past in baggy red shorts, counting money and whistling. Dudu noticed Kilanda's expression change. He no longer looked tired; he sat up, alert, ready for something. "What is it?" Dudu said. Kilanda raised a finger to his lips. *Quiet!* The boy in red shorts put money through the little window of the kiosk and Dudu noticed a green tattoo on his forehead, shaped like a question mark. The boy spotted them watching, took his new scratch card and quickly backed away.

"Hey, wait," Kilanda said. But the boy was already gone, slipping through the gap between two women approaching the kiosk. Kilanda barged through them, yelling after him to stop. The women seemed surprised. Dudu scrambled to his feet and followed Kilanda across the road, dodging cars. The boy was running too, faster now. Dudu caught up with Kilanda at the junction but they could not cross because of traffic. "What, Kilanda?"

Kilanda pointed. "Don't lose that kid!"

"Why?"

"Because he's got the tattoo. Where did he go?"

"The *tattoo*?" Dudu said, but Kilanda was halfway across the junction.

They reached a line of high bushes. The boy had vanished like steam from a pot. Kilanda pointed to a hole in the foliage and squeezed through it. Dudu followed, a thorn pricking him halfway. On the other side, Kilanda said, "Still don't believe me?"

They stood at the edge of a field, surveying neat rows of cassava bushes with pointy green leaves reaching for the sun. The tattooed boy was halfway across, standing among old headstones and wonky wooden crosses, watching his pursuers, as if daring them to follow. Kilanda called out but the boy turned and trotted on, towards ramshackle huts. Figures wandered about outside them: men and women, a few wobbly-legged infants. Smoke drifted up from a campfire. Kilanda whooped, striding ahead. "This must be it. I'll do the talking!"

They walked through rows of cassava plants that reminded Dudu of home; he pictured Mama thumping her stick into her bowl, making *fufu*. Perhaps tonight he and Kilanda would eat decent food, get washed and sleep in a bamboo bed, rather than an alley.

"There's Luc!" Kilanda said, laughing. "Big guy in the purple shirt, see!"

Dudu shaded his eyes and wondered how Kilanda could tell from this distance, especially through a heat haze that rose from the field like rippling water. The fellow in purple was leaning on a stick, watching and waiting. The boy in red shorts stood behind him, peeping out. Dudu followed Kilanda. *What will Lucky Luc do when we march in with strange tales? Will he hug his long-lost little brother or chase him like a stray dog?*

Kilanda was trotting ahead. He reached the wonky crosses

and sunken headstones in the middle of the field and stopped. Dudu stopped too, scanning the ground. "Snake?" He inched forward, stood alongside his friend and looked down. The nearest little cross bore a name and date, the letters and numbers scorched onto the grey weathered wood.

LUCKY LUC 1999

Kilanda sank to his knees and gurgled as if someone had just cut his neck; Dudu looked up and saw the big fellow in purple walking towards them, swinging that stick.

Chapter 52

The Catholic mission in Kisangani sat solid as a medieval fort, lacking only a moat and men in pointy helmets. Its walls loomed twenty feet high and were stained with patches of silky green lichen. The entrance was a flat arch big enough for a troop of cavalry at a gallop. Frank read the large white letters above the arch. La Procure. It was a regional logistics centre and, apparently, it offered cheap rooms. It also had an in-house radio station, and might be the perfect base for Unicorn's final seminar in Congo. At least, in theory.

The old guy sitting in the guard hut had a transistor radio and few teeth. Frank offered him a peep at Dr Hitimana's email, the paper grubby by now. The man read it and asked Frank where he had come from. "Bukavu," Frank said, "I train journalists. See, here?"

"No, what country are you from?"

"England."

The guard seemed to have heard of it. He passed the note back and Frank walked through the arch into a big cobbled courtyard flanked by flowerbeds and arcades. It looked like an Oxford college, very respectable, but the nun in reception had a first-class degree in rudeness; Sister Edwige listened to Frank's pitch and said, "Really? Your friend Matt from MO-NUC *told you*? Well, Mr Kean, he didn't tell *me*. What does he think this is, a *hotel*?"

She wanted cash up front and no funny business. Holy Mass would be at 7 a.m., breakfast would be at eight. Frank was tempted to ask if there would be any lunatics praying in the kitchen at 4 a.m. Sister Edwige scribbled in her ledger. "A *seminar*, eh? Well, Père Augustin runs the radio station, but I have no idea where he is. And please don't think you can just *wander about*, because you can't. Key." She dangled it for him, without looking up.

"Thank you, Sister. Please say I've arrived, if you see him?" Frank took the key and walked away. He sensed the nun's bright eyes burning two holes in his presumption.

His room was a monastic cell with a cot, basin and mosquito net. The décor was murky green and brown, like some military hospital. There was something joyless about the place. Then again, according to Matt-from-MONUC, several of La Procure's priests and nuns had been chopped to bits in the Mulele Mai rebellion of 1964. Kisangani certainly had a troubled history, anarchic even. Frank rinsed red dust from his face and went back to reception. It was time to explore the town. Sister Edwige barked *key* and he handed it over.

In the road outside, a group of men stood chatting by their bicycle taxis. Frank chose the tallest fellow with the aquiline nose, because he looked sort of Rwandese and might be able to shed some light on Congo's tiny eastern neighbour that had proven so influential, to put it politely, over the years. The man slapped the rear passenger seat.

"I'm Biroko Ruzerwa, sir, at your service. Tour of the town on my *toleka*?"

"Just down to the River Congo, please, I'd like to go across." Frank climbed aboard and watched the taut calves work the pedals. Biroko was all questions and Frank answered the easy ones. "I'm English, Biroko, married with two kids and another one coming. You?"

Sure enough, Biroko hailed from Rwandese stock. His father had moved here to work as a clerk in the diamond trade. The war had brought hard times but he loved Kisangani and he was hoping his six kids would see peace. Frank was hoping not to fall off the wobbly bike.

Kisangani had wider boulevards than Bukavu; less traffic too, and gentler slopes. The crumbling villas offered tantalising glimpses of a prosperous, long-gone colonial era. But here and there he spotted bullet holes, buildings blown apart by artillery. The modern white bungalows with red roofs hinted at a better future, but Biroko would know.

"How are the peace talks?" asked Frank, as if he didn't.

"RCD-Goma rejected the Sun City Agreement," said Biroko, legs pumping up and down. "Probably because they don't want to lose control of Kisangani and the diamonds. They like this town!" Sun-baked earth whizzed below as the bike cruised down a long incline bordered by tall palms. Elegant young girls marched single file carrying huge loads on their heads; weary-faced youths ambled around selling car radios, toys, fat rolls of sticky tape.

The riverbank was packed with people and livestock. Huge wooden canoes or pirogues nuzzled the quay, fifty feet long, six or seven feet deep, all coughing diesel. The water in the river was deep brown and flowing to Kinshasa a thousand miles south. Henry Morton Stanley had passed this way too, long ago, taking his boats apart and walking around the local rapids. Meanwhile, his sponsor King Leopold of Belgium had taken the country apart. Frank noticed a line of women staring at him, the curly blonde stranger. Their mystified gaze reminded him, oddly enough, of a night dive off Java, the time he had shone his torch at a huge shrimp suspended in the inky infinity, its fluorescent eyes gawping back. *Who are you?*

"And how is Kinshasa la Belle?" Biroko asked, as they disembarked from the bike.

"Not very *belle* at all, sorry to say." Frank climbed into a pirogue carved from a single tree. It rocked and bumped. Biroko lowered his bike in and slithered down.

"And sir, what would you like to do on the other side, when we reach Lubunga?"

"Walk around and come back," said Frank and Biroko nodded, looking baffled. He had bloodshot eyes and his white shirt clung to his sweaty torso.

Frank gripped the edge of the canoe as it puttered across brown water to the opposite bank, five hundred metres away. The river had looked tame from the shore but a swirling current soon offered a hint of its power. No wonder Joseph Conrad had described it as *an immense snake uncoiled*. In fact, hadn't this very city provided the model for Conrad's Inner Station, where Mr Kurtz lost his marbles in pursuit of ivory? Mr Kurtz, he should have stuck to seminars.

When they arrived at the opposite side of the Congo, Frank bought cold drinks at a kiosk and squatted to look back at the river. Biroko pointed out the landmarks: La Procure. Kisangani Cathedral too, like a small Westminster Abbey. Frank clicked photos with his second disposable camera. A kid joined them, his hair orange and black like a scorched field.

"Malnutrition," said Biroko. "He should be in the food hospital." He pointed to a wire fence. In the compound a few metres beyond, a man wearing a white tunic was addressing a group of women on benches. His flip chart showed brightly coloured sketches of fruit and vegetables, food groups. The little boy nestled between Frank and Biroko. They asked his name and age, and he said, "I'm Pons. Thirteen. I think." He looked about seven.

"Thirteen?" Frank said to Biroko, who nodded and pointed to the hospital. *Nutrition.*

Frank bought little Pons a Fanta and some snacks. The kid trotted away on bowed legs, swigging at the bottle. Three more kids appeared and Frank dipped in his pocket.

Biroko shook his head. "Please don't, sir, it just encourages begging."

"You sound like my father-in-law," Frank said. He gave the kids some cash and lit a cigarette, thinking about Anwell pottering around his cottage on the Swansea coast. Lovely place for a weekend, but Mr Goodall had all the answers when it to came to saving money, and all the questions about making it: *Time to get a real job, boyo?*

Frank stood up. "Let's go, Biroko. I've got work to do. People to meet at La Procure."

Back in the pirogue, rolling across the river, he told Biroko about the seminar. "Do you listen to local radio? Do you trust it? How would you change it, if you could?"

"Me?" Biroko seemed at a loss to answer. Turned out he didn't catch much radio – too busy working. But, back on the Kisangani side, walking uphill, he added, "Sir, this town feeds on rumour and it comes mostly from the market. Gossip spreads like fire. We don't know what to believe, sometimes. A radio station there could help us?"

Frank paused for breath, looking at some old villas. "It's an interesting point. But what kind of rumour?"

"The kind that starts trouble, and ends in a curfew, although these days, as you see, we have a lot more freedom than before, to travel. In fact, if you like, I'll transport you to Mangobo, to meet my family. They would enjoy that, sir. We'll relax, and drink tea like in England?"

"Maybe another day, thanks. As I said, I need to get back to La Procure. Hey, *there's* a picture."

Frank took out his camera. The dilapidated villa up the road looked ancient, its walls sagging into the ground, doors and windows long gone, stucco curling like lilies. He imagined some keen young Belgian in a starched collar surveying his garden long ago, his wife nearby, bored whalebone-stiff; dreaming every sultry afternoon of distant Antwerp?

Today, a little Congolese girl stood on the cracked veranda, her green frock matching the lush foliage all around her. Woodsmoke spiralled from the backyard where a hunched woman was poking at a blackened pot; she stood upright, spoon in hand and staring at him. Frank nudged Biroko. "This light is just right. Please, could you ask her if I can take a photo? I don't mind paying."

Biroko called out and the woman waddled quickly through the overgrown garden, hips swaying, one hand out. Frank gave her a few banknotes. She folded them into her cleavage and returned to her fire. He crouched to frame the veranda, at an angle. The girl's huge brown eyes glimmered in the airless afternoon. *Perfect.* He snapped again, to be sure.

"Stop that, now!" A small, baldy man in a polo shirt came striding along the street. Frank watched and waited. The fellow marched up and snatched the camera away. Frank tried to swipe it back. "Hey, not again! That's mine! Who the hell do you think you are?"

"Show me your authorisation for photographs. Who gave you permission?"

Frank paused, pointing to the garden. The woman had vanished, cooking pot too. "She was there. Just now," Frank said. "A woman. I gave her money. Who are you?"

"*Money?* Come with me." The eager stranger seized Frank's arm and signalled to a taller colleague standing a few metres away at a brown car with black windows.

Frank squirmed. "Hey! What's the bloody problem? Who are you?"

"I'm Theodore, he's Roosevelt and you're under arrest."

Chapter 53

Frank sat between two sharp elbows in the back of a speeding Peugeot and watched Kisangani whizzing by outside. His captors were RCD Security. They were not fools, and he was not a media consultant, here to train journalists. The small baldy fellow, Theodore, flipped through Frank's passport and Roosevelt spoke with a stammer, his mouth quivering under his attempt at a moustache; it wisped and curled like pubic hair.

"You were d-d-disturbing the p-p-peace. Probably selling b-b-bad photos of Congo for thousands of d-d-dollars to m-m-ass media in the West." He looked about seventeen, more kid than cop. He had halitosis and studied Frank's face like some Victorian criminologist, seeking tell-tale physiognomy.

Frank looked away. In the rear-view mirror he glimpsed a white smudge in the dusk – loyal Biroko on his bike, trying to catch up. The car slowed for two boys dawdling in the road. Theodore leaned forward, told the driver to use the siren. It jangled like the bell of an ice cream van. The boys scattered and Roosevelt said, "Mr Frank, where do you s-s-stay?"

"I'm at La Procure."

"W-w-why not at P-P-Palm Beach Hotel, don't you like g-g-girls?"

"La Procure has a radio station and big rooms. I'm hoping to hold my seminar there."

"We'll see about that," said Theodore. The car nosed through black gates with barbed wire above. In the courtyard, men in blue uniform sat holding guns and chatting to pneumatic women in miniskirts. Discussing drill, perhaps. "Out," said Theodore, and Frank obeyed.

They led him up steep steps and told him to sit on the bench at the top. He sat on the bench. The sleepy-eyed guard opposite looked like he would have preferred courtyard duty.

Theodore vanished and reappeared, glaring at Frank as if to say *just you wait*. Frank waited. Forty minutes.

Theodore led him into a big office with folders stacked in wonky piles, bureaucracy gone bonkers. On the desk, pens sprouted from a jam jar next to a Newton's cradle, made of wire and steel, its balls tarnished but intact. Theodore stood against a wall, hands behind his back, legs apart. A middle-aged man with a big belly entered the room. He had a holster on his belt, with a gun in it. He pulled up a chair and straddled it backwards, like he was in a cop film. His skin shone blue-black, the whites of his eyes were yellow as egg yolks. *Malaria, probably.* Frank watched stubby fingers bend his passport under the glare of a lamp. "Sorry for the delay, Mr Kean. Now, tell me why you are here."

"With all respect, I was hoping you might tell me."

"Because you were disturbing the peace. Why are you in Kisangani?"

"To train journalists."

"You entered our territory illegally. Where is your *carte de séjour*?"

"I didn't know I needed one."

"So you bribed our immigration officers. How much?"

"I did not bribe anyone. I respect your laws."

"How so, if you do not know them?"

"I took a photo of an old house with a child on its veranda. Is that a crime?"

"Tell me what you know about RTNC," said the cop, slowly turning pages.

"RTNC?" Frank scratched his head, to show he was trying.

"Radio-Télévision Nationale Congolaise. A media consultant would not have to ask."

"Sure. RTNC. State broadcaster. Some of its journalists came to my seminars in Kinshasa, Goma and Bukavu. I try to recruit at least two. Same here, next week, I hope."

"Tell me the names of your RTNC contacts in Kisangani."

"I don't have any. I was planning to drop in, introduce myself." Frank watched the big cop toss his passport in a drawer and lock it with a key.

"Mr Kean. I can detain you for forty-eight hours without charge. Once charges are filed, I can hold you a further two weeks before I transfer you to prison. So, is there anything you wish to tell me? A name, perhaps?"

"Dr Hitimana."

The cop looked puzzled. He flicked his Newton's Cradle, *click-click*. "Go on?"

"Your colleague Dr Hitimana approved my request from your HQ in Goma. He did not mention a *carte de séjour*. Perhaps I'll mention it, next time I see him. Would that help?" Frank stole a glance at the guy who had arrested him. Theodore looked stunned, his macho frown unravelling kink by kink. The big cop beckoned the small cop for a quiet word and when they were done, Theodore led Frank out. Roosevelt was sitting on the bench, chewing a fingernail.

"What d-did he s-s-say?"

"Never mind." Theodore led Frank up the corridor, out through a back door and down a fire escape. They walked single file along a narrow path through tangled weeds. Theodore strode ahead, steaming. Roosevelt stumbled along at the back like the class clown, first to be bullied and last to be picked. Frank noticed a brick hut, up ahead, in a secluded corner of the compound. When they reached it, Theodore kicked open the door and pointed at Frank. *You. Inside. Now.* Frank obeyed. The hut contained one wardrobe, one desk and three chairs.

"Sit down," said Theodore. He opened a drawer and took out a big black book, its pages swollen with damp. He used a pencil and ruler to draw a margin down one of them, tongue poking out as he worked. "You will give us a statement. You will describe how you were surprised, in the act. And you will tell me your contacts at RTNC, here in Kisangani."

"As I said, I don't have any contacts. Not in Kisangani. But I know Dr Hitimana."

Theodore slammed his palm on the desk. "Stop lying!"

Frank unfolded Dr Hitimana's printed email and slid it across. "Read this."

Theodore read the paper and flicked it back. "Anyone can forge an email."

Frank took two photos from his bag. "And these? I had these pictures developed in Bukavu, just last week. Look, here's me with Dr Hitimana after my Goma seminar."

Roosevelt came for a peep. "Anyone c-c-can f-f-fake a photograph."

"We were also on Goma TV, on the news. Did you see it? Was that fake too?"

"We don't get m-m-much TV here. K-K-Kisangani is *enclavé*," said Roosevelt, "too isolated. We can't even s-s-see the f-f-f-football, s-sometimes."

"Sorry about that," Frank said. "Which team?"

"I support A-a-a-a—"

"Stop trying to change the subject." Theodore sat sharpening a pencil.

"Arsenal," said Roosevelt, finally, with a proud grin.

Frank winked at him. "Theodore, may I suggest you call RCD-Goma, ask about me?"

They eyeballed each other. "Mr Kean, *I* will decide what to do. I can lock you up, I can stop your seminar if I like." He sat erect, stiff backed. "Statement, I want a statement."

Frank sighed, eyeing the ceiling. "Fair enough. I flew from Bukavu this afternoon in a MONUC helicopter. I checked into La Procure, I rode a *toleka* to the river. I took a pirogue across to Lubunga. I came back. I took a photograph. You arrested me. The question is why?"

"I will ask the questions. Who took you to the river?"

"Some guy on a bike."

"Who did you meet in Lubunga?" Theodore was scribbling fast. And possibly furious.

"A little boy with malnutrition. I bought him some snacks and a bottle of orange *sucré*." Frank paused to scratch his head. "Wait, rub that out. I believe it was *lemon sucré*."

Theodore paused to look up. "Do you think this is a joke?"

"I think you should call Dr Hitimana. He personally organised my seminars after extensive talks with the US government. According to what I saw on Goma TV. Presumably, if you prevent me from staging my seminar in Kisangani, he'll have to call the White House."

Theodore spoke sideways to Roosevelt. "Call Goma."

Roosevelt strode to the door. "But what if I c-c-can't get through?"

"You'll keep trying, won't you?" Theodore said, and Roosevelt slipped away. Theodore licked his pencil and leaned over his pages. "Start in Kinshasa, Mr Kean. Talk."

Frank talked. About hyacinth on the Congo and flags on poles; about talented musicians; about a priest who helped vulnerable street kids, and a vox pop that sparked a spat among a gang of violent ones. Theodore glanced up. "Do you enjoy causing trouble in my country?"

Frank avoided his gaze and looked at the wardrobe instead. Its door was ajar and he noticed names and dates carved inside. Theodore leaned closer. "Answer me."

"Certainly. I'm just thinking what to say. Please write this down, word for word. *I did not come here to cause trouble. I came to help journalists, to foster objective reporting of community issues, to promote tolerance and prevent conflict at the grass roots, to help build a sustainable peace.*"

"Peace? Hah! Kinshasa is not interested in peace. You are wasting your time."

"You sound like my father-in-law. To be honest, I'm starting to wonder if he's Congolese. Not Welsh."

"Let's talk about America. You mentioned USAID in the

car. Tell me more."

"I feel hot. I can hardly breathe. Why don't we go out, chat over a beer?"

"USAID."

They played verbal tennis until Roosevelt returned twenty minutes later with Frank's passport and whispered words for his colleague. Theodore grimaced, drew a line under the three-page statement and read it aloud in a droning voice. Frank stopped him after two lines. "Wait, I never said, *I was caught disturbing the peace.* I said, *I was photographing a child with her mother's permission when* RCD *security officers approached me.* So please change that bit. I won't sign this version in case I incriminate myself. You might lock me up."

Roosevelt shook his head. "We w-w-won't l-l-lock you up."

Theodore erased the offending words, scribbled again and read to Frank the amended text. After three pages and several more tweaks, Frank signed and said, "Thank you."

"Just d-d-doing our j-j-job," said Roosevelt.

Frank smiled. "And doing it well, I might add. Now, gentlemen, may I leave?"

Theodore snapped his book shut. "You said beer."

Darkness had descended by the time Frank emerged through the big gates. He spotted a friendly face – Biroko the *toleka* driver was still waiting outside after all this time. Frank invited him for a beer with his new friends. Biroko looked worried. "Your *friends?*"

They walked a few blocks in balmy air. Roosevelt suggested his favourite sports bar because it had a TV. They were in luck too, the place was showing live soccer for a change. Theodore chose a long table with eight seats and Biroko muttered, "Frank, are you sure?"

"Why, what's the problem?" Frank said. He found out soon enough. Three more plain-clothes RCD men joined the party and he sat watching their beer bottles multiply.

Nevertheless, he was a free man. They even returned his cheap little camera. He swigged beer, *cheers guys,* and tried to inveigle Theodore into explaining why the RCD had been so interested in his non-existent contacts at he state broadcaster in Kisangani. But Theodore preferred to discuss The Iron Lady, "Because I am a fan of your Magritte Thatchur. Did you meet her?"

"Sure." Frank obliged with an anecdote. The waiter brought more drinks plus a menu. The RCD boys were hungry; famished, as it turned out. They ate, drank and argued among themselves. Frank paid the bill. By 11 p.m. he was drunk, like them, and stood under a street lamp listening to Theodore espouse *the purity of Hitler's vision,* watching moths flutter in kamikaze delirium. Roosevelt was peeing in a bush and the other guys were cracking jokes with a woman in a short skirt and red lipstick who seemed willing to help with further inquiries.

Frank walked unsteadily backwards, waving farewell to his new friends, promising to stay in touch. Biroko, who had not touched a drop all night, insisted on transporting him to La Procure, *now.* They climbed onto the bicycle taxi and off they wobbled. Soft rain glistened on the peaceful boulevards and frogs croaked from the grass.

"I have a question," Frank said. "Who would carve names and dates in a wardrobe?"

"The people who were locked inside it," Biroko said.

Hopping off outside La Procure, Frank paid his loyal driver a handsome fee and agreed to visit his home across town sometime. He walked on, into the dark and dripping courtyard, past a wrinkle-faced priest who stared as if he had seen a curly-haired ghost.

There was no sign of Sister Edwige in reception, so Frank lifted his key from its hook and walked to his room. He sat on his bed, turning his disposable camera in his hands; he was glad Theodore had given it back but something did not add up: *why all those questions about the state broadcaster, which is under* RCD *control here in the east? Shouldn't they be more concerned about private radio stations, which are not?*

He undressed, thinking through his schedule for the next few days. His brain was pickled but, still, best to plan ahead. Tomorrow, he would try to find Père Augustin here at La Procure, who would probably know a good fixer. Then tour the local stations, recruit trainees. Different town, same routine. Congo was blurring into one big bloody seminar. Frank burped and wrapped a towel around his waist; time for a shower then bed? Cot, actually.

He locked his room and walked up the brown-walled corridor to a bathroom containing four stalls lit by a one-naked bulb. The water in the shower was cold but clean. Frank stood under icy jabbing bullets. He lathered soap and whistled "Singin' in the Rain".

The water spluttered to a stop and the light went out. *Great.* He stood in roaring darkness, listening to tiny bubbles of lather pop like distant guns. He tapped the water pipe. Nothing. After three minutes he lost hope but found a solution: *I can rinse off from the water bottle in my room.* He slithered back up the corridor, groping the walls like some desiccated extraterrestrial. He heard clawed feet pattering, an animal running towards him? A small dog came barking and snapping at his ankles in the darkness. Frank yelled and cursed, hopping aside, lashing a kick. The dog scampered off. Frank froze as a torch beam flooded the floor and slowly lit him up, head to toe, inch by soapy inch. "Mr Kean, what you are doing?"

He squinted into dazzling rays. "Sister Edwige?"

"This is a house of worship. Please dress accordingly." The torch beam circled away like a spotlight in a POW camp and he stood in the dark, counting the days until his escape.

Chapter 54

Saturday morning, driving to the prenatal clinic, Ruth got stuck behind a long, fume-belching lorry at the sharp corner on Lavender Road. She pulled out her phone and texted Frank: *How r u?* She poked her head through the window to check on the lorry and got a blast of acrid diesel. She covered her mouth and nose; you could never be too careful about fumes, especially if you were expecting a baby. She twisted towards the back seat. "Hey, Dylan, close your window." But her son ignored the advice, too busy thumbing his Game Boy.

In the lobby of the clinic, she paused to read a poster about cleft palate kids in India, poor mites, something to do with arsenic in their parents' drinking water. She spotted a website address for donations, but you never knew, with charities. Dylan shuffled behind her up the corridor, thumbing his buttons. "But how can we see the baby if it's in your tummy?"

"You'll see," Ruth replied. They reached the waiting room and she sat next to a pregnant Indian woman in a sari, who seemed no more than eighteen years old; she had big gold earrings, big brown eyes and a red dot on her forehead, as if a sniper were aiming his gun in some movie. Ruth was tempted to mention arsenic, but this was London not Lucknow.

Her phone beeped and she read Frank's reply. *I'm good, in Kisangani. Can I call?* She texted, *Yes but I'm at clinic, ultrasound.* Her phone rang moments later and she left the room, telling Dylan to stay put. He nodded, staring at a poster of a womb with a foetus in it.

Frank's voice was clear but he sounded strange, not quite himself. She walked out to the car park and asked about Kisangani but he changed the subject rather too soon.

"So, how's baby, good-looking like Mum?"

"Actually, I'm still waiting, next in the queue. Is everything OK?"

"Sure, Ruth, why not?"

He sounded breezy but something was amiss, she just knew it. Nor would he say a word about whatever was bothering him, until he got home; it was always the same, like getting blood from a stone. So she waited and Frank said, "Been thinking about your text."

"Which one? I lose track. If you mean the childminding, so far so good."

"No, the one about Billie's boyfriend asking about Max, or something?"

"Callum asked about the suicide, yes. I told him to mind his own business. Why?"

"I was wondering if Billie put him up to it, that's all."

Ruth watched a jet flying to Heathrow. Or from it. "Frank, can we talk about something else? Such as, when are you coming home? Kisangani is your last seminar, yes?'

"Yes. And you'll have to tell Billie sometime. Why her dad killed himself, I mean."

His tone made it sound a simple task for any good parent; easy like Sunday morning. Ruth waddled in circles, one hand on her huge belly. "I will, but not because of some pushy boyfriend. Or maybe I won't tell her at all. Probably do more harm than good, anyway."

"I'm just saying …"

"Frank, I just replied. Now tell me about Kisangani. What's up? Don't say *nothing*."

"It's hot and sticky. The water goes off in the shower. You'd love it."

"Did you know that arsenic in drinking water gives kids in India cleft palates?"

"Sounds grim. Good job you haven't been to India—"

The line dropped with a dry click before she could say, *but you went, Frank*. She texted it instead, strolling the car park, and got no reply. She passed by a shiny Audi. The middle-aged Indian driver wore a scarlet turban, probably waiting for the girl in the clinic. He was reading a newspaper. Ruth squinted at the headline. THAMES TORSO MYSTERY. What was that about? London could be a nasty place. Noisy too. She tracked the sky, watching the next plane. *Be nice to live someplace quiet. South Wales?* She felt a strange and unexpected longing to be back there, and not just to visit. Frank had still not replied to her text so she scrolled to her father's number and pressed *Call*.

She pictured Dad in a shirt and tie, standing on his sunny balcony and sipping tea – or possibly scotch and soda – and staring down at the surfers in Rum Cove. *Nincompoops, the lot of 'em.*

"Do I owe you money?" Dad said, cackling down the line. He sounded in rude health but was soon complaining that his days were numbered; when would she visit?

Ruth gawped up at the grey belly of a huge aircraft and said, "When Frank gets back."

"From bongo-land. Why doesn't that boy find a job here, like normal people?"

"Good question and don't be racist."

"Not me. Some of my best friends are bus drivers."

Ruth let it pass; Dad might never forgive the Asian driver of the charabanc that had flattened Mum, but at least he could joke about it. Was this racism or progress? *Both*.

The jet overhead was too loud. Another soon followed. Ruth's chat was drowned by almost constant noise so she ended her call, keen to go back into the clinic. She paused in the lobby to read the poster about cleft palate surgery, this time forcing herself to look at the photos, before-and-after. One of the grinning kids looked like someone had swiped him in the gob with a machete. *What a world.* Ruth closed her eyes and said a prayer for her baby, and one for Dad, that the gash in his spirit might heal. She prayed for the bus driver too. It had not even been his fault; Dad seemed to have forgotten, over the years. There was a word for that, when you tweaked history to suit yourself. Revision? Revisionism. She remembered how it had foxed Frank one time, in a crossword, and he should know, changing his tune as soon as he got home from a trip. *Well, Ruth, when I said* fine, *what I meant was…*

She went back to the waiting room and sat with Dylan. When the young Indian woman reappeared, Ruth caught her glance and asked, "All OK?"

"I am hoping so, thank you." The woman walked on, gathering her sari, *swish-swish*.

Ruth watched her go and wondered about arsenic in India. You probably had to live there, in a poor place. Not in west London, with a nice Audi. Dr Ryan poked her head out of the ultrasound room and grinned, *who's next?* She was wearing her lab coat and a stethoscope dangled from the pocket, black and wormy. Ruth ushered Dylan inside. "Time to see the baby, big brother."

Dr Ryan exuded the calm authority of someone who knew just about everything, except that her silver hair was too long for a woman her age. Her dark blue blouse was buttoned at her skinny neck; that ruby lipstick did not look right with her pale skin. All a bit ghoulish. Dr Ryan grinned at Dylan, who looked ready to pee his pants. She rubbed stinky cold gel across Ruth's distended tummy and moved the hand-piece back and forth. The ultrasound squelched. Dylan edged forward, looking wary but curious. "What's that thing?"

Dr Ryan poked a button. "My sonic transducer sends waves into Mum's tummy."

"*Waves?* Like at the seaside?" Dylan turned to Ruth. "Like at Grandad's?"

"Waves of sound," said Dr Ryan, pointing to the monitor. "There's your sister."

Dylan gawped. Ruth watched the monitor over the tight swell of her tummy, her excitement gnawed by anxiety as she gazed at the grainy image flickering onscreen like a triangle of black and white pizza. The baby nestled in the middle of it, curled up and sucking her thumb. Either that or she was growing a beard like King Tut. Baby had Frank's nose too.

Dylan hoisted himself on his elbows, heels swinging. "Actually, it's a boy."

Dr Ryan winked at Ruth and said to Dylan, "Are you sure?"

"Yup. A girl would have long hair."

After a few more twists and turns with her hand-piece, Dr Ryan turned off the machine and swabbed Ruth's belly, nice and clean. "All done, you can get down now." A flat-footed medic came in with a foolscap file and Dr Ryan reached inside to take a document. "Here are your triple test results, Ruth, you did well. Congrats, see?" She passed the sheet.

Ruth blinked at the bewildering columns of data: *alpha-fetoprotein, human chorionic gonadotropin* and *unconjugated estriol.* "I'll borrow Frank's dictionary."

Dr Ryan chuckled. "And how's your morning sickness, through the worst?"

"Thank God! A three-month hangover that was, men just don't get it do they?"

"Lucky them." Dr Ryan watched a sheet of white paper spool from the printer on her desk and gave it to Dylan. "And here's a pretty picture for you, until next time. Bye, Donald!"

Dylan frowned and it was time to go home. Ruth explained the printout as they walked down the corridor, past noticeboards and potted plants. She stopped for a cup of iced water from a cooler, but changed her mind. "Let's go to Auntie Carol's for a cuppa. She's got one of those scanners. I'll ask her to scan this and email it to Daddy. What d'you reckon? Shall we go to Auntie Carol's? On the way, we can think of a name for our baby."

"Not Donald," said Dylan, gazing at the drum of water. "Can we get a goldfish?"

They spent the afternoon at Carol Watt's fairy-tale cottage on Anne Boleyn Walk. Ruth wiped a smear of Devon cream from her lips and imagined life in this cosy nest. She liked the William Morris wallpaper and vintage Japanese quilt blocks under glass – *very Zen*. The shrubbery out back was glorious – *classic Kew* – but she did not care for the framed black-and-white photo of the hungry African kid, ribs like a concertina. Nor the spooky grandfather clock going *bong* every time she reached for another scone. Dylan sat at the inglenook fireplace stuffing cake into his face – *don't mind if I do* – and Carol stood at her scanner, wearing clogs and a gorgeous hand-knit Fair Isle jumper that probably cost a bomb.

"How's my scan?" Ruth asked, sipping Earl Grey from a posh china cup that she was scared of dropping. Nice motif, gold-leaf trim. Carol had good crockery, too.

"Almost done, Ru. I'll email you the attachment, then you just forward it to Frank."

"*Just?* I can't even download that Google-engine. I did try. Not as easy as you said."

"You must persevere. It's useful. It can find stuff about anything. As good as Explorer if not better. I've asked my staff to try it at Kew. Look what happens if we enter QUILT." Carol tapped at her computer keyboard. Ruth watched the results fill the screen.

Dylan came to see. "How come you and Mummy always talk about quilting?"

"We talk about other stuff too," Ruth said, but her son looked unconvinced.

"Quilting made us friends," Carol said. "When you were very small, Dylan."

"In Mummy's tummy?"

"Actually, you were in your pushchair; waiting with your daddy, in a queue for beer."

Dylan shrugged. "Which supermarket, Tesco or Waitrose?"

"Actually, you were all at the summer concert at Kew,"

Carol said. "I spotted a neat little patch on your daddy's linen jacket and I thought, *Interesting, someone likes to sew*."

Ruth shook her head. "If it was so neat, Auntie Carol wouldn't have spotted it, eh?"

"*Nice block; just needs a border*, I told your mummy. We've been pals ever since."

"Why?" asked Dylan, and Carol scratched her Einstein curls. "Why not, Dylan?"

He had no answer and Ruth smiled over her teacup. Few people could flummox her young chatterbox, but this blunt northerner with the southern gloss had his number. You never quite knew what to expect with Carol, which was part of the fun. Sentimental but not soft, sensitive but sharp, she was loving but never seemed to be *in* love. How come? Were men scared of her, as Carol herself had once suggested? Or plain terrified, as Frank had insisted? Ruth pointed at the computer. "Can Google search for *P. Price, risk management?*"

Carol typed it in and peered at the results. "Let's see. The top hit is an article by *Patricia Price-Garland* about *the risks of managing twins in labour*. No thanks."

"What happens if you search for my name?" Dylan said, munching a scone.

"Let's try. How do I spell DONALD?"

Dylan stopped chewing to stare at her in silence.

Ruth edged closer to the computer. "Just a sec Carol, what if we type *Pippa Price?*"

She watched Carol's nimble fingers fluttering fast and precise. *No wonder her quilts turn out so nice*. The Google-engine thing did its stuff and Carol clicked the top line.

"Here we go. She's on Biz-Link, like me. I can log in, view her profile, like this…"

Carol typed a password. "OK, I'm in. Wow, nice horse. Is this Pippa in the saddle?"

The photo onscreen showed Pippa Price riding a sleek black horse at a gymkhana. *Oh, bravo*. She looked amazing, fit as a fiddle and confident of her abilities, showjumping with the best of them. The photo was about two years old, dated *Aug 12, 2000*, in small red letters, bottom left corner.

Carol pointed to the text below. "No, sorry Ruth, this can't be your Pippa. Look, if we scroll down, under this stuff about work and MBA, it says *single, no children.*"

Ruth looked closer. Carol was right but something was amiss. For sure, the woman in the photo was Pippa Price; those cheekbones, the distinctive eyebrows; Ruth would know them anywhere, no problem. The problem was *August 2000*. She sat doing sums in her head. The daughter Aubrey would have been what, *five*? So how come Mummy was *single, no kids*? Either clever Pippa had checked those boxes wrong or she was taking people for a ride.

Chapter 55

Frank sipped chicory-flavoured coffee in the corner of the breakfast room of La Procure, watching two arthritic priests in black cassocks solemnly nibble their bread and jam. They looked sun-dried, worn out; to smile would be a sin. A third priest sailed into the room, humming a melody as he edged along the buffet, stacking his plate with boiled eggs, toast, crepes, the lot. He spotted Frank and came weaving through the tables and chairs like a heavyweight boxer closing in. His handshake almost yanked Frank's arm from its socket.

"Mr Kean, I presume! I'm Père Augustin. Sister Edwige told me all about you."

Frank pictured himself soapy, half-naked. "I'll bet she did. How's Radio Éternel?"

"Excellent! Well, excellent until we rebroadcast the BBC World Service. The RCD claims the BBC is biased, anti-rebel. They'd probably like to shut us down." Père Augustin chuckled at the very idea, sipping his coffee. He peered into the mug. "Not bad, today."

"And how often to do you rebroadcast the BBC?"

"Every day."

"Sounds risky. Why don't the rebels shut you down?"

"Politics, Frank! First, we have the biggest transmitter in the region. Second, we also use it to broadcast RCD announcements. Third, if the rebels banned the BBC they would alienate Rome, which would be undiplomatic in a Catholic country like this. So, welcome! I heard you've been wandering in the dark, frightening our little dog? Be careful, Bosco bites."

"Not to mention Sister Edwige," said Frank and the priest grinned.

After breakfast, walking across the courtyard, Frank noticed that Père Augustin's soutane had buttons from collar to feet, shining like a line of blackcurrants, and asked, "Why so many?"

"One button for each year of Christ's life. I'd prefer a zip."

The studio of Radio Éternel was small but functional, with digital gear in sturdy steel racks. Frank half-expected to find a DJ nun spinning hymns. Instead, a youngster in a tracksuit was playing rap music, and raised a thumb. *Yo*. Frank followed Père Augustin into an office with wood-panelled walls, faded framed photos of priests, and a pile of old paperback Bibles zigzagging up a corner. The dust lay thick, the flowers were plastic.

"Let's discuss your seminar, Frank. The RCD says certain stations cannot attend."

"I can still invite them. I just need a fixer. Someone connected, who drives something faster than a *toleka*."

"I have a motorbike. I'll take you wherever you want, far easier. Besides, Kisangani is bigger than you might think and quite unpredictable. I have good contacts."

"Thanks for your generous offer. And I agree about *unpredictable*." Frank told him about getting arrested by the RCD. The priest shrugged. "You got off lightly, Frank. They can be quite severe. It was generally easier in the old days." He nodded at the framed photos. "But that was then."

Frank looked at the wall, and looked again. One frame contained a poster of the boxer Joe Louis in US Army uniform, clutching a rifle, poking his bayonet. The slogan read, *We're going to do our part, and we'll win because we're on God's side.* "Nice poster. The Brown Bomber; my dad liked him. Actually, Père Augustin, you look a bit like Joe. Is that an original?"

"Yes, from 1942. It was an ordination gift in '72, from

America. But let's discuss the seminar. We should start organising, as soon as possible. Will you fill my tank with petrol?"

"If you fill my class with students. When do we begin recruiting?"

"Now, why not? Three journalists from here, plus me. That's four already."

"That's greedy, already."

"What about my *generous offer?*"

Frank smiled. This was some town; out of the frying pan, into the Vatican. "Three places including you, Père Augustin, or I'll phone the Pope. Do you have a seminar room?"

"Yes, but I can't host your training here. The RCD will say we manipulated you."

"You're doing your part, with God on your side," Frank said, and got a strange look.

"I'll get you a seminar room, I know places. But first, let's meet some radio people."

Fifteen minutes later, they were roaring around the town on a Yamaha 500, shimmying through traffic, cutting low on turns. Frank clung to the pillion seat, saying his prayers. They rode along a boulevard bordered by red earth and huts under palm fronds. Young men lined the roadside selling stuff nobody seemed to need. Tiny girls carried jerry cans and firewood, while boys wobbled across a deserted intersection, three to a bicycle.

Most of the radio stations Frank visited with Père Augustin were tiny – Radio Reveille was the size of a pantry with a mixing desk and mangled wires snaking up the wall. Some stations earned revenue from NGOs keen to spread a message. Most – like Radio St Paul – had church support. News-wise, there seemed no shortage of community issues in a town of half a million people – health and sanitation dominated the agenda, despite the deluge of political polemic from the good offices of the RCD. The radio station managers told Frank a familiar tale of woe – there was little commercial advertising revenue. They seemed worn out, weary of an economy on its knees. Ironic, somehow, in a town famous for diamonds. But, when he visited Radio-Télévision Nationale Congolaise he noticed something different; not so much the buzz of a newsroom, more a palpable tension. Perhaps job cuts were looming at the state broadcaster. Frank pitched his seminar to RTNC's radio editor, finishing with a question.

"So, could you spare two journalists to attend? It's free. Location to be confirmed."

"Expect so." The editor fingered her pearls, glancing at her watch. "Are we done?"

Over the next two days, Frank and Père Augustin honed their double act: the burly priest with the local touch – all head bumps and friendly gossip – and Frank the newbie foreigner with training for free, per diems too. They chatted with two dozen managers and journalists; it went well until Père Augustin got a phone call from the RCD, who had heard about Frank and wanted to meet him. "Not for beers, I hope?" Frank said.

"For information conversation," replied Père Augustin, turning the bike around. They rode to a different RCD office, where Frank was lightly grilled by an anxious official in horn-rimmed specs, pencil poised. "The names, Mr Kean. The names of your contacts at RTNC."

Frank sipped tepid water from a glass with lipstick on the rim. "I met an editor."

It lasted twenty minutes. On the way out Père Augustin said, "Something's brewing."

Frank followed him down well-worn steps. "A cup of tea would've been nice."

Chapter 56

With help from the big priest, Frank hired a seminar room at a local NGO called Mother & Baby. Plenty of space, good desks, chairs and a huge whiteboard. Best of all, it was located on a busy street and the restaurant down the block – Apollo Grill – offered buffet lunches. Père Augustin suggested they drop in, his bear-like hand caressing his sizeable belly.

The restaurant's grizzly Greek manager sat rolling topaz prayer beads through sallow fingers and said to Frank, "Are you serious? Can I *feed twelve journalists?* I can feed twelve tribes."

Frank treated Père Augustin to a buffet lunch and they sat down to enjoy their kebabs, humus, and succulent Kalamata olives. "How does a priest get into radio?" Frank asked.

"I attended a seminary in Kinshasa but came back here. I'm local, I missed Kisangani. It's an interesting place and Radio Éternel keeps me rooted in the community. Our missions keep me on my toes. I like the combination. There's always a crisis out there somewhere."

"Were you here for the big one, Rwanda versus Uganda, two years ago?"

"Yes, I was." Père Augustin chewed an olive. "Short and savage. Next question."

Frank sat back to survey the other guests; most seemed to be Congolese. Two *mindele* and a MONUC Blue Hat were sipping at tiny glasses of luminous limoncello. "Do you think Dr Hitimana from the RCD will turn up, to launch my seminar?" Frank said. Père Augustin shrugged hefty shoulders and poured mint tea. "If he does, your life will be easier."

As it turned out, Dr Hitimana stayed away. The journalists arrived on time for their first day: six women and six men. Frank tried to memorise names from their folded tags: Bouazizi, Guychel, Mabi, Ekanga, Sharufa, Bibiche… it was like poetry, curling his tongue.

They seemed serious-minded, no clowns or prima donnas, not even the young woman who resembled Naomi Campbell. Frank started with basics – headlines, short paragraphs, comparison and analysis. They took notes, asked sharp questions. The mood was friendly until the afternoon coffee break, when hackles rose during a chat about the RCD. He spotted a clear divide between those who felt the RCD had been right to spurn the recent Sun City peace deal, and those who felt the RCD had squandered a chance at that conference for peace, thanks, allegedly, to meddling by their political godfathers over the border, tiny little Rwanda. It was a feisty class and Frank was unusually tired by home time. It would be a good week.

He slept well that night, relishing the heavy silence that numbed Kisangani like a natural narcotic wafting in from the surrounding jungle.

He woke at six and was in the breakfast room by seven, enjoying a fried egg. Père Augustin strode in and poured a huge mug of coffee. He sat opposite Frank, grim-faced with a tiny radio pressed to his ear.

Frank chewed yolky bread. "On a diet?"

The priest frowned, finger to his lips. "Heard this? Someone is broadcasting hate messages on RTNC. *We must kick all Rwandans out of Kisangani.* This means trouble, I bet."

"What? Who's *we*?"

"*We are the RCD Originel.* It's a mutiny, Frank. We must get to your seminar, soon."

They rode out through the flat arch of La Procure five minutes later. Kisangani seemed like a ghost town minus the tumble-weed. Even so, Père Augustin seemed cautious, stopping at every intersection. He cut no corners, today. "Can you hear that, Frank?"

Frank nodded. "I hear something. Sounds like footy fans. But where are they?"

A gang of chanting youths trotted from a side street, most of them swinging wooden clubs or iron bars, one lad waving an upside-down American flag on a bamboo pole. Frank stared and wondered about the millions of dollars that USAID was pumping into this country, some into his own seminar. He spoke over Père Augustin's shoulder. "What's going on?"

The youths trotted across the road towards a tall, skinny fellow carrying a briefcase. He tried to run. They blocked him, dragged him down, kicked him in the guts, whacked him in the head. His skull popped like a firecracker and red mush flooded the gutter. They bashed his brains out and moved on. A skeletal dog moved in. Père Augustin and Frank sped away.

Chapter 57

The youths living at the cemetery called themselves *The Living Dead,* and Dudu was getting used to it. After a few days, he considered this quite an appropriate name, because the cemetery certainly seemed lively most of the time, even fun, with its cosy little homes in ramshackle huts and old cars, the campfires and meals cooking every day. These youths were not wandering troublemakers like some other *shegués* in Kinshasa; The Living Dead were like a family. Plus, most of them seemed to feel sorry for Kilanda, after all that weeping at his brother's grave. Their leader Chintock even offered him Lucky Luc's old hut to live in.

It contained rusty pots and pans, a broken bike, piles of dusty documents. Some of the gang refused to enter in case of ghosts, but Chintock stood poking his stick through the junk.

"Place just needs a clear out, and about time. Dudu, you can stay too, if you like?"

"Thanks. We can tidy it," Dudu said. He looked at Kilanda, who seemed to disagree.

Chintock clapped his hands. "Good! Work hard and you're in." He seemed a decent sort in his smart purple Lakers singlet and gold earrings glinting in the gloom. That green question mark tattoo on his arm made him seem mysterious. He walked out, towards his own hut, the biggest of all, the one they called *The White House,* although the paint was old, grey.

Dudu wondered about that tattoo. The rest of the gang had the same one in different places – on their ankles, shoulders or neck – but only Alain who wore red shorts had the tattoo on his forehead, and if you asked him why, he just gazed with glassy eyes. "Because." He seemed to spend most days smoking *diamba*; it made his movements slow and his mouth slack. *So how had he run as fast as a rabbit to escape Kilanda, that first day?* "Because."

The gang numbered about a dozen. Second in command was Bruno; he wore a black beret, a washed-out jacket from the militia and cool, bug-eye sunglasses. He seemed wary of the two newcomers and asked Kilanda at least one new question every day, as if checking the *kadogo's* story. Bruno's girlfriend Lady Chantal had red-painted toenails that shone like ripe coffee beans, nice eyes and lips ready for kissing. Most nights she stood in the road by the cemetery, waiting for trucks to stop and flash their lights. The rest of the girls went too, including pretty Jacquette with long legs like an okapi, and even Joelle who was only ten. They would all return with money tucked in their tops, to share with Chintock, Bruno and the rest, to buy food and supplies. "One day, you'll have to go and get some," Mama Marie told Dudu. She never went to the road. Perhaps because she was the cook, up early and tying on her pinafore. Mama Marie was about sixteen; she had calloused hands and tired eyes but her pretty ribbons and beaded hair reminded Dudu of Ginelle in Mavuku.

Some of the gang teased the fat boy, Tubbi, if he ate too much of Mama's *fufu* at lunchtime. His favourite T-shirt had blue hoops that made him look as round as a ball and his bottom wobbled like a girl's when he walked. He had a friendly face but a surly manner and a sharp tongue. Tubbi had asked Kilanda and Dudu only one question: *when are you leaving?*

Rémy was friendlier, although he spent most of his free time alone, training. For what, was not clear, but he had big muscles from one-arm push-ups and could lift bags of sand until his sweat dribbled. One time, when he got sand in his eyes, Lady Chantal helped him wash it out.

Water came from a well across the field. The well had a long wooden pole with a handle; you had to turn it a long time, to bring up the heavy bucket. Dudu learned how, from a boy with crossed eyes, nicknamed Miso 5 Heures; this was a cruel name about him not seeing straight. Miso soon invented a nickname for Dudu too: *mbokatier,* country hick.

"Hey *mbokatier,* turn the handle!" Miso said, laughing. The name soon spread. Dudu did not mind but Kilanda disliked being called a *country hick,* as well, especially by strangers who would turn up, puffing *diamba* day and night and ask, "So, do you like Kin, *mbokatier?*"

Some visitors stayed a few minutes to bring messages for Chintock and Bruno, others stayed for hours, sitting around and talking nonsense. At least, this was Kilanda's opinion. Nor did he respect the keen young boys who earned money running errands or working as porters on the street. One night, in the hut, Dudu suggested that it might be worth a try. "I hear there are jobs in the market, uptown. It would be better than fetching water and firewood all day."

"No, we'll be businessmen, remember? Why don't you carve little animals?"

Dudu lay watching a lizard, overhead. *Businessmen?* It sounded as likely as them walking upside down on the ceiling. "Kilanda, here's what I remember. The last time I carved some little animals, a man put a sack over my head and threatened to shoot us."

Next morning, when he was gathering empty bidons to take to the well, Dudu noticed Bruno lounging with his hands behind his head, watching Kilanda with suspicious eyes as if he were trying to think up another question to test the country hick. It came soon enough. "Hey Kilanda," Bruno said. "Remind me, your younger sister's name?"

Kilanda looked up from his task, sorting through a pile of old documents he had found in their hut; they were just faded lists of numbers that Luc had scribbled long ago, stuff bought and sold, but seemed to fascinate Kilanda. "We had no younger sister," he replied. "Maxi was older.. Luc called her

Maxi Taxi – first you ride, then you pay."

"Sounds like Luc. He was always fun. But tell me, why did he leave your village and come to Kin?"

Kilanda gazed at the sky. "Tata and him had a row. Luc never told me what about."

"Luc certainly told *us*," Bruno chuckled, as if he had known the answer all along. Kilanda continued sorting through the documents and seemed to think this was important work. Or perhaps he was just too proud to ask Bruno any questions of his own. Dudu threaded a length of nylon twine through the handles of the bidons and carried them from the dusty yard. Filling bidons was hard work but it reminded him of home, so he did not mind.

Weeding the cassava field was hard too, especially on very hot days. Dudu did a lot of weeding and Chintock gave him an old yellow hat to protect his head from the sun. But Kilanda refused to help, because Luc's grave was in the field and the sight of it made him weep. Dudu could not tell whether this were true or just another fib, but Kilanda did seem sad a lot of the time. Except, of course, when Mama Marie served hot food from her pot.

One afternoon, Marie made tasty pepper soup and roast bushmeat. Kilanda licked his fingers. "Not bad, Mama, but this meat has pellets in it, from the hunter's gun." Marie went to her hut and stayed there for the rest of the evening.

Dudu noticed Kilanda becoming lazier and more miserable every day – mooching about with his hands in his pockets, avoiding chores, and cadging *diamba* cigarettes. Dudu worked hard so they would not get kicked out. And anyway, he preferred to be with Chintock and the others, asking questions and listening to their stories.

"How did we end up in this cemetery? That's a good one,

Dudu," Marie said, one morning, peeling a sweet potato. "We had all been kicked out by our families; we were living alone on the street, scraping by, you know how it is. But Luc brought us together. He was always running errands, working as a porter. He knew people, kept his ears open, heard about this disused cemetery. He rounded up the people he liked and suggested we move here to work the land, grow this stuff." She passed the potato. He cut it up and put it in a pot of water.

"It was OK for a while, I suppose," Marie continued, "but now we can make more money, in other ways." She nodded towards the road where the lorries came at night. "My dad's a driver, you know? He stopped there once, spotted me and drove away, quick as you like. I often wonder – was he ashamed of me or of himself? Probably both. That's why I stopped going to the road; I did not like the look in his eye. I like cooking. Someone has to."

"Why did your tata kick you out?" Dudu said, chopping the next potato into neat cubes.

"Can't you guess, Du?" Marie said, with a sly smile, and he reckoned he probably could.

He looked away and spotted Kilanda slouching on a tree stump, staring at the field of cassava. Perhaps Kilanda was thinking about the grave in the middle, or the noisy city beyond. Perhaps he was bored and disappointed with this camp, ready to move on. Dudu wondered about that and decided he would not follow, if so. *No, best to stay, make a home for a bit.* Kilanda seemed adrift, like a pirogue with nobody to steer it. He was no longer the clever *kadogo* making shelters and telling stories; he was someone else now.

Most nights, Chintock would strum his battered guitar for the girls to sing and dance around the fire. Dudu danced too, *like a hick,* the boys said. Kilanda would sit apart, hardly speaking, just watching the flames flicker and die, with a strange look, as though something was smouldering and cracking inside him too, like those red hot embers.

"Are you thinking about Lucky Luc?" Dudu said later, curling on his mat to sleep. The gecko was back, watching and listening. Kilanda nodded, staring at the wobbly shelves stashed with dusty odds and ends. "Luc died from *Slim*. They should have got him a virgin."

"To stop AIDS?" Dudu said.

"Exactly. But they were too stupid to think of that."

"They're not stupid."

"You know what Chintock told me, about that field of cassava? They forgot to renew the annual lease on it, after Luc died. Now some VIP wants to kick them off the land."

"I know, Bruno told me. But he also said it will take years, so they'll have time to find somewhere else, and, in the meantime, at least we've got somewhere to live."

"Yes, in a junk cupboard. This place is falling apart."

"We just have to clean it up a bit more, muck in like Bruno said; there's jobs to do."

"*Bruno said, Bruno said*. What are we, slaves?"

"No, we can join The Living Dead, if we want. Get their tattoo. Rémy said so."

"Who wants some stupid tattoo, do you?"

"Why not? Rémy told me Lucky Luc got it first, and later they all copied him."

Kilanda fell silent but was soon wagging his finger. "Exactly! They can't think for themselves! That's why my brother is dead and gone!" He slipped outside, and Dudu watched through a hole in the tarpaulin. Kilanda stood hunched in moonlight, quietly sobbing, and Dudu wondered when the *kadogo's* troubles would be over, as he had promised.

Loud voices and barking woke them in the night. They got up and ran with Chintock to some bins in an alley; two dogs were fighting over the body of a baby with its tummy tube dangling like blue rope. The white dog pulled at an arm, the brown dog at a leg. The girls with money in their tops wept and howled, and Jacquette said, "We are all damned!"

Next morning, Dudu was sitting with Chintock and Marie, stirring sugar into his black tea, when Kilanda came marching across the yard and said, "Chintock, I want a green tattoo like Luc, like you. I have every right."

Marie gave him an inquisitive glance. "Why, Kilanda, are you a witch too?"

Chapter 58

Frank sat with his arms folded, gazing at the coating of red dust on his shoes from the ride across town on the back of Père Augustin's motorbike, and wondering how it would feel to have your head cracked open with an iron bar. It was 10 a.m. and nine of his journalism trainees stood before him, rattling off their versions of events. Their shoes were dusty too.

A consensus soon emerged. It seemed that fifty renegade RCD men had seized control of Kisangani's state radio newsroom, between 6 and 8 a.m. "I taped their broadcasts, want to hear?" Bibiche said. She pressed a button on her cassette recorder and Frank cocked an ear.

Congolese compatriots! Go out to kill Rwandans, do not be afraid! Take rocks, machetes! After four years of suffering, we want peace. Let's chase the Rwandans!

Bibiche pressed the stop button. "It goes on for ages, all the same. He even appealed for help from Bana Etats-Unis. That's a local youth group, Children of the USA. He's nuts."

Marthe, the Naomi Campbell lookalike, seemed to agree. "He even appealed to President Kabila, as if Kinshasa gives a damn about some little mutiny up here, in the RCD."

"Even asked MONUC to help," said Mabi in the granny specs. "Talk about naive."

Bibiche disagreed. "Talk about *killers*. Civilians are getting lynched, right, Frank?"

"Saw it with my own eyes. The question is why?" He turned to Père Augustin, hoping for answers.

The priest shrugged. "The fellow we saw was probably Rwandese, or looked it."

Frank wiped red dust from his shoes with a paper tissue. "So what happens now?"

"Now it gets worse. The snake and the crab cannot sleep in the same hole."

Guychel arrived, out of breath. He dumped his red baseball cap on a desk and chattered in rapid bursts, like a machine gun. "RCD is rounding up ringleaders! God help any they find! I hear Foxtrot Charlie is flying in from Goma with crack troops. That guy is crazy. His men once beat a cop to death for stopping his car." Guychel paused, chest heaving, his shirt stained with dark patches of sweat. "I've been running. Had to file for my station."

"Breaking news," Bouazizi said. He stood up, with a phone in each hand, reading from one and quickly thumbing the keypad of the other. "Governor blames... NGOs for mutiny... local human rights groups deny... involvement. I'd better chase this, sorry Frank."

Marthe glanced up from her work. "Who sent you the breaking news?"

"Kamwanya, my colleague at Radio Reveille."

Marthe rolled her eyes. "Kamwanya on your sports desk? It must be true, then."

Père Augustin took Frank aside. "Sorry, but I need to go back to La Procure, supervise Radio Éternel's broadcasts. I must be careful how we cover this." He was gone in seconds.

Three more journalists wanted to leave too, to check the streets and file for their own newsrooms. Frank agreed but requested updates for his seminar's hypothetical radio station. It also needed a name. "Trouble FM," Bibiche suggested. "Raise your hands if you agree."

They all raised their hands, except Frank. "Trouble FM. We're sure that's appropriate?"

"You're outvoted," said Sharufa in the big earrings. "That's democracy."

Frank asked each journalist who stayed at the seminar to write a short despatch on the mutiny. Their efforts soon exposed the ideological fault lines among them. Guychel wrote of *brave dissidents facing a brutal crackdown;* Mabi had *local authorities decisively outwitting terrorist insurgents.* Frank checked their copy, deleting howlers with his red pen. "I want news, not polemic." He stood at a window, watching the street. A semblance of normality had returned – trucks and mopeds – but people looked worried and walked quicker than usual.

The gunfire started around lunchtime – a distant dry clicking followed by short bursts, then all hell let loose. Marthe's phone rang and she said, "It's Bouazizi with a despatch for us. But he needs to file for Reveille, all afternoon. Will you still give him a Unicorn per diem?"

"If he survives," Frank said. "Tell him to keep his head down, this will be a long and dangerous day."

At twenty to six, Frank rode a *toleka* back to La Procure, where he found Père Augustin dozing in the radio studio and Papa Wemba pumping from the speakers. The news desk was strewn with scribbled copy, phone numbers and an empty coffee mug with the Pope's face on it. The big priest opened an eye. Frank sat in a chair, spinning it slowly around. "What's the latest?"

Père Augustin uttered a leonine groan. "Not good. It seems those early-morning mobs we saw killed six Rwandans living here in Kisangani, including a personal friend of Rwanda's president Paul Kagame. My guess is, someone in Kigali then phoned Goma and raised hell. Next, RCD-Goma sent troops to restore order. At least, that's what they call it."

"What about the gunfire, early afternoon? State radio didn't explain it, so far."

"Hardly surprising. Rumour has it, state troops have been targeting the Mangobo area, raping women, beating up local policemen, shooting on sight. Dozens dead, I gather."

"That's restoring order?"

"That's what they call it. Actually, they went on the rampage. The gloves are off, as you say. They even arrested Father Patrice from the Christ the King, for helping victims."

"This is one heck of a story. Did you call the BBC?"

"They called me. The story is out. Perhaps you should phone your wife."

"I tried. My sat-phone has a gremlin. I'll try later."

"I'd better prepare my bulletin. Any chance of a coffee, keep me awake? You look pale."

"I feel pale." Frank reached for the empty mug. "What's your lead story, for the six?"

"I'll announce the name of the *toleka* driver. I got it from the family, confirmed."

Frank paused in the doorway. "*Toleka* driver?"

"The one killed in Mangobo. Shot in the leg, died at home, Biroko Ruzerwa." Père Augustin scribbled a line of copy. "By the way, four sugars and no milk, God bless."

Frank leaned back against the door frame. "They shot Biroko?"

It was dark in the cobbled courtyard; stars dotted the black sky, as if someone had flung a bag of Congo diamonds to entreat the gods; *please stop what you're doing*. Frank positioned his sat-phone on a low wall and dialled Ruth. The phone signal was strong but she sounded worried. "What's up, Frank?"

"Nothing, darling. I'll be leaving in a few days."

"Don't you *darling* me, not from the middle of the jungle. I can tell from your voice. What's wrong?"

"Well, there's trouble and you might hear about it on the BBC. But don't worry."

He heard *tak-tak-tak* from the town and so did she. "What sort of trouble, Frank? What's that noise?"

355

"Woodpecker," he said. "Or possibly gunfire. As I was saying—"

"*Gunfire?* My God, what's going on? When are you coming home?"

"Not sure."

"You said *in a few days*. Which day, Frank?"

"I meant leaving Kisangani. But I'll need to write some stuff in Kinshasa."

"What stuff?"

"My report for Unicorn and USAID, about how my work might affect media in DRC. I want to strike while the iron's hot." He could tell, from the long silence, she was displeased.

"What about how your *work* affects our family? When are you coming home, Frank?"

"In two weeks, maximum. There's a place I need to visit, first."

"Two *weeks?* I'm pregnant, ready to drop! Don't tell me you're thinking of a holiday?"

So he didn't. He told her about a Catholic priest who helped street kids, about how he would be interviewing Yom and some of the lads at his centre, for *Perspective*. Ruth eased up but not for long; her questions were as accurate as a sniper's bullet, bang on target from afar. Yet the more she badgered, the less he listened; the sharper her queries, the less compliant his replies. He did not mention child witches or brutal exorcisms in Kinshasa. Bad idea. Instead, he directed the discussion back to Kisangani. *Tak-tak.* "We've heard gunfire all day. But I'm OK, promise."

"What if you get chopped up? *Angry mobs,* it says here, I've got it on Teletext."

"Ruth, I'm safe."

"In Congo? Why can't you get a job in London, at *Perspective*, stop saving the world?"

"This is my job. It's just… the situation is abnormal."

"I know. I've been telling you that for years."

The battery light flashed red and the line went down.

Frank cursed, shoved the sat-phone into his bag and stalked around the courtyard, walking in circles until the anger left him. *Anger?* Frustration, more like. If he told Ruth everything she would worry; but if he kept it inside, it festered. He walked past the guard and under the arch of red bricks. He lit a cigarette in the street, looking at the taxi rank where, only last weekend, Biroko, RIP, had slapped the seat of a rusty bicycle. He recalled a poem from high school: *We are the Dead, short days ago, we lived, felt dawn, saw sunset glow.* He had forgotten the rest, something about a field in Flanders. He looked to his right and shuddered in fright, almost shit his pants.

An emaciated figure emerged from the shadows dressed in a white shirt, eyes wide and a hand reaching, like a ghost. The teenage *shegué* raised two fingers to his mouth in a V. Frank fumbled him a cigarette and they smoked in silence. The *shegué* was holding a mucky plastic bag, probably of solvents. Frank slipped him some cash but, really, a lad like this needed a future, not another fix of hydrocarbons. Frank had an urge to scoop the poor kid from this troubled town engulfed by jungle. What if he told Ruth that? She would text DIVORCE.

He looked again at the taxi rank, then tilted his head back and blew two perfect rings of smoke and watched them float away, two little grey wheels in the black sky. "Bye, Biroko."

The ghostly *shegué* gave Frank a worried look and offered the glue bag. *Try this.*

After a sleepless night, Frank spent the next morning in a caffeine daze listening to his trainees squabble about mutiny and murder, ethical principles and malicious gossip. The rumours kept coming. Every few minutes, a phone would beep with another text about chopped bodies floating down Tshopo River. Some sources claimed the victims had been beheaded, mutilated, or shot with their hands tied behind their backs, execution-style.

"If they had any hands," said Marthe.

"By the way," said Bouazizi in the red cap, "it seems you look like someone famous."

"Who?"

"Naomi Campbell," said Frank, watching the street. *Vogue* magazine would probably fly to Kisangani, ten years from now, on principle no doubt, to shoot its African special.

Friday afternoon, Frank wore his worst tie and best smile. He presented Unicorn diplomas to the journalists and bought them a round of drinks at the Apollo Grill; the mood was solemn and most of them left early, diplomas folded into pockets and purses. Dr Hitimana did not show up and the rebels' press corps evidently had bigger fish to fry.

Saturday, Frank rode with Père Augustin to the airfield. They bumped heads Congolese-style at the gate, but when they shook hands, the burly priest held on for a final word.

"Frank, listen to me. We need a radio station, in Kisangani's central market, like in the old days, to stop all the rumours. Tell your boss. That would be far more useful than seminars."

"Will do, and thanks."

Père Augustin roared off on his Yamaha, cutting low to the ground, waving like a stuntman in a fairground. He was right about one thing, in Kisangani things changed fast.

At the departure desk, an affable RCD goon in epaulets said, "Mr Kean, please give my regards to Kin la belle. And how were your training sessions, are you happy with the performance of my compatriots, here in Kisangani?"

"I met some nice people," Frank replied, and the fellow beamed. *Come again soon.*

Frank got a window seat in the pristine UN jet and watched the palm trees alongside the runway fluttering adieu. He closed his eyes on take-off but it did not help. When he opened them, he spotted lanky Matt in the aisle with a pen and clipboard, slapping high fives and signing people up for the Namibia trip. Frank watched, sorely tempted after a week like this.

His alibi appeared to him in a flash: he could tell Ruth that Unicorn would be hosting a business retreat in Namibia, he had been invited to speak, and it would look bad if he refused.

Perfect!

Matt strolled up with his hand raised, ready to slap a high five, but let it fall and oozed sympathy instead. "Oh, look who's here, married-with-kids. Can't come, right?"

Frank reached for the clipboard. "Wrong."

Chapter 59

"Why don't you help?" Dudu said, tidying the hut.

"Shut up, I'm thinking." Kilanda turned away, curled on his grass mat.

Thinking about what? Kilanda seemed more sullen every day, carrying his ill humour like a bad smell, wandering off alone and kicking stones around the yard when he returned. He did not fetch firewood or bidons of water. Some of the smaller kids would flee in fright when he came by swishing his stick; he was copying Chintock, probably. He would sit in the yard and stare at Marie's shoulder, Chintock's arm or Chantal's ankle, ogling the tattoo of a green question mark. They wore it like a badge and only they knew why; something about a witch. "Are you ok?" Dudu said, sweeping dust from a corner.

"Leave me alone, I'm thinking."

One evening, Kilanda seemed to have finished thinking. He planted himself on a bench beside Chintock and stared into the licking fire. "Luc's tattoo," he said, "the one you all copied. What's it got to do with sorcery? I want to know. So, just tell me."

Chintock blew *diamba* smoke and said, "We thought you'd never ask. It's simple. Your brother left home because your tata accused him of sorcery and kicked him out."

Kilanda stared, open-mouthed like a dead fish. "Bullshit."

"Let me finish. You asked about the tattoo, I'm going to tell you. So, Luc came to Kin. He won money at cards and, soon, people called him *Lucky Luc*. They would say, *why are you lucky?* It was a good question. Even he didn't know, so one day he got this tattoo." Chintock pointed to the green question mark inked high on his arm. "In time, Luc brought us all together. Started this gang. We were on the run like him, so-called *witches*. That's it."

"Bullshit."

"It's the truth. He had a nice girlfriend too, Nina, but they got sick and died."

"Luc would've told me about Tata when he sent his letter. My sister read it out."

"*Dear-bro'-I-got-accused-of-sorcery?* Lucky Luc wouldn't write about that."

"How do you know? Was he your brother? No!"

"He was my best friend and he's gone, Kilanda. So please, cool down."

"Cool down? My brother started your gang, helped you start a business, got *Slim* from some Kinshasa *pute* and died like a dog and you didn't even try to help him?"

Marie stood up and crossed the yard, steaming with anger. "Hey! My sister was no *pute*! So watch your tongue or I will cut it out and feed it to those dogs, you stupid hick!"

Kilanda rose and trudged alone into the darkness, towards the fields. Dudu got up to follow but Chintock blocked him. "You can't help. We all have to grow up, sometime."

Kilanda did not return that night. He reappeared next morning covered in dust, looking like he had slept in the field. He shuffled around the fire and said, "Sorry, Marie."

She tossed him an empty bidon and he walked away to the well. He came back with the bidon full and firewood under both arms. He dumped the wood in the stockpile and pointed to the green question mark on Chintock's arm. "I want the tattoo."

Bruno offered his *diamba* cigarette. "Are you sure? Some people say it's the mark of a witch."

Kilanda smoked. "I'll tell them to jump in the Congo river. I want a tattoo."

Chintock chuckled. "In time, brother. Why did *you* leave home? And no bullshit."

"Guess."

Chintock turned to Dudu. "And you, big man?"

"Same." Dudu looked at Kilanda. So, that was that. No more secrets, no big deal.

"But we're not witches," Kilanda said.

Bruno was laughing. "Who is, round here?"

"It's not funny. When do I get my tattoo? I just collected water and wood for you."

Cross-eyed Miso walked by and muttered. "Not enough, *mbokatier.*"

Kilanda raised his stick but Chintock blocked it with his own. "Easy. I'll call Bones."

"Bones?" Dudu said, picturing Tata's skeleton, bleached white in the jungle.

"He's our tattoo man," said Bruno. "He'll do you an *M* for *mbokatier,* if you prefer."

"No, I want one," Dudu crouched to carve in the dirt with a twig, "like this…"

?

Chintock smiled. "That's our mark. You'll get yours soon."

"And you'll earn it," said Bruno.

Bones turned up a few days later – a raggedy fellow stinking of beer, his eyes all yellow from malaria. He had a little wooden box, a glass ink pot and a needle that hurt like hell. Dudu sat watching the steel point go in and out, at the top of his arm, with the ink that Bones was putting in, forever. The pain made him gasp. Bubbles of blood shimmered dark red and green and Bones said, "Keep still, son. You know what this means, the tattoo?"

"It means I'm lucky."

"If you were lucky, you wouldn't be here."

"So what does it mean?"

"It means nobody can question how you live. If they do, tell them to go to hell."

"Good idea," Kilanda said, looking at his own tattoo, wrapped tight in cling film.

"Almost done, son." Bones dipped his needle into the glass ink pot and poked out his tongue as he worked. When it was over, he smeared petroleum jelly on the tattoo and wrapped it in cling film, like Kilanda's. "Leave 'em covered, boys, two days to stop infection."

Bones wobbled away on bandy legs to see Chintock. "I need money and a drink."

Kilanda peeled off his cling film after two hours and went strutting around the yard, showing off his glistening tattoo to anyone who cared to see it. "What do you think?"

Bruno raised his shiny sunglasses and looked. "Now you have to earn it."

"How?"

"Tubbi will take you to Kalamu market to fetch supplies, right Tubbi?"

"Right. Just in case the hicks get lost and don't come back. That would be a pity."

"Like we got lost coming eight hundred clicks from Kananga?" Kilanda said, sarcastically.

"Eight hundred clicks, hicks from the sticks? This is the city. You're with the big boys now."

"Speak for yourself," Kilanda said, and everyone laughed. Except Tubbi.

"We'll see how clever you two are in Kalamu," he replied, sour-faced.

"How do you mean?" said Dudu.

Bruno stood up. "Here's what we mean." He beckoned Tubbi, Chintock, Rémy, cross-eyed Miso and some of the smaller kids. They gathered around. Bruno whispered for a few moments and they all nodded – *sure, got it.* Marie was sitting on a bench, slowly beading the hair of a tiny girl with eyes like moons. Tubbi and the others took up positions nearby.

"Kilanda and Dudu, pay attention," Bruno said. "Imagine we're in a busy market. Marie is a woman selling phones. Here they are." He reached into a dusty sack, took out two sweet potatoes and put them on the bench. "Two mobile phones, yes? Rémy, Miso, come!"

Rémy and Miso walked from opposite directions, bumped into each other and started arguing. Soon they were pushing and yelling. Marie stood up to watch the fuss, Tubbi grabbed the potatoes from her bench and slipped them to Chintock, who strolled away. It was done in seconds and Bruno looked pleased. "And that, hicks, is how you earn your tattoo."

"We *steal*?" Dudu said, looking at their happy faces. Kilanda was grinning too.

"Don't worry, hick. It's easy," said Tubbi. "We start trouble, grab what we can."

"And get the hell out," Miso added, with a cross-eyed wink.

"Distraction, action, extraction," said Chintock, puffing smoke from his nostrils.

"Your turn soon, Dudu," Bruno said, with a smile. But Dudu did not smile back. He felt strange, almost cold. Maybe living in the cemetery was not such a good idea.

"Why so sad?" Lady Chantal said softly, crouching by him. "You're one of us, now."

"Not yet, they're not." Tubbi said. "Any questions, hicks?"

"Yes," Kilanda said. "Who the hell are you going to call on your mobile potato?"

While they were all laughing, Dudu tugged back the cling film to inspect his tattoo. The big question mark seemed bigger than before; the slimy mush of ink and blood made him feel sick and he heard Mama whisper deep in his head, *Do not shame us, son.*

Chapter 60

When Frank emerged from the airport in Kinshasa, he found a less-than-happy Claude waiting in the Unicorn jeep wearing his sky-blue MONUC cap at a jaundiced angle. Perhaps he had heard about Kisangani and was worried about the state of the nation. They drove across town and Frank avoided the subject, instead speaking in glowing terms of the volcanic lava of Goma and keen journalists in Bukavu. The jeep stopped at a red light and, eventually, he mentioned the murder he had witnessed, the mayhem that had followed. Claude shrugged. Perhaps only peace and sanity would be news in DRC. "Anyway, how's Ellen?" Frank said.

"My girlfriend says I am not a serious person."

"This might help." Frank passed him a small wooden figure on a leather lanyard. "Present from Goma, hotel gift shop. Apparently, it brings us luck with our special lady." Claude hooked it to his mirror alongside the rosary and Frank wished he had bought one for himself.

He phoned Unicorn to postpone his flight home and Bernadette said, "Why?"

"Because I'm going to Namibia, long weekend. I need a break."

"I can imagine. So it's all true about Kisangani? Some people say its propaganda."

"Truth is a matter of perspective," Frank said, and Ruth would probably agree.

They drove on and Frank told Claude more about the misguided mutineers, which brought a smile.

First thing he did, in the Unicorn flat, was open every window. The place smelled stale, thanks to the stinky old sofa that belonged in a skip. He found a coffee mug with six weeks of fungus inside and examined the gossamer spores with interest, wondering what a fortune teller might make of his fuzzy future. It was easy to predict, for example, that Ruth would be peeved about Namibia, whenever he told her. But she would also be glad he was writing a piece for a big newspaper, because by now, in her fertile imagination, *Perspective* would be ready to offer him a full-time job in London. *Yes, Ruth, of course.* He would disabuse her of that notion, let her down lightly, if and when his Kinshasa feature were published. She would be upset to read of child witches, but happy to know that a certain Father Yom was rehabilitating the poor mites. If *Perspective* wanted the story.

He emptied his rucksack and scrubbed three pairs of khaki jeans in his cracked bath. The dust of eastern Congo gave the water a blood-red tint and, among soap bubbles, he pictured a mush of battered brains, red and spongy. He thought about Biroko the *toleka* driver, wondered how long it took to die from a stray bullet. Ruth did not need to hear about that either, just yet. He rinsed his hands, watching pink froth swirl away. The worst was over.

For dinner he strolled two blocks down the boulevard to Pizza Pazza and sat in a corner munching thin-crust Neapolitan, looking at the black-and-white photos of Muhammad Ali and George Foreman on the walls. *Hadn't Yom promised a trip to the famous stadium?* Better get in touch, set up the interview and remind him. Frank sipped Chianti, listening to some ponytailed ex-pat bore, at the next table, regaling a silent, doe-eyed Congolese woman.

On the way home, Frank stopped for cigarettes and watched two slack-jawed *shegués* trading slow punches, high as kites. He called out to them, *Muhammad Ali, boom-aye-yay!*

They spotted the plume of smoke from his ciggie and trotted over. *Papa, donnez-moi!*

Sunday, he went swimming at Cercle Sportif and lounged under a weak sun, one eye on a crossword and one on the bikinis. The stick-thin French women stood in a line, chatting, about as sexy as marathon runners. He pictured his curvy Ruth back home, with her mummy-tummy, big as a medicine ball. He phoned her on his mobile. She was *busy sewing, actually.* Frank asked her about the baby, the kids and the quilt. She cut to the chase, soon enough.

"When are you coming home, Frank?"

"Not sure, there's talk of a staff retreat. I'm invited."

"Really? You're not on staff, you're a consultant."

He peered at his crossword and wrote ULTIMATUM. "Sure love, but the thing is…"

He ambled home along a quiet street, enjoying his downtime; there seemed to be less traffic in Kinshasa today and his mind was clear, even if his conscience was not. He went to the cybercafé, bought a chilled *sucré* and squeezed into a corner seat next to a couple of young local lads in their spotless Sunday best – white shirts, black ties, grey shorts – zapping computerised monsters. They huddled at the screen, hardly speaking, taking turns to click the mouse. Frank logged on, wondering if Dylan ever shared his Game Boy. *Er, no, Daddy.*

His inbox contained an email from Saul with good news. *Perspective* would most definitely be interested in child witches, if Frank could manage *eight hundred words plus a few photos?* He typed a quick reply and promised *a thousand plus a pint (or three) in London.* He texted Yom for an interview, emailed Ruth the latest developments in his brilliant career and promised to find her a nice gift – *you wanted something ethnic, antique?* He sipped *sucré* and typed *Namibia Walvis Bay.* The screen flashed with tourism options. The sand dunes looked huge. Not to mention the shrimps.

Frank's phone beeped and he read Yom's reply. The priest was *rehabilitating kids in Mbandaka*. But there was more. Frank cupped his hand to the Nokia screen, blocking light from the window nearby, and looked closer. *Sorry, not sure when back. Too many* MONUC *VIPs, too few helicopters. Will contact u.*

Frank frowned at his phone, wondering if his big scoop was about to fall through, and whether this was what you got for lying to your better half. He looked towards the window, watched the sun disappear behind huge downy clouds and imagined the angels debating his case with the Almighty. What would their verdict be, on a fibbing atheist who wanted to write about a worthy priest?

God was a clock and time would tell.

Chapter 61

Ruth chose an easy recipe, a good treat for kids, the weekend Aubrey came to stay. She mixed a tub of plain yoghurt with sugar, eggs, lemon zest and sultanas; placed a sheet of filo pastry in an oblong dish and brushed it with sunflower oil, taking care with the delicate edges. She did four more sheets of filo and poured some of the yoghurt mixture on top. Then she started over – filo, oil, yoghurt mix. Aubrey approached the marble worktop. "Mrs Kean, what are you making? May I help?"

"Sure, you can do the oil if you like. Yoghurt Pie."

Aubrey reached for the brush. "You like being in the kitchen, don't you? I've never heard of Yoghurt Pie."

"Helps me relax. Frank got this recipe in Romania. What does your mummy make?"

"G & T mostly, then she listens to opera. Except, when we stay at Uncle P's, she plays piano. Uncle P likes to cook. We ate venison injected with brandy, at his house in St John's Wood. Except there isn't a wood. Uncle P used a syringe. To put it in. The brandy, I mean."

Ruth stared at the pastry. It drooped from her hands like flayed skin. Someone had using a syringe in her kitchen too, in Wales, long ago; yes, some creepy smack-head DJ who called himself a *business advisor*. Got his claws into Max. She shuddered at the memory. "And what about Daddy, does he cook?" Ruth placed the sheet of filo, inch by careful inch.

Dylan slid off his chair and came to peep into the oven. "It's not true."

"What isn't?" Aubrey asked, sharply. Dylan ignored her

and said, "Mummy, guess what my friend Baxter said? He said you've got a bun in the oven. But you haven't."

Aubrey tittered into a fist. "Baxter meant *baby*. Don't you know anything, Dilly? You can be such a *moron*."

"Language, Aubrey," Ruth said. "Anyway, enough about Uncle P. Tell me about your daddy."

"Why do you keep asking me about Daddy?" Aubrey said. Ruth forced a smile, and longed to say: *because every time I ask your mother, she changes the bloody subject.* But there was a fierce fragility to Aubrey; like a kitten that might scratch you, if mishandled. Ruth poured yoghurt. "We're just chatting, Aubrey. I'm sure Mummy chats, in the kitchen?"

"We eat out, or from Fortnum's."

"I'll bet."

"What do you mean?"

"I mean Fortnum & Mason is a nice shop. Makes lovely food, I would imagine."

"You don't *imagine*; you just buy it. May I be excused? I need to go to the loo."

Aubrey strode out of the kitchen. Ruth poured herself a generous glass of wine and stood at the back window, staring at the dark garden beyond. The kid's father was none of her business; she had no right to pry. Just as Billie's boyfriend had no right to ask about Max's suicide. Callum's innocent questions had annoyed her, yet here she was, pumping a kid for family details like a hungry dog chewing on a meatless bone. Talk about a hypocrite.

Aubrey returned, composed and smiling, the glossy hair brushed and tied. Ruth slid the yoghurt pie into the oven and they went into the sitting room. Aubrey pointed at the dusty chess set. "Shall we, Mrs Kean?" Ruth agreed to play three games. She lost two and folded it away again. Dylan sniggered. "I knew that would happen. Aubrey always wins." Ruth sipped her wine, feigning indifference. *How come kids are so clever, sometimes?*

They chatted about Harry Potter for a bit – Aubrey was

keen to see the new film when it came out – and Ruth went back to the kitchen to pan-fry tuna steaks. She opened the French windows to let out the smell; the kids trotted out into the garden and she heard Dylan telling Aubrey why it was wrong to squash worms. "They help the soil," he said. Ruth gave him a thumbs up, chewed a morsel of tuna and wondered if it contained mercury. Tasty, even so. She walked into the hall and called upstairs, "Billie, time to set table, there's a good butler!"

Over dinner, she noticed Aubrey's impeccable table manners – the knife and fork held just so, the erect posture, the appreciative words. "Excellent fish, Mrs Kean! Don't you agree, Dilly?" Aubrey turned to Dylan. He nodded, gob stuffed with garlic bread.

Billie nudged him with an elbow. "You're *Dilly*, eh?"

Dylan nodded again. "And Aubrey is Strawberry. And Callum snogs you at the gate."

Billie flashed a citrus smile. "Want a knuckle sandwich?"

"No thanks, *Billie babe*."

After dinner they settled to watch a video. Aubrey wanted *The Sound of Music* but Dylan insisted on *The Three Musketeers*. "You can choose when we go to the cinema," he said.

"Oh well, never mind." Aubrey sighed, trailing fingers through her hair. "*C'est la vie*."

"*Mais oui, quel dommage*," said Billie, with a wink.

At bedtime, Ruth asked Billie to read a story to Aubrey in the guest room while she read one to Dylan. The two kids soon nodded off. Childminding was money for old rope.

She went downstairs and settled on the sofa, browsing a quilt magazine. Billie flipped the TV channels and found a preview of upcoming concerts. The tousle-haired presenter mentioned Summer Swing at Kew, and Ruth said, "Too right, matey, we'll be there." Billie groaned in mock despair, but when the guy plugged Glastonbury Festival, she hooted, "This is more like it. I can't wait. Guess what, Mum? Cal's writing a new song, about me."

"Nice. Your dad wrote poems for me, sometimes."

"Dad wrote poems?"

"Well, *tried*. Lost his inspiration, then his marbles."

"How do you mean?"

"By the way, did I tell you, Frank is going to write an article for *Perspective*?"

"You never tell me anything."

"Something about a priest who helps orphans, in Congo. I think that's nice."

"Callum's dad reads *Perspective*. For the tourism bits. I mean, the travel bits."

"How is Callum, these days? I hope you two are revising for your exams, not just snogging at the gate. And be careful, Billie, one *bun-in-the-oven* is enough for this house."

"I'm not stupid."

"Oh really. Are you sharing Callum's tent at Glasto? Or are you sharing with Chloé?"

"Chloé's not coming, changed her mind. Cal's tent is one-man. I'll need my own."

"Good job I asked, eh? There's a big sale at Great Outdoors, I saw a sign. They stock tents. I'll buy you one, if you're good. And a few condoms, for when you're not."

Billie rolled her eyes. "Here we go again."

Ruth plumped a cushion and lay back, with her hands on her bulging belly and fatigue gluing her eyelids. Her dreams came short and sharp in quick flashes; she glimpsed an ultrasound image of her baby – grey and white and precious – then it was gone, into black.

She was standing in her favourite shop on the Saturday afternoon, feeling jolly breezy and browsing a piece of vintage

Japanese silk, when a text from Frank soured her mood.

Ru, I have to go to that thing in Namibia, staff & consultants conference. Very sorry xxx

She thumbed a curt reply. *If that makes 100 countries, my deepest condolences.*

Staff *and* consultants, eh? She stared at a bolt of fabric and longed to drop it on Frank's curly head. The owner of the quilt shop strolled up – blue-eyed Mikki with the cute Dutch accent – as if attracted by the scent of a dilemma. "Hi Roof, so everythink, it is OK?"

"Everything is fine," Ruth said, and it certainly was for Mikki, with her ideal job and a converted windmill in Norfolk whenever she felt like it. Ruth had a sudden urge for retail therapy. "How much did you say, for those, from Japan?" She pointed at the silk display.

"The quarters? Oh, so *expensive*! Cut from a vintage kimono, pre-war."

"Good. I'll take ten quarters. Five fat with the grain, and five long against the grain. Plus a packet of your best needles, Japanese titanium, sharps and betweens."

Mikki smiled, the wind of profit in her sails. Ruth stood in her doldrums, paid with plastic. She waddled out, through side streets to the cinema. The sun was far too hot. Billie, Dylan and Aubrey were already waiting outside the Odeon. Ruth led them inside and bought tickets to see *Ice Age*. She cooled down, eventually. Laughter was the best paracetamol.

Sunday morning, she prepared roast beef for lunch then walked with Dylan and Aubrey to the newsagents to buy newspapers and comics. Mr Singh beamed from behind his counter, his elegant grey turban complementing his increasingly bushy silver beard; he really did look like Ernest what's-his-name, that author. The shop just needed a few deer heads on the wall. Mr Singh peered at Aubrey. "And who is this lovely lady, Dylan's twin?"

"They're just good friends." Ruth left it at that, ruffling Aubrey's blonde curls.

She took the kids to twelve o'clock Mass at St Edward's and chose a pew near the front for a decent view. Aubrey seemed mesmerised by the priest in his creamy vestments, the red-robed altar boys with their cruets, and tinkling bells at the consecration. Ruth whispered to her, "The priest changes the bread and wine into Our Lord's body and blood." Aubrey turned to listen, blinking her big eyes like an owl. Her head swivelled back to face the altar.

Ruth watched the sun flood through stained glass windows and listened to the warbling choir, the ladies of the parish, jolly hockey sticks giving it loads. They sounded a bit batty but their efforts soothed her, after another busy week on her feet. Church helped her to relax, think. She breathed deeply in the bright light, which was surely coming from heaven.

How did people manage, without something like this? Would Frank always be an atheist? Or was it agnostic? Something beginning with *A*, she knew that much. The other puzzle was her first husband; why had Max, raised a Catholic, rejected the faith? Then again, why had she embraced it, upon his death? Perhaps because it had called to her, after the cremation, like a grieving lover from his past, a kindred spirit offering friendship. And yes, she had responded, moth-to-flame. She could still picture the sacristy door in Cardiff, where she had knocked, to thank the nice priest for the requiem. The rest was mystery, like now.

She rose from the pew to go to Holy Communion and queued in the aisle, watching candles flicker, little tongues of holy fire, as she waited. Imagine being burned at the stake; *did you choke on the smoke?* She moved forward, stood before Father Lynch, his salt-and-pepper beard neatly trimmed. She opened her mouth, closed her eyes and felt the wafer melt on her tongue, a brief taste of better times beyond. She returned to her place and knelt to pray – for her new baby to be born healthy; for Dylan to grow up safely in a decent world; for Billie's exams and Frank's safe return. She prayed for her dad in Rum Cove and asked God to hide the gin bottle. She prayed for Frank's widowed mum up north and promised God they would all visit her soon. She prayed for Aubrey not to be lonely in Daddy's absence. *Where was the bugger anyway, had he emigrated? And who was this Uncle P with his brandy venison? What a stuck-up, pretentious ponce.* Ruth paused – was it a sin to think such thoughts? She glanced sideways at the black door marked CONFESSION. No, probably a minor offence; like parking in a zone for the disabled. The wafer on her tongue coagulated to a sticky blob, slipped down her gullet and God was in her. She prayed for herself: *Please forgive all my sins, including the stuff I just said.* She gazed at the big crucifix over the altar. What a death. Aubrey was gawping too.

After Mass, they waited outside on the steps to chat with Father Lynch, but he seemed a bit busy, wandering about, meeting and greeting in his shiny vestments, flanked by a flock of elderly ladies, the praetorian guard in pearls, reeking of mothballs and Chanel No. 5. Dylan stood picking his nose; Ruth picked her moment and slipped through the phalanx to introduce little Aubrey, who said, "Hello, my mummy plays piano. She's better than your organist."

Father Lynch was all smiles. "Music to my ears. When is Mummy coming to church?"

Aubrey shrugged and Ruth was tempted to say, *when it's Harrods,* but if she did, she would have to confess, in the grisly cubbyhole with its unholy whiff, for being a sarky bitch. Father Lynch gestured to Ruth's big belly. "How's our next parishioner doing? And your African explorer?"

Ruth cradled her bump, making small talk about the baby and Frank, but three ladies with candyfloss hair came to engulf the handsome priest, plotting marmalade. Time was up.

On the drive back, Aubrey had questions, mostly about how Father Lynch turned bread and wine into body and blood. "So, Mrs Kean, does he know magic, your priest?"

"It's not magic, Aubrey; the consecration is about... faith."

"But you told me, *body and blood*. That means you did what cannibals do."

"Cannibals?"

"They eat people. You ate Jesus."

Dylan sat forward. "You're a cannibal like in *Robinson Crusoe*."

Ruth looked at them in the rear-view mirror. "I'm not a cannibal." She saw them exchange dubious looks in the back seat – *oh sure*. She stopped in traffic at a red light and turned around to face them. "I'm a Catholic. You too, Dylan, we're Roman Catholics."

"Roman Cannibals. Will I have to eat Jesus?"

Ruth spent the rest of the drive trying to explain the subtle difference between savages and salvation, like a Victorian missionary. She thought she had succeeded, but walking up the garden path, Dylan said, "What did you put in our oven today? I know it wasn't a bun."

Ruth served the roast with Yorkshire pudding and steamed veg for lunch; Aubrey complimented her on the roast spuds, Billie sat thumbing her phone under the table and Dylan eyed his plate warily, eating around the meat, until Ruth said, "Hey, it's beef."

Late afternoon, Billie took the kids to the swings at Tiller's Field and Ruth settled in an armchair to stitch squares of fabric under her reading lamp. This quilt would be pink, lilac and brown; nice colours for her baby to treasure forever. She held it to the light – *something wrong with my blocks?* She rose from her chair and yelped as her palm pressed down hard on a needle buried in the armrest. God, it hurt. She had only herself to blame. She sucked a blob of glistening blood and shuffled in her socks down the hall to the kitchen to brew a cuppa.

The kids came back flushed with fresh air and Pippa Price turned up around six in tight jeans and a leather windcheater with elasticated cuffs. She updated Ruth on her busy weekend at the Frankfurt conference. "Hectic but fun!" That was about it. Ruth noticed a faint plum-shaped mark under a dusting of make-up on Pippa's neck. *Yikes, a love bite?*

"And here…" Pippa handed over a bag of duty-free, "is a little something!"

"You shouldn't…" Ruth tried not to stare at the love bite. *Mrs Price already had?* Pippa turned sideways, checking that perfect bum in the hall mirror. "Had fun, Aubs?"

"Certainly did, better than boring Berkshire. Thanks for having me, Mrs Kean! Ciao, all." Aubrey flicked her bubbly hair and was gone. No tears, no fuss: a class act.

"Bye, Strawberry," Dylan said, and Billie added, "*Au revoir, mon amie.*"

There was no chauffeur-driven limo this time, just the dark blue Range Rover, purring away into Sunday evening, and Ruth gently closed her front door. Their home seemed diminished, somehow. Dylan was wiping his eyes, either at the sudden departure of his new best friend or at the joyful prospect of guzzling posh chocolates. He peered into the duty-free bag and said, "I haven't seen this type before."

Ruth draped her arm over his shoulder. "Nor have I."

She was helping Dylan tidy his bedroom later, when, amid the usual mess of toys, Lego and comics, some new items on his little desk caught her eye: a crucifix, two tea candles with their wicks burned down and a stainless steel ice cream goblet – it was one she never used, usually stashed in the kitchen.

But here, it shone like a chalice. "What's all this?"

"We played priests," Dylan sat cross-legged, flicking through a *Batman* book.

"Lighting matches? Dylan, you'll roast us alive. Where did you get them?"

"Kitchen. But we're not cannibals, don't worry. Oh, and I want an iPod."

Ruth pictured her house in flames, imagined how she would feel, standing in the street, watching it burn down. She perched on the bed and patted the space beside her, "Sit, Dylan." First, she warned him about fires then moved into matters spiritual. "If Aubrey wants to come to Mass more often, we'll take her each Sunday and drop her home afterwards, OK?"

"Or bring her here afterwards. She likes our little house."

"Aubrey told you our house is *little?*"

"Yes, and she predicts we'll have a summer full of fun here. What's *predicts?*"

Ruth felt a sharp kick in her womb. She lifted her T-shirt and reached for Dylan's hand, guiding him to the right spot. "Did you feel a kick, Dylan? That's your baby sister. And Dr Ryan *predicts* that she'll be out and about, before you even know it. *Predicts*, you see?"

Dylan stared. "What's this black squiggle, down your middle?"

"My *linea nigra*, it means *black line*. Most mummies get one."

"It looks like a zip; is it for the baby to come out?"

"Not exactly."

"So where, then?"

Ruth raised her wrist to check her watch. "My goodness, so late? Almost bath time!"

She led him out and ran him a deep one. He sank into lemon-scented bubbles and said, "Oh, I lent Aubrey *The Sound of Music*. Her mummy would like to see that film again."

"Thanks for asking." Ruth plunged a little plastic battleship into the fragrant foam. "By the way, *your* mummy would like to see it again, too, so make sure the video comes back." She hauled him up and towelled him down, his tiny pink penis curled like a prawn.

Tonight's bedtime story was *Six Dinner Sid* and, afterwards, they discussed whether the black cat next door could be as clever as Sid and con six neighbours into feeding him. Dylan seemed unsure. "Willow is stupid, can't even catch a bird. Can I have a skateboard?"

"We'll see. Goodnight, Dyl." She kissed his forehead.

He yawned and slumped into his pillows. Ruth turned off the bedside lamp and whispered, "A summer full of fun sounds nice, Dilly. Sleep tight."

She walked downstairs humming "The Lonely Goatherd" and stopped halfway to peep through the oblong window at a pink sky, smooth as watered silk. A swooping smudge of black descended suddenly from above, landing on the garden fence. The mucky-looking crow danced closer, eyeing her with interest, as though it might share a dark secret, for a price.

Chapter 62

Frank sat in Hector's office at Unicorn, wondering about the verb, *to debrief.* Surely, he should have been providing the answers, here? But Hector didn't need any, because Hector knew all about the Kisangani mutiny – *nothing new, matey* – and stopped talking only when Frank mentioned the two RCD goons who had arrested him. "Arrested, Frank?" Hector ran his tongue around his lips like a snake alert to a sudden change in its environment. Frank savoured the silence, the privilege of knowing something that *was* new. He looked out at the crusty garden, at the ancient janitor in faded overalls stooping over a generator that refused to chug. "Well congratulations," Hector said. "But best not tell Misti, in the conference call."

"What conference call?"

"Misti wants to chat with managers of all the Kinshasa radio stations whose hacks you trained. Bernie will set it up and you'll moderate. I hear you're staying on for a bit?"

"Unless you need the flat in a hurry. So when's this conference call? I'm going to Namibia on Friday."

"The call is Wednesday, 11 a.m., our time. That's what, six in the morning, DC time? Misti likes to start early. Namibia, eh? Buggies down the dunes and sand up your arse."

"Why don't you come?"

"Already been, my Army days." Hector tried his desk lamp. Dead. "Anything else?"

"I'm filing a story for *Perspective,* about street kids. Interviewing an ex-pat priest."

"What do you want me to do, cartwheels?"

"I thought you might be interested in giving me a quote too, from the ex-pat…"

"Negative. What I'm interested in is why my fucking generator is bust, yet again."

Frank got out of Unicorn pronto and took a taxi to the cybercafé near his block. He read the latest email from Misti, conference agenda attached. One of her bullet points was entitled: *Africa: reversing the polarity*. He stared at the blurb. Where did she get this stuff?

He went back to his flat, read his scribbled notes from Goma and transcribed them into his laptop. He smoked a cigarette on the balcony, watched the distant Congo shimmer to the ocean and wondered about *reversing the polarity*. Misti should try reversing the tides.

Out of the blue, Yom the wandering priest phoned on Tuesday afternoon to tell Frank he had just landed in Kin and would pass in ten minutes. "If you want to do the interviews?"

Frank was downstairs in five. "How come," he said, climbing into the priest's Beetle, "you get to fly with MONUC?"

Yom tapped a finger at his Gallic nose. "Friends in high places. Although the VIPs take precedence of course, hence my late return." He looked tanned in his old Popeye T-shirt, but he did not look like a VIP. "So, what were you up to, exactly, in the sticks?" Frank said.

They puttered along Avenue M'siri, wide and leafy. "I rehabilitated two of my boys with their family in Mbandaka; they were dumped here two years ago, accused of sorcery."

"So how did you persuade the family to take them back?"

"When the time comes, the words come." Yom said, and changed the subject. They talked about Kisangani, and it turned out he knew Père Augustin. "Looks like a boxer?"

"Exactly, Joe Louis!" Frank said. "Oh, any chance you could show me the stadium, from Rumble in the Jungle? I leave Wednesday and time flies."

"If you insist. Actually, you could interview me over dinner, at Mama Colonel's place. It's near the stadium. Plus, the boys won't bother us or eavesdrop. You eat chicken?"

At Centre Tosalisa, Frank lined the musicians up for group shots and portraits. The bright sunlight was perfect for his cheap camera; if the shots looked rough and ready, so much the better. He started his tape recorder and asked Jo-Jo and Mamba to tell their stories.

"My stepmother kicked me out," said Jo-Jo, "after she lost her cleaning job."

"I ran away when I was ten," Mamba added, pulling his shirt up to reveal lumpy skin that curled over his ribs like melted wax. "After Tata set fire to me. Here, see?"

"Why?" Frank said, tilting the tape recorder. A small boy came to sit at his feet and Mamba shrugged.

"The neighbours told Tata I was doing bad stuff."

"Sorcery?"

"Of course. But that was a lie. And those phoney pastors? They trick people."

"How did you survive, so young?"

"Joined a gang. You had to, really, in those days."

"Then what?"

"Go on operations," Jo-Jo said, with a grin. "Stealing, fighting with other gangs, all sorts."

"We were bad kids but, Mr Frank, I'm telling you, it was the only way."

Jo-Jo showed an ugly scar on his arm. "From a knife. It festered. *Mr Maggot*, the others called me. Yom took me to some nuns. They sewed me up, in their little hospital."

When the tape ran out Frank proposed a final photo, with Yom sitting between the two lads. The contrast worked well – the skinny, solemn-faced nerd in his owlish specs flanked by grinning, streetwise dudes with their guitars and drums. Jo-Jo borrowed a smart grey Homburg, Mamba tilted his dusty black bowler, and they posed in their cut-off jeans and flip-flops like a couple of swells. Frank rose to take the photo, but stopped to look down, on a hunch. His shoelaces were tied together and the little bugger responsible had vanished. Crouching to untie them, he said, "Hey, Yom, I'm getting wise to their tricks."

The priest laughed. "You want to bet?"

Chapter 63

According to Yom, Mama Colonel's restaurant served the best fried chicken in Kinshasa, but you had to arrive early to get a table. They drove quickly across town and he groaned when he spotted tatty string spanning the road. "Rambo's roadblock. Perfect timing."

Five young soldiers sat near a long-barrelled machine gun on a tripod; one ambled forward, with a pistol holstered high on his hip. He leaned in at Yom's window, smelling of booze, gun oil and more. His maroon beret was moth-eaten. "*Bonsoir,* Yom. Who's your friend?"

"*Bonsoir,* Rambo! My friend is Frank, a good journalist."

Rambo clicked his teeth. "Journalists talk shit."

Frank looked at Rambo. The soldier glared back. "I'm thirsty, Yom. I want a *sucré.*"

Yom gave money *pour un sucré* and Rambo raised the string. They drove on, Yom checking his rear-view mirror as he pressed a button on the dash. He was soon humming along to Chopin, fingers tinkling the high notes. Frank sank deeper into his seat and after a few blocks he could hear the black dog of depression growling in his weary head. *Journalists talk shit.*

Mama Colonel's seemed a bit of a cliché – a rowdy place crammed with grizzled ex-pats swigging beer and telling whoppers. Rumba pounded from a scuffed speaker the size of a wardrobe. This was no location for an interview but the menu he spotted scrawled on a big blackboard looked interesting, if you believed less was more: *fish, chicken, plan-tain, fries.*

They found seats but no waiter and Yom said, "What's up, Frank, sorry you came?"

Frank studied a wonky fan whirring in the ceiling; it looked ready to drop on their heads, slice them off. He spoke above the din. "It's bit loud here but no worries! Actually, I was thinking about that Rambo guy. Thing is, what if he had shot me, on a drunken whim?"

"You'd be dead!"

"Obviously! Having achieved what, in Congo? Or rather, *for* Congo?"

Yom clicked fingers in the air, trying to attract a waiter. "You came to teach journalists. That's your job!"

"Sure, but to be honest, I'm starting to think, the longer I'm here, that what I do is nothing, compared to what you do. I watched a man get beaten to death in Kisangani; my *toleka* driver Biroko died from a bullet in his femoral artery, *bang,* gone! And what did I do? I sat in my seminar, *talking shit,* probably, all theory! Maybe Rambo is right? You should see the emails I get from DC. *Reversing the polarity.* What do they know? What do *I* know?"

Yom turned aside to talk to a waiter who nodded and wriggled away between the tables. Yom turned back. "Sorry, you were saying?"

Frank took out his tape machine and poked a button. "Just talk about you, your work."

Yom's answers proved evasive and his boffin smile a little tiresome. Pressed on his background, he offered precious lit-tle. He had trained, for a while, as a chef near Strasbourg. The rest of his life, pre-ordination, seemed to be under embargo. "Alsace, eh?" Frank said.

Yom folded his pipe-cleaner arms. "Can we stick to the subject?"

"Can you make *tarte aux quetsches? Tarte flambée?*"

"Yes. But now I'm a priest. We agreed to talk about Centre

Tosalisa, not cookery."

"You don't dress like a priest. You never wear a dog collar. How come?"

"I'm not a dog."

"Can I quote you?" said Frank. Yom reached for the recorder and turned it off.

The waiter returned through the labyrinth of packed tables, bringing chunks of crusty baguette and a pitcher of wine. Frank smacked his lips and looked into the glass. "Not Bogle, but it's not bad. This should open up nicely, as they say. Unlike some people I know?"

Yom chewed bread and sat looking around. Perhaps he considered the interview over. Frank sniffed the wine's bouquet. "I had a chat with my wife the other day. Our son accused her of being a cannibal, for eating Jesus at Holy Communion. It got me thinking: when you say Mass, do you really believe wine becomes his blood, and a wafer becomes his body?"

"No, Frank, because that would be a miracle."

"You told me that every boy at Centre Tosalisa is a miracle."

"I *believe* in miracles. I just don't *perform* them. Bread and wine are symbols."

Frank sat back, with a warm feeling in his guts, which was partly the wine snaking home, and partly the realisation that even if Yom might not talk to *Perspective* about himself, as a person, he might talk theology, which could suffice, if beliefs reveal who we are.

They paused to watch a pink-faced woman at the next table give a drunken speech; she was flanked by friends – beaming females in posh frocks and ribald men in funky shirts. She was *sorry to be leaving, but not that sorry.* How they laughed. Yom turned back to Frank.

"Since you ask, here's how I see it. At the Last Supper, Jesus knew his time was up and his life was in danger. He wanted to leave a strong message. So, like any after-dinner speaker, he needed a hook, and told his friends he had a little trick to show them."

"Jesus the Magician. I wish my wife could hear this. Go on."

"He took the loaf, broke it up and said *if you eat this, I'll put it back together again.* So, they ate the bread. Then, he asked them all to hold hands and said *See? If we are one, the bread is one. Remember this when I'm gone.* And guess what, Frank? They did."

"Some trick. No wonder Judas left early. Maybe he was bored."

"He certainly didn't leave to betray Our Lord; that's another myth."

"You'll get excommunicated."

"Doubt it. I studied all this for my PhD, my tutor was from the Vatican."

"You have a PhD? Talk about hiding your light under a bushel. Continue."

"Judas did not *betray* Jesus; Judas just got him access to the high priest, through his connections, which was actually what Jesus wanted. When he told Judas: *Do what you must,* he meant: *Get me to Caiaphas. Tell him you can deliver the loud-mouthed yokel.* Judas got thirty pieces of silver because that was the standard tip-off fee, for an informer."

Yom knew all sorts and he did not stop for half an hour, even when the food arrived. Frank sat there chewing chicken, sipping robust house red and listening, enthralled, trying to keep up, hoping to trump Ruth the stout convert, on a point or two, in a week or three.

"Jesus wanted to confront elitism, at Passover, for maximum impact," said Yom, "that's why he ejected the moneychangers who minted special currency at very high rates, which you had to buy in the temple. It was a mockery of Jewish law – *love thy neighbour* – so Jesus mocked them, when Jerusalem was packed with poor pilgrims, all under Roman occupation and a puppet Jewish government. It was a tinderbox, and he knew it."

"Blessed are the troublemakers?"

"No, Jesus didn't raise a militia like some *messiahs*. He was a hillbilly healer who told clever stories. *The Good Samaritan* is my favourite. It's not really about love your neighbour; it's about love your *enemy*. Samaritans were foes. So he celebrated them!"

Frank chewed the best fried chicken ever – white and fluffy outside but bloody at the bone – and swigged his big glass of house red, as Yom said, "Ever heard of haematidrosis?"

"No, but if it's caused by wine, I'm getting there."

"It's a rare medical disorder caused by extreme mental stress. Some people get it before their execution, or, say, in a storm at sea, because they think they're going to die."

Frank gnawed meat. "That's what I had, when we met Rambo. Symptoms, doctor?"

"Your arteries burst, blood enters the sweat glands and you sweat blood. It may explain what the disciples saw in the Garden of Gethsemane, the night before Jesus died."

"Plus, he probably didn't use antiperspirant. But what about the empty tomb?"

"Flavius Josephus records at least three people surviving crucifixion. You look confused. He was a historian. Look him up. By the way, you know what mandrake is, by any chance?"

"Some duck?"

"Mediterranean plant, the roots contain hyoscyamine. It's used in surgery, in pre-meds, it makes people insensible to extreme pain; they seem lifeless. Even Shakespeare mentions it, when Cleopatra says: *Give me to drink mandragora… that I might sleep out this great gap of time, my Antony is away.* You should know that. You're English."

"I'm lost. What's the connection?"

"Roman military took mandrake into battle as an anaesthetic. First, they soaked a sponge in mandrake solution and let it dry out. Later, they would put the dry sponge in vinegar to release the painkiller. *That's* the connection. Jesus was on the cross and a Roman soldier gave him vinegar on a sponge.

We think he was taking the mickey, right? But, what if that sponge was secretly laced with hyoscyamine? Its vapours would knock Jesus out cold."

"For three days? Then he woke up and flew to heaven? Explain that."

"That's faith. Science and history don't explain Jesus, but they do offer context. He predicted the temple system would collapse within a generation, and it did. In AD 66, the Jews revolted and in AD 70 the Romans burned Jerusalem. Miraculous, wouldn't you say?"

"Food for thought." Frank peeped into the bowl of chicken. "Want this last leg?"

"No, I'm full. I told you it was good."

Frank scratched his ankle, hard. "But you didn't tell me about the mosquitoes."

"You don't use repellent? In that case, maybe we should forget the stadium."

"We're going. You promised. *Ali, boom-aye-yay.* Now *that* was a miracle."

"Oh, really," said Yom, clicking his fingers at the waiter.

Chapter 64

"We'll get drenched, earning our tattoos!" Dudu said, trudging on. Kilanda did not answer. They walked behind Tubbi and the others, single file, on their mission to the market. Dudu watched rumbling clouds gather over Kinshasa; the humid air seemed to wrap him in a heavy cloak and the sticky pavement was packed with people hurrying about, in case of rain. *Ten million souls in this city,* Bones had told him, and Dudu reckoned it was true. Cars honked and bikes beeped. This part of Kinshasa was noisier than the cemetery. He wanted to go back and stay in that quiet place, as a member of The Living Dead. *After I earn my tattoo.*

The task ahead of him wriggled in Dudu's head like a worm on a hook. He raised his sleeve to check the green ink; it seemed to be healing well, the scab falling off in crumbs of dried blood. He ran a fingertip along the question mark. *Does it mean I'm lucky? Had Luc been lucky? Not really. So this tattoo just means I live by my own rules, like Mr Bones said. But if he's right, why live by the rules of The Living Dead? Hmm. Because their mark is on my arm and soon I must earn it.* Dudu glanced at the rolling sky. *Yes, and get drenched, probably.*

Tubbi raised his stick to call a halt; he wanted a *sucré.* They stood at a drinks place and Kilanda showed his tattoo to a pretty girl, said he was *a businessman.* Alain with the tattooed forehead wandered off to watch TV outside a shop selling satellite dishes, but the screen was fuzzy. Dudu sat on a wall and took his picture book from his satchel. He turned the pages, showing Tubbi the nice pictures of Eiffel Tower, and London Bridge with arms that went up for ships to go under.

"So what?" Tubbi said. "Look over there." He pointed at a line of smiling *shegués* standing on a kerb with plastic bidons in a row at their feet. "If you two hicks really want to be business-men, you should sell fuel like those *kaddafi,* see them?"

"*Kaddafi?*" Dudu said. "What would we do?"

"Easy. You just need empty bidons and money to fill 'em with petrol, kerosene, whatever. Client brings you an empty bidon, you sell him one already full, at a profit."

"Then what?"

"You go to the garage, fill the empty one, and do it again. But you need a good spot."

A car stopped and Dudu glimpsed a wad of blue bank-notes as the deal was done. Those clever boys were getting rich. "So, why do you call them *kaddafi?*" he asked.

Tubbi shrugged and his belly wobbled. "How should I know?"

Dudu nudged Kilanda. "We should sell petrol, kerosene. What do you think?"

"About what?" Kilanda sat picking at his tattoo, pretend-ing not to hear Tubbi's idea.

Tubbi chuckled and unfolded a piece of paper. "I'll check the shopping list. Mama Marie wants oil, salt, sugar, tea, sar-dines, matches, candles and condoms. Lady Chantal wants toys for the kids. You hicks will get the toys. Let's go. It's quite a walk. Don't get lost. Unless you want to."

"Yes, Tata," Kilanda said.

By the time they got to the market, Dudu was tired and his head was woozy in the heavy heat. Tubbi wandered about chatting to stallholders, checking prices, buying stuff and dropping it into canvas bags. Kilanda stopped at a clothes stall and reached for a belt with a D & G buckle, but the big man who owned the store blocked him. "Can you afford it, *shegué?*"

Tubbi led them away, swinging his stick, down back al-leys, hopping ditches filled with smelly rubbish and worse.

The air seemed heavier by the minute but Kilanda insisted on carrying a canvas bag full of supplies, perhaps to show off his muscled arm with a big tattoo. Tubbi bought a bag of broken biscuits and they stood munching them, watching weary-faced porters and busy shoppers, mangy dogs and mean-looking *shegués* who stared too long. The rain clouds sank lower, the light was fading fast; reggae music throbbed from speakers on a truck and Dudu remembered what Mikey Dread had said, on their final ride into Kinshasa:

Now let us go, before darkness don come.

Tubbi ate the last biscuit. "Time for you hicks to earn your marks. We need something for the kids, good toys. So let's find some. Stick close and wait for my word."

They walked on, glancing left and right. Alain nudged Tubbi and pointed to at a stack of baby shoes and sun bonnets. Tubbi shook his head but, finally, he seemed to spot what he was looking for – a busy stall stacked with dolls, toy cars, crayons and colouring books, combs and mirrors, elastic hoops for girls' hair, vases of plastic flowers, plastic guns, even soldier dolls in camouflage clothes standing in a line at the front, like miniature militia. Tubbi drew Alain and Kilanda aside, speaking in a low voice. Alain nodded, *got it.* Kilanda listened too and seemed to understand, *got it,* but Dudu missed most of Tubbi's instructions because he was at the edge of the group, next to loud music from a boom box and a porter with a trolley who stood yelling, "Make way!" Kilanda turned, grinning as the group separated.

"Don't look so worried Dudu. It's just like Bruno showed us, remember?"

"OK, but…"

"No *buts*. It's time to show these guys what we can do." Kilanda put down his bag of groceries. "Take care of this stuff. Wait here for me, and be ready!" Kilanda sauntered off, peeping into a stack of tin buckets, as though he wanted one. Tubbi and Alain drifted away in different directions. Dudu looked at the stall of toys and noticed a man in a black shirt leaning in the shadows, gazing back at him. The man spoke to a bigger fellow nearby, in a grey cap, who was wiping shelves with a rag and paused, to listen, wringing water. *Oh, really?*

Tubbi reappeared among the shoppers and porters, walking quickly. Alain came from the opposite direction. They bumped into each other, cursing and arguing, *watch your step!* Tubbi thumped Alain in the arm. Alain produced a knife and they grappled, round and round, soon tumbling to the ground. People moved aside. Tubbi lumbered to his feet, brandishing Alain's knife. The man in the grey cap stepped out with the wet rag and lashed it smartly in Tubbi's face. Tubbi yelped, reeling away. The man in the black shirt got him in a headlock. Kilanda came from the crowd, clutching toys and phones. "Dudu, open your satchel!"

Someone yelled, "Stop, thieves!" Kilanda pushed past Dudu and raced up an alley, dodging people but dropping a doll. Dudu followed him, scooping up the doll as he ran and stuffing it into his satchel. He glanced back to check on Tubbi and Alain. Lightning cracked the sky. Thunder boomed and fat raindrops bounced off the litter-strewn ground. He glimpsed the big man coming after him, but it was easy to escape among people trotting for cover. He whipped off his bright yellow hat, just in case, and shoved it in his bag; he ran on, after Kilanda.

The storm proved more of a friend than a foe, swirling down in great silver sheets to cover their retreat from the market. Dudu tailed Kilanda up a muddy path towards an old stadium. Puddles pooled along the ground because the drains were blocking up, and water was soon glittering, ankle-deep, under the neon floodlights of the stadium. The sky flashed and the booms made Dudu's bones shake. Kilanda ducked into a brick alcove. "We'll stop here!" He flicked raindrops from his brow. "You messed up, Dudu! I told you to be ready!"

Dudu stood in the alcove, panting. "They got Tubbi and Alain. I didn't know…"

"Where's bag of the food?"

"Oh…"

Kilanda groaned. "You really messed up, just wait until Chintock finds out."

"I got scared. What should we do now?"

"Shut up, let me think." Kilanda sat sighing for a bit and shaking his head, and said, "It's not our fault Tubbi chose the wrong stall, but Marie will get angry about the groceries."

"You left the bag, not me."

"I told you to keep an eye on it! My job was to deliver and get away."

Dudu sat watching three girls wobble past on high heels. "What was my job?"

"To receive! Didn't you even listen? You screwed up. You'd better not, next time."

"I'm not doing it next time. Stealing is bad."

"So go home to Mavuku; tell Mama what a good boy you are."

They sat without speaking for a long time, listening to the sky crack and boom. Dudu thought about Tubbi and Alain. They would surely blame the country hicks, the *mbokatiers*.

"What are we going to do, Kilanda?"

"We'll dry off here tonight and walk back to the cemetery tomorrow." Kilanda patted a pocket, found half a cigarette and soon the alcove smelled of *diamba* smoke. He emptied his other pockets and laid his haul on the ground: three phones, a male doll dressed like a pastor, elastic hoops for ponytails and a pack of red bootlaces. Dudu opened his satchel, took out the doll he had picked up and placed it alongside. Kilanda smoked, smiling.

"Well, not bad for ten seconds' work, I suppose. I can sell these phones, easily."

"What will Chintock say?"

"He won't know, unless you tell him. Why the long face?"

"Never mind."

"You probably think I should give the phones to Chintock,

after I did all the work, is that it?"

"No. That's not it. I don't even care about the phones. Do what you like. It's just…" Dudu pointed. "This pastor doll, in the black clothes. It reminds me of someone bad."

"Bruno? He likes to wear black."

"Never mind."

"Dudu, tell me, before I give you a good slap. You certainly *earned* one. Did Bruno hurt you?"

"Of course not." Dudu stared at the doll. "It reminds me of… the pastor who said I was *ndoki*."

"This one, really?" Kilanda laughed, grabbing the doll. "So let's teach him a lesson." He sucked his cigarette and poked the glowing tip into one of the doll's eyes, making the plastic melt. He did the same to the other eye. "Do you *see*, Pastor? Not any more, bastard."

"But that was a present for Chantal's kids," Dudu said. Kilanda tied a red bootlace around the doll's neck. "Present for you. String him up."

Dudu heard laughter as he took the doll. He peeped out of the alcove. Four men were walking up the alley outside, chatting away, one of them swinging a bidon as they approached.

"And this doll," Kilanda said, reaching for the other one, "can be my tata. I'll teach him a lesson too. My brother Luc would be alive, if this bastard hadn't called him *ndoki*."

Kilanda poked the hot tip into the second doll's eyes. He put the cigarette between his teeth, squinting through smoke and chuckling as he tore the doll's shirt off, took a penknife from his pocket and carved its belly open. He folded his knife and sat admiring his work.

"I smell *diamba*," said a voice from the darkness. One of the men in the alley had paused to crouch outside the brick alcove. He stank of beer. "Having fun, boys?"

"Yes thanks," Kilanda looked towards the entrance. "So get lost."

The man smiled. "Hey, *shegué*, watch your mouth." He leaned in, spotted the doll in Kilanda's hands and snatched it from him, quick and easy. "What's all this?"

"None of your fucking business," Kilanda said.

Dudu backed into the bricks and quickly shoved the pastor doll into his satchel.

The man turned Kilanda's doll slowly in his big hands; they bore nasty scars and his left thumb was a gnarled stump, as if someone had bitten it off. He scratched his whiskery chin and the small Jesus Cross on the chain around his neck glinted in the gloom; a tiny bead of rain – or sweat – clung to the end of the cross, shining like a wobbly pearl. He backed out of the alcove on his heels, to see the doll better, under neon light. He stared at its torn belly and melted eyes. "My God," he said, looking at Kilanda. "Are you sick in the head, *shegué?*"

Kilanda said nothing. Dudu huddled into the wall, his heart banging in his ears. The man offered the doll to his nearest companion, who would not take it. "A fetish? No thanks."

They lunged for Kilanda's ankles and dragged him out of the alcove, into the alley.

Kilanda wriggled on his back, punching and cursing, "Get off, motherfuckers!" But the men just laughed and took turns kicking him in the ribs, like a football, until he howled.

Dudu moved into the shadows, hot pee trickling down his pants. The fourth man stepped into the alcove. He raised his bidon and shook it at Dudu, making the liquid inside slosh about. His eyes glittered like raindrops. "Guess what we do, with witches like you?"

Chapter 65

Lightning exploded across a black sky and rain hissed down in great swirling arcs, silvering the little windows of the vw Beetle. Frank sat scanning the road for the famous stadium but saw only houses and shops – *Alimentation de la Victoire, Alimentation la Divine*. The car cruised through steaming puddles and passed a drenched drunk pissing into one. Yom turned the music up and a Chopin nocturne tinkled like the raindrops on the car roof. "Welcome to the commune of Kalamu," he said, pointing, "where you'll find Matongé, home of Papa Wemba's Village Molokai music foundation… and there… is your famous stadium, Stade du 20 Mai. Although these days, it's called the Stade Tata Raphaël. Not to be confused with Stade des Martyrs, which used to be Stade Kamanyola but is now affectionately known as *Le Grand Libulu* – the big hole. This one is smaller. Happy now, fight fans?"

The stadium sat on waste ground off the main road, wide and low, with floodlights on pylons. The car trundled the perimeter, weaving around potholes. Frank lowered his window. The place was smaller than he had expected but still… magical. "I just wish my dad were here," he said. "We watched the Rumble together, early morning, whooping for Ali. Mum let me stay up. *Ali, boom-aye-yay!* That's what the fans sang, yeah?"

"Yes, and, in case you don't know, it means *Ali, kill him*. What a disgusting sport."

"Actually, one journalist described this fight as *opera for the 1970s*."

"Oh, shall we sing an aria? Perhaps 'Ich Bin Der Welt

Abhanden Gekommen', by Mahler? Lovely song. It means, 'I've Lost Track of the World'. Or of reality, in your case." The rain eased, Yom stopped the car a few metres from the stadium wall and they stepped out. Three teenage girls strutted by, wearing low tops and high heels, touting for business.

Frank walked alongside the wall, nicely tipsy from red wine, caressing a stanchion of pitted steel. "I feel like a pilgrim. Remember you said *Jerusalem was a tinderbox,* in the restaurant? Well, let me tell you: on October 30, 1974, *this* was a tinderbox. Know why?"

"I can hardly wait." Yom stood checking his watch.

"*Context,* as you like to say. First, think about the age difference, that night: Foreman is twenty-four, world heavyweight champion. Muhammad Ali is thirty-four, wants his crown back. Add politics: President Mobuto puts ten million dollars in the pot, fifty-fifty split, biggest purse to date, to showcase *Zaire,* so-called. Also, consider the contrasting styles – Foreman coops up in a hotel, Ali hit the streets; he was the underdog with the common touch, like your Jesus."

The flyweight priest leaned on the car. "Fascinating. Please don't stop."

"Consider historical background, as you might say. Seven years earlier in 1967, Ali had been stripped of his title for *refusing* to fight, in the Vietnam war, that is. He was a pacifist, went to jail. Meanwhile, Foreman stepped into the ring, knocked out thirty-seven opponents and took the title. Invincible. We Brits refused to recognise Foreman as champ. Ali liked that. We'd loved him since the '60s. Yes, he beat *our 'Enry* but, what a gent, on our chat shows."

Yom walked about, arms folded, gazing at the ground. "Objection. If this Foreman fellow was so *invincible*, how come Ali won, in there?" He pointed at the old stadium.

Frank raised his guard, boxer-style. "Rope-a-dope, of course. Ali tricked him, kept backing into the ropes, taunting the enemy, saying, *Is that all you got, George? That didn't hurt!*" Frank shimmied around a puddle, jabbing balmy air.

"Hey, George, you're in trouble!"

"Hey Frank, how much did you drink tonight?"

"But in round eight, Ali unleashes a left hook followed by a right cross, *boom!*" Frank wobbled like a puppet, reeling back under neon dazzle. "Foreman is down, he's out!"

"The End," said Yom, jangling his car keys. "I'll drop you home."

A mangy dog scampered past, ears cocked. Frank walked to the car. "You know something else? Ali wrote the shortest poem in the world: *Me, We.* And come to think of it, I reckon that's exactly what your Jesus said when he was using his loaf. Pardon my paganism."

Yom seemed to have lost interest. "Do you hear voices, Frank?"

"All the time."

"I'm serious. There it is again. Listen."

Frank burped and listened. "Oops, pardon me. All I hear is a dog, what's it saying?"

Yom hopped into the car and revved the engine. "Get in! Now!"

Frank slithered into the car and fumbled for his seatbelt. The sudden acceleration jerked his head back. The car sped past oil barrels stuffed with rubbish, a cat on a wall, a rat with a tail like a fat worm, nosing in a bin. Yom slowed down, circling the stadium with his head out of the window. Frank leaned out and, yes, he heard it too – yells and howls? Yom spun the wheel and roared back the way they had come, turning into a wide alley. The brakes squealed and the car skidded to a halt. He put his headlights on full beam, the two bright silver tunnels piercing the gloom. "Thought so," he said, pointing, "and I'll need your help."

Frank watched two men kick a kid huddled on the ground. A third man stood with a jerry can, watching. Yom was already out of the car, running towards them and yelling in Lingala. Frank followed and saw, twenty yards farther up the alley, a fourth man taunting a second boy, slapping him and jabbing a finger. The boy was yelling, "*Non, ce n'est pas vrai!*"

Liquid cascaded from the jerry can, drenching the boy on the ground. The man pouring it shouted, "Boom-aye-yay!" A flaring match glowed orange as it sailed through the air; Frank heard a rumbling *whoosh* and the first boy was up in flames, scrambling and screaming, running blind, a human torch, arms flailing fire; he ran towards Yom, who lunged at the pumping legs as he passed and brought him down, rugby-style. Yom rolled the bawling boy into a puddle of rainwater and called out through steam, "Frank! Help the other kid!"

Three of the men had scattered into darkness but one remained, punching the second boy into the wall. Frank ran on, shouting, "Hey, leave him alone!" He saw the boy buckle and fold, watched the man step back and kick him in the face. Several teeth came out, dancing like popcorn. The man trotted off, whooping like a warrior drunk on blood, "*Ndoki!*"

The boy was crawling on all fours, moaning like an animal at the death, trying to stand but tripping on the strap of a leather satchel, tangled around his knees. He reeled backwards and fell against the wall, sliding down, hands grasping the air. Frank crouched alongside and clasped the puny shoulders, helping him to sit. Blood seeped from the mashed mouth. The boy was weeping, mumbling some mantra through his sobs, over and over, barely audible through the popping froth of scarlet bubbles; he looked up, shaking like a giddy pup, one bashed eye closing tight as a bloodied clam. Frank leaned closer, turning his head, listening between the tearful gasps to catch the boy's words, "*Je ne suis pas un sorcier!*"

I am not a witch.

Chapter 66

Dudu sat back against the wall, crying and sniffling. The bullies were gone, but his left eyelid felt big and tight from those punches. Something was wrong with his mouth too; he ran the tip of his tongue along his gums, over gaps and stumps that tingled and hurt. He noticed tiny stones scattered at his feet, sharp and white. *My teeth? Yes, some of them.* The *mundele* with curly blond hair crouched beside him. "*N'ayez pas peur. Je veux vous aider!*"

They walked slowly towards a strange-looking car, shaped like a bug. Kilanda was standing beside it, howling and groaning; his back was a mess of raw flesh and his T-shirt hung down like burnt rags. A *mundele* in spectacles was talking to him. Dudu sat in the front seat of the car, dribbling blood. Kilanda and the blonde *mundele* got in the back and the other *mundele* drove, while speaking into a phone. "Sister Berthe? It's Yom, another emergency…"

The car roared up deserted streets. Dudu gazed out at flooded gutters and scuttling rats. His bashed eye was almost closed and Kilanda yelped like an animal caught in a trap.

Eventually, the driver stopped. They all got out and walked past a frowning security guard with a walkie-talkie, into a long courtyard. Lights flickered at the far end and two worried-looking women appeared on the low veranda of a house, wrapping gowns around their pyjamas. Sleepy-eyed girls peeped from windows to watch Kilanda weep and whimper as he went hobbling by. Dudu followed him up some steps into a small room with glass cabinets, a sink and two empty beds. The women told the two *mindele* men to wait outside.

Frank sat in a wicker chair, listening to hideous shrieks and gazing at a palm tree in the courtyard. Someone had recently watered it, judging by the damp soil at its base. Sister's Marceline's Home for Abandoned Children seemed well tended, spick and span. He got up to take another peep into the emergency room, watching the nuns. They exuded a calm authority, accustomed to emergencies, their gaze steady above their face masks, their voices low, those hands quick and careful. Under the neon glare, the burnt boy's back looked like someone had poured diced tomatoes over it; he slumped, straddling a bench, dribbling ruby-coloured strands of saliva. His sodden T-shirt seemed to have melted into his spine and Frank caught the cloying stink of fried flesh. The little emergency room was starting to smell like a cheap hamburger stall, the sort Frank avoided back home. He returned to his seat on the veranda and lit a cigarette. He took a long drag. Yom sat picking grit from an elbow. "No smoking, Frank."

Frank exhaled and stubbed out his cigarette. "Sorry, should've asked." He sat thinking about the time little Dylan had fallen from a swing, put a tooth through his lip. The dash to the doctor's. First, you react; later, you blame yourself. *That was then. This is now.*

"Ever play rugby, Yom?" he asked. *And you joke about it, as soon as you can.*

The priest nodded. "Once upon a time; you should've seen me at the seminary."

"Thought so. Hell of a tackle you did." Frank spotted a sea of young faces at a window across the yard, keen eyes going left and right. "Do all these kids live here?"

"Twenty-five girls, long-term. Sort of an orphanage with an A & E unit tagged on."

"Who's Sister Marceline? Does she live here as well?"

"No, she's in heaven. She was a Belgian nun, one of the first to help the homeless kids."

"So, what happened outside the stadium tonight? Was that… what I think it was?"

"If you mean an exorcism, you're probably right. And he's lucky, the bigger lad."

"*Lucky?* His back is like fried bacon, extra ketchup. They tried to burn him alive!"

"But it smells like kerosene. If they had used petrol, he would be in the morgue."

"We should tell the police, that's attempted murder."

Yom laughed hard. "The police? Oh, the *bobbies?* You're so English, sometimes."

"It could be worse; I could be French, all the time. Anyway, what happens now?"

"I love that word, *anyway*. The English can say whatever they like, then say: *anyway,* and that's that. It's the perfect rhetorical device, for any non sequitur. "

"Anyway," Frank said, firmly, "what happens now?"

Yom shrugged. "Never can tell, with burns. He'll have to stay here a while. The smaller kid seems OK – black eye, bust tooth – the sisters will let him go in a few days."

"I counted four teeth at least. They came out like money from a slot machine."

"He'll live. I'll drop you home. We're done, here." Yom took out his car keys. Frank checked his watch. It was late. He wanted to stay, check the kids were OK, but Yom was right, it was time to let the diligent nuns do their stuff. Plus, at home, he could smoke.

Dudu sat very still. The nun peeped in his mouth and shone a torch in his eye. She went to her tray and dabbed lotion on his face; it stung and made him wince but he tried to sit still, like she asked. She placed a gauze pad on his bashed eye, unrolled a bandage, snipped the ends with scissors and wrapped it around his head. "Tell me if it's too tight," the nun said, but it wasn't. It felt just right.

The other nun was tending Kilanda who gasped and writhed like a fish on a riverbank. If she asked a question, he did not speak; he just moaned and whimpered. His back looked as if someone had painted it red and pink. He gazed at the floor as if watching the flames of Hell.

Frank did not speak much on the ride home. Yom turned the CD up and Chopin's rolling piano made a pleasant change to the moans of a half-roasted boy. When Yom reached the apartment block, he stopped the car and rummaged behind the passenger seat to retrieve something: a leather bag. "This yours?" he said, and Frank looked at the scuffed satchel.

"No, it belongs to the little fellow. But I'll keep it safe, until next time we swing by."

"*We?* If you want to take the bag, I'm afraid you'll have to use a taxi, or ask that driver of yours. I'll be busy these next few days. And if I were you, I'd go soon, because as you saw, the nuns only have two emergency beds. And a high turnover, by the way."

"No problem. What's the address?"

"Forgotten already?"

"Yes, because when you drove there, I was in the back with Kentucky Fried Kid."

"I'll text it later. You sure you can find your way home? Twenty yards, that way."

Frank chuckled. "You're quite competitive, at the end of the day. A real rugger bugger, just like my father-in-law, in Wales. A better man than I, and doesn't he know it."

"I don't care whether I'm better than you, only whether I'm better than yesterday."

"Did they teach you that stuff in the seminary?"

"No, I made it up, just now. *Anyway,* could you spare me a cigarette? Just one?"

Frank gave his pack to Yom. "No such thing as *just one*. Consider these my donation to Philosophy Cabs, and thanks for the ride. If I call the police, I'll update you."

Yom took a cigarette and passed the packet back. "Don't get involved, Frank."

"With what?"

"Anything. The police can't help. Neither can you, so go home and get some sleep."

"I'll try." Frank got out and walked to his block. He could still smell that burnt boy.

Chapter 67

Frank woke on his sofa, fully dressed with a tight headache, and a mosquito buzzing in his ear. He lay dazed, replaying the final scenes of a bad dream – foul-mouthed Congolese soldiers in maroon berets burning kids, with flamethrowers. He studied the ceiling. The bubbled finish on the polystyrene tiles looked like blisters. How would it feel to be doused in kerosene, set alight? He blinked at his watch. Almost noon. The brimming ashtray on the coffee table stank to high heaven. He rose slowly and stared at the bloodstained leather satchel on the floor. It looked well travelled, worn out. *I know the feeling; time for coffee.*

He went to the kitchen, set a small pan of water to boil and sat at the table, wondering what to do with his day. *Take that bag back to the kid?* He patted his pockets in vain for his phone, wondering if Yom had texted the address. No phone. On the balcony, probably? He had spent too long out there, drinking beer and smoking into the small hours. Got bitten to hell.

The old Nokia was where he had left it and Frank checked for a message. The battery was dead. He plugged the phone into an electric socket and was pouring boiling water into a mug when he heard a sequence of beeps. He paused to check his phone. No text from Yom, but six missed calls? Two were from Hector, three from Bernadette and one from Claude.

Oh, shit. He dialled Hector, fearing the worst. *Misti's conference call, was it today?*

"Two hours ago," Hector growled down the line. Frank apologised and explained. Hector sounded intrigued, but mostly he sounded pissed off. "I sympathise with the two *shegués,* but not with you, Frank. You sat up half the night because… you were *upset?*"

"I couldn't sleep."

"You couldn't *wake up,* is the problem. Misti was in our DC office at 6 a.m., expecting you to chair a conference call with local radio managers about our wonderful seminars. Instead, she gets an earful from Bizima, while you were in the land of Nod."

"Bizima?"

"Hope FM. You had a disagreement about sodomites and sorcerers, remember?"

"Oh, him."

"*Oh, him.* A big city is still a village, Frank, especially in Africa. When we let people down, it resonates. Then again, by the time this reaches the ears of Alberto Rossi at USAID – and rest assured it will – you'll be in London, feet up, watching Wimbledon, won't you?"

"Yom and I stopped a lynching; will that resonate with USAID?"

"What do you want, a Congressional Medal? You're not paid to worry about a scrap between *shegués.* You work for Unicorn, not Mother Teresa. You told me, on your first day, *I'm here to help,* remember? I was impressed by that, Frank, but I'm starting to wonder, because you arguing with Bizima is not helping, you getting arrested in Kisangani is not helping and you pissing off seven local bigwigs with your no-show is a PR fucking disaster."

"Hector, I'm sorry. What do you want me to do?'

"If you have to ask, you'll never know. Enjoy Namibia." The phone clicked, dead.

Frank sipped coffee and stared at the bloodstained leather satchel. He peeped inside and found a grubby cap and a dog-eared book entitled *Let's Go!* He flicked pages showing faded cartoon of world landmarks, including London's. Home seemed far away. In a side pocket, he found a doll like an Action Man but wearing a black suit, its eyes burned out, a noose around its neck. *Nice.*

He took a hot shower, washing the stink of kerosene from his hair. He put on a clean T-shirt, baggy shorts and flip-flops. He rode the rattling elevator to the lobby, gazing at his bloated face in the mirror. He looked a mess; a man who needed rest, time out, a holiday.

For breakfast he bought two fresh almond buns from the *boulangerie* under his block and, when he emerged, two *shegués* trotted up, yelling, *"Papa! Papa Boulanger!"* They held out their hands. He offered a bun and walked on, leaving them to wrestle for their shares.

The Internet café was mercifully quiet with few clients. Frank bought a Coke from the friendly clerk at the front desk and settled at his usual terminal by the window. The *shegués* soon reappeared, sitting on the wall outside, grinning in at him, their fingertips dancing above their knees, as if typing. Frank could only laugh – it made a welcome change.

He emailed a brief apology to Misti for his no-show, citing *unforeseen circumstances;* he mentioned the two injured lads at the nuns' place and wondered how she might reply. Hopefully not with a lecture on why his modus operandi had reversed the polarity of her beneficiary indicators. His update to Ruth proved trickier to write. Less was more and a grisly tale of kids and kerosene would only fan the flames of her habitual anxiety. So, he emphasised the positive: he had done his interviews for *Perspective* and would be home in seven days, after the retreat in Namibia for staff. And consultants. Finally, he emailed Saul, promising *a dramatic new angle on child witches,* so-called. He sipped Coke, wondering about that doll.

Walking back to his block, he felt a rush of nausea, and, by the time he reached the apartment, his guts were ready to explode. He made it to the lavatory just in time and emerged ten minutes later, flopping on his bed, ready for the knacker's yard. Because of a late night? Mama Colonel's fried chicken? Or that *fufu,* perhaps cooked in dodgy water?

He lay listening to the rumble of beeping traffic, grateful he did not have to be out there, monitoring vox pops and cajoling a team of journalists. His work was done, for better or worse. He pictured himself, in a few days, riding a quad bike down the tallest sand dunes in the world. Actually, no, his work was not done. Not quite. *Misti wants a report.*

The apartment seemed hotter than usual, and Frank had difficulty concentrating. He sat at his desk, typing slowly, his mind wandering back to a dark alley where a kid in flames was howling for his life. By nightfall, he had drafted less than two pages, and even that had been hard going. He lay on the sofa with a wet cloth across his forehead, listening to the tape of his interviews at Centre Tosalisa, instead. It had seemed easy, at the time, chatting with Jo-Jo and Mamba; but now their accents, impenetrable slang and tendency to swallow words baffled him. Maybe it was the bug in his guts. Even the cigarette he smoked on the balcony tasted like bleach and the city swam below in a honking blur. He was soon scooting back to the toilet. He noticed the empty loo roll, *great.* Or, as Ruth might say, *men.* He sat on the lavatory with his head in his hands. Something inside his body was chewing him in half.

He slept fitfully and got up at 3 a.m. He sat sipping camomile tea, watching a gangster film on TV. The bad guy wore black, head to toe, which made things easier.

When he phoned Yom, mid-morning, to ask for the nuns' address, the priest apologised for not sending it; far too busy. Frank asked about the mutilated doll he had found in the satchel.

"Probably a fetish," Yom replied. "Bin it, less said the better. Are you still planning to visit them?"

"Sure, maybe this afternoon, if I can shake off this bug. How are you feeling, ok?"

"Our water pump is kaput and my cook resigned. I'm on kitchen duty. One of the lads has fever. I'll take him to the nuns at the weekend. When you'll be on holiday."

"Touch wood," Frank said, tapping his head. It hurt.

Chapter 68

When Frank arrived at the nuns' A & E room, the boy with the burned back was hunched over a chair and seemed to have aged years since the attack – haggard and gasping, perched upon a precipice of pain. A Congolese nun in a surgical mask gently swabbed his raw flesh, murmuring encouragement. Frank watched and winced from the doorway, toes bunching in his flip-flops. A second nun appeared, pale as milk. Frank asked, "Do we know his name?"

"Kilanda. But he has not spoken yet. The other one told us, Dudu. Lucky boy, that Dudu, to get off so lightly. No real damage, as far as we can tell. We'll let him go, soon."

"Go where? I brought his bag, by the way." Frank patted the satchel under his arm.

"Oh, that's a relief. He's been asking me about that. You'll find him in the yard."

Frank found the smaller boy squatting under a palm tree with his left eye patched and bandaged, his lip split like an overripe damson and a sticking plaster on his jaw. He resembled a survivor of the Somme and was nudging an upside-down beetle with a twig, helping it to flip right side up. Frank raised his thumb. The boy froze, his good eye fixed on the satchel and Frank said, "*Bonjour,* Dudu. *Je m'appelle* Frank. *Vous me reconnaissez?*"

Dudu wondered what to say to the *mundele* with curly blonde hair. His eyes were blue like the sky and his white shirt had no holes. The way he spoke French sounded a bit strange. *I'm*

Frank, remember? Dudu nodded. They shook hands. Frank's pink arms had golden hairs like the moss on trees in Mavuku at dawn. His nostrils had hairs too. "How are you, Dudu?"

"My mouth hurts. Some words, I can't say them right. A man kicked my teeth."

"I saw it happen. Sorry about that."

"You've got my bag."

"I cleaned it up. Washed your hat, too. Here you go." Frank the *mundele* offered the bag.

It looked better, not dusty anymore. Dudu took his bag, peeped inside and saw his picture book and his hat, bright yellow now, not so dirty. The *mundele* crouched down. "Nice book, too. I had a read, hope that's OK. Big Ben, eh? I'm from London, by the way."

Dudu took out his book, turning the pages to see if any were missing. The *mundele* stood up again. "Do you know who hit you? If so, we can call the police. What do you say?"

Dudu shook his head, put his book in the bag and shut the flap. The *mundele* was glancing around the yard. "As you wish, Dudu. So, what will you do, when you leave here?"

"Go somewhere else."

"Do you have family?"

"Too far away."

"Some friends waiting, perhaps?"

Dudu thought for a moment. "They're probably waiting. But they won't be friendly."

After five minutes of evasive answers, Frank walked back around to the front of the villa to thank the nuns, *adieu*. He paused on the veranda, breathing hard. Sister Berthe approached and he shook her hand, *bye then*. She cocked her head at him, with a searching look. "You're unwell."

"Just a tummy bug, Sister. Too much of Mama Colonel's fried chicken, perhaps. Ever tried it?"

She told him to sit and placed her cool knuckles on his

brow. She peered in his eyes, at his tongue, and took his pulse. "If this is fried chicken, I'm Donald Duck. Wait here." She strode off, like a matron on a mission. She was fun and all, but... why the fuss?

Frank saw Dudu peeping through the railings and made a funny face to amuse him. Dudu's cautious smile revealed stumpy white fangs; a little African Dracula. He was what, seven, eight? Handsome under those bruises, but destined to live out his days looking like the village idiot. The question was why? Frank had a fair idea but it seemed pointless to ask. *Least said, soonest mended.* Sister Berthe returned clutching cotton wool swabs and a syringe with a three-inch hypodermic needle. Frank cowered in his chair. "I don't need an injection."

"But I need a blood sample. You've got mosquito bites on your ankles. See?"

Frank glanced down at his bare feet. "*Blood sample?* What for?"

"Malaria, dengue, who knows? Arm, please."

Chapter 69

Frank took two painkillers in the taxi home, no problem. The travel advice from Sister Berthe, however, was harder to swallow. He phoned Matt at MONUC, for an update on the Namibia schedule. He mentioned his tummy bug and Matt chuckled. "Stay home, Frank."

"I'll be fine. Namibia will be my hundredth country. I like to travel."

"So did a buddy of mine, named Steve. One morning, he pulled his back in Lagos, reaching for his alarm clock. Ex-pat doctor gave him a shot for the pain. Four hours later, Steve flew coach to LA. Wife met him, took him straight to the hospital. He died next day."

Frank had not been listening very closely, but he was now. "Died from what?"

"Septic shock. If we travel when we're ill, all bets are off. Your call, buddy. See ya."

In his apartment, Frank sat rocking on his heels, reading the packet of pills Sister Berthe had prescribed. *Take another one?* He paced the rooms like a tiger in a cage; a tiger with flu or worse. He sat at his laptop and tried to work but the words swirled like alphabet soup. He stood on his balcony watching *shegués* steal from the vegetable cart below. He watched a woman buying comics for her kid from the newsstand nearby. Lucky boy.

Friday morning, he felt better; he put on a crisp white shirt and took a taxi to the nuns' place. The security man at the gate grinned, as if to say, *can't stay away?* Frank spotted Yom on the veranda, chatting with a nun. They fell silent as he approached, which made him wonder; as did the twinge of exhaustion he felt walking up three steps. *Better? Not much.*

Yom gave him a stiff smile and a limp handshake. "All packed for Windhoek, Frank?" There was something in his tone, like he knew better. Or perhaps it was just envy.

"Walvis Bay, actually. Depends on my blood test. Where's Sister Berthe?"

Frank found her in the A & E room; tending the scorched whorls of puffy flesh on Kilanda's back. The boy was catatonic, constantly whimpering. Frank noticed a new boy, in the second bed, on a drip feed. Sister Berthe glanced up and said, "Give me two minutes."

Frank went back to the veranda and listened to Yom blabbing on about some broken water pump, his belligerent cook and little Alex, the boy on the drip with a mystery fever.

Sister Berthe appeared soon enough, her surgical mask tucked under her jaw. The mole on her chin had crinkled hairs growing from it, about a centimetre long. "The good news," she said, wagging a document, "is that you do not have malaria or dengue."

"Namibia, here I come!" Frank grinned at Yom, who looked pleased, or was trying to. Sister Berthe frowned.

"The bad news is, you *do* have something, so I'll prescribe a safety net and you should avoid travel, if that was your intention?" Her tone seemed to suggest Frank's intention had been to pinch the lead off a church roof. She handed him her sheet of graphs and God-knows-what. Yom perused it eagerly. "Interesting case, Frank."

Frank stared, flummoxed, at a row of numbers. "You sound like a bloody doctor."

"I am a doctor, remember? Oh, and your friend Dudu is asking after you. He's around, somewhere. You're just in time, actually. He's on his way soon. Mending nicely."

Frank thanked Sister Berthe, stuffed the data into his back pocket and stalked off the veranda. He found little Dudu crouched in the back yard, eating slices of papaya from a cracked blue plate with doves on it. He looked pretty cool in his eyepatch. *Short John Silver.*

"Bought you these." Frank offered three comics from his bag and stood to watch the boy turning the lurid pages, slow and careful. It calmed Frank somehow, until Yom's high-pitched laughter echoed from the veranda. *What's so funny?* Frank lit a cigarette but discarded it after two drags. It smelled like horse dung and the strange taste made him nauseous. Even worse, he realised that he could not go to Namibia. It was as clear as a kick in the teeth. He pictured the shiny sabre of logic severing the Gordian knot of his travel plans. So, that was that. His hundredth country was out there somewhere and, someday, he would see it, but not this weekend. He took out his phone and texted Matt at MONUC: *You're right. I'm staying. Bon voyage.* He wondered about Dudu's travel plans, and squatted down. "When do you leave?"

"When it's dark. So nobody will see me."

Frank looked at the sky. Heavy and grey, rain on the way. "You'll leave tonight?"

"Yes. Want to see a dead bird?" He produced a tiny rag containing a scrawny chick, its neck limp and eyes closed. "It fell down from that nest, see?" Dudu pointed into a tree. "I tried to feed it. It did not like papaya. Then it died. You want some papaya?"

Frank chewed a slice. The fruit tasted so bitter, his arse puckered. "Wow. Poor bird."

"We should bury it."

"Good idea. And where will you go, tonight?"

Dudu shrugged puny shoulders. "Somewhere else. Can I keep the comics?"

"That's why I bought them."

"*Matondi mingi.*"

"Whatever."

The boy poked a twig into the ground, dug a tiny trench and placed the dead chick inside, almost sitting, wrapped in the rag. Frank watched, entranced, as the scrawny bird disappeared under the tiny mound of ochre earth that Dudu scooped carefully on top. The battered boy's simple act of compassion seemed to act like a hissing brake in Frank's spinning head. He heard birdsong, very clearly; noticed it perhaps for the first time since he had left the UK, and it resonated. An adult bird looking for a little one it had lost, perhaps.

Dudu looked up with split lips. "What shall we do now?"

"You wait here, bird-man." Frank walked back to the front yard and found Yom strolling up and down, barking into his phone, *turn the pump handle right, not left!*

When the call ended, Frank said, "Yom, why can't you take Dudu to Centre Tosalisa?" The priest walked back to the veranda, took the lid off a teapot and peeped in.

"No space, Frank. All of my boys have friends, on our waiting list. They'd lynch him for jumping it. Cup of tea? Numerous recuperative qualities. Sit down, you're not well."

Frank sat, woozy-headed. "What if I were to make a donation, to your Centre?"

"We don't take bribes. Strange but true."

"What does *matondi mingi* mean?"

"*Thank you very much.* And you might say it to Sister Berthe for the blood test."

"I will." Frank sat kneading an eye. That nun was right; he had something, a bug, throbbing joints and a drum kit in his head. "But we can't just put Dudu back on the street."

"The boy will be fine, they bounce back every time."

"What about love thy neighbour, Krishna karma, *God is the best we can be?*"

Yom offered a flinty-eyed stare. "I'll do my job; you do yours, even if you feel it makes no difference. You've been here what, a month or two? Try a *year* or two, then we'll talk. You need thicker skin. There are twenty thousand children in

Kinshasa just like Dudu. He'll manage. Do you take sugar?"

"Was he *managing* when he got beaten up outside that stadium a few nights ago?"

"If you're so concerned and so capable, why don't *you* find him a place?"

"Me?"

"Exactly. So, with all respect for your newfound spirituality, may I suggest you stick to organising seminars? You wouldn't last five minutes in my line of work."

Frank tried to think of something clever to say, but Yom seemed to be floating, the veranda pitching like a pirogue. He fought the urge to puke. He closed his eyes and let the world spin, his mind with it. The savvy priest was right, just like these clever nuns. What did Frank Kean know about fever, Congo or rehabilitating street kids? His expertise lay in journalism, mostly theory, shaking hands that were tied, up and down the merry land. And he could get shot at a roadblock and nobody would know the difference, certainly not Bizima and all the other zealots, like the pastor preaching at 3 a.m., on his first night in-country and that daft bat bellowing in her kitchen in Bukavu. *This is how I pray.*

And what did a journalist do?

They talk shit, someone had told him, not so long ago, and maybe they were right. So, thank you for your opinion, west Congo. And as for the wise guys in the wild east, the RCD had advised him, *stop wasting your time.* And here he was, stuck in the middle with flu.

But to find a safe place, for a battered boy; might that make a difference?

It was not so much the best he could *be*, as something he could *do*. If he were able to last more than five minutes, *naturellement.*

Frank opened tired eyes and looked at the priest sipping tea. "Want to bet, Yom?"

Chapter 70

Dudu opened one of the comics but Kilanda seemed more interested in the concrete floor of the emergency room; he was sitting on his chair, the wrong way round as usual, arms draped over the back, mouth dribbling shiny bubbles, tired eyes staring at the floor.

"Oh well," Dudu said. "Here's one, just in case. I'm leaving now. The nuns have no space. But Frank promised to help. The big *mundele*, remember? I'll visit you, promise."

Kilanda grunted and looked up with glassy eyes, his mouth half-open as if he wanted to reply, but could not. The boastful *kadogo* had no more words; he was burned like bushmeat on a stick. He shrank back like a beaten dog when Dudu offered to shake hands. He looked confused, as if he no longer recognised his companion. Dudu placed one of the nice comics on Kilanda's bed and went out.

He found Frank in the yard with the other *mundele,* Yom, and a nun holding a mop and bucket. Dudu thanked the nun, said goodbye and walked down to the gate. Outside in the alley, Yom told him *be careful* and gave Frank a scrap of notepaper. The two *mindele* bumped heads. A taxi arrived and Dudu got in the back. Frank got in the front seat, reading the note.

The driver kept glancing in his mirror as if a wild creature were sitting behind him, ready to bite his ears. Frank showed his note; the driver nodded and drove quickly along a busy street, squeezing between lorries with high loads that might fall off and squash you like a beetle. Frank twisted around, grinning. "The adventure begins, Dudu, let's find you a place to live." Dudu wanted to reply, *I've had enough adventures.* But instead, he read a comic about a man who wore a red cape and could fly around the world whenever he wanted to. He turned the pages, wondering if anyone would say to the man, *you're ndoki.* But nobody did.

After several turns, the car stopped in a narrow lane, where rubbish sat piled against a wall. The driver pointed to a sign; it showed Jesus Cross surrounded by children looking at golden clouds. Frank went to ask at the gatehouse and returned, shaking his head. "Dump."

The next place had barbed wire on top and noisy locks on the door. Dudu watched Frank chatting at the entrance with a man in a denim shirt who seemed quite friendly, lots of smiles, *yes, come in.* Frank returned to the taxi and said, "Another weirdo."

They tried three more places. Dudu stayed in the car. Frank came back each time, to say he had *serious misgivings;* he had serious misgivings about hygiene, about a bossyboots and a dormitory with few beds. By mid-afternoon, Dudu was having serious misgivings about Frank, who appeared confused and irritable, and whose adventure was becoming a problem.

The driver sat fanning himself with a newspaper, complaining about the heat, with his tongue hanging out. Frank said, "OK, I got the message." He went to a shop that had plastic streamers for a door and bought chilled *sucrés.* Dudu got out of the car and sat with Frank on a low wall to drink; the driver sat apart, as if these clients had a bad smell. After a while, two dusty *shegués* strutted past and one yelled, "Hey, kid with the eyepatch! Better look out, or your friend will take you home and poke his pink dick up your back door. You'll see."

"Or maybe you won't," said the other *shegué,* laughing.

When they were gone, Frank said, "I've just had a good idea."

Dudu bumped his heels back and forth against the wall. "Another one?"

"You can stay at my place. We'll try this another day. I feel a bit sick, right now."

Dudu looked at the sky. It was getting dark and would probably rain, like the night the bad men had come. He looked at Frank and said, "Have you got a television?" Frank nodded.

They took the taxi along the big boulevard and got out near some tall blocks. Frank walked as stiffly as an old man and had to stop for rest against a tree; he screwed up his face and said *Jesus*. He pointed with a wobbly hand. "My flat is up there. Can I lean on you?"

They hobbled past a man with a cart selling fruit, vegetables and the sort of herbs that Mama grew in Mavuku. Dudu pictured her bubbly soup and wished he were home to eat it. Some mean-looking *shegués* came out of an alley and watched him helping Frank. The biggest wore his tatty cap sideways and shouted, "Wait, punch bag, who the hell are you?"

The boys followed, saying rude things all the way, until a guard with an AK in the lobby chased them. Dudu went with Frank through sliding doors into a tiny little room that went up so fast, he wanted to puke. "Elevator," Frank said. Dudu pressed back flat against the wall and looked in the mirror opposite; his face resembled a purple cabbage that someone had kicked. Numbers flashed near the sliding doors. Frank stood moaning and holding his head.

The doors squeaked apart. They walked down a dark corridor that smelled of cooking, but it was hard to tell what. Frank opened a door. "An Englishman's home. It's no castle."

They went in and Dudu looked around. Five rooms and water from shiny taps. Frank pointed. "In there is the bathroom and toilet. Pull the chain. And here's the lounge. TV, see?"

"Does it work?"

"Of course it bloody works."

In the kitchen, Dudu noticed a little yellow face smiling

from the door of the nice white fridge; it was a magnet and you could easily pull it off. "Now put it back," Frank said.

Dudu put it back and Frank opened the fridge door. "Food and drink, see? Help yourself, except beer. Don't eat anything with fungus on it, that's for me. Anyway, welcome, make yourself at home, at least for a day or two, until I feel better. Right now, I need a shower. I also have a special request, something you can do for me later, OK?"

Dudu walked out of the kitchen. From the balcony you could see the river. And white jeeps with UN on the roof.

Frank shut the bathroom door, peeled off his clothes and sat cross-legged in the shower under a hissing storm of water, trying to think. *I fly home Wednesday. Tonight is Friday. Is tonight Friday?* He counted on dripping fingers; *yes, four days to help the shegué; Bernadette must know a decent orphanage?* He closed his eyes, leaned forward and let the water bullet into his aching shoulders. So bad it felt good, like Thai massage, no holds barred.

Washed but wobbly, he wrapped himself in a towel and padded up the corridor to his bedroom. He pulled on a fresh singlet and candy-striped boxers. The disco in his skull was getting louder. He checked his pulse – *still racing, I need a pill.* He rooted in his bag, peering at packets of painkillers, at the tiny printed instructions dancing like ants on the march. He swallowed two pills, swigging water from his bottle by the bed. *Need something else; what? Ah yes, vitamin C.* Time to call in a favour. Send Dudu to buy some oranges.

The TV was booming from the lounge and Frank went to find his guest. No sign of life. He checked the balcony, likewise. *Where's the kid?* He went back inside the flat.

"Dudu, where are you? I want you to do something for me."

As Frank entered the kitchen, he heard the cutlery drawer slide open, fast and rattling. Dudu spun around brandishing a bread knife and said, "Stay away or I'll stab you."

Chapter 71

They chatted from opposite ends of the lounge. Or rather, Frank listened, sprawled on his sofa and nursing a mug of tea that tasted like hot tar. His young guest spoke from a seat at the dining table, chewing mashed banana sandwiches and sipping warm milk from a tall glass.

Dudu's account of UN peacekeeping made Frank's blood boil; he pictured a paedophile Blue Hat beckoning kids into a forest. Frank stared at the ceiling, his ears ringing. "I hope that creep woke up with a headache."

"Perhaps he didn't wake up," Dudu said. "Is this what English people eat?"

"Sometimes. Milk is good for your teeth, so drink up."

"Will mine grow back?"

"Doubt it. You're what, about eight or nine years old?"

"Twelve. How old are you, about?"

"Probably the same age as your dad."

Dudu gazed into his milk. "Tata's dead. The soldiers took him."

"Soldiers?" Frank sat up.

Like most "official" autobiographies, the silences in Dudu's were deafening. Apparently, a marauding militia had forcibly conscripted his father, who, at some point in their service, had stepped on a landmine. Dudu's home was in a village far away. The war had swept through it several times. The survivors included his mama, his kid brother Emile, a bad-tempered, shady-sounding, live-in Uncle Moses, and their neighbour Ginelle, sweet but not always, with whom Dudu seemed besotted. He declined to explain clearly why he was in Kinshasa, and the green question mark tattoo on his arm. As for friends, he and Kilanda ran with a gang that lived in a cemetery and he did not want to return, which sounded reasonable.

"It's better here, Frank. I'll have a room, you said?"

"For a few days."

When they were all talked out, Frank led his knock-kneed lodger up the corridor and prepared the guest bed with musty sheets. Frank's skull was pounding with the effort.

"Sleep tight, Dudu, and please don't slit my throat?"

The *shegué* gazed out of the window at the big city and said, "*Matondi mingi.*"

It was neither *yes* nor *no*, but at least it was *thank you*. Frank went to his own room.

He scarcely recognised the sallow bag of bones in the mirror. He wrote his pill dosages in big easy-read digits on a jotter and placed the packets close by, red and blue. He also scribbled *Call Bernadette*. His bottle of water and bucket were the final precautions. He sat on his bed hoping for the best, but sensing worse would come. *Should I text Ruth?* No – least said, soonest mended. If she thought he was having fun in Namibia, that was better than the truth, right now. He struggled to remove his socks – the sweat had superglued them to his feet. The last thing he did, before turning off his lamp, was forget to hide the bread knife. *Oh, well.* He lay down and slipped into a sulphuric fever of hot sweats and troubling dreams.

By morning, Frank's tongue was furred and he felt if someone had rammed a hot coal down his gullet. He heaved himself off damp sheets, fumbling for pills. He called Bernadette but could not remember why. She sounded equally confused. He terminated the call and yanked a fleecy jacket from a drawer. He huddled into it and was trying to zip it up, when a Congolese boy with an eyepatch peeped into the room and said, "Feeling better?"

Frank gawped. *Perhaps I'm dreaming.* He wondered how to reply. The kid picked at a scabby tattoo. *Ah, it's not a dream, just Dudu.* "Well, I'm alive," Frank said.

They drank tea on the sofa, watching Road Runner cartoons. Dudu inspected the contents of his cup but seemed unimpressed. "This tea won't help, but I know what will."

"I'll bet," Frank said, "but I don't sniff glue." He went back to his room, tied his Sri Lankan sarong around his head and curled on his bed, like a foetus, shivering to his rubbery bones. His phone rang and the name HARRIS flashed on-screen. Probably time for another hectoring? Frank turned it off. Whatever HQ wanted, they could wait.

He slept in waves of vivid nightmares; in one, he was stark naked, interviewing a gang of nuns who pretended not to notice. In another, he was hosting a seminar for child soldiers armed with rocket-launchers. He awoke huddled in the shower stall, wrapped in a wet towel. He knelt by the loo retching bile.

A voice boomed through bathroom door. "Frank, answer me! Are you OK, in there?"

"Top of the world. Whoever you are, go away."

Hector barged into the bathroom, as if its occupant owed rent to the SAS. Burly arms hauled Frank, fireman-style, up the corridor, and, en route, he received useful advice about the benefits of pomegranate juice. He was folded into bed and Hector stood guard in a corner, his keen eyes blazing in that big ruddy face made from girders. Frank nodded at the window.

"Nice weather we're having. Did Misti send you?"

Hector spoke through a hissing haze. He looked and sounded like a video out of sync. "Bernie sent me. You called her mobile, talking shite. *Frank's losing his mind,* she said. I phoned you, no answer. So, I came round. Young Dodo with the eyepatch let me in. I gather he lives here? Smart move,

Frank. Does the kid always carry a bread knife? Intelligent *shegué,* by the way, he described your symptoms with admirable brevity. *Frank is dying.*"

"I already did," Frank said, through lips crusted with gunk. "So save your breath."

"You look like shit. You need a blood test."

"Done it. Inconclusive. Not malaria."

"Could be dengue, but I see no rash. You can't fly home Wednesday."

"I'll be fine. Today's Saturday."

"Today's Sunday."

"What?"

"*Fever* is what. Time flies when you having one. Let's hope it breaks before you do."

Dudu joined them, minus his eyepatch and Frank said, "Was that a good idea?"

"Felt too itchy," Dudu said, all gummy grin. His bruises had the glossy sheen of boiled beetroot with a patina of Dijon mustard. "Are you feeling better, Frank?"

Frank gave him a thumbs up. "Magic, thanks."

"You want some more of my tea?"

"Your tea?"

Dudu glanced at Hector and backed out. Hector rose, a giant in his tie-dye shirt. "You're unwell, Frank, so I'll be polite. What the fuck is a *shegué* doing in the Unicorn flat?"

"His name is Dudu."

"He's a street kid, they're trouble on legs. Playing Oxfam, are we?"

"Just trying to make a difference. I'm here to help, remember?"

"You're a mess. Get well and go home. Oh, and one more thing, just in case you might be tempted, you cannot take African Grey parrots to the UK. It's against the law."

Frank stared. "Fascinating. Does Bernadette know any orphanages?"

Hector put on his bush hat as if he were planning to go

and look for one in the jungle. "Orphanages? Probably does. I'll ask her. Anything else I can get you – wine, women, song?"

"Fruit. From the cart in the street. Bananas for Dudu, oranges for me, please."

"I'll sub the *shegué* some petty cash. I'll also contact Misti, tell her your report will be delayed. Bernie will hold your flight. This bug might take a while. You should call the wife."

"I'm saving that for later." Frank sat back and closed his eyes.

Frank's room seemed to take on a warm, yellow glow when a pretty young woman turned up, unannounced, and perched herself at the end of his bed, wearing holed jeans and a silky red bodice that complemented her dark brown skin; she looked slightly familiar and very displeased, arms folded with a tight smile. "You should've used a condom, Frank."

He raised a finger to his lips and glanced at Dudu, but the *shegué* was slouched in the corner chair behind a comic. The woman tittered and Frank recognised her mischievous grin. Sabine, the Senegalese student he had once dated? Yes. Maybe a dozen times actually, in London. He remembered something else. She loved dancing. "Takes two to tango," he said.

"But only one of us had an abortion. And it was your idea. You told me, remember?"

"I didn't *tell* you anything, Sabine. I paid for the clinic and you bloody vanished."

"Go to hell."

"We probably will. Wait, Sabine? Sabine, why are you… Sabine?"

She was gone, fading into the fog of fever. Dudu giggled into his comic and peeped over the top. He came towards the bed, offering a mug. "Drink this up, Frank, it will help. You liked it last time. With some honey."

"I did?" Frank took little sips, then big ones. The dark green tea had bits of twig floating in and it smelled of cut grass, of turning leaves, of a horse's arse. "Not bad. What is this?"

Dudu plumped Frank's pillows. "You talk in your sleep. Who's Sabine?"

"An old friend." Frank gazed at the pale light beyond his bedroom curtains. The sun was coming up or going down. The oranges on his shelf glowed like golden cannonballs. His bones ached less than before. Perhaps Dudu's bitter concoction was working. He drank more.

Sexy Sabine, eh? He recalled their brief and disastrous fling. They had always liked to argue, it had been part of the attraction and made for great sex, impulsive passion, *shut up and shag me, yes here, now.* But had he ever dreamed about her? He could not remember. And that stuff about the abortion? He thought of the unborn kid they had terminated in the late 1980s, what, fifteen years ago? The memory still made him uneasy. Had his guilty conscience summoned Sabine as a key witness? Freud would be a good judge. But why now? *I should have asked sooner, before she vanished. Forever.*

He looked up from his drink, into Dudu's gummy grin. Some synaptic spark flashed and died like a shooting star in Frank's throbbing brain, but he saw it clearly. *Holy smoke. Sexy Sabine and I wronged the gods, wherever they live. And perhaps this battered* shegué *is my chance to make amends?* The African connection was alive and well, just about. He sat watching Dudu, the kid flicking through comics as if he could live here forever, as though Frank had all the answers. But Frank didn't, and more questions were coming.

Mr Kean, if your conscience sent Sabine, who sent this street kid to test your mettle – was it the angels of redemption or some horny little devil with malice in mind?

Is this beat-up boy a bridge to a better future or a trapdoor over a mighty river?

Wait.

Isn't there a Sabine River in Texas?

And that boring Belgian cowboy in Bukavu, hadn't he lived

in Texas?

And you, Kean, truth be told, were a bit of a bloody cowboy in London, no? Yes.

Oh, yes. Oh, yes, Oh God, Sabine, yes...

Therefore...

Therefore what?

He was burning up again and fingering his pulse, checking. *BOOM-BADDA-BOOM.*

Jesus, this fever could spin your head like a kick from a cross-eyed mule.

Chapter 72

"Ruth?" Simon was staring at her over his surgical mask. "I need a syringe with microcapillary tips. Preferably this week." His unblinking gaze said *buck-the-buck-up*.

It was a slow day, and Ruth's mind was wandering. *Why hadn't Frank called? What time would he land, Wednesday? Had he met some gorgeous Namibian over the weekend?* She prepared a syringe and wished she could ram it into his buttock. She glanced at the stupid, tooth-shaped clock on the wall, as the pale-faced teenager lying on his back in the chair said, "Micro what?"

In her break between clients, Ruth quickly dialled Congo from the car park. Some drunken loser answered. *Wrong number.* She called back. The drunken loser was her husband; he had the flu, he had no idea when he would be back, and he had a girl in his flat. The bitch was giggling in the background.

Ruth tried to remain calm. "Who's that, love?" She paced circles around the gravel drive, listening to Frank's garbled explanation: he had found a street kid in trouble, who had been badly beaten, Frank did not know why; a kid named after Che Guevara who made wicked tea from eucalyptus, fennel and God knows what. "Ruth, I think Dudu's parents kicked him out. He's had a bad time. But he's a good boy. I want to help. I had this dream."

"Hey, Martin Luther Kean, what did you take for your flu, LSD?"

"Ruth, I'm serious. It's a bit complicated. I'll tell you more when I come home."

"That'll be the day." She sat for a while gazing at the rhododendrons then went back inside and told the boss, first chance she got. Simon stood at the window, peeling a latex glove, probably planning a round of golf. He turned to observe her; he looked wary somehow, as if she had arrived from Mars with a little green toothache. "Tricky," he said.

She thought it over. "You know, maybe I'll go to a quilting festival. There's one in Paris; Carol Watt usually attends. Maybe I'll tag along, stay a month, visit a few orphanages and make quilts for some good little kids who've had a hard time. See how Frank likes that." She slammed the autoclave door and Simon asked her not to, please. It was time to leave.

Driving home through Richmond she stopped at traffic lights outside the train station and noticed a commemorative blue plaque on the wall to her right, outside the pub where The Rolling Stones had played some of their earliest gigs. To her left, a lady of a certain age gave her a haughty look from a huge car, perhaps a Bentley. Ruth rummaged in her glove box, found her *Best of Stones* CD and shoved it in the slot. She cranked it up and rolled her windows down, so madam alongside could hear "Get Off of My Cloud". Nice and loud.

She passed Jagger's Georgian mansion perched on Richmond Hill, high above the Thames, a few minutes later. She thought about Jerry Hall and men who always get what they want, except that gorgeous pile – Downe House with its balustrades and Doric piers. She thought about Frank. OK, he was no philanderer, but his solo world tour had lasted ten years.

She parked outside St Edward's Primary and ambled through knots of parents to fetch Dylan and Aubrey from Kids' Club. They came trotting towards her, coats flapping and blonde curls wisped by the breeze. They looked like twins. She told Dylan his daddy would be delayed, and why. "He's got fever, not very well. But he'll be back soon."

"What sort of fever?" Dylan asked, goggle-eyed.

"Jungle fever," Aubrey said, "your daddy probably got bitten by a tarantula."

Ruth drove into Kingston listening to "Wild Horses". The twanging slide guitar and sad words hit her deep, made her weep. It was probably hormones. *Or perhaps it was love?*

When Ruth got to the camping shop, Billie was already inside ogling the tents. The young sales assistant came a-smiling, with his freckles like muesli. He wore the obligatory Great Outdoors T-shirt, red neckerchief and waxy pants that rustled. "Climate?"

Billie gave him a lopsided smile. "Somerset."

"It's for Glastonbury. A present from me," Ruth added, and Billie rolled her eyes. The assistant led them past the sun hats to a section marked EXTREME, as in prices.

They emerged half an hour later, Dylan sporting a red bandana, Aubrey a pink one and Billie carrying her new tent like a big green sausage. Ruth told her about Frank, and how she had a good mind to fly to Congo, help him get well and make sure he came back.

"Good idea. Book a flight, Mum. I'll look after the house."

"I'm joking. You look after your tent," Ruth said, waddling to the Bentall Centre.

They rode the escalator up five floors of pristine white colonnades linked by glass box elevators and suspended walkways, a modern shopper's safe haven of biometric buy and sell. Ancient Greece meets *Blade Runner*. At the top, Ruth herded her party into a sushi house with dark wood panels, heavy linen napkins and a demure Japanese waitress who said, "Hey."

"We normally go to McDonald's," replied Dylan and Ruth could not deny it.

After their meal, stuffed full of Omega-3 fats and *matcha*, they went to a bookshop because Billie was getting into psychology. It was news to Ruth. "Since when?"

"Since she met Callum," Dylan said. "They snog at our front gate."

Billie wandered off in search of books with big words and Ruth sank into a comfy chair to wait. She spotted something among a stack of bargains, one of those classy-looking door-stoppers that nobody buys. *Art of Africa*. She opened it up, perused the glossy photos of eerie masks, bracelets, carved wooden figures with pointy tits and donkey-size dicks. *All very fascinating, I'm sure.* But Africa had put a bug in her husband's gut and cast a spell over his feeble mind, whereby he now had to help house a street kid. *So bugger this.* Halfway through the book, she snapped it shut and dumped it on the low table in front of her. Billie returned, perched on the arm of the chair and picked the book up, nodding approval.

"*Art of Africa*, eh? Looks interesting, Mum, dead ethnic. Cheap too."

"Weighs a ton."

"You should ask Frank to bring a few carvings home, our house would look more eclectic, like Callum's place. They've got a bonsai tree. Seen this section at the back, about fabrics? Check the grass mats! This is right up your street. You should buy it. I mean, even if we never read it, it would look good on our coffee table, and people might think we do."

Ruth angled her head, gawping at the stunning geometric designs. "They're quite nice, actually. How much is it?" She checked the price. Red sticker. *Certainly a bargain.*

Driving home in the drizzle, she played various CDs, but little Aubrey did not like The Rolling Stones, or Bowie or even the classic disco of Frankie Goes to Hollywood.

"Have we got *Frankie Goes to Congo And Stays An Extra Month?*" Billie said.

Aubrey asked for some opera and Billie dug out *Best of Pavarotti*. Dylan leaned forward with his head inside a paper bag with holes for his eyes. "Suits you," Ruth said.

The kids' giggles lifted her spirits; the music helped too. The good thing about opera was that everyone sounded unhappier than you. That was probably why she had never been. Then again, a night out with Pippa at Covent Garden, watching some *Welsh tenor chappie raising the roof,* would have been nice. Ruth checked her watch. The traffic was easy now, Aubrey's home not far. She asked Billie to send a quick text to Ms Price: *E.T.A. 5 minutes.*

Ruth turned left into The Lindens with its lovely trees that smelled sweet from the rain. *Linden tea, don't health shops sell it?* Maybe Pippa would invite her in for a nice cuppa. She inched up the cul-de-sac of desirable homes, mostly ivy-clad, with sumptuous lamps and gilt-framed paintings. Aubrey squealed, "Stop, Mrs Dean! Thanks, ciao!"

Ruth watched Aubrey hop from the car and scamper towards a classy Edwardian house whose windows needed a clean and whose shrubbery was a mess. She waited to wave when Pippa opened up. But Aubrey disappeared into the alley and that was that. Almost.

Ruth drove on and made a careful U-turn, clocking her wing mirrors to avoid the vintage Merc with bulbous headlights and the eye-popping yellow sports car with a bonnet that sloped into the road like a wedge of Pecorino cheese. On the way back, she spotted Pippa's silhouette in the front room downstairs and got a discreet wave – *ciao* – for her trouble. Ruth glimpsed movement upstairs too – a silver-bearded man arranging a red coat on a hanger, in a bedroom. She glanced at Billie and said, "Who's that, Father Christmas?"

"Uncle Patrick," said Billie, "he owns the house, stays over now and again."

Ruth's eyebrows shot north. "And who told you?"

"I did," said Dylan, watching the road through the holes in his paper helmet.

Chapter 73

A big glass of ruby red Bogle Petit Shiraz helped, but not much. Ruth slumped on her sofa, sewing a pink block on the quilt for her new baby. But she couldn't concentrate. She was thinking about Frank and she had one eye on a TV chef, whose soufflé was as tall as his hat. Dylan nestled close, reading and fighting yawns. Music boomed down through the ceiling from Billie's room above, drowning the TV. Ruth dumped her sewing and marched upstairs. Dylan scampered in her wake. "Mummy, kick her ass, she's a goddamn party animal."

"I see, and where did you learn to speak like that?"

"From Baxter. He lost our frog. His brother can spell *Mississippi* in one burp."

"Charming." Ruth reached the landing. Billie's bedroom door flew open and she stormed out in bra and knickers, hands on hips, looking pretty good but pretty angry too.

Dylan stood picking his nose. "We can see all your bits."

Billie pointed a finger. "Watch it, you little creep."

"I'm not little."

"Mum, I've lost my socks. The ones with skulls on. I need them. I'm going out."

Ruth glanced at her watch. "It's almost nine, bit late isn't it?"

"Just to the park."

"Oh, I see. Because you love walks, I assume? I want you back by ten."

"Or you'll be in trouble. Won't she, Mummy?" Dylan said. Ruth nodded, *exactly.*

Billie rolled her eyes. "OK! But have you seen my socks? They were a present."

"They'll be in some drawer, let's have a look." Ruth went into her daughter's room and reduced the volume on the throbbing music. Dylan settled at Billie's computer to browse her emails and Billie sank to her knees to peep under her bed. Ruth spotted a big blue X just above Billie's bum, swollen at the edges. It looked grotesque. Billie spun up, boobs heaving, hair mussed. "My best socks! Shit! Where are they? Mum, did you—"

"Never mind socks, turn round," Ruth said. Billie stood sheep-eyed, surveying shelves and ledges. Ruth stepped closer. "Billie, look at me when I'm talking to you."

"What?"

"Is that a tattoo, on your hip?" Ruth reached to turn Billie by the arm.

"Oh, this? Yeah, it's runic. Medieval alphabet." Billie was squirming away. Dylan circled her like a hungry hyena, eyeing the prize. "Cool. I want one. What does it mean?"

Billie yanked at a drawer. "X means *gift*. A present from Cal. Shit, they're not here."

Ruth rubbed her temple with her fingertips. "Billie, what have you done?"

"I'm eighteen. It's my body."

"Seventeen. Oh, you silly girl. And when you're sixty-five? What's in your head?"

They eyeballed each other for a generation or two; Ruth felt the walls of the teenage den pressing in and squeezing her out. She marched to the door and spoke firmly from the threshold. "Billie, X also means *wrong*. So forget the park. You're grounded, for tonight." She slammed the door and lumbered downstairs, ignoring Billie's banshee shrieks.

Dylan came trotting behind her. "Nice one. Hey, can I get—"

"No, you can't get."

She went into the kitchen, poured herself another glass of Shiraz. Her mobile phone rang and she watched it buzz and spin across the dining table like a demented bug. *Probably*

Frank. She let it ring. If she answered, she would only yell and disturb the neighbours. Them and their stupid pottery kiln; what kind of a job was that? The phone buzzed on. She reached for it, checked caller ID. It was Carol Watt, who said, "Ruth, are you watching TV?"

"I was. Now I'm drinking alcohol. I'm ready to blow. I think I'll go to bloody Paris."

"Good idea. I'll come too. What's up?"

"I'll tell you what's up." Ruth let it all out in a torrent of quiet rage. She told Carol about Frank's fever; about a street kid that needed help and how Frank was the only person in Congo who could oblige; about the tattoo on Billie's bum; about Pippa's big posh house where you would be lucky to get a cup of tea. "In other words, I feel like my life is a merry-go-round and I'm about to fall off. So, what's on the box? And don't say rhubarb soufflé."

"You've probably missed it, but try the BBC. Something about Congo. It was in the headlines. And, Ruth, if I were you, I'd tell Frank to come home, the sooner the better."

"I've told him! I may as well talk to next door's bloody cat." She aimed the remote at the TV on the kitchen wall and watched bloated bodies rolling like barrels down a river. The caption said *Kisangani.* The presenter in the snazzy tie was talking about *Congo's volatile political climate, ravaged infrastructure and five million dead.* "Good God," Ruth said.

"Get him home, Ru. I'll see you tomorrow, I'm coming in for my check-up. Hopefully you'll be in a better mood."

"Indeed. And hopefully you'll floss first."

When Ruth put Dylan to bed, he asked wide-eyed, "Did I do something wrong?"

She tousled his hair. "No, Dyl, I'm sorry, it's me. I'm just tired."

They shared a bedtime story about a cuckoo who could not sing. Dylan's eyelids drooped and she kissed him goodnight.

Walking out, she stooped to retrieve a coloured drawing pin from a rumpled rug. It had probably fallen from the map of the world on Dylan's cork-board. She stood before the map. It was dotted with dozens of pins – ninety-eight, no doubt – all exactly the same colour as the one between her fingers, because Dylan was his daddy's loyal son, and good at keeping track of travels. Fair enough. Congo had a pin but Namibia did not; nor did England, oddly enough. Ruth thumbed the pin into LONDON and wondered if Daddy might notice, next time he passed through.

Chapter 74

Dudu stood in Frank's bathroom, dabbing his sore face with nice-smelling soap. His swollen eyelid was a bit smaller today but more yellow than ever. His teeth were still jagged stumps and, when he tried to smile, he looked like a crocodile having a rest in the sunshine.

He drank milk from Frank's fridge, then a bit more, to help his teeth grow back. Soon there would be no fridge with milk, because Frank would return to England where the Queen wore a diamond hat and London Bridge had arms that went up. Frank would write letters, send comics. That was a promise. *But I need an address, Dudu?* That was the tricky bit.

He stood in the corridor listening to Frank snoring, in-and-out. It sounded like a big whistle. He peeped into the big bedroom. Frank was lying with his mouth open, but he did not look like a crocodile. The doorbell rang and Dudu stood on a chair to look through the spyhole. A man was standing outside wearing a baseball hat, and Dudu said, "Who is it?"

The voice from the other side said, "I'm Claude. Special delivery. For Frank."

Frank awoke, clear-headed, which made a pleasant change. He had dreamed of seagulls soaring over the peaceful beach at Rum Cove, Ruth's childhood home. He sat up slowly but felt no wave of nausea. *No more fever?* His watch showed *10:21*, very civilised.

He found Dudu sprawled flat on his tummy the lounge, knees up, bumping heels to a tune on MTV. The swelling on

Dudu's face had reduced but the spectacular colours suggested someone had cracked an egg over his eye. Frank heard a squawk and said, "Was that a bird?"

Dudu nodded, flashing his jack-o'-lantern grin. "Special delivery, on the balcony."

"What?" Frank went onto the balcony and found a large aluminium cage containing two grey parrots with scarlet tails. "What's all this?" he said. The parrots gawped. *You tell us.*

"Mr Claude brought them," Dudu said, with a shrug. His shoulders were bony, as if a wire hanger was stuck under his ragged T-shirt. The kid needed food, clothes. Frank circled the shit-speckled cage, got a strong whiff of ammonia. The birds sidled away, as if he stank a bit too.

He rang Claude, who said, over beeping traffic, "Parrots? Your journalists sent them."

"Which journalists and why?" Frank watched the bright-eyed birds. They looked intelligent. *Yes, we are.*

"Thony from Choice FM. He organised it. You liked the parrot on the balcony, opposite the seminar?"

"Claude, I also like polar bears. Doesn't mean I want one. Certainly not two."

"Oh well. Just open the cage door. I'll tell Thony they escaped. Problem solved."

Frank opened the cage. The birds cowered on their perch, hopping and flapping. Their wings had been clipped. "To stop them flying away," Dudu said. "Have we got any peanuts?"

Frank felt queasy when walking to the Internet café; the sun was too bright and the street too noisy, but it was good to be out, back on his feet, even though they felt more like roller skates. Dudu was all talk, about parrots and more. "It takes a long time, Frank, for their wings to grow back. Uncle Moses sometimes catches parrots to sell to traders, with glue and nets. One time, Kilanda and me met some men who had caught a leopard. They made a wooden cage, put bait inside it, then used poison darts. That way, you don't damage the fur."

"I thought you said Moses was the manager of a some bar, Hero something?"

"Heroes' Corner. But he catches parrots and bushmeat, sometimes. I'll do it one day."

Frank paused for a breather. "What if I bought you a bus ticket, back to Mavuku?"

"No, I prefer Kin *la poubelle*. Look, we can buy clothes in here, like you promised?"

They entered a clothes shop near the Internet café and Frank kitted Dudu out with T-shirts and jeans, underwear and decent shoes to replace the outsize army boots that made him look like a circus clown. They left the boots on the low wall outside the Internet café, for whoever, and went inside. Frank sat at his usual terminal by the window and booted up.

Ruth had emailed about tropical fever and corpses on TV from Congo, *so come home!* Bernadette had sent names of orphanages. Dudu stood sucking on a carton of milk, watching a youth terminate monsters from a banana-shaped handset. "What's that, Frank?"

"A waste of time." Frank printed out Bernadette's list. "Let's go, second time lucky."

The woman in charge of Centre Gabriel looked sweet in her pearls and simple grey shift, but the kids in her yard looked bored shitless and several had rust-coloured hair from poor nutrition. Dudu peeped in and backed out, as though he would rather live in a tin bucket.

Next on Frank's list was the House of Eternal Light, but the name reminded him of Bukavu and some strange woman caterwauling at 3 a.m. He scribbled a red line through it.

Casa Kids sounded more promising, like Dylan's after-school club. The taxi trundled up and down the boulevard, their veteran driver carefully explaining how he had lost his way.

They found it, in time. Casa Kids had a rainbow logo, a boom box in the yard, and two over-friendly pale-faced Brits, named Debbie and Dodge, as managers. Dodge's shaved head bore unsightly scars; Debbie wore a washed-out WOMAD top and her hair in a Mohawk. They smiled a lot but their teeth were a disgrace; strewn with debris, like great white sharks high on chum or whatever. Frank reckoned Ruth would have a fit. Dodge beckoned him in, with a crouching gesture like some creepy medieval fool. "Yay, enter the fun house, bro!"

Debbie Mohawk took a long look at Dudu. "Wow, who dropped from the ugly tree?"

Frank did the rounds, spied shit on the loo seat and said, "Keep up the good work."

The next few orphanages were little better. Those with spare beds had a dismal air and a cloying religiosity; the staff seemed too keen to discuss cash and Dudu seemed uneasy.

Frank led him to a café terrace overlooking the noisy boulevard. Dudu ordered *fufu* and fish, but had problems eating it. Frank drank cardamom tea with honey and browsed his shrinking list of prospects. "We'll try one more. Refuge des Petites Saints. Let's hope they're more interested in you, than in my money. To be honest, I need a lie down, I'm whacked."

"You should give it to me."

"The list?"

"The money."

Frank pointed to a raggedy kid inhaling solvents from a bag. "So you can do that?"

"So I can buy milk, drink lots. Make my teeth grow back."

"They won't. You need somewhere to sleep. If we find a place, I can *send* money. And comics, remember?"

"I can sleep anywhere. I learned from Kilanda. I just need money for food and milk."

Frank lit a cigarette, thinking it over. His brilliant idea, when it came, dazzled his feeble brain, as bright as a dentist's lamp. He clicked his fingers, grinning. "I've got it."

Chapter 75

Ruth checked her email in Simon's office. Her boss stood hunched nearby with his golf putter, practising on a strip of lurid plastic grass. "Maybe Frank has malaria, Ruth?"

"Amnesia, more like. No email, see? I'll call his mobile from home, see if he's come to his senses. His Internet is often dodgy, not to mention his priorities. I could strangle him."

"Cade would probably hug him. Or, at least a tree. Call Frank now if you like, use the office landline."

"Thanks, that's generous; maybe I will. What's got into you, back in love again?"

"Hole-in-one, see?" Simon pointed his putter and Ruth checked Frank's number.

The line was good and she could hear the traffic beeping in Kinshasa; it sounded more like a fairground, a royal din. But at least her wandering husband sounded a bit more sensible this time, less driven, even breezy. "I'm on the main drag, Ru, looking for a dentist, actually."

"Don't tell me you've got another abscess?" She listened, fearing the worst. But what Frank told her was something he called *Plan B*. She rubbed her temple, incredulous, as he blabbered on and on, until she could take no more of it and cut him off, mid-bullshit.

"Stop. You're looking for a dentist for Dodo? Are we made of money? If you're well enough to tramp the street, you're well enough to sit in a plane; so get on a bloody plane!"

"I'll book my ticket after I find out the price for four crowns. I'm sure I saw a dental surgery up here, some logo. Dudu says he doesn't need a home, but he does need teeth."

"Frank, come home or *you'll* need teeth. I'll fly down and kick 'em out myself."

"Can you call me back in, say, an hour?"

"One hour. And you'd better find a bloody travel agent. Or *I* will." She slammed the phone down and Simon asked her not to, *please*. She stood at the window in silence, watching sycamore leaves sway in a breeze. Simon came alongside. "What's the forecast?"

"He's off his head. It's probably the medication, Lariam or whatever. "

They walked down the corridor to the surgery, Ruth talking in a daze, updating Simon who seemed to find Frank's dilemma interesting, as opposed to infuriating, probably because he wasn't married to the prodigal prat. "Bridgework in Congo? Tough call, Ruth."

Their next client was the creaky pensioner Wilfred Jennings, back again in his tweed jacket, and by God he could talk, mostly about escorting allied convoys in the North Atlantic and watching sailors drown in a sea of fire. Sure, his war stories had been interesting, first time you heard them. But that was yonks ago and he smelled of TCP. "Open wide," Simon said, and Ruth was tempted to add, *so we can shut you up.*

With Jennings done, she stood checking the client list and Simon said, "Maddox next. I'll need hypochlorite solution, put a kink in his ponytail. Tell me about the kid."

"No kids booked today; we've got Stinky Maddox then my mate Carol Watt."

"I meant the kid in Congo; Frank is willing to pay for bridgework, you say?"

"Don't remind me. On central incisors, maxillary and mandibular I reckon; two up and down, perhaps laterals. Not sure, although it seems the kid was kicked in the face by some thugs, so use your imagination. Whereas Frank got kicked in the head by an elephant."

Simon folded his arms, plucking at his neat beard. "Difficult age, twelve."

"I'll tell Frank next time I see him. My little Dylan will probably be twelve by then."

"Tell Frank, if he brings the kid here, *I'll* do it. Win-win. And by the way, Maddox has osteitis and a pocket on four-four. He'll be with us a while and he stinks, so best open a window."

"What?"

Simon pointed, discreetly. "Window. Open. Before smelly tracksuit arrives."

"No, the other thing: *bring the kid here, win-win,* what are you on about?"

"Frank comes home, the kid gets the best care in town, and perhaps Cade will stop badgering me to donate to charities. I don't trust them. Goes on salaries in the UK, I reckon."

Ruth gawked. "Fly the kid from Kinshasa to London? Simon, are you nuts?"

"No need to raise your voice. Goodness me, I'm only trying to help."

"Fly the kid here and pay *you* for the bridgework?"

"Who said anything about *paying?* I meant *pro bono,* you nit. Well, as long as I get something for my wall. An African mask would be nice, or whatever. If Frank agrees."

"Bugger me," said Ruth, and Tom Maddox strutted in with an obliging grin.

In her tea break at 3 p.m., Ruth went to the tiny kitchen off the corridor, filled the kettle and leaned against the counter, gazing down at her white shoes. They needed a clean. Simon popped his head in. "Cat got your tongue, Ruth?" She shrugged and said, "I'm still thinking."

"Well, when you stop, I'll have a cup of Earl Grey. Carol's in the lobby, by the way."

Ruth reached for the teabags, wondering what to tell

Frank. Sure, this would be her chance to take control, call the shots for a change, but how much would flights for that kid cost? Still, Father Lynch would approve. There was a word for Simon's kind offer. It began with *A*.

"Altruism," said Carol Watt, reclining in the chair in the hygiene suite, her hair spouting like silver weeds from her headband. Ruth prepared her tools. "*Altruism?* Easy for you to say."

"Jolly decent of Simon to offer; I'd also say you're looking a gift horse in the mouth."

"Or just a horse, in your case. How often do you floss, Carol?"

"Why, what are you going to do to me?"

"Remove your plaque with Gracey curettes and ultrasonics. Any more questions?"

"Yes." Carol blocked Ruth's hand and gave her a piercing look, as if addressing one of her computer-challenged botanists at Kew Gardens. "What if I paid the kid's airfare, Ru?"

Chapter 76

Frank raised a thumb at Dudu to encourage him but the *shegué* looked terrified, lying back in the big black chair, gripping the arms like an astronaut who had changed his mind.

The petite Filipina dentist wore a crisp white coat and a green name tag – *Dr Julie.* She looked about seventeen, cute as a button even when she frowned. She raised a dainty hand to her chin.

"His jaw got swollen, here and here, so I can't see enough. Also, my X-ray machine too old; cannot do panoramic. Also, this boy is vulnerable age. You know about teeth?" Dr Julie's almond-shaped eyes widened in anticipation. Frank half expected to see dollar signs.

"My wife is a dental nurse, and she knows the score. So, how much, best price?"

"Can I get down?" Dudu said and Dr Julie nodded. He slithered from the chair and she watched, all smiles. Frank caught her eye. "Dr Julie, I asked you how much?"

"Oh, sorry. No, you see, I cannot help this young gentleman. You know about teeth?"

"Not as much as you. What do you mean, you *can't help*?"

"A tooth has root, develops as child grows. Apex may not be fully formed. I can't tell."

Frank wondered what an *apex* was. "Can you recommend another dentist?"

"For bridge, rich clients from Congo usually go in South Africa, Botswana, Kenya, India, Thailand, USA, all places like that. And also for the shopping – *Gucci, Louis Futon.*"

"Impossible. I can't go to those places. Too expensive.

Plus, I'm due in London."

"They also go in UK!" said Dr Julie, twinkly-eyed, as if savouring the sudden silence.

She went to a porcelain basin to wash her hands. Dudu stood admiring himself in a mirror, checking his new jeans and his bright T-shirt with the logo, HELL YEAH. The dentist glanced over her shoulder at her young ex-client. "Red nice colour, is good luck for you!"

They walked back up the boulevard, slowly this time. Dudu noticed some *shegués* looking at his nice new T-shirt and they were probably wishing they had one like it.

"Frank, you promised me Dr Julie would help. Why can't she help?" he said. Frank did not reply. He seemed unhappy, not sure of Plan B anymore. Or perhaps he had not heard the question, with all this noisy traffic. They sat on a bench. "Frank, you said—"

"Yes, I know!" Frank put his head in his hands. "Could you do me a favour, Du?"

"Depends what."

"Be quiet." Frank lit a cigarette, blew smoke at the sky and said, "Fuck."

Frank's phone rang soon enough. He let it jangle in his pocket. *Probably Ruth, keen to drill my ears.* The other pedestrians waiting alongside him at the intersection turned to look; *isn't anyone going to answer that?* Frank heard a beep and checked his screen. The text from Hector said, *Bell me.* Frank called back, exhausted now but listening hard amid the mopeds.

Hector sounded far away, a voice from a previous life, almost. "Hello, Frank. I can hear traffic, you up and about? How's the fever? How are the parrots? How's the *shegué?*"

"His name is Dudu. We're on the boulevard, having a wonderful time. What's up?"

"I need the Unicorn flat in a week. Chance and Melody are coming. You're going."

Frank quickly reached out to prevent Dudu from getting mashed by a truck with a lion painted on the front, and said, "Chance and Melody? Who are they, folk singers?"

"Unicorn staff, home office kids in DC, friends of Misti. She forgot to tell me."

"Just like she forgot my rent. Someone needs to wake up, in DC."

"You can talk, Rip Van Winkle. She's been asking about your report, by the way."

"I'll get back into that tonight, if I can think straight. I'm knackered already."

"Get some sleep and get to work. Christ, this one's a bit of alright."

"Excuse me?"

"Oh, some tasty wench preparing tonight's buffet. Rotary Club. Wish me luck."

Frank stalked across the road, with Dudu alongside asking about new teeth. But Frank had no answers, just a report to write and bags to pack. He flagged a taxi and climbed aboard, feeling woozy and worn out. Dudu sat alongside. "Frank, what will we do now?" Frank closed his eyes. "Don't worry, son, everything's OK." But it was a lie, and they both knew it.

When Frank entered his flat, he could hear the two parrots squabbling in their cage on the balcony. They ceased as soon as he approached. Perhaps they were just a bit fed up with each other's ways, like any married couple. Gorgeous-looking creatures, though, up close.

Their silky grey plumage had an off-white penumbra where their black eyes glistened. Their stubby scarlet tails thrust left and right as they sidled about. He clicked his fingers; the smaller parrot let him scratch its neck with his fingertip, the feathers soft and fluffy with taut sinews beneath. The bigger bird grasped a peanut shell in its talon and prised it apart with its beak, before inserting its touchpaper tongue for the goodies. Dudu chuckled and Frank held his friendly gaze, glad to be in Congo, making a difference at last. Sort of.

Mid-evening, Frank settled at his laptop, tapping a thumbnail at his teeth and reading the paltry first page of his report. What next, add the aims and methodology? Assess the likely impact of the Unicorn seminars given the media landscape and political context that pertains in Congo? The buzzwords were budding in his head – green shoots of inspiration. Perhaps he should suggest something practical, urge USAID to fund a community station in Kisangani like Père Augustin wanted. No, Misti Puffer and her bosses would prefer to hear how Unicorn *had inculcated a fostering of dynamic confidence, a multiplicity of commonalities.* She would also appreciate *a paradigm shift,* and doubtless it would help if *local stakeholders would own their gradual transformation and grow their own potential.* He should probably allude to Hector's work on the business side *and the synchronicity thus engendered.* Yes, exactly, pile on the verbiage for the VIPs. Come to think of it, who even reads this stuff? He had no idea of his wider audience, not really. And it would not hurt to find out, especially if the secret of writing blurb lay in knowing your *blurbee.* It was time to recap on Unicorn's top brass and their overarching McMission. Plus, he needed a break.

Frank pulled the NGO's most recent annual report from a stack of documents on his desk. *Unicorn: Changing Lives, Seeding Hope.* The cover shot showed two pale-skinned westerners in their mid twenties, the woman in sunglasses and the unshaven dude festooned in bracelets and swathes of keffiyeh. Or was it *kuffiyah?* A checked scarf anyway, presumably to prove he got around the menswear department. They were chatting to grateful-looking, leathery-faced peasants, and the caption cited *all four corners of the world,* a curious cliché, since the world was spherical, sort of. Frank flipped pages to the Africa section and looked at a photo of one Konrad Mott II, dressed casual smart with a silver moustache the size of a deck brush. So this was the boss, too busy bee to sign fifty diplomas for Congolese journalists, one of whom had walked fourteen kilometres each day for a week to earn it? Mott sat in a huge leather chair, gentleman's club-style, under an oil painting of a lighthouse, with his four female acolytes, petite and blonde, left and right: Bella, Chance, Melody and yes, keen-eyed Misti, all grinning like piranhas. The text below suggested world peace and grass-roots economic stability was just a matter of time, because this quintet was on the job, bless their fair trade cotton socks. Frank tossed the report onto the sofa and watched it slide off. He started typing. His work in DRC would amount to a little check in their boxes and a big one in his bank. If he used enough syllables, Misti might even reply.

His phone rang – perfect timing. He took the call and walked around, listening to his wife, on a two-second delay. He made no mention of his resident *shegué.* He led their chat elsewhere. There was nothing to say, no options left. "So, how's the garden? How's Dylan?"

"Grumbling; wanted to watch *The Sound of Music* but forgot he'd lent our vid to Aubrey."

"Right. And Billie?"

"She loves her tattooed bum and wants an iPod. Do you know what that is, Frank?"

"Expensive gimmick; she should save her cash, they'll never take off. How are you?"

"Let's just say I've had an interesting day. How did it go at the dentist?

"Oh, that? Not good. I feel like I'm a mouse and God is a cat."

"I thought God was a clock?"

"Correct, you win a Unicorn diploma, with a genuine

451

fake signature, Konrad Mott."

"We have to talk. Have you booked your flight?"

"We're talking. I've asked Bernadette to call the travel agent."

"And what about Dodo?"

"His name is Dudu. I can't help him, not really. I can't find him a home, I can't find him a decent dentist. This place is beyond me, Kinshasa is a brick wall. I'll give him some cash to help him on the street, maybe wire more one day, through Hector or Yom. Glad to hear you're concerned, at last." Frank instantly regretted the last bit and expected a riposte.

"Is this Plan c? You dump him, looking like, what was it you said, *the village idiot?*"

"Unless you have a better idea." Frank walked onto the balcony to watch the parrots squawk and flap in a blur of grey and scarlet. Dudu was sitting nearby, gazing at the city, but turned to mutter into the cage. The birds froze, good as gold, and Frank smiled. *Knows a trick or two, this kid.* But what would become of him, growing up? And what girl, in her right mind, would settle for a homeless guy who resembled a vampire? Oh well. You try your best and fail. That's life. Yom was right. *Shegués* learn to manage alone, soon bounce back.

"I do." Ruth sounded if they were getting married. Frank had expected a divorce.

"You do what?"

"Have a better idea, if you'd care to hear it."

"Shoot."

"Don't tempt me," Ruth said, with a chuckle. She sounded almost amenable.

Frank listened, gazing out at the dusky city. The sun was dipping. Ruth was talking. About her boss, Simon being willing to work *pro bono,* especially since his boyfriend had been giving him grief about charities, priorities, his Rolex. Carol Watt would fund Dodo's flights, because she had more money than sense. Dylan would enjoy having a little African friend for a few weeks. Billie could help out with the street kid, practise her French language for Uni. Ruth was able to speak a bit of the lingo herself, had always liked French at school, *oui*? Frank watched the sun smear the horizon like melting butter. His world was looking slippery, from up here. The parrots were quiet. Dudu was watching. Ruth was rounding up.

"*Et voilà,* Frank, there it is. Perhaps *you* can't help him, but *we* can, all of us. Win-win, see? And I'm sure Father Lynch at St Eddie's would love to meet a Congolese kid; he was a missionary, don't forget, adores Africa, always asks about you. So, please come home, soon. And bring what's his name, Dodo. I mean Dudu. I'll pick you up at Heathrow."

Frank took a long drag on his ciggie. Ruth's idea sounded very generous, a stunning *Plan c*, like a fluffy white rabbit pulled from a shiny black hat. There was only one problem – she had not asked his opinion, even a question, so he put one to her, as politely as he could.

"Ruth, have you lost your bloody mind?"

He heard a click as she hung up.

Chapter 77

Frank stubbed out his ciggie, folded his arms and thought about that click, down the line. It had signalled Ruth's displeasure, which did not surprise him, but on further consideration, perhaps it had also been the sound of a penny dropping in his problem, which intrigued him. He looked at Dudu, at the two birds and at the sprawling city where, to be honest, none of them belonged, not really. Just like him, in fact. Fish out of water. Parrots in a cage. *Shegué* in a spot. Husband in deep shit. So sod this. It was time to go home, return to England, where humble pie would be served cold, a welcome change from warm, sticky *fufu*.

He phoned Ruth back, gushing remorse and agreeing to try her idea. She accepted his apology but sounded as if she had been weeping. Frank said, "I'm sorry Ruth, I love you."

"If you loved me, you wouldn't be in fucking Africa."

"Hey, we'll be dancing at Summer Swing before you know it. *À bientôt.*"

Ruth sniffled and said, "Does that mean *see you soon?*"

"*Exactement.* That's my girl. Now I have to make some inquiries, so bye for now."

Frank signed off and thumbed a text to Hector: URGENT, *big question.* His phone rang soon enough and Hector said, "Frank, you're missing an inferior buffet and a tasty waitress."

Frank outlined the altruistic offer from Ruth; Hector said they were *a classic pair of tits.* Perhaps he meant the waitress. "So, Hector, can I get Dudu into the UK?" Frank replied.

Hector sighed down the line. "I thought you were working on our report?"

"I am, but please answer the question."

"Tell me again, you want to take a *shegué* to live with your family?"

"For a few weeks, yes. It's the best I can do and it feels right."

"Not to me, it doesn't. Don't be a fool, matey, you hardly know him."

"I know he helped me through my fever. I know he's basically a good kid."

"Frank, he's a *shegué*. Do you understand what that means?"

"It means he's down on his luck and survives any way he can."

"So slip the wee blighter fifty dollars and go home! Your work is done here!"

"You mean those four Unicorn seminars that won't make any difference?"

"Whereas this will, I presume?"

"To him and to me. You saw the mess he's in – no teeth, no home."

"You came to train journalists, not to play social worker."

"Maybe I came to meet Dudu."

"Come again?"

"I've been thinking about what you said in your office on my first day. About how Congo could be the engine of Africa? About your trainees being tomorrow's *movers and shakers*? Well, maybe my little *shegué* is one too; maybe one day he'll *sell the sizzle,* as you say? He just needs a push, someone to change his life."

Hector stifled a guffaw. "Cosmic destiny, eh? I thought you preferred facts?"

"This isn't about journalism and I'm not his trainer; just a friend."

"You're crossing the line. He's feral. Things *will* get messy."

"They were messy when I found him. Have you read any Jean-Paul Sartre?"

"Excuse me?"

"*Les choses s'arrangent toujours.* Sartre said that. *Things always work out.* And they do, too. You just have to be brave enough to take a chance. Like in business."

"I'm impressed. And I'm sure that your little *shegué* will be, when he sees how the other half sip their bleeding Chardonnay. But tell me this: how will he feel when you bring him back, dump him on a street in Kalamu or Camp Luka?"

"Where?"

"The poorer parts of Kinshasa. I rest my case."

"Forgive my ignorance, I'm new around here."

"Precisely, and Sartre was a pretentious frog-in-a-beret, from what I hear."

"You know something else? I had a dream, first night in Hotel Maisha, about trying to help a Congolese boy. I had another dream during my fever; an old flame was trying to tell me something, urging me to take responsibility for a kid. For this kid, I reckon. Spooky but true, Hector; I can't ignore that stuff. Yes, you're right, as ever, my work here is done, but not quite. I have unfinished business. Can I get Dudu into the UK?"

"You know who else has dreams? The pastors you complain about."

"That's their problem, this is mine. Can I get Dudu into the UK?"

"Stubborn bastard, aren't you?"

"I'll take that as a compliment. Now answer my bloody question. Is it possible?"

Hector gave a long sigh. "Of course it's possible, this is Kinshasa."

"How do I do it?'

"You call Godfrey."

"Godfrey?"

"Godfrey. And you ask him nicely to find you a credible courier, preferably someone who's already bought a ticket to the UK and can add the kid as family."

"Godfrey the *expéditeur?*"

"Unless you know a different Godfrey, with better connections."

"Excellent. What will he need from me?"

"What do you think?"

Chapter 78

Dudu was lying in bed, facing the wall and thinking about promises and the people who make them. People such as Major Monuc, Kilanda and Frank. Even Mama.

The door squeaked and Dudu slid his hand under his pillow. His fingers closed around the handle of a knife. Smaller, easier to hide. He turned his head. "What do you want?"

"A little talk." Frank was peeping into the room, as if he needed permission to enter.

"What about?"

Frank came in and squatted against the wall, smiling. His curly hair looked like a cloud of silver dust and his knees were poking from his shorts like two pink pigs. "You got bored on the balcony, I see? Sorry to neglect you, I've been making some phone calls."

"But why so long? You were talking very loud. I can't even sleep."

"Sorry, I had to chat with Hector and then someone else, named Godfrey, and then with my wife. Anyway, it's done and I have a question: do you want to come to England?"

Dudu released his grip on the knife and sat up. "What do you mean?"

"We'll fix your teeth. You can stay in my house, meet my family. Well?"

"*Nakei poto?* Go to other places, far away?"

"Well, sort of, yes. Fly in a plane to London, how about that?" Frank came to sit on the edge of the bed, laughing and shaking his head. "Hah! You should see your face!"

"Fly in a plane?" Dudu backed into his pillows and looked

towards the window. "London is in Europe. There are many worlds. *Mikili*. Will I see the Eiffel Tower?"

"No, sorry. That's in Paris, France."

"Will I see Atomium like Mikey Dread? He lived in Europe, as a *mikiliste*."

"Hmm. I'm not sure who Mikey Dread is, but I know Atomium is in Brussels, so you won't see that either. But you'll see the London Eye and other places. And, most important, Simon will fix your teeth, good as new, I promise. Simon's nice. He's my wife's boss."

"But what about Dr Julie on the boulevard?"

"Change of plan. So, will you come?"

Dudu wrapped his arms around his shins, wondering. *Frank's plans never work, so why should this?* He shook his head. "I have serious misgivings."

Frank laughed. "About what, England?"

"About you. First, you promised to find me a place to live. And then you said that Dr Julie would fix my teeth. Now you're saying I can go to Europe and …"

"But this is different, trust me, Dudu."

"Why should I?"

"I see. You'd prefer to stay in Kinshasa, looking like the village idiot?"

"I'm not an idiot."

"Agreed. But who will fix your teeth, The Living Dead? Mikey Dread?"

"What's London Eye?"

"A big wheel that we can ride in, high above the city, you'll like it. And before we leave Kin, I'll put your name on Yom's waiting list, so that, if he has space in Centre Tosalisa when we get back, you can live there. It might work out. Well?"

"Does the queen wear a diamond hat?"

"Sometimes, but never mind about her. Let's talk about you and me."

They sat in silence for a few moments and Dudu looked at the pink sky.

"Why the long face?" Frank said.

"Kilanda. What about Kilanda?"

"Don't worry about Kilanda. He's safe and sound. The nuns will help him. I want to help *you*. So, would you like to come to England, yes or no? I need your answer, now, because, if you say yes, I'll have to make preparations and the sooner the better."

"What preparations?"

"I have to pay Godfrey."

"With money?"

"No, with buttons. Any more questions, Mr Journalist?"

Dudu looked at his empty glass on the shelf. "Can I have some more milk?"

"After I get a straight answer. You have to decide, tonight. And one more thing: don't worry about whatever happened here in Congo, because it will be different in England. I promise that nobody will hit you or say bad things or call you *ndoki,* ok?"

"I'm not *ndoki.*"

"Sure, and we must never mention that, ok? I promise and you must promise. But right now, I need to know if you want to come to England. So, yes or no?"

Dudu felt strange, unsure whether to laugh or weep. "Yes, *matondi mingi.*"

Frank stood up and pressed buttons on his phone. "You're very welcome."

Dudu slid off the bed and stood at the window. Lights from the traffic were filling the city and questions were filling his head. About going to places far away. *Nakei poto.*

If I go, will I ever see Mama again? Emile and Ginelle? He ran his tongue over stumpy teeth, watching trucks and cars and motorbikes. But he could not hear them, or even the parrots now, because his head was spinning with promises that had not come true and others that might. Frank came to shake his hand and smiled, but Dudu could not. The room seemed to be sinking underwater as Frank crouched down beside him.

"Hey Dudu, *mon ami.* You'll be ok, I promise. Don't cry."

Chapter 79

By morning, a trip to England seemed the only solution and Frank lingered in bed enjoying the inner peace of the newly converted. *Was this how Ruth had felt about Catholicism?* He wondered about Simon's generous offer, too. The dentist had clearly forgiven that drunken jibe last summer about his little BMW being a *hairdresser's car*. Better take him a thank-you gift. *And apologise, on the record.*

Mid-morning, Frank took Dudu to a photo studio where the little *shegué* stared at the lens like a murder suspect. "We need snaps for your ID card," Frank explained. "Do you want to go and tell Kilanda about London?"

"No, he'll be sad if I say *nakei poto*, because that means I will travel and see many different worlds and I will be *mikil-iste;* one who lives many lives. So, he will be envious."

They took a taxi to Matongé and passed Tata Raphaël stadium, the boxing place, but Dudu seemed oblivious. Perhaps the location had been erased from his traumatised mind. Frank spotted words painted on a tyre outside a shop: *Maison Meubles Mabiala*. He tapped the driver's shoulder. "Stop, this is my rendezvous."

They waited on the forecourt near rough-hewn wooden beds wrapped in polythene. A salesman in shirt and tie was talking to a young couple, the girl pinching her mouth between finger and thumb. A dusty brown Mercedes slewed to the kerb, its black window jammed halfway down and Godfrey the *expéditeur* peeped out; a grin split the handsome face but the eyes were all business. "*Bonjour*, Frank!" He gave a high-pitched giggle as if he thrived on discreet dilemmas, and climbed out, adjusting his black fedora. He gave Dudu the once-over. "Kid will pass for ten, easily. Birth certificate and ID takes three days. I've found a relative."

"Really? A relative?" Frank said. Godfrey gave him a puzzled look.

"No, Frank, but from today, they're family. When do you want to leave?"

"Ah, as soon as possible. How does this work, I pay you today? And the *relative*?"

"Don't buy the salt if you haven't licked it. How is your fever, all better?"

"I've felt worse. What do you mean, *don't buy the salt*?"

"I'll take half of my fee today and half when you get the documents. As for Adrienne, give her one payment when you all depart, and one when you all return."

"Who's Adrienne?"

"A friend. Kinshasa hairdresser with a big family in London, she travels there often. She's your courier and *Dudu's auntie*, yes? You'll hook up at the airport."

"Ah yes, *a relative*, I see. And how will I recognise her, do I get a photo?"

Godfrey rapped his knuckles on the Merc roof. The passenger door opened and a pretty Congolese woman stepped out wearing pink Adidas trackpants and a denim jacket. She had braided hair and her bum was the size of a space hopper.

"*Bonjour, messieurs!*" she said in a husky voice, offering Frank a well-manicured hand. But Dudu shook it first, grinning from ear to ear. The glamorous woman smiled down. "*I* am your Aunt Adrienne. *Mon Dieu*, how do you *eat*?"

Godfrey beckoned Frank into the Mercedes. It smelled of Adrienne's perfume – roses marinated in gin. Frank sat in the passenger seat and gave Godfrey some photos of Dudu and a wad of dollars. Godfrey counted the cash with a stubby thumb. "Big-head presidents, good." He opened the glove box and Frank glimpsed six mobile phones and a pistol inside. Godfrey selected one of the phones and made a hurried call. Frank turned to watch Dudu and Adrienne, through the tinted window, chatting away. *Yes Auntie, no Auntie.*

So far, so friendly. It seemed Ruth had found the solution to an intractable problem. It was easy, in the warm light of day. Too good to be true, almost.

Godfrey put the phone away and Frank said, "So, are we done for today?"

Perspiration pearled on Godfrey's blue-black skin and his perfect teeth shone like tiny marble headstones; the whites of his eyes were yellow from malaria, and bloodshot with tiny red rivers. He was grinning again. "There's just one more thing."

He looked as if Satan had sent him to close a deal.

Chapter 80

"How do you mean, *one more thing?*" Frank said.

Godfrey pointed through the car window to the furniture shop, Maison Meubles Mabiala. "You see the shutters next door? That's my sister's shop. She sells dresses. My brother sells artefacts. His place is out at the back. They'll arrive soon."

"And?"

"Well, I heard that you would like to buy something, for your wife, I believe?"

"How convenient," Frank said, watching little birds in a tree, warbling their gossip.

"And while we wait…" Godfrey reached under his seat for a bottle of Chivas and two shot glasses. "I propose a toast, Frank, to your journey and safe return. I think Hector has doubts and envies your entrepreneurial spirit. Me? I admire it."

Frank watched the amber liquid trickle. "Bit early for Scotch, isn't it?"

"Better late than never." Godfrey flashed a mischievous smile. "I insist!"

They clinked glasses and sipped. The *expéditeur* pushed back his fedora and explained why he liked Chivas, something about his days in the élite Special Presidential Division. Frank closed his eyes, letting the alcohol work its magic while Godfrey rambled on about some mission to the Central African Republic. "Our president toasted me personally, after I led a squad to rescue his niece from being eaten by Bokassa."

Frank opened an eye. "I beg your pardon?"

"Interesting, yes? Emperor Bokassa was upset with President Mobuto and had promised to eat the poor girl, *to make the payback,* as you say. So, Mobuto sent us to stop him." Godfrey rotated a broad finger in the air. "We went by helicopter. Dead of night. We took our witch doctor to charm the crocodiles in Bokassa's moat. We waded across, killed the palace guards, rescued the girl. Smash and grab, as you say! Bokassa telephoned, gloating about his plan to cook her, until Mobuto said, *did you check her room, lately?* We got medals and a case of Chivas on our return, oh yes!"

Godfrey held his glass to the light, admiring its contents. His misty-eyed gaze suggested the anecdote was based on fact, even if those crocodiles' tails had perhaps grown in the telling. "Down the hatch!" Godfrey said, and drained an inch of Scotch in one go. He smacked his lips, pointing. "And there's Miriam and Daniel, see?"

A woman was rolling noisy steel shutters up on the shop next to the furniture place; the young man with her resembled a younger version of Godfrey; the same bull neck. Frank got out, head spinning in the sunshine, and floated towards them.

Miriam in the snazzy headscarf had a dazzling smile and a cramped shop stacked with dazzling fabric. He bought a green robe for Ruth, slipped out the back, eyes popping, and moved on to Daniel's place in the yard beyond. Daniel's shop appeared to be two shipping containers bolted together end to end, with a doorway cut where it said KLG ROTTER. Frank perused this as he would a crossword clue. *Rotterdam?* Whatever. It seemed unlikely KLG would see these big steel boxes again. Daniel was waiting in the shadows, in a linen smock and hooped earrings – the artisan look – beckoning Frank. Godfrey and Dudu were already inside, browsing the artefacts. The place looked like Aladdin's Container.

Frank stepped through the door hole. The place smelled of woodsmoke, wood oil, wood everything. Exquisite carvings packed the shelves: little ebony hippos, ivory chess sets, toy trucks and helicopters. Bigger items dominated the floor, including a life-size carving of a nude woman, her body twisted and face contorted.

"This is a fetish," Daniel said, "to stop polio. Or so they thought."

He seemed less garrulous than his elder sibling and, as Godfrey approached, beaming on booze, Frank said, "So you believe in this gris-gris stuff, Godfrey?"

Godfrey's gaze was steady. "*Stuff*? I believe that I crossed Bokassa's moat."

Daniel laughed; perhaps he had heard that story before. He tapped a wooden mallet on a hollow log, two metres long: *bip-bop*. "Buy this talking drum? We call it *lokole*. Slit in the top makes five different sounds. I'll ship to London, just for you."

Frank whacked the drum with the mallet. It sounded like a hollow log. "Nice, but no thanks, Daniel. It's far too big. Besides, I have a mobile phone."

Daniel chuckled. "Yes, and we call that *progress,* until the battery dies."

"Then we call it a nuisance," Frank said, and Godfrey tittered. Godfrey-six-Nokia.

Daniel moved to a rack of spears. "These were for *bokeke* – a party after the death of a chief. They make fine gifts, from Équateur province. Try." He offered a spear and Frank held it aloft, getting the heft of it, picturing himself in a grass skirt and chasing prey – or the neighbours – along the equator. "No thanks, Daniel. My son would skewer next door's cat."

Daniel looked disappointed. "Perhaps a little helicopter? Or some crocodiles?"

"Perhaps. But first, something for my wife?" Frank patted a tall, sinew-bound drum, wondering if it could send texts. Godfrey and Dudu were chatting before a wooden figure with nails sticking from its torso. Frank cocked his head, stepping closer. "What's this?"

"*Ekeko*," Daniel said, more emphatic now, *take-it-or-leave-it.* "A Power Figure."

"It's a good one, Frank," Godfrey said. "For that *gris-gris stuff.* If you know how."

The wooden statue stood approximately twelve inches high. Rusty nails protruded from its chest and back, the gaps between encrusted with cowrie shells, shards of mirror, rusty wire, feathers and beads. It looked heathen, antique and completely bonkers. Daniel pointed. "Nails represent favours it has granted. People would make offerings, ask requests."

"Power Figure, you say?" Frank remembered one similar, in Hector's office, but this was better. A lot older. More... powerful. He affected disdain. "How much, minus a zero?"

Daniel extracted a pocket calculator from a pocket of his smock. "Well, for you..."

When Frank emerged from the shipping container into scorching sunlight, clutching his bag of ethnic antiques, Auntie Adrienne promptly cornered him. She seemed fascinated by his curly head, or rather, the price his hair might fetch. "Been thinking. I know an Indian lady in Peckham who makes wigs, I'll get you a fair return." She peeped into his bag, briefly distracted. "Power Figure, nice. My grandma had one; she used to burn offerings at his feet."

Godfrey rested a hand on Frank's arm. "I have a feeling your journey will go fine."

"Let's hope so, but how do you mean?"

Godfrey gestured at Dudu talking to Daniel at the doorway of the artisan's shop. "Your little companion there? Our gris-gris is in his blood; Dudu's tata was *nswendwe*."

"Was what?"

Godfrey grinned. "But never mind that *stuff*. I'll bring your tickets to the airport. I'll find you easily. I know it well." He stood rotating a stubby finger, like a little helicopter.

Chapter 81

It was time to clean the guest room, prepare it for a new occupant. *From Africa, how exciting.* Ruth scooped Aubrey's hairbrush and Harry Potter comic from a shelf and put them in a plastic bag. She added two blouses from the wardrobe and, from the bedside drawer, a pencil case with a rabbit's foot attached to the zip. Ruth stroked the fur. *Not very lucky for bunny.* She heard movement on the landing, as Billie peeped into the room, her eyes tight with sleep. "Cheers Mum, you woke me up, rattling drawers. What you doing?"

"Morning camper, just tidying up. I'll be seeing Pippa later. I'll give her this lot."

"Aubrey won't be happy. She likes coming here."

"Too bad. This is *my* little house, not hers. Besides, we all have to make sacrifices."

"Including me."

"What's that supposed to mean?"

"I make extra dosh when Aubrey stays over. From childminding. Or did you forget?"

"I'm just doing my bit; you too. It was Frank who started this, so complain to him."

"Don't worry, I will. Perhaps Frank could get me a job in France, to make up for it?"

Ruth slid the drawer shut on the bedside table. "What are you on about, *France?*"

Billie yawned, a big stinky one. "Me and Callum have decided to do a gap year, take some time out. See the world. That's the plan, anyway."

"I see. And were you planning to ask me?"

Billie rolled her eyes. "Sorry. I forgot. Mum-can-I-do-a-g ap-year-please?"

"If you mean, *Mum-can-I-hack-some-shitty-job-for-twelve- months,* I doubt it, Billie."

"I don't want a shitty job. I'll ask Frank. Where did he work, before college?"

"No idea. All I know is if you don't hurry up, you'll be late for school."

In the kitchen, Ruth poured a cup of coffee for Billie and some milk over Dylan's cereal. He sat with his chin in his hands. "When is Daddy coming back from Africa?"

"I told you, he has to see some people. About Dudu."

"But we're people. *I'm* people."

"He'll be here in a few days. You'll be glad when he brings Dudu, I bet."

"Except *that* means Strawberry Aubrey can't stay over. So, probably, I won't be."

"Won't you feel good that we're helping someone less for- tunate than ourselves?"

Dylan shrugged. "Can Aubrey come to play, sometimes?"

"Certainly, just no sleepovers, we have no space. Besides, she has nice grandparents in posh Berkshire, she can stay there. Dudu has nobody. Now, eat up and let's hit the road."

Dylan gazed at the French windows. "In Africa, do ele- phants walk in your garden?"

"Lions," said Billie, stirring coffee.

Dylan's eyes widened. "Did Dudu ever see a crocodile, Mummy?"

"Saw one and killed it," Billie said. "He wears a necklace made from its teeth."

"Wow. And does his belly get big and round, when he's hungry, like on TV?"

Ruth said, "Well, I know he loves Cheerios." And Dylan reached for his spoon.

She drove the kids to school and proceeded to Richmond listening to Ladysmith Black Mambazo, drumming her fingers with the baby kicking inside her big, round belly.

There was no sign of Pippa at the dental surgery, even though she had requested an early appointment; *La Price* eventually breezed in, half an hour late, suited and booted, with Aubrey tagging along, big smiles, *Hi, Mrs Kean!* All went well until they were leaving, when Ruth offered Aubrey the plastic bag containing her spare clothes and the other stuff, explaining why. Aubrey skulked away to the shiny Range Rover without another word.

"Gosh," Pippa said, in the lobby. "Aubs was quite looking forward to summer, she rather enjoys her sleepovers. And how long will this little African chappie be staying?"

Ruth shrugged. "The bridgework shouldn't take long, Simon reckons four or five weeks. Sorry Pippa, perhaps you could tell Aubs we're all helping someone less fortunate?"

Pippa donated a tight-lipped smile and walked away to her nice car. Ruth followed, watching from a safe distance. Pippa slid into the driving seat and seemed to be trying to reason with her daughter. Aubrey was slumped in the back seat, bawling into dainty fists.

Chapter 82

In the taxi home from the artisan's place, Frank sat sneaking glances at Dudu, his eye drawn to the question mark tattooed on the boy's arm. It seemed increasingly appropriate somehow, in the light of Godfrey's spooky aside about gris-gris, about how *Tata was a rolling stone* or whatever. *Yeah right. Godfrey should know, on the sauce at 11 a.m.* Frank looked out at the dusty street. A few blocks up, he spotted a familiar logo – *Choice* FM. He told the driver to stop, paid the fare and led Dudu towards the rickety staircase around the back of the building.

"Ever seen a radio station, Dudu?" Frank asked, walking up. He pictured keen-eyed Thony racing down it, flying past him all those weeks ago, hungry for news. "The guy who sent the parrots works in this place. Time to send them back."

Inside, they paused at the window of a studio to watch a DJ in wraparound shades, all blather and bling. Dudu cupped a hand at the glass. "Can I wait here?"

Frank nodded and went to the newsroom; no sign of Thony, but Deputy Editor Leo seemed keen to discuss news writing. Frank mentioned African Grey parrots, *protected species*. Leo looked puzzled but promised to send a driver. Frank scribbled on the whiteboard. "Here's my mobile. I'd be very grateful." He paused, the pungent smell of ink transporting him back to a hundred training sessions, here, there and everywhere. "Maybe I could attend your next seminar?" Leo said.

"You bet, bye for now," Frank said, and they bumped heads.

He found Dudu in the corridor, talking to a skinny woman in hipster jeans. Frank recognised the shape of her shoulders, the staccato voice. She sounded angry. He sauntered forward, affecting a breezy smile. "Hi, Nadine! Everything ок?" Dudu backed into the men's room. Nadine turned and glowered. "Talk of the devil! *Bonjour,* skeleton. You've lost weight. Not that you had much to start with. So, I hear you don't want our gift. What's up, you don't like African parrots anymore?"

"They're beautiful, thanks, but I can't take them to England."

"But you can take a *shegué?*" Nadine's cute nostrils flared, her blood up.

Frank poured himself a cup of water at the cooler, watching bubbles rise and pop. "That's the idea. Just waiting for a friend to confirm tickets. How's Choice?"

"Why him, Frank? When I needed help, you asked me, *are you nuts Nadine?*"

"This is different."

"How is it different? You know what he told me? *Nakei poto.* He's going to London. The queen wears a diamond hat. He's going up the Eiffel Tower. Because you're a liar!"

He raised his cup. "Cheers. Please shout a bit louder. When's your bulletin?"

"Mind your own business." She walked backwards and raised a skinny arm as if seeking permission to speak, her lips pouted like plums and her pink tongue rolling between them. "*Brrr-brrr!* Please, sir, do you think God won't punish you?"

Frank sipped the icy water and watched her go, around the bend.

He led Dudu out, down the iron steps and onto the busy street. They walked the rest of the way home, stopping briefly en route at the cybercafé, where Frank bought a couple of floppy discs and quickly emailed Ruth, updating her on his deal with Godfrey. He read a short one from Dylan, who had sent a misspelled, unfinished joke:

Knock-knock, how is there? Freddy.

Back at the flat he cooked pasta with pesto and grated cheese on top. They ate on the sofa, watching cartoons on TV. Dudu offered to wash up and Frank went back to his desk. He added a few paragraphs to his draft report, explaining how, if Unicorn could set up a small radio station in Kisangani's central market, it might help prevent rumours and save lives. He glanced at his jotter. Père Augustin had scribbled stats – such a station would reach forty-five thousand people per day – including *la population riveraine* – by word of mouth. Frank keyed it in but he could already guess Misti Puffer's response. She would dismiss the idea, unless USAID expressed interest and then, no doubt, it would be hers. Dudu came to peep.

"Do you have any games in that computer?"

Frank shook his head and let Dudu click the mouse, showed him how to create and save *Dudu.doc.* The kid seemed bright and keen, quick to catch on. "But now," Frank said, reaching for the mouse, "I need to write to my boss. Sorry."

Dudu washed the dishes, then sat on the sofa to watch TV, changing channels whenever he wanted. He liked watching the singers with their caps on backwards, but also watching football, when he could find some. He thought about Emile kicking stones and pressed the remote. He watched men in smart black suits using big words; one looked like Pastor Precious except his spectacles did not have pink lenses and he wore no ring. Frank was calling for something, *glass of water, please Dudu?*

He went to the kitchen and stood at the sink, turning the tap on and off, listening to the water swirl through the pipes in the cupboard underneath. He crouched to watch the drips where the pipes leaked onto an old rag. There was a bin with a lid that swung if you poked hard enough, and inside the bin he saw a plastic doll, dressed like a pastor with a shoelace noose around its neck.

The doll lay observing him through the smelly rubbish, with melted black holes for eyes, as if it were lost, asking for help, waiting to be lifted out. *The doll Kilanda had stolen from the market and burned with a cigarette and strangled, just before some bad men…*

"Hey, Dudu, what happened to my glass of water?" Frank said, from behind.

Chapter 83

Frank held the doll. "ok, let's try again, Dudu. You took this from my bin, because you were *curious*, and because you've *never, ever seen it before*. But, the thing is, I found this doll in your bag. So, I'm curious too. Is this gris-gris?"

Dudu stared back in silence from the other end of the sofa, his gaze unflinching, his eye still bruised from the attack at the stadium. This *shegué* had met meaner opponents in his time, no question about it. Frank blinked first and looked away; perhaps gris-gris was a family secret and Dudu felt bound by some Congolese version of omertà? But if so, why had he chatted so openly to Godfrey about his tata being *nswendwe, who worked for a great sorcerer*? And why clam up, now? Did he not trust a *mundele* – even a helpful one? It was a crossword without clues. Frank placed the mutilated doll on the sofa and sat back, hands behind his head. He watched Dudu slip away to settle on the balcony, beside the parrot cage.

Frank's phone rang, and Bernadette told him, "I've booked your flights for Monday. You can pay at your local travel shop and Godfrey will bring the tickets."

"You and your connections," Frank said. "Thanks, I owe you." He went to the balcony to tell the stern-faced *shegué* but got no response. They sat in silence, watched by wary birds. "How's your amnesia, Dudu?" Frank said, after a while.

"I don't know big words."

"But you know something." Frank poked a finger through the bars and caressed the friendlier of the two parrots. "Will they ever talk, do you think?"

"About what?"

"About anything. They're very quiet today. Maybe they're sad about their clipped wings. Maybe they would rather be free, go where they want. And you?"

"Me what?"

"Perhaps you would rather be on the street, down below, free to do what you like and go where you want? Instead of here, listening to an inquisitive *mundele?*"

"I don't know big words."

"But you know about that doll, in my bin. Can't we discuss it, as friends?"

Dudu sidled back into the lounge. Frank decided to stop fishing. *Least said, soonest mended,* as Yom might put it. He lit a cigarette and this one tasted good, not like bleach or tar. He blew smoke at the boulevard. *But where the hell was this driver Choice* FM *had promised?* He called the deputy editor's mobile; Leo did not reply. He dialled Thony. *Out of area.* And Nadine? She would peck his eyes out. He caressed one of the parrots through the bars, clucking sweet nothings. The other bird puffed up its silky grey plumage, wiggled its scarlet tail and glared. *Watch your tongue, stranger.*

On Saturday, Frank hunkered down and finished his Unicorn report – thirteen pages. He rang Hector with the good news and promised to email it from the cybercafé. Hector sounded in ebullient mood, having spent the night with his *tasty waitress.* "So, bon voyage, Frank, but do not email your report from a café; USAID will be unhappy if it leaks. Kindly give it to Claude, on a floppy, in a sealed envelope. I'll send him to drive you to the airport."

"Thanks, roger that. And who should I give the parrots to?"

"Fuck knows. Look, just leave your key with Claude, he'll sort that bollocks out."

Sunday afternoon, Frank polished his feature story for *Perspective,* and his shoes. He was stuffing clothes into his rucksack when Yom phoned him, about some letter he wanted posting in England. The priest turned up later, with a stooping Congolese Jesuit who resembled an ageing headmaster, gnarled but natty in a grey suit and suede boots. Père Gustave was Belgium-based, visiting for a conference. They asked how Dudu was doing.

"Busy sulking right now," Frank said, leading them up the corridor of his flat. "Comes out of his room for food and cartoons. I think he's memorised the TV schedules."

Père Gustave seemed impressed but not surprised. "Intuitive intelligence, you see."

Frank knocked at the guest room, en route. Dudu opened his door and closed it again, as soon as he saw Père Gustave's clerical collar. Frank knocked gently, twice.

"Hey Dudu, Yom came too, to say bye." Frank heard a muffled reply, *go away please.* He winked at the two priests and tried again. "Hey Dudu, Père Gustave lives near Atomium in Brussels and he's come specially to see you. What am I supposed to tell him?"

He heard feet shuffling back towards the door, then Dudu's reply, low but clear, *Longwa kuna.* Yom chuckled and walked away. The elderly Jesuit sighed and followed.

Frank served iced Coke in tall glasses on the balcony. They spoke about Dudu, about the trip to London, and Simon's offer. When Frank outlined his cash deal with Godfrey, Yom almost choked on his drink. "*What?* I could buy *ten* water pumps for that money."

"Except you don't take bribes," Frank said. "And Dudu needs teeth, not a standpipe."

They watched a fuzzy sun bleed into the horizon – orange and red, then a vast bruising of dark blue that arched high over the humming city. Père Gustave craned his neck towards the corridor, perhaps hoping Dudu might show. Frank mentioned the mutilated doll.

"Dudu says he never saw it before; *doesn't know* how it got in his bag. Such fibs!"

"What do you expect?" Yom said, "I told you to bin it, not have a tête-à-tête."

"It was in the bin. Dudu pulled it out. What was I supposed to do, clap my hands? By the way, he also told my fixer he has gris-gris in his blood, Tata worked for a sorcerer, and Grandad before him, carving fetishes. But when I mention any of that, he just clams up. One minute he's my big buddy; the next minute he's like a total stranger. I can't work him out."

"Stop trying," said Père Gustave, steepling his waxy fingers like a hermit with all the answers. His hooded eyes and slit-trench mouth reminded Frank of someone – an African politician but not Mandela. *So, who*? *Ah yes, Robert Mugabe.* It was a little disconcerting.

"Mr Kean, how many of *us* are consistent? We all have two sides, little secrets. And every *shegué* guards their secrets too, as indeed they must, in order to survive. But I doubt there's any cause for concern; in all my years, I've met only one genuine *enfant sorcier*."

"Did he tell genuine fibs?"

"Something like that," said Père Gustave, sitting back. "Imagine a boy so disruptive, his entire village wanted rid of him – *pure evil* according to his parents, respectable folk at their wits' end. In time, they decided a Jesuit education might prove beneficial and so, as a junior priest, I was assigned to collect and drive the boy to our boarding school. En route, I had to stop at a girls' school to see a teacher friend. I left the boy in the yard. He caused pandemonium; the girls were howling, running for their lives. Yet apparently, all he had done was to whisper in their ears."

"Whisper what?"

"I have no idea. No girl would repeat it, and nor would he; I duly delivered the boy to our own school but he absconded after a week and was never seen again."

Frank swirled his ice cubes, dying for a cigarette. "Is that it?"

"My point is this," said Père Gustave, "some people have a knack for getting into scrapes and causing trouble – we've all met such pests and buffoons. However, the true *sorcier* is a rare thing, because he's a genius of sorts, in the sense that Mozart was a good one and Hitler a bad one; individuals who leave their mark on any community and the wider world, through their charisma, rare personalities and particular talent, for better or worse. They turn heads, change minds and influence events through a form of social hypnosis, during which the extraordinary becomes normal; so that when we finally awake all our reference points have somehow shifted. That *charisma* is the difference between a follower and a leader, between a child full of beans and a child who has the power to influence those around them by force of will or through a special ability, often both. At least, that's my theory, as explained in my master's thesis. Do you have a slice of lemon?"

Nicely hypnotised, Frank wandered to the fridge. Yom followed and said, "Frank, don't worry, everything will be fine. And if not, remember: *least said, soonest mended.*"

"What do you mean, *if not?*" Frank asked, slicing lemon. He arranged the results on a plate, and Yom said, "Nicely done. You could be a chef." They returned to the balcony.

"How much did you tell your wife?" Père Gustave said. It was an astute question.

"About Dudu?" said Frank. "Not a lot; Ruth would only get upset."

"Indeed. And how is London; still in the grip of Bin Laden fever, I expect? Now *he's* a clever one." The Jesuit pinched a lemon wedge between strong fingers.

The priests chatted on and Frank listened in a daze. Père Gustave's anecdote and Yom's casual *if not* roared in his head like a jet engine. He watched the tail light of a plane sloping into the night and wondered about the difference between gossip and fact, between doing right and getting tangled in a web of mistrust, between the two sides of Dudu's personality. Père Gustave gestured at the lights winking across the evening sky. "Tomorrow that will be you! Bon voyage. I do miss London."

Frank managed a smile. "What does *longwa kuna* mean, by the way?"

"*Go to hell,*" Yom said, and drained his Coke.

Chapter 84

Dudu stood in his room, listening at his door to Frank in the hall saying *bye-bye Yom, bye-bye Père Gustave*. He sat on his bed, bumping his heels, thinking. *Have they really gone, or is it a trap?* He waited a bit then opened his door, peeping both ways before he came out to look for Frank. He found him soon enough and said, "Did they want to do an exorcism?"

Frank was packing stuff into his rucksack, but stopped and leaned against the bedroom wall, rubbing his head. "Listen, my boy, we need rules for London. You won't ask me about exorcisms, and I won't mention gris-gris or *ndoki*. We won't discuss any of that, promise? Because if my wife hears, she won't be happy, OK? Pass me that red one, please."

Dudu handed Frank a crumpled shirt. "I'm not your boy. And I'm not *ndoki*."

Frank was clearing out his desk, binning jotters full of scrawl, when he heard Dudu screech like a skidding car. He raced to the balcony and found the *shegué* spinning in circles clutching a bloodied finger and bawling at the parrot cage. The African Greys cowered inside as he yelled at them through the bars. "*Longwa kuna!* This one just bit me, Frank! Throw them off the balcony, I don't care if they can't fly!"

The wound was small but deep. Frank fetched his first-aid kit and tended it with antiseptic and calm words, applying gauze and tape. "Easy, Du, keep still. You know, we have parrots in Richmond, green ones, you'll see. Nicer than these guys."

481

Dudu sniffled. "Do they bite?"

Frank shook his head. "No, they stay in the trees. Don't worry about England. Nobody is going to bite you or beat you up or call you names."

"What sort of names?"

"Let's make some sweet tea. It'll help."

"Are there pastors in England?"

"Yes, but they're not quite as enthusiastic as some of the ones here."

"Will I see the queen's diamond hat? And London Bridge?"

"Sure, all sorts. But our priority is teeth, not tourism. OK, better?"

Dudu examined his dressed digit and nodded. "*Matondi mingi.*"

Frank got to bed around 11 p.m., their bags packed. He lay listening to a barking dog and counted the weeks back to his first night in-country with its noisy alleys and raucous choir. All that seemed a lifetime away, and so did London. He smiled in the darkness, musing on the summer ahead. He pictured himself pottering about in the shrubbery with Ruth, caressing her big tummy for kicks; taking Dylan to the park; watching Wimbledon on TV and sipping warm beer at Kew Gardens, bopping to a good band under a regal sky. And, tooth-by-tooth, Simon would fix little Dudu's battered gob and give him back a smile. Oh, and they would try to avoid churches, although Ruth would probably have other ideas.

He rose early next morning, selected comfy chinos and his emerald shirt with the button-down collar, Ruth's favourite; *makes your eyes look green*. He filled his steel-handled saucepan with bottled water and set it to simmer on the stove.

Dudu was cross-legged before the TV, glued to a cartoon and carefully munching mashed banana from a plate. Frank went to pack his laptop. It was lying at an angle to the edge of his desk, not parallel. *Odd.* He spotted small fingerprints on the mouse and said, "If you've been looking for games in my computer, forget it."

He unlocked the balcony door and went outside to watch the buzzing boulevard. A smattering of grey feathers wafted towards his feet, light as gossamer. He tugged the shawl from the birdcage. One parrot lay wedged between the aluminium bars, as if trying to escape, its head hanging down, with dark blood congealed around a hole in the nape of its neck. The other was slumped, slashed and torn at a bowl of peanuts. *Jesus, what the hell?* Frank opened the cage door, reached in and poked one of the parrots. It was dead as a dodo, cold and stiff. The other one too. Dudu came out to blink at the carnage. "Parrots fight."

"Now you tell me." Frank stood with his arms folded, surveying the blood and cack and feathers. *Fight over what, food?* It seemed unlikely somehow, as they had two bowls of peanuts. Perhaps parrots were prone to jealousy, like one-man dogs, so-called? Had the timid parrot been envious of the friendlier one? He wrapped the dead birds in newsprint.

He washed his hands and changed the dressing on Dudu's finger. The pink wound gaped like the mouth of a tiny fish. Dudu winced. "Parrots fight, Frank, don't blame me."

Frank paused. "For what?"

Dudu turned towards the TV. "There's Road Runner."

Frank went to the kitchen, spooned Nescafé into a mug and frowned into the empty saucepan on the stove. *Thought I filled it?* His fingers closed around the steel handle. Pain raced up his arm and exploded in his head, a starburst of agony that seemed to send him floating to the ceiling. The scorching pan crashed to the floor and he squealed like a stuck pig. He thrust his throbbing hand under the cold tap and stood sucking air through clenched teeth. Brown water dribbled from the tap. His phone beeped in his pocket. He read a one-word text from Claude. *Ready?*

They arrived at the airport around noon. Frank gave Claude his keys and a floppy disc in a sealed enveloped for Hector. Claude spotted the gauze on Frank's finger. "Congo war?"

They bumped heads and Claude pointed at Dudu. "Bring me back a T-shirt, or else."

Adrienne tottered up on vertiginous heels, hauling a battered Prada bag – genuine tat. "*Bonjour, messieurs!* Oh, dear, our poor fingers. Shall we, Frank?"

"You first, Auntie Adrienne. I should probably keep my distance."

Her huge false eyelashes fluttered like moths. "My boyfriend thinks so too."

Frank spotted Godfrey's fedora bobbing through the crowded lobby. The fixer slipped him the airline tickets and accepted another envelope of cash, which vanished into the black leather waistcoat. "Not counting your fee, then?" Frank said.

Godfrey tapped his nose. "I have your address, I know people in London."

He peeled away, shepherding Adrienne and Dudu to a VIP gate. Frank saw a guard extract a bread knife from Dudu's satchel. *C'est quoi, ça?* Adrienne sashayed through. Other travellers tried but the guard shut the gate, ignoring their protests.

Frank stood in line, perusing his ticket. *Flight 555.* At least it wasn't 666. He watched sweating porters and listened to incomprehensible announcements on the PA. So this was it, his last day, for a while at least, in the Democratic Republic of Congo, *soi-disant.* He offered his scuffed passport to the clerk in gold epaulets.

Once through, he wandered around the departure lounge, talking to Ruth on his mobile, using the last of his airtime. She sounded excited, breathless. "I'm just polishing the Welsh dresser and I stink of lemon oil. Anyway, love, how are you?"

"Tickety-boo. Except I scorched my hand on a pan, multitasking."

"You should leave that to a woman. I'll kiss it better. How's Dudu?"

"Packed a big knife in his carry-on. I hope we're doing the right thing."

"Line's breaking up. *Doing the right thing,* I agree. How's sexy Adrienne?"

"Not as sexy as you."

"Promises, promises. I hope you took lots of photos, of Congo, I mean."

"Some sod stole my camera. In a church, of all places."

"Really? You kept that quiet. And what were *you* doing in a church?"

Frank stared at his shiny shoes. "Breaking up, love. How's Dylan?"

"Tugging at my sleeve. I think he wants a word. Big news for Daddy."

The *big news* was Billie's tattoo. Frank laughed. "Dyl, you've already told me three times! By the way, Dudu's got one as well. You'll be coming to the airport with Mum?"

"Yes, before school. Got to get up extra early. Will Dudu bring a spear?"

"Just a leopard," said Frank and heard Dylan gasp, *no way.* He could hear Ruth's aerosol too, hissing in spurts, and then her voice: *Tell Daddy ethnic antique. Tell him to buy Bombay Sapphire. Tell him you want to hear Foghorn's Horses.* Dylan said *no, you tell him* and Ruth was back on the line, listing goodies she had procured.

"I got your Oxford marmalade, some cans of Guinness and the latest *Private Eye.*"

"Great. But try and get some *fufu.*"

"Some what, Frank?"

He mooched about the departure area, keeping his distance from Auntie Adrienne and her long-lost nephew Dudu. He stood watching the jets. Hector phoned, sounding gruff as a goat; perhaps his tasty waitress had found pastures new.

"Question, Mr Kean. I just got the floppy from Claude. Where's my report?"

"In the folder marked *Unicorn*."

"Negative. This disc you sent contains one blank document entitled *Dudu*."

Frank stared at the code on the tail fin of a plane. It made no sense. "What?"

"This isn't good, Frankie; please email your report from London, first thing."

"Wait, it must be there. Try the folder marked *Perspective*. Can you see that?"

"Are you deaf? I see one file on this disc. It's not your report. Bon voyage."

Frank pocketed his phone and stood watching aircraft. Had he given Claude the wrong floppy? Probably. Definitely. Things had been a bit mad lately.

He sat down and slid his laptop from his bag. Sweat glistened on his forearms and his blistered fingers hurt as he pressed the keys. He heard Dudu giggling from across the lounge, and turned to look. Adrienne caught his gaze but quickly turned her head, playing strangers. The laptop flickered, its screen pale in the midday sun. He opened two folders but found no trace of his Unicorn report or the story for Saul at *Perspective*. He whimpered like a trodden pup, rammed a backup floppy into the slot and stared, bug-eyed. It was empty, not a sausage, *how the fuck*?

Frank snapped the laptop lid shut and strode across the lounge, stepping over sprawling teenagers, and around dapper travellers in their business suits. He planted himself in front of Dudu and glowered down. "What were you doing in my laptop?"

The *shegué*'s bruised eye was healing nicely; Dudu no

longer resembled the half-chameleon sci-fi ghoul of the previous week but he did look baffled by Frank's accusation. Adrienne wobbled upright and said, smiling, "Do we know you, sir?"

Chapter 85

Dudu held Auntie Adrienne's hand as he walked across black tarmac, smooth as a midnight lake. The aeroplane was big, shiny and white. He could smell oil, but not mucky oil like on trucks and barges. The high whistling sound seemed to come from all sides. He trotted up steel steps and a smiling lady at the top said *bonjour, monsieur*. She wore a gold pin, red lipstick. Dudu turned to look back one last time, before leaving. *Nakei poto*. What would Mama think about him going to faraway places? Would she ever find out? Maybe one day.

Inside, the plane was like a bus but the seats looked more comfy, with boxes above and lids hanging down. Two kids ran giggling up the aisle, not stiff and nervous like him. He sat by a small window and Adrienne fastened his belt. When the plane got full, a lady showed everyone how to put on a yellow bib. They would land in the sea and slide down a chute to get off. You could blow your whistle. He tucked his satchel under his seat and looked in a shiny magazine, free, for keeps. It had maps for *bonnes vacances*, with nice little photos of Eiffel Tower, Big Ben and famous London Bridge.

The plane rolled forward. Slowly then quickly, wobbling a bit. He watched grass swishing by outside and suddenly his tummy seemed to sink into his bottom and he felt himself tipping back as the plane went up. Thick grey clouds swallowed the shrinking city below. Frank was a few rows away, just across the aisle, rubbing his head, as if it ached.

Soon, the nice ladies brought trays with food in silver packets that were hard to open. If you pushed some buttons you could watch a film on a little screen, or a different one if you didn't like it, with headphones. When his tummy rumbled, Dudu nudged Auntie Adrienne. *I'm going to be sick.* Frank turned and they looked at each other but did not smile. Things were different now, somehow. Dudu puked into his lap and Auntie said, *oh-la-la.*

The story continues in...

ChiLD WiTch

L O N D O N

Frank Kean returns home to England, but brings too much of Congo in his baggage; not least twelve-year-old Dudu, whose behaviour and beliefs soon clash with life in London.

Frank battles to keep the peace, but when he tells his wife and kids about their guest's mysterious past as a 'child witch', his cosy suburban routine spins out of control. Tragedy strikes and family life implodes.

Is it bad luck? Or black magic, retribution by sorcery for betraying Dudu?

Fear and friendship collide in the peaceful setting of suburban UK.

Author's Note

I began writing *Child Witch* in 2003 and finished in 2013. I am indebted to my wife Angela Nicoara for her unwavering support and editorial input throughout that time. She is the ink in the nib.

The initial idea for the story came to me in Kinshasa, 2002, when Angela and I visited a 'halfway house' for street children, run by Oeuvre de Reclassement et de protection des Enfants de la Rue (ORPER). We were greatly impressed by the friendly youngsters and the dedicated adults helping to rehabilitate them – notably Fr Zbigniew 'Zibi' Orlikowski, Père Nzuzi Bibaki and Ange Bay-Bay. Later, we visited a children's home run by Mother Teresa's Missionaries of Charity, where we met a boy named Kilanda, who had horrific burns after a recent 'exorcism'. Those experiences inspired this novel. We also saw an opportunity to intervene locally, and, since we were due to leave within a few weeks, we had to act quickly. I had been training local journalists and Angela had been working as a freelance camerawoman, so we decided to collaborate and make two short films about children accused of sorcery.

You may view both films at *www.childwitch.com*. They have received more than 55,000 hits on YouTube, to date.

The first film is a documentary; we used it at a seminar for sixty Kinshasa-based journalists, to encourage objective reporting on this divisive and dangerous phenomenon. The second film is a music video about a small boy forced to leave home after his parents accuse him of sorcery. That film was intended for the general public and Congo's state TV broadcasted it after our departure in 2002. Angela and I moved to Rwanda in 2003, where I started writing *Child Witch*. So that's the background, and now a word of thanks to friends and family.

In Kinshasa, I received extensive help and advice from Fr Zbigniew 'Zibi' Orlikowski who first introduced us to his charming *enfants dits sorciers* and the talented members of L'Orchestre La Chytoure. Without them, there would be no story. Père Nzuzi Bibaki shared his interesting theories on rare and charismatic 'sorcerers'. Ange Bay-Bay deserves credit too, for her advice and work as a lawyer dedicated to children's rights. Christian Kakesa-Kasanza and Kapete Benda-Benda were our resourceful fixers. Simon Lawson at Search for Common Ground proved a solid ally during a frenetic but memorable schedule. Kate Mary at Internews in DC was ever helpful. Tony Gambino and Marty Schulman at USAID were shining beacons in a stormy sea. In eastern DRC, Abbé Celestin Bwanga Malekani and Dr Jean Pierre Lola Kisanga offered welcome encouragement and timely assistance, as did my various fixers, whose names, alas, I lost somewhere between Congo and here.

My limited experience of life in Congo – all of five months in 2002 – has been greatly enhanced by detailed suggestions from my trusted advisor Félicien Wilondja Basiku-Ngoma and his wife Marceline. So, *matondi mingi* Fély and Marceline, and also, *multumesc mult,* Gabriela Tuftedal, for introducing us. Likewise, my thanks to Gina Isale, Tito Farias and Henriette Ngongo for clarifying points of vocabulary. Violeta Cojocaru provided a useful introduction, in Niger, to Das Longondo Eteni, and Guy and Marie-Claire Mbayo Kakumbi whose advice on sculpture, linguistics and sorcery was illuminating.

Extra special thanks to globetrotter Tim Short for his exhaustive and encouraging response to my 'big ask' despite his busy itinerary somewhere warm.

Nimble-fingered Margaret Martindale scrutinized the quilt sections, Derek Martindale advised on matters Kingston, Kew and Richmond, while John Martindale provided tips on life as a London youngster, when he was one. *Tempus fugit!*

I spent considerable time chewing over dental terms and technique with Adrian Angelescu in Bucharest and Janet Dolluri Dela Cruz in Kigali. I appreciate their expertise and goodwill. They endured my drilling without anaesthetic.

Thank you Eddie Startup, radio marketing guru, for your inspirational panache.

I am especially indebted to Ascanio Martinotti and Callum Ormsby, for sharing two goldmines of information from their personal journeys, continents apart.

Simon Davies provided technical details on military issues. Kim Gjerstad's photos of *shegués,* from our time together in Kin, were a constant inspiration. Mark Blackburn, Jody Bogle VanDePol, Brian Cooper, Charlie Cooper, Colette Cooper, Joe Cooper, Michael T. Coyne, Ivor Gaber, Bob Saijad Hussain, Arabella McIntyre-Brown, Frank O'Connor, Andrea Ormsby, Eddie Ormsby, Hannah Ormsby, Lucy Ormsby, Henry Peirse, Sarah Popp, Gary Pulsifer, David Rees, Peter Rees, Rhiannon Rees, Nick Supple, Tim Supple, Tim Vallings and Caroline Vaudrey provided helpful advice on numerous other aspects. Thank you all.

Intrepid traveller Ben Dowson shared with me his impressive 'Country List', and is probably adding another location as I write. Bon voyage!

I am extremely grateful to the beady-eyed Steven Miscandlon for editing my final manuscripts and offering pertinent suggestions. Also, Dominic Cassidy's partial edit, advice on the ICTR / UK police procedures, and evocative anecdotes from driving big trucks across DRC were crucial.

If I have omitted anyone who also assisted over the years, I apologise.

Finally, thank you, Vera Ormsby, for being my mum, and so supportive, especially as you 'never read fiction, unless it's true'. I hope you'll try, just this once.

Mike Ormsby
Baku, September 2013

Further reading

Should you be interested in learning more about D.R. Congo, or the themes and places in *Child Witch*, you might find useful the selection of books and websites below. Since Congo's future is inextricably linked to Rwanda's past, I have included a few titles that cover both countries, and more.

Blood River: *A Journey to Africa's Broken Heart* by Tim Butcher (Grove Press, 2009)

Congo Justice: www.congojustice.com & www.congojustice.org

Heart of Darkness by Joseph Conrad (Penguin Classics, 2007)

Congo by Michael Crichton (Ballantine Books, 1992)

Mandela, Mobutu, and Me: A Newswoman's African Journey by Lynne Duke (Doubleday, 2003)

Leave None to Tell the Story: Genocide in Rwanda by Alison Des Forges (Human Rights Watch, June 1999)

The Economist – various articles: www.economist.com

Friends of the Congo: www.friendsofthecongo.org

Voyage au Congo by André Gide (Folio, 2001)

We Wish to Inform You that Tomorrow We Will Be Killed with Our Families: Stories From Rwanda by Philip Gourevitch (Farrar, Straus and Giroux, 1999)

An African Dream: the Diaries of the Revolutionary War in the Congo by Che Guevara (Panther / The Harvill Press, 2001)

King Leopold's Ghost: A Story of Greed, Terror, and Heroism in Colonial Africa by Adam Hochschild (Houghton Mifflin Harcourt, 1999)

Human Rights Watch – various reports: www.hrw.org

Congo deal boosts hope for street kids by Katherine Irie (AlertNet, ReliefWeb report, 29 Aug 2002)

Stanley – The Impossible Life of Africa's Greatest Explorer by Tim Jeal (Faber & Faber, 2011)

Emil Torday and the Art of the Congo, 1900–09 by John Mack (British Museum Press, 1990)

The State of Africa: A History of the Continent Since Independence by Martin Meredith (PublicAffairs, 2005)

Oeuvre de Reclassement et de Protection des Enfants de la Rue: www.orper.org

The Scramble for Africa: White Man's Conquest of the Dark Continent from 1876 to 1912 by Thomas Pakenham (Random House, 1991)

Fragments of the Invisible: The Rene and Odette Delenne Collection of Congo Sculpture edited by Constantine Petridis (Five Continents, 2013)

Africa's World War: Congo, the Rwandan Genocide, and the Making of a Continental Catastrophe by Gérard Prunier (Oxford University Press, 2008)

The Rwanda Crisis: History of a Genocide by Gérard Prunier (Columbia University Press, 1997)

Dust Devils by Roger Smith (Serpent's Tail, 2011)

Dancing in the Glory of Monsters: The Collapse of the Congo and the Great War of Africa by Jason Stearns (PublicAffairs, 2011)

Mayombe: Ritual Statues from Congo by Jo Tollebeek (Editions Lannoo, 2011)

And We Ate the Leopard: Serving in the Belgian Congo by Margaret Wente (iUniverse, Inc., 2007)

In The Footsteps of Mr. Kurtz: Living on the Brink of Disaster in Mobutu's Congo by Michela Wrong (HarperCollins, 2009)

My character Dudu's knowledge of his father's work as a carpenter and traditional African sculptor, or *nswendwe,* and of the role of such sculptors within a social community, derives from my interest in the research of art historian and anthropologist Hans Himmelheber (1908–2003), who travelled in the then Belgian Congo in 1938 and 1939. Himmelheber collected Songe art, including monumental power figures, and learned about the great sorcerers or *nganga buka*. I invented the name of Dudu's grandmother (Nana Kima) as a respectful nod to the Songe power figure *yankima*. Himmelheber published his research in the 1930s Belgian journal *Brousse*. Part of his sculpture collection was lost in the Second World War, but some of it survived and is held by the Ethnographic Museum of Basel and the Rietberg Museum, Zurich, among others. One of Himmelheber's Songe power figures sold at auction, in New York in 2004, for $489,600.

I travelled in Congo mostly by UN helicopter, or by car and motorcycle, although not by rail or river except for a brief ride in a large pirogue at Kisangani. To find out what Dudu and Kilanda might see, hear and otherwise experience on their travels across more isolated regions, I watched numerous documentaries, notably *Congo River* (2006), a remarkable film directed by Thierry Michel, which I highly recommend. I am very grateful to Mr Michel for his permission to adapt for my book some scenes and locations from his film.

If you would like to hear the song "You Don't Listen", that my character Callum Xavier sings in chapter 49 of *Child Witch Kinshasa*, please visit: *www.childwitch.com*.

About the Author

Mike Ormsby was born in Ormskirk, England. He is the author of a short story collection, *Never Mind the Balkans, Here's Romania*, and of *Spinner the Winner*, a children's book about a wind turbine, translated into four languages. His screenplay *Hey, Mr DJ!* was filmed in Kigali in 2007 and topped the bill at Rwanda's first Hillywood Film Festival. His short script *Enfants dits Sorciers* was filmed in Kinshasa in 2002. Mike is a former BBC journalist/World Service trainer. He is based in Transylvania, Romania. *Child Witch* is his first novel.

27009395R00303

Made in the USA
Charleston, SC
27 February 2014